D1557187

Arboriculture

History and Development
in North America

Arboriculture

HISTORY AND DEVELOPMENT
IN NORTH AMERICA

Richard J. Campana

MICHIGAN STATE UNIVERSITY PRESS
East Lansing

♾ The paper used in this publication meets the minimum requirements
of ANSI/NISO Z39.48–1992 (R 1997) (Permanence of Paper).

Michigan State University Press
East Lansing, Michigan 48823-5202

04   03   02   01   00   99   1   2   3   4   5   6   7   8   9

Library of Congress Cataloging-in-Publication Data

Campana, Richard J.
        Arboriculture: history and development in North America /
Richard J. Campana
        p.   cm.
    Includes bibliographical references (p.   ) and index.
    ISBN 0-87813-497-3 (clothbound: acid-free paper)
    I. Arboriculture—United States—History. 2.
Arboriculture—Canada—History. I. Title.
    SB435.5 .C26 1999
    635.9'77'097—do21
                                                    99-6658
                                                        CIP

Book and cover design by Sharp Des!gns, Inc.

_____

Visit Michigan State University Press on the World-Wide Web at:
http://www.msu.edu/unit/msupress

Dedicated to the late

D R . L E W I S C . C H A D W I C K

Professor and Horticulturist
at the Ohio State University
for thirty-eight years

For almost sixty years Dr. Chadwick was a leader in the field of arboriculture in North America as both an educator and a mentor. At different times he was editor, secretary, treasurer, and director of the National and International Shade Tree Conference, and director emeritus of the International Society of Arboriculture.

Dr. Chadwick was a pioneer in the field. He was influential in taking a small, annual, regional meeting of the National Shade Tree Conference, and making it grow to a nationwide, and then to an international force of ever-increasing professional standing. The end result was the establishment of the International Society of Arboriculture. Always a professional of high achievement, he inspired arborists everywhere to reach for high standards and quality performance.

Contents

Tables

Acknowledgments

The initiative and enthusiasm for this history were shared by the executive officers and the board of directors of the International Society of Arboriculture (ISA), and especially by Dr. Alex Shigo, previously of the U.S. Forest Service. Members of an advisory board of ISA provided the basic framework from which the chapters emerged, contributed illustrations, made helpful suggestions, and provided thoughtful leads. Members of a review board examined the entire manuscript and contributed to its improvement. Special thanks should go to Bob Dewers, Jim Kielbaso, Dan Neely, and Sharon Lilly. Funding to support the research and preparation was provided by contractual arrangement between the board of directors of ISA and the author.

Office, library, and preparation facilities and materials were made available by the Fogler Library, Department of Botany and Plant Pathology, and College of Forest Resources, University of Maine, Orono; United States National Agriculture Library and National Arboretum, Washington, D.C.; National Offices of the International Society of Arboriculture, Champaign, Illinois, and the National Arborist Association, Amherst, New Hampshire; the University of Massachusetts Shade Tree Laboratories, Amherst; National Headquarters and archives of The Davey Tree Co., Kent, Ohio; the F. A. Bartlett Tree Expert Company, Stamford, Connecticut; the Asplundh Tree Expert Co., Willow Grove, Pennsylvania; and the private manuscript collection of A. Winslow Dodge.

Additional information was obtained from library facilities at the Arnold Arboretum of Harvard University; Yale School of Forestry and Environmental

Sciences; Connecticut Agriculture Experiment Station; University of Nevada at Reno; University of Vermont; Longwood Gardens, Kennett Square, Pennsylvania; Pennsylvania and Massachusetts Horticultural Societies in Philadelphia and Boston; American Horticulture Society, Alexandria, Virginia; Dumbarton Oaks Agriculture Library, Washington, D.C.; Fairchild Botanical Garden, Miami; the Northeast Forest Experiment Station, New Haven, Connecticut.; Thuja Gardens, Bar Harbor, Maine; Texas A&M University at College Station; and Farnsworth Museum, Rockland, Maine.

I am grateful to many individuals and institutions too numerous to mention in detail. Special thanks goes out to the International Society of Arboriculture for making this work possible, to the University of Maine for its constant support beyond tenure obligation, and to Donna Wilbur and Diane Mazerolle for many long hours of patience and efficiency in typing and revising the manuscript.

The following individuals and organizations provided information requested: Walter Bench, Massachusetts Horticultural Society; John Rosenow, National Arbor Day Foundation; Charles Ritz, Karl Kuemmerling, Inc.; Walter Dages, the Bartlett Tree Expert Company; Librarian, New York Botanical Garden; Dr. R. L. Taylor, Chicago Botanical Garden; Dr. Lafayette Frederick of Howard University; Dr. T. H. R. Hall, Oxford, England; Gary Moll, American Forestry Association; Dolores Keith, Tree Trimmers Log; Nancy Bechtol, Longwood Gardens; Bartlett Manufacturing Company; Bert Taylor and L. N. Albrecht, Deep Root Corporation; Roger Mellick, the Doggett Company; Peter Hanon, Arbor Computer Systems, Inc.; J. J. Mauget Company; Dr. Howard Waterworth, U.S. Plant Introduction Station; Bruce Parliman, National Plant Germplasm Quarantine Center; Ken Morrison, *Chain Saw Age*; W. J. Barrows, Clovis, California; Dr. John Peacock, USDA-Forest Service; Gerald Farrens, Jacksonville, Florida; Thomas Taylor, Worcester, Massachusetts Parks and Recreation Department; American Horticultural Society, Mt. Alexandria, Virginia; Janet Evans, the Pennsylvania Horticulture Society; M. Lindberg, University of Florida; James Foster, Boston; Jerry Roche, *Trees and Turf Magazine*; Dr. Dennis Ryan, University of Massachusetts; June Scanlon, Ohmstead Falls, Ohio; Denise Britton, St. Helena, California; Dr. E. Charles Nelson, Dublin, Ireland; L. M. Hume, Pacific Tropical Botanical Garden; Pesticide Publicity Policy Foundation, Washington, D.C.; *Arbor Age Magazine*; Arthur Knof, Bloomfield, New Jersey; Dr. T. G. Andreadis, Connecticut Agriculture Experiment Station; Dr. W. A. Sinclair, Cornell University; Dr. A. L. Shigo, Durham, New Hampshire; Dr. Henry Gerhold, Pennsylvania State University; Randy Fox, Arbor Day Lodge, Nebraska; Harry Banker, W. Orange, New Jersey; Dr. Robert Cook, Arnold Arboretum; Dr. Frank Santamour, Jr., National Arboretum; and Dennis Townsend, USDA-ARS.

In addition, many individuals have searched their archives to find photographs for this publication. I am indebted to: Dr. Wayne Sinclair, Cornell University; Dr. Dennis Townsend, USDA-ARS; Lillian Steiger, the Asplundh Tree Expert Co.; Walter Dages, the F. A. Bartlett Tree Expert Co.; Jennifer Matthews, the Davey Tree Expert Co.; Dr. Frank Santamour, the U.S. National Arboretum; Chris Dunn, The Morton Arboretum; Carol David, the Arnold Arboretum Library; Kathy Wheeler, the National Arbor Day Foundation; Harry Banker, E. Orange, New Jersey; Dr. Alex Shigo, Durham, New Hampshire; Dr. Terry Tattar, University of Massachusetts; Cheryl Oakes, Forest History Society; Peter Gerstenberger and Pat Felix, the National Arborist Association; and Jerri Moorman, Beth Crozier, Derek Vannice, Jim Skiera, and John Geissal with the International Society of Arboriculture.

Finally, I am extremely grateful to the many individuals who reviewed portions of this manuscript and made valuable suggestions that have clarified and enhanced the book. For their help I extend my sincere thanks to: Dr. E. B. Himelick, Urbana, Illinois; Dr. Frank Santamour, the U.S. National Arboretum; Gary Brienzo, the National Arbor Day Foundation; Dave Shaw, Freehold, New Jersey; Dr. Roger Funk, the Davey Tree Expert Co.; Walter Dages and Dr. Thomas Smiley, the F. A. Bartlett Tree Expert Co.; William Lamphear, Forest City Tree Protection Co.; William Kruidenier, Sharon Lilly, and Peggy Currid, the International Society of Arboriculture; Robert Skiera, Milwaukee, Wisconsin; Peter Gerstenberger and Pat Felix, the National Arborist Association; William Rae, Wolfeboro, New Hampshire; Jim Orr, Hyland Johns, Kristin Wild, and Lillian Staiger, the Asplundh Tree Expert Co.; Dr. Alex Shigo, Durham, New Hampshire; Dr. Gary Watson, The Morton Arboretum; Don Blair, M. F. Blair Tree Experts; William Ostrofsky and Richard Hale, University of Maine; and Larry Hall, Hendricksen, The Care of Trees.

Preface

Arboriculture: History and Development in North America may be the first book of its kind. The author is aware of only two histories of arboriculture at even a national scope (England and Ireland); and has been unable to find any record or indication of a history for Canada, the United States or North America. The present history is confined to Canada and the United States. This does not mean that arboriculture is not practiced in Mexico or Central America, it means only that I have found no evidence of the conscious recognition of arboriculture as an institution or a profession beyond Anglo-America.

Because history is a record of past activity and performance, there are some who question the value of spending time and effort reviewing it. In a paper entitled, *International Society of Arboriculture*, Director Emeritus L. C. Chadwick gave four reasons to support such reviews. He noted that everyone interested in tree care should know that arboriculture is not new, that most of the basic practices used today were established in ancient times, that in the earliest years of arboricultural practice there was a certain "love of trees" not apparent nor stressed in many operations today, and that it is well to be able to show young arborists (as well as old) facts that they may have overlooked from old established journals.

To supplement Chadwick's reasoning, the present history will show that the origins of some of our basic practices, such as planting, transplanting and pruning, antedate writing. It will become clear also that the "love of trees" to which he alludes was common through most early civilizations. This love is shown in the respect that influential, national leaders give in recognition to the significance of trees as one of the dominant aspects of our environment. Someone said "those who ignore history are doomed to repeat it." In addition, as time passes, new information comes to light, perspectives change and further insights are possible. Thus, historical review is a continuing learning process.

Finally, every human practice begins with a *need*, evolves (by repeated application and improvement) to a *skill*, and is followed by a *concept* (of what the practice is and what it means). This leads to the discovery, accumulation and organization of related knowledge by *research*. And thus makes possible sets of approved *standards* for wise and competent use, ending in *professional* practice. Arboriculture has gone through such an evolution. We have reached the point where we want to know how it began, what road it traveled, where it is now and where it may be headed in the future. Such an aspiration is a hallmark of professional development.

This account of arboriculture is not meant to be an unbroken historical treatise. Its primary purpose is to review some of the significant historical information that led to the development of arboriculture in North America. The book is written for arborists ranging from the manual workers in trees to corporation presidents and for sophisticated scientists using complex tools in the laboratory. It provides breadth, depth and understanding of how arboriculture became what it is today. There is no intent to record histories of arboricultural firms or persons in the industry, except to the extent of the roles that they played have a primary significance. Since the "International Society of Arboriculture" and the "National Arborists Association" have dominated the arboriculture movement in the twentieth century, this history necessarily includes their histories in some detail.

This history was sponsored by the International Society of Arboriculture to provide a factual account of the origins of arboriculture in general, and its development in North America from crude practices to professional skills based on scientific principles. It is designed in particular to provide a sound basis for arboriculture as a profession, and as a reference for those interested in the role of amenity trees in our society. Arborists, city foresters, landscape designers, nurserymen, contractors, park and city managers, superintendents of institutional grounds, educators, students, workers in land management, government and public utilities should be interested.

For convenience in treatment of subject matter in Part I is arranged chronologically. Each chapter describes chronological developments within significant aspects of arboriculture. The book is abundantly illustrated, with descriptive terminology, glossary, index, tables on organizations, events, key individuals and selected references. No attempt was made to be exhaustive. The scope of the book is too large and the allocated time and space too small, to do more than review the highlights of each area. Reference to specific chemicals and other commercial products were omitted because regulations concerning their use are constantly changing.

This volume condenses the views, ideas and writings of numerous, dedicated scholars and observers, not the least of whom were practicing arborists. An effort was made to interview as many older arborists as possible or obtain from them statements on their views. The author has reviewed books and journals too numerous to mention, but has given special attention to business proceedings of the International Society of Arboriculture (and its precursor organizations), the National Arborist Association and histories in botany, gardening, horticulture, parks, forestry and other related disciplines.

CHAPTER ONE

The Early Roots of Arboriculture

"Histories make men wise" —F. Bacon

The history of arboriculture is the story of practices used in the care of trees, from before the time of written history to the present. It is clear from both archaeology and anthropology that trees were highly valued and used by prehistoric humans for food, shelter, and worship. The earliest writings indicate that certain tree care practices such as planting, transplanting, and pruning were already well known. The development of such practices is attributed first to a practical use of trees for food and protection, and second to the veneration of trees as gods or the dwelling place of gods. The earliest humans had a deep sense of awe for the size of trees, for the spirits associated with growth and change, and especially for the enormous age and apparent durability of trees transcending many human generations. There is little wonder then that trees were both loved and respected in almost every primitive society, and that the care of certain trees became a sacred obsession.

Arboriculture in North America has origins in the old worlds of Europe and Asia. As with medicine, horticulture, botany, agriculture, and forestry, we can only surmise its earliest beginnings. Arboriculture as a *science* did not develop until after horticulture, agriculture, and forestry were well established. From the Renaissance to the twentieth century, the terms *arboriculture* and *forestry* were almost synonymous. Although many basic principles and practices of what we now call arboriculture have been established and well known for more than 2,000 years, arboriculture did not become a crafted art until late in the nineteenth century. Following the development of arboriculture as a small business, it became a science with the beginning of research in the 1930s and is only now emerging as a profession. Development of arboriculture from a small business to a great industry in the United States was due largely to the men who initiated and developed the major tree companies that are dominant today. The Davey, Bartlett, and Asplundh tree companies and their successors initiated professional arboriculture, as we know it today. Likewise, contributions have been made by those who started commercial tree care services, with their offerings of tree pruning, pest and disease control, utility line clearance, tree selection, planting, fertilization, and planned tree maintenance.

Dr. L. C. Chadwick was an important influence on more recent arboriculture. A professor of horticulture at the Ohio State University, he was simultaneously chairman of his university department and secretary/treasurer and later executive director of the National and International Shade Tree Conferences (now the International Society of Arboriculture) for a period that spanned thirty-two years (1937–69). Chadwick was a solid rock around which the swirling currents of time and change fashioned the steady growth of the first professional society of arboriculture.

ANCIENT ARBORICULTURE

Tree cultivation originated before writing. Domestication of fruit trees was well established in ancient civilizations. In some cases the original fruit tree ancestor-types, such as the olive, are still extant, but with most, the original wild types of fruit trees are extinct. By contrast, most of the ancestral types of cultivated shade and ornamental trees are known. Thus, the evidence is clear that human use of fruit trees has a longer history in cultivation than any other group of trees.

The practice of arboriculture among the ancients was known from the Sumerian culture of the Middle East in 5000 B.C. to the western realm of the Roman Empire until its fall after five millennia. The oldest written evidence on ancient concern for arboriculture is found in the Gilgamesh epic of the Sumerians, one of the oldest works of literature known. Engravings on earthenware tablets illustrate "sacred gardens of cedar trees." In the area between the Tigris and Euphrates Rivers, often called the cradle of civilization, ancient gardens evolved into architectural parks for the sole enjoyment of the rich and powerful. Such parks were early precursors of the present-day arboreta.

Following the Sumerians, between 3000 and 200 B.C., the Egyptians developed the earliest foundations of tree care; for this they are considered the fathers of ancient arboriculture. The Egyptians experimented with trees and shrubs as early as 2000 B.C. and were involved with the introduction of new species, as well as transplanting and cultivating trees on a massive scale. According to archaeologists, the pictographs made 3,500–4,000 years ago in the Temple of Hatsheput, Dur-el-Bahri near Thebes in Egypt, depicted men transporting "frankincense" trees in containers. In 1570 B.C., Queen Hatsheput brought foreign seeds and trees from the east coast of Africa to Egypt to produce aromatic incense in her gardens. The story is told in reliefs carried in temple walls. Her boats were loaded with six-foot trees in large baskets suspended by ropes from poles. This is perhaps the earliest record of the introduction of trees from another country.

The Egyptians were skilled in moving large trees, placing them in pots comparable in size to our large outdoor urban planters of today. Large trees were transported in ships at least as early as 2000 B.C. In one recorded case they were transplanted with a root ball of soil after being moved over a distance of 1,500 miles.

Within the Assyrian realm were the cedars of Lebanon, famous for their majestic size, age, and use. Initially covering the mountain slopes of what is now Syria and Lebanon, they were so heavily depopulated that they had almost disappeared by 1000 B.C. This must have had a sobering influence on the rulers of the period who needed wood for construction, and probably created a respect for the value of trees in general, and for this tree species in particular. The cedars of Lebanon may be the most famous in history because of their place in the development of Western civilization. While initially prized for their use as forest products, because of devastation and scarcity they became symbolic for the preservation of trees in general. Thus, we see them now as a historical beginning for tree preservation and the spirit of arboriculture.

In a later age in the same land, the Babylonians used the wealth of their culture to develop a new quality of life by using trees and gardens for comfort, beauty, and art. Circa 650 B.C., in the reign of Sennacherib, the Babylonians were known as the garden makers because of the phenomenon of "hanging gardens." Many kinds of trees and shrubs were moved from mountain areas to adorn public parks, one of the earliest examples leading to the concept of an arboretum. It was King Nebuchadnezzar in 600 B.C. who built the famous "Hanging Gardens of Babylon," one of the seven wonders of the ancient world. Famous for their architectural splendor and elevation, these gardens had reservoirs for watering plants, wells, streams, groves, and avenues of planted trees, which included cedars and cypress. This may be the earliest evidence of elaborate art and landscaping in arboriculture.

The Persians, who followed the Babylonians (ca. 500 B.C.), were no less known for their high regard for trees. The great king, Cyrus, is said to have cared for trees with his own hands even though he had hundreds of slaves. Persian gardens (ca. 300 B.C.) were probably the most opulent of all ancient times, and garden trees were cultivated for beauty as much as for fruit. The Persian king, Xerxes, in his campaign to conquer Greece (330 B.C.) halted his army in Asia Minor (now Turkey) to observe a single tree. Seeing an oriental plane for the first time, he was so impressed with its size and beauty that he paused for three days to honor and decorate it before crossing the Hellespont to put fire and sword to Greece.

There are literally hundreds of references to trees and other woody plants in biblical literature. The Old Testament is a historical treasure reflecting a way of life from 1000–500 B.C. in southwestern Asia. Of all the plants mentioned in the Bible, greatest importance is attributed to trees because they are noted most frequently. The tree as a source of food is an important concept in the Bible; fruit trees were supposed to be spared from destruction, even during periods of war and upheaval.

The olive (*Olea europaea*), considered the most sacred of all biblical trees, was reported to be cultivated on a large scale in Sumeria as early as 4000 B.C. In a biblical reference Jesus is said to have given special attention to the fig tree and the use of fertilizer to produce fruit (Matt. 24:32; Luke 13:6–9). From the Song of Songs (8:2) we learn that wine was made from the fruits of pomegranate and other trees.

In the Far East the early arts of tree cultivation were probably as active as in ancient Europe, western Asia, and northern Africa. Although historically separated from the West, the Chinese were not completely isolated. As early as 2000 B.C., the apricot (*Prunus armenica*), native to Armenia in Europe, was said to be cultivated in China. According to the earliest Chinese sources, the Emperor Sheng Mung had built a garden in 2800 B.C. for cultivation of medicinal herbs and trees. By 1120 B.C. the highways of the Chou dynasty were said to be lined with trees. Nearly 1,000 years later, in 200 B.C., when China was unified in a single empire, thousands of miles of military roads were lined with pine trees. In that period, the Chinese were known to use pine, willow, sophora, chestnut, and elm in street tree plantings. The Chinese were also responsible for the origin and development of ornamental dwarf trees (bonsai). By 1200 A.D. this practice had reached a high point as a recognized feature of Chinese art and culture. The Japanese, who are more famous for bonsai art, were not preeminent in the field until 500 years later, in the 1700s.

Of special interest to arboriculture was the practice by the Greeks of establishing the "groves of academe." These were secluded areas designed for serious study and quiet reflection. The seclusion was created by hedges of woody plants and trees were planted for shade. The first trees in the gardens of academe were the plane trees so admired by Plato (427–347 B.C.). Native to Greece, the plane tree was one of the most popular and widely used trees among the ancients. It was introduced into Sicily circa 400 B.C. by the Greek tyrant, Dionysius. It was so highly valued that when introduced to Italy, the Romans were said to have watered its roots with wine.

One of the first Greeks to comment on trees was the philosopher, Aristotle, probably the world's first naturalist. He ascribed the longevity of trees to their low water content (but provided no explanation). Aristotle denied the existence of sex in plants and because of his wisdom and fame this view persisted for another 1,700 years despite the knowledge at that time of caprification. Caprification involved the hanging of pollen-laden fronds of palm in nonpollen (female) palm trees to ensure production of fruit. Aristotle noted also that destruction of roots and branches is often followed by sprouting of new shoots from the stump, and that new roots regenerate from older ones.

Most of the reliable information on trees known to the ancients up to the time of the Greeks (ca. 300 B.C.) was recorded by Theophrastus (327–287 B.C.). His list of more than 170 woody plants included not only trees and shrubs native to Greece, but others (e.g., peach, persimmon, and cherry) introduced from other lands. As a student and disciple of Aristotle, he loved plants and gardening and wrote extensively on many things including kinds of trees, their diseases, and care. He is credited as the author of 400 volumes and he taught 2,000 students in his lifetime. Of special interest are his two large botanical treatises, *The History of Plants* and *The Causes of Plants*. He was the first to make and record critical studies of plants. Because of his early and accurate observations, he is properly regarded as the father of botany.

Theophrastus's observations of trees are of special interest because they are the first records of value that go beyond the arboricultural practices common then, such as planting, transplanting, and pruning. He had an unusual opportunity to study newly imported trees from Asia Minor (Turkey) following its conquest by Alexander the Great in 300 B.C. From him it is clear that ornamental trees and shrubs were cultivated for their own value throughout the world of his knowledge. Theophrastus is credited for establishing the only known botanical garden in the ancient world. His garden differed from all others in that it was used for the study of plants themselves in an effort to see how and why they functioned.

Theophrastus was the first to recommend treatment of a wound to induce "healing" when he advised the use of a mud plaster with leaves. In this he was first to use a medical principle for plant wounds that would persist in tree wound dressings for more than 2,000 years. He also noted that juice in tree (sap) flows upward through the outer zone of wood in the stem (sapwood).

The Greeks introduced a new concept in the use of plants, not only with flowers around their homes, but in particular the use of trees in groves around their temples, and in rows along their streets and marketplaces. They were among the first to introduce a living style involving the use of trees and woody vines as arbors, using trees and shrubs skillfully with open or shaded patios and porches. Thus they blended living inside with outside space, partitioned and embellished with plants and trees. The establishment and maintenance of such planting required much knowledge of arboricultural practice including planting, transplanting, pruning, and such general care as watering.

By 300 B.C. the Romans cultivated olives and figs introduced into the area at an earlier time by Greek colonization. They had cottage gardens where fruit trees were protected by outer screening walls of other tree species such as plane, cypress, laurel, pine, and fir. There is early evidence of planned landscaping design so highly advanced later in Italy. The villas of prosperous Romans were landscaped with many varieties of ornamental trees such as oleander, bay laurel, box cypress, myrtle, and the oriental plane tree.

The Romans spread their knowledge of trees around the ancient world. They utilized the formidable knowledge of the Greeks in natural sciences and improved on it. Through military conquest from England to Persia, they extended knowledge of trees and arboriculture throughout the known world of the ancient west. In addition, they increased the range of many woody plants through the constant traffic and commerce for hundreds of years.

The Romans were the first to give the tree worker a name—*arborator*. Used originally only for a tree pruner, this term was later used to include those who cared for any and all trees, including fruit species. Obviously, this is the origin of the words *arborist* and *arboriculture*. They also gave the gardener a name—*topiarius*. In this we see the origin of *topiary* the adjective describing the art of shaping evergreen ornamentals by pruning and shearing. The use of *topiarius* for gardener suggests that amenity woody plants may have been given the highest priority of all the plants in their gardens.

The only literature of significance on trees or arboriculture to emerge from the Roman Empire in the first century was written by Pliny the Elder (23–79 A.D.), a distinguished statesman and author. Pliny gave numerous directions on the care and planting of trees as well as on tree wounds and their treatment, but offered nothing new. He noted, however, that trees found in both hills and valleys grow larger in the low places, an observation reflecting the favorable influence of water on tree growth. He was among the first to note numbers of different but similar trees belonging to a single taxonomic unit not yet described. His best example is the enumeration of ten different kinds of maples. And finally, he was interested in cultivation and care of mulberry trees for the production of silk. Although China was unknown to the Romans in his time, the mulberry tree had

TABLE 1.1

SELECTED ANCIENT PRACTICES IN ARBORICULTURE

5800 B.C.	Earliest known written record of trees
4000 B.C.	Earliest known street tree use
3500 B.C.	Earliest known transport of trees
2800 B.C.	Earliest known garden of trees
1500 B.C.	Earliest known planned introduction of trees from afar
	By this year, large trees were moved by water
	By this year, a royal park of trees had been established
1200 B.C.	Earliest known use of root ball
	Earliest specific record of planting for shade
650 B.C.	Early concept of *arboretum*
600 B.C.	Earliest known tree protection laws
300 B.C.	Earliest known use of tree groves for study and retreat
	Earliest authentic botanical garden
	First record of the words *tree worker* and *gardener*
175 B.C.	Earliest known book on tree care
100 A.D.	Earliest known interior tree planting

made its journey over the oriental silk trail from China to Persia, and westward to Rome.

Following the conquest of the Mideast, the Romans, borrowing from the regal splendor of the Persians, built large, ornamental pleasure gardens. In the second century of the empire, such developments occurred on such a large scale that they threatened the food-producing acreage of the Italian peninsula.

The Romans had a marked effect on arboriculture in other ways. With their ability for organization and engineering, they developed the original ideas of others and achieved more with them. Their development of landscaping exceeded anything seen before in the ancient world, and provided a basic framework of tree culture, style, and design that would survive the demise of the ancient world and would emerge again in the Renaissance. The need to organize the extensive resources of the empire for productivity led them to create and organize the first programs in state forestry, and literally the only effort to regulate or manage trees in the ancient world. But their greatest contribution was to spread their knowledge on culture and care of trees into wild and barbarian lands around the Mediterranean basin and into Great Britain. By the time the Romans arrived in England, the cultivation and care of trees was a highly developed practice that could be applied immediately to a wild and barbarous land. As a result, southern England "flowered" in the declining warmth of the Empire as it approached its final days.

The knowledge of ancient arboriculture was lost along with most of the civilized learning of the ancients after the fall of the Roman Empire circa 500 A.D. As the Norsemen conquered Europe, they destroyed most recorded knowledge. To the east and the south, the wars against Huns, Vandals, and Muhammedans left a path of destroyed libraries and dead scholars. Even the surviving knowledge of the ancients was lost during that long period, and there was little progress in the practice of arboriculture. The practices of the Romans, however, were kept alive by Christian monks in a thousand monasteries, although even some of them were destroyed.

POST-RENAISSANCE EUROPE

The development of arboriculture in this period was characterized by a renewal of scholarship, the initiation of botanical gardens, the beginning of practical forestry, the discovery and publication of specific tree care practices, a call for organization of tree workers, the advent of the arboretum, and landscaping by tree scraping.

The period from 1500 to 1800 was one of intensive naval maneuvering in Europe, involving the colonization and development of the New World. This favored the development of "amenity forestry" or arboriculture with the discovery by Europeans of thousands of "new" plants including trees of great interest and value. It was further stimulated by a fashion among the newly wealthy for collecting exotic plants. This led to the rise of extensive landscaped gardens. The collection of specimen trees in private arboreta and "artificial" landscaping was well under way in the 1700s, especially in England and France. By the 1800s it reached its highest point requiring the services of "estate foresters." This was the origin of arboriculture as we know it today. For a hundred years (1800–1900), the care of individual trees on a large scale evolved by trial and error from crude practices to a crafted art.

Many basic principles of arboriculture were established largely by repeated trials. Observations along similar lines were made in many European countries, but because of North American familiarity with English history and language, our knowledge of arboriculture was derived primarily from England where many significant contributions were made. James Lyte first used the term *arborist* in his book *Dodens* in 1578. The term *arborist,* like the Roman *arborator,* included not only pruning activities but other aspects of tree care. The earliest English reference book of note is a *Boke of Husbandrie* by Fitzherbert in 1534, in which he discussed the care of trees among other aspects of rural life. Also in this period, in a *Treatise on Fruit Trees* in 1553, Austin discussed fertilization by soil application. Probably the first to recommend the application of fertilizer in holes punched in the soil with an iron bar, he had the insight to recognize that overfertilization could be damaging to trees.

Austin was followed by John Lawson, whose book *A New Orchard and Garden,* first published in 1597, underwent numerous editions over the next eighty years. This publication included the first comprehensive treatment of the principal arboricultural practices in that period, such as planting, tree moving, pruning, fertilizing, wound treatment, and cavity filling. Over a forty-year period, dating back to 1578, Lawson actively opposed the planting of trees too close together, believing it shortened the life of trees. One of the first to note the significance of root development to soil depth and density, he also noted the need for balance between roots and tops for the best transplanting result. Probably the first to recognize that most absorbing roots were near the soil surface, he anticipated the need to replant at the original ground line.

In pruning, he called attention to the creation of wounds by leaving stubs to die, where rot could enter and result in a hollow tree. He advised, "cut him close," "fill his wound," and "close with cerecloth nailed on to prevent air and water." He recognized that several small cuts are better than one large one, because they close more quickly. In this, he established the principle of early corrective pruning. He recommended pruning back tops of trees after transplanting as did Theophrastus in 300 B.C., but with the added purpose of balancing branch and root structure. He also advised sloping a pruning cut, having a twig on the upper side of the cut, and painting all large cuts or wounds. Lawson is also considered one of the earliest authorities on treatment of tree cavities. He recommended "filling the hole with well-tempered mortar (concrete)." Finally, he recommended fertilization with liquid manure. As a practical horticulturist and the earliest arboriculturist, he may well be considered the father of European arboriculture.

John Evelyn is the most famous English writer on arboriculture, and his 1664 book was considered the most important work in this area at the time. It is our richest source of information on early arboriculture. On assignment by request of Charles II, Evelyn wrote his long and detailed *Sylva: Or a Discourse on Forest Trees and the Propagation of Timber in His Majestie's Domain.* At that time and for at least another 200 years, *arboriculture,* the care of individual trees, was synonymous with *forestry,* the management of trees in forests, or *silviculture.* Evelyn was the first to advise that cavities in tree stems should be cleaned out by removal of dead and decaying tissue, and the first to recommend treating the cavity with oil or tar. His basis for the use of tar is unknown to us, since the nature of wood decay was not discovered until 200 years later. His recommendation suggests knowledge on the use of coal tar products as preservatives. This recommendation anticipated the widespread use of creosote in the pole-treating industry. He also advised that a new tree, whether fruit, forest, or ornamental, should never be planted in the same spot where an old decayed one had been recently removed. He properly sensed that the same thing might happen to another tree in the same place, because the same environmental conditions would prevail.

In his historical account, Evelyn reviewed numerous tree care practices such as nursery methods for growing trees for transplanting, transplanting and moving large trees, pruning, age and size for felling trees, infirmities of trees, laws and statutes for preservation of trees, characteristics and care required by different species, the sacredness and use of standing groves, insect and disease problems, and wound treatment after pruning.

In 1790 T. Austin Forsythe (gardener to King George III) took the first definitive stance on how to treat cavities in his book, *The Culture and Management of Fruit Trees.* He stressed the importance of cleaning out the cavities thoroughly. For this he is considered to be the father of tree surgery as a science. He devised a formula for filling tree cavities with cow dung, old lime, wood ashes, and sand. He received an annual grant from Parliament of £4,000 as a reward. His method was considered so effective that it was practiced for more than a hundred years. The name Forsythe was honored for posterity, not in arboriculture, but in botany, when the great Linnaeus created the genus *Forsythia* in his honor.

Soon after Forsythe published his recipe for wound healing ingredients, his formulation was severely criticized by others. Sir Arthur St. Clair offered a new superior product, involving hot tar in dusted chalk. This may have been the first use of a petroleum product for this purpose. Its use to prevent wood decay before science knew the cause of decay was a good example of progress by trial without knowledge.

Another critic was William Nicol. In his book of 1803, *The Practical Planter,* he agreed on the need to cut away dead, decayed, and injured tissue to expose sound wood. But in contrast to Forsythe, he recommended tar as a "plaster" to keep water out of the wound. In strong words he challenged the Forsythe formula for filling cavities as less effective than tar. Nicol also noted the need to undercut when pruning off limbs to prevent "laceration" (stripping).

William Pontey was a nurseryman and ornamental gardener to the Duke of Bedford in England. The duke directed him to conduct a series of experiments on the effects of poor pruning practices and neglect of trees. In 1810 he wrote *The Forest Pruner: A Treatise on the Training or Management of British Timber Trees, Whether Intended for Use, Ornament or Shelter.*

Pontey was even more critical of Forsythe for implying that wounds not treated with his own composition would fail to close, ignoring "the astonishing and successful exertions of simple nature in healing wounds of trees." In this he preceded Shigo by more than 150 years by calling attention to the ability of wounds to be closed by the tree itself without benefit of a dressing. He believed strongly that Forsythe's implication discouraged pruning generally because of the perceived "need" to treat pruning wounds.

In 1864 Des Cars, of France, devised a practical system of tree pruning. As director of parks in Paris, Des Cars used coal tar as a wound dressing in preference to all other preparations. This became the accepted practice by the first American commercial arborists circa 1900.

The first to clearly differentiate the cultivation of individual trees for purposes other than fruit or timber was Sir Henry Stuart in 1828. Stuart was an arboriculturist and author of the *Planter's Guide,* which included specific recommendations on transplanting. He was the earliest to use a rule for measuring the size of a root ball, essential for success in moving trees. His standard was the diameter of a tree trunk one foot above the ground and recommended a ball one foot in diameter per inch of stem diameter. These specifications became common practice and are still used by arborists today. He was the first to call for an organization of arborists for the care of individual trees, but nothing came of it. Critical of the arboricultural practice in his day, Stuart saw with great perception the underlying status of arboriculture throughout most of its history—that it was universally practiced but nowhere understood.

TABLE 1.2

A CHRONOLOGY OF EARLY ENGLISH TREE CARE PRACTICES

DATE	PERSON	NOTES
1750	Miller	Warned against severe topping
1759	Greenwood	First used ropes for climbing
1760	McIntosh	First used tile for drainage
1775	Boutcher and Marshall	Recommended top pruning for root/shoot balance
1790	Forsythe	Recommended treating wounds and filling cavities
1803	Nicol	First use of the term *undercut* pruning
1828	Stuart	Wrote earliest tree pruning standards
		Issued earliest call for research
		Issued first call for arboriculture organization
1838	Loudon	First used the word *arboriculture* in current meaning

Following Stuart's new conception of modern arboriculture, J. C. Loudon published a book in 1838 entitled *Arboreta and Fruit Trees*. In his text he was the first to use the term arboriculture within the context that we know it today. Probably the most eminent authority of his day (author of *Encyclopedia of Gardens* in 1865), he also was the first to use the term *arboretum* (pl. *arboreta*).

Summary

No one can ever know when or precisely how the first tree care practices began. Tree cultivation originated long before writing. The ancient Egyptians, however, were the fathers of ancient arboriculture. European arboriculture was characterized by the origin of modern botanical gardens; the beginning of practical forestry; the discovery, use, and publication of basic tree care practices; the advent of the arboretum; and landscaping with trees. The terms *arboretum* and *arboriculture*, were first used in the nineteenth century with continued confusion between arboriculture and forestry and an abortive call for an arboricultural society. Significant during this period were the beginnings of forestry as a profession, a resolution of the cause of wood decay, and a golden age of tree planting with early evolution and development of landscaping.

CHAPTER TWO

Development of Arboriculture in America

"All trees in the New World are unlike those of Europe . . ." —Columbus

When the Europeans began to colonize North America in the sixteenth century, knowledge on the use and care of trees was still at a low level in Europe. Thus, development of arboriculture in colonial America followed that of Europe. It was in fact heavily dependent on Europe and, especially, on England and France. It was not until after the American War of Independence that tree care in America began to diverge from that in Europe. The first book in England on the flora and fauna of North America, written by Hariot in 1588 and published in London, was *A Brief and True Report of the New Found Land of Virginia.* While a keen observer and explorer, Hariot was not a professional botanist.

Marie Victorin Cornuti wrote the first history of Canadian plants, *Canadiensium Plantarum Historia,* in 1635. He wrote: "On peut dire, sans trop solliciter les faits, que la Botanique Amèricaine est neé chez les Canadiens français" (It can be said without exaggerating the facts that American Botany originated with the French Canadians). Cornuti, however, never went to North America and his account, published in Paris, was based on collections and site observations made by nonbotanists.

Before the European colonists arrived in America, the resident Indians had been using trees in their own ways. In all of the Americas more than 200 species of trees, shrubs, vines, and small fruits were then known. In North America more than 100 were used for food, shelter, weapons, transportation, and ornament. Native mulberry fruits (*Morus rubra*) were so well liked that the southern Indians planted their seeds around their villages. When the Spanish explorer de Soto visited Georgia in the 1500s, he was met by local tribes bearing gifts of twenty baskets of mulberries. The Indians planted the peach tree, introduced to Florida and Mexico by the Spaniards in the early 1500s, in large numbers. Indian peach orchards were developed from the Atlantic coast westward to Arkansas and Texas before the English settled Jamestown in 1607.

The Indians used or abused trees in much the same way as the white man would do later, in farming, burning, clearing, and planting. Trees were planted to shelter their crops from the sun. The English captain John Smith noted that the Indians on the James River in Virginia planted mulberry, locust (*Robinia* sp.), grapes, roses, and sunflowers in their villages and around their homes. Often certain forest trees were preserved in clearings to shelter such crops. In the north the French explorer Cartier in 1534 found plum plantings (*Prunus nigra*) around Iroquois Indian villages. Indians prized the black locust for bow wood and their plantings extended its range. Kentucky coffee (*Gymnocladus* sp.) and dahoon holly trees (*Ilex cassine*) were planted to make coffee and tea.

Some of the earliest native trees to be cultivated by colonists in North America included sugar maple, American elm, red oak, and catalpa. The English practice of favoring English elms at home was adopted by the colonists with the American elm. This led to widespread planting of elms, first in northeastern America and then into the Midwest. The first public shade tree planting for the relief of travelers occurred in "Boston Towne" in 1646. It was a mass planting of American elms along the Boston "neck" connecting the town to the mainland. One of these trees became famous as the "Liberty Elm." Lord Butte, author of the Stamp Act, and Andrew Oliver, the king's appointed stamp dispenser, were both hung in effigy from its limbs in 1765. A symbol of colonial defiance for ten years, the Liberty Elm was destroyed by British troops when the American Revolution erupted. By 1665 trees had been planted extensively along colonial streets, in and around the edges of towns, and especially on the commons. The elms were preferred, but other native trees were present along with the lime trees (*Tilia*) from Europe.

William Penn was the first person to plan and build a city in America. In the late 1600s, he advised putting every house in the center of an assigned landed lot to provide room for gardens, orchards, and fields. As a result, colonial Germantown houses, with grounds of twenty-five acres along the Delaware and Schulkyll Rivers, were beautiful colonial homes surrounded by small tree-studded parks. By 1760 Philadelphia and its immediate surroundings had been transformed from an uncultivated desert into a series of villas, gardens, and luxuriant orchards.

In the South, expansive gardens created late in the 1600s had a lasting influence on the discovery and use of native trees, and the importation of trees from abroad for ornamental purposes. One of the oldest and best known of these gardens is the

Magnolia Plantation and Gardens outside Charleston, South Carolina. Settled in 1671 by Thomas Drayton of a noble English family, this is said to be the oldest large garden in North America. Still remaining in the hands of the Drayton heirs, this garden is resplendent with magnificent oaks and cypresses, as well as hundreds of imported species of azaleas and camellias. Now open to the public, it is said to be America's oldest man-made tourist attraction.

The earliest list of native trees in Virginia was prepared by Thomas Hariot in 1595. His list included oak, walnut, fir, cedar, maple, witch hazel, holly, willow, beech, ash, and elm. By 1660 many native American trees had been introduced to England by John Tradescant. These included the tulip tree, American plane, witch hazel, sumac, red maple, persimmon, dogwood, mulberry, locust, and others.

The earliest scientific approach to recording the botanical resources of North America in a systematic way was made by John Bannister, a young clergyman sent in 1678 to save souls and collect plants. From his chapter post, over the next fourteen years, he sent back to England 340 plant species and began a natural history of Virginia that was never finished.

The second naturalist to explore in the South was John Lawson who arrived in Carolina from England in 1700. Lawson was financed by James Petiver, naturalist and apothecary of London, to explore the Carolinas and send back specimens. After eight years and a thousand miles of travel, he returned to England and published *A New Voyage to Carolina*, in which he described the flora and fauna. Better informed than Bannister, he was the first to introduce in his records a holistic natural history of the New World.

The next botanical explorer-collector to appear in Virginia was Mark Catesby. In 1712 he came to visit relatives in Williamsburg, but remained to explore, collect, and sketch the natural history of the area. He sent seeds and plants to England not only from Virginia but also from Jamaica. After Catesby returned to England in 1719, his paintings (of birds) won financial support from wealthy members of the Royal Society. He returned to America in 1722, landing at Charleston, South Carolina, and in four years amassed collections and records for what would be the first great natural history of the American colonies. His great work was published in sections beginning in 1729, but was not finished until 1747. He was supported financially by the generosity of Peter Collinson, a Quaker merchant who would become the patron of American horticulture. Catesby's masterpiece, *Natural History of Carolina, Florida and the Bahamas Islands,* was dedicated to the reigning Queen Anne and included the flora of Georgia as well.

The last of the early botanists in the southern colonies was the first born in America, the younger John Clayton of Virginia. Beginning about 1722, Clayton sent his own records to the Dutch botanist, Gronovius in Leiden, who published them without Clayton's permission or even knowledge. Although Clayton had given his work the title, *A Catalogue of Plants, Fruits and Trees Native to Virginia*, it appeared as *Flora Virginica* in two parts in 1739 and 1743.

John Bartram (1699–1777) was the most interesting, famous, and productive botanist in the colonial period. Bartram's interest, skill, and industry in collecting and raising plants soon attracted the attention of influential men in Philadelphia, among them Benjamin Franklin. As a result he was soon in touch with a wealthy dry-goods merchant in England, named Peter Collinson. In 1732 Bartram began a correspondence with Collinson that lasted thirty-eight years. He began collecting plants and seeds for Collinson and sold them in England in 1734. To find more and different plants he began traveling in 1735. He visited parts of New York, Ontario, New England, New Jersey, Maryland, and Virginia in search of plants to satisfy his clients. By 1763, with extensive backing from Collinson, Bartram had built a huge following in Europe, where his activities and abilities were widely known. Among his correspondents were Queen Ulrica of Sweden and the medical botanist, Peter Kalm, a student of the great Linnaeus. Linnaeus himself considered Bartram the greatest contemporary natural botanist.

TABLE 2.1
EARLY HORTICULTURAL ACTIVITY IN AMERICA

DATE	PERSON	ACTIVITY OR EVENT
1642	Drayton	Earliest tree planting for ornamental garden (South Carolina)
1680	Penn	Earliest city design for trees in parks (Pennsylvania)
1728	Bartram	Earliest botanical garden (Pennsylvania)
1730	Prince	First commercial nursery (New York)
1741	Middleton	Earliest landscaped garden (South Carolina)
1773	Marshall	Earliest arboretum in North America
		First book on native trees published in America by an American-born citizen
1790	Washington	His estate was a model for ornamental planting
		Engaged the first landscaper for U.S. Capitol
1803	Jefferson	Initiated introduction of foreign trees
		Commissioned Lewis and Clark Expedition to collect specimens of unknown trees

Financial support from King George made it possible for Bartram to finance substantial collecting trips through the Carolinas, Georgia, and even into Florida.

He discovered a new small, hardwood tree near the Fort Barrington ferry in 1765 and named it Franklinia after the "illustrious" Dr. Benjamin Franklin. This tree became the famous "lost tree," because it was not seen in its wild state from 1803 until a few years ago, although many naturalists tried to find it for almost 180 years.

Collecting and preserving plants was unusually difficult in the 1700s when Bartram was active. Travel was by horseback or canoe. Indians and animals were a problem, and collected plants often perished. At Peter Collinson's urging, Bartram stored his plants in bladders of oxen and cows, with roots and soil inside and stems and tops in the air. It is estimated that many of the 150–200 plants he sent to Europe were trees.

Robert Prince started the first commercial nursery in North America in 1731 at Flushing, Long Island, in the colony of New York. Nursery operations were at first limited to importing and growing fruit trees from Europe. Later its scope was broadened to include both native and introduced shade and ornamental trees and shrubs. By 1774 the nursery was shipping native magnolias and large catalpas to England. The nursery contained some of the oldest and largest exotic trees in North America, including cedar of Lebanon, atlas cedar, purple leaf beech, and Asiatic magnolia. By 1793 the Prince Nursery had evolved into the Linnean Botanical Garden and Nursery and was producing more than a million trees annually. This garden, under the direction of the son and grandsons of Robert Prince, had a strong influence on the development of American horticulture, forestry, and arboriculture.

In 1785 John Marshall of Pennsylvania was the first American to publish on native trees and shrubs. He entitled his book *Arbustum Americanum* (The American Grove). Marshall was inspired by his cousin John Bartram.

Both George Washington and Thomas Jefferson were products of the Southern landed aristocracy of "great estates with broad lands." Each had a passion for landscaping and gardening with a hands-on approach. After the war Washington made his Mt. Vernon estate a showplace by using ornamental trees to grace his garden, orchards, and roadways, and by planting peach trees, grafting cherries and pears, and transplanting English walnut. In his second term as president he called on the eminent landscape designer from France, Pierre Charles L'Enfant, to plan the site designated for the U.S. Capitol and the federal city. Within an area of ten square miles of dense woodlands, L'Enfant designed two large parks around which the city of Washington would rise.

Jefferson used his estate as a huge experimental botanical garden and kept accurate records of all that was done. After his presidency ended in 1808, he gave his plantings all his attention, with special care to trees. He put flowering peach fences around his fields, planted allees of trees along his roads, and lined his first carriage roundabout with rows of mulberry, honey locust and evergreens. The gardens of Washington and Jefferson are known as two of the best-documented sources of plant materials during the first four decades of the United States (ca. 1785–1825).

Jefferson initiated the first expedition to explore western America in 1803, and bought the Louisiana Territory from France in 1804. This territory was the largest section of land in North America to become part of the United States until Alaska achieved statehood. The expedition (1803–6) was an army operation under the direction of Captain Meriweather Lewis and Lieutenant William Clark. It was sent by Jefferson to explore the vast reaches of the upper Missouri River Valley and cross the Rocky Mountains to the Pacific Ocean. Lewis and Clark had specific instructions to collect new plants and animals. Some of the collections went directly to the White House. Most of the plants and seeds were sent to the American Philosophical Society, which distributed them to seed houses and nurseries.

After the American Revolution, French botanists sought contact with the "Anglo-Américicaines." The French government sent Andre Michaux (1770–1855), a trained botanist, to America to find new plants, especially trees useful to France. He came to America in 1785, established a nursery in New Jersey, and began sending tree shoots and seeds to the Royal Gardens at Versailles. Through him the Marquis de Lafayette sent the first seeds of a pyramidal cypress to George Washington, who first grew these trees at Mt. Vernon. Michaux and his son, Françoise Andre, documented the flora of the eastern North American forest from 1785 to 1810. The elder Michaux published *Flora Boreali-Americana* (North American Flora) in two volumes in 1803. His son published *North American Sylva* in three volumes from 1817–19.

Following the botanical discoveries from the Lewis and Clark Expedition, Dr. Benjamin Smith Barton of Pennsylvania University sent his botanical assistants to collect Western plants for a comprehensive flora. Barton was the author of the first American text on botany (*Elements of Botany*) and the leading American botanist of that period. Pursh, a recruit from England, was his first collector. On returning to England, Pursh published *Flora Americae Septentrionales* in London in 1814, the first publication on North American flora on a continental scope.

A second recruit from England, Thomas Nuttall, arrived in Philadelphia in 1808 to begin his American career. Nuttall was directed by Barton to explore the South and West. Although English-born, he became the first American botanist to visit the West Coast and Hawaii. He collected more new plants in the United States than any other person up to that time. According to Asa Gray writing in 1844, no botanist had ever visited so large a portion of the United States or made so many observations in field and forest. Nuttall published *Genera of North American Flora and a Catalogue to the Species* in two volumes in 1817. His most significant contribution to arboriculture was a second work, *North American Sylva: Trees not described by F. A. Michaux,* in three volumes from 1842–49. This included the newly discovered Western species.

In 1836 Asa Gray published *Elements of Botany,* the first American text in botany to leave the Linnaean system of classification for the natural one. John Torrey and Gray worked together on the most comprehensive flora of North America to that time. Begun in 1839 by Torrey, the second volume was completed in 1843. With numerous other studies, this was the basis for Gray's famous *Manual of Botany of the United States.* First printed in 1847, it continues (revised) as a masterpiece today as *Gray's Manual,* a literal bible of plant taxonomy for eastern North America. Gray was the last man to dominate botany in the United States, and one of the last American botanists trained initially in medicine.

EARLY USE OF TREES

In colonial Virginia more extensive planting began as soon as the settlers knew they could survive threats of inclement weather, Indians, and starvation. In fact, they literally had to plant trees for food in order to survive. In Massachusetts, fruit trees from England were planted extensively. There was hardly a settler's home without pear trees planted nearby. Such trees were so highly valued that Massachusetts enacted a law in 1642 awarding triple damages to tree owners for theft of fruit or damage to trees. Tree planting in the new colony of Georgia was stimulated in the 1720s by its English backers. To encourage both settlement and a new silk industry, a grant of fifty acres was offered for planting imported white mulberry trees. For his fifty acres a settler had to plant fifty trees—one for each acre. Although the project failed to establish a silk industry, it resulted in the permanent naturalization of white mulberry in North America.

Tree planting began in force with the westward movement of settlers beyond the Appalachians, progressed westward to the Pacific, and experienced a resurgence in the East with shade trees as the nineteenth century came to a close. Closely associated with the rise and development of tree nurseries and horticultural societies, tree planting extended well into the twentieth century with the development of forestry.

During the 1800s as settlers established new homesteads in North America, they carried seeds of cherished trees left behind in eastern states, so that many of the same species in the East were established around their homes in the Midwest and West. These seeds were primarily those of fruit trees needed for newly settled

Fig. 2.1 All across the United States, American elms were planted to line streets. Courtesy of L. Schreiber USDA-ARS.

lands. Later their needs would extend to windbreaks and woodlots, creating both a demand and stimulus for the production of deciduous tree seedlings. Although shade trees were given less thought and attention, even these were prized by settlers homesick for those trees left behind. Thus, William Bringhurst planted an American elm in Utah in 1856. As a seedling the tree was taken from the bank of the Susquehanna River in Pennsylvania and rooted in a wooden tub. Transported in an oxen-drawn wagon across the plains and mountains, it was set in what is now Springville, Utah.

Any review of the planting of trees in America would be remiss if it failed to recognize the tree planting record of Johnny Appleseed (John Chapman, 1774–1847). Born in Massachusetts, he moved to Pennsylvania where he had a farm and apple orchard near Pittsburgh. In 1800 he sold his property and began to travel, intent on making the wilderness bountiful. In his travels, which included Ohio, Michigan, Indiana, Iowa, and Arkansas (and probably parts of interconnecting states), he is said to have walked barefoot, and slept only on the open ground or cabin floor. In the winter he collected apple seeds from cider presses. In the spring he did the tree planting for which he became famous, carrying a bag of seeds; wearing his cooking pot as a hat; and toting a bible, hatchet, hoe, and rake.

As interest in tree planting developed, some towns took collective action to increase urban plantings. In 1816 planting of elms on Boston Common was made possible through funds raised by popular subscription. In later years (ca. 1830) the feeding of cows on the commons was banned to save the residual trees. One of the earliest small towns in this period to begin a tree planting program was Lynn, Massachusetts, a suburb of Boston. By 1831 tree planting in general had become an accepted philosophy, at least among farmers.

As the settlers moved west they not only planted their fruit trees in the prairie soils, but began to establish other trees such as cottonwood, juniper, elm, ash, and hackberry for windbreaks and fencerows. Trees had special significance for the settlers of the plains, where native trees and the desire for them led J. Sterling Morton of Nebraska to establish the institution of Arbor Day in 1872 in his state. This gave tree planting a new status, which continues today. Arbor Day is described in detail in chapter 4.

The first tree planting by Canadians for nonforestry purposes occurred in Western Upper Canada (now Ontario) in the 1860s. One early project was undertaken by David Smellie in Concord just north of Toronto. Smellie was a strong advocate for planting trees bordering farms and fields.

The Horticultural Societies

The origin and growth of early horticultural societies had a significant influence on the development of arboriculture. In 1769 when America was still colonial, the indefatigable Benjamin Franklin organized the American Philosophical Society in Philadelphia. Soon thereafter, in 1780, an American Academy of Arts and Sciences was founded in Boston. Collectively these societies dominated intellectual leadership in this period, and the earliest American papers in botany were presented to these societies. Each of them spawned societies for the promotion of agriculture, the first in Philadelphia in 1785, the second in Boston in 1790. Both agricultural societies provided support to our first president, George Washington, who in his first term made agriculture a priority in calling for a federally sponsored program to support it.

The first horticultural organization—the New York Horticultural Society—was created in 1816. Its founder and first president, Dr. Joseph Hosack, was a medical botanist. The society did not survive more than fifteen years but it was followed by societies in Pennsylvania and Massachusetts. The first horticultural society in Canada was established about 1830 in Montreal and the second in Toronto in 1834.

The Pennsylvania Horticultural Society (PHS) was established in 1827 by the Philadelphia Society for the Promotion of Agriculture. It is the oldest continuing horticultural society in America. The Massachusetts Horticultural Society (MHS) was established in 1829 in Boston by the Massachusetts Society for the Promotion of Agriculture. It is said to have had more influence on horticulture in America than any other organization. Through its Harvard alumni leadership, it was influential in the founding of the Arnold Arboretum in 1872. By the 1880s, the Arnold Arboretum was interested in the relative value of introduced and native ornamental trees and shrubs. Later it compiled lists of the best trees for different uses, initiated the first listing and documentation of the oldest and largest trees, and gave awards for the finest trees.

As one of the earliest, largest, and most famous intracity parks in North America, because of its landscaping and trees, Fairmount Park in Philadelphia owes much to the PHS. Although not created until 1855, its physical origin dates from 1812 when the city purchased five acres in Fairmount for use as a pumping station and reservation for water supply. By 1825 it had expanded to twenty-four acres. Landscaped with terraces of shade trees, it was considered the showplace of the city. Beginning in 1827 the land around the waterworks at Morris Hill was cultivated for recreational purposes. In 1856, after the society helped to establish the new public park by urging voluntary subscription of funds, it clashed with the city on selection of trees. This was only the beginning of the society's many battles over trees. In 1863, when the society sponsored subscription from private sources to plant memorial trees in the park, it publicly deplored the quality of the tree planting and landscaping. In 1876, as part of an exhibition, the city built a Horticultural Hall for the society.

The Massachusetts Society made other contributions of interest to arboriculture. One of its endowed funds was used to support a course in landscaping at the Lawrence School of Landscape Architecture at Harvard University. This was the first of its kind, and the man selected as lecturer was Frederick Law Olmsted. It also supported the conservation and forestry movements which would ultimately establish the United States Forest Service. In 1884 the Massachusetts Society hosted the National Forest Congress.

The Pennsylvania Society was first and foremost in developing a horticultural library. Begun in 1828, by 1834 it had voted to allocate $250 to collect literature in horticulture, botany, agriculture, and natural history. In 1842 it hired its first librarian, and in 1852 claimed to have the largest horticulture library in the United

States. Parallel in much of their development up to 1900, the Pennsylvania and Massachusetts Horticultural Societies supported one another in friendly cooperation and rivalry for seven decades. Their dominant influence helped to bring about the emergence of arboriculture from conservation and forestry, which they supported strongly in this period.

TABLE 2.2

EARLY LANDSCAPERS IN THE UNITED STATES

DATE	PERSON	NOTES
1806	M'Mahon	Early book on design and planting
1820	Parmentier	European-trained landscaper; introduced natural landscaping
1841	Downing	First native landscape designer; emphasized landscaping of small homes
1850	Vaux	English trained; sponsored by Downing; designed New York's Central Park (with Olmsted)
1857	Olmsted	First American large-scale landscaper; created Boston Parks System; designed Arnold Arboretum; taught first course on landscape design
1893	Eliot	Created "Trustees of Public Reservations"; known as the "Father of Metropolitan Park Commissions"

THE EARLY LANDSCAPERS

Landscaping in America did not get under way professionally until the nineteenth century. Beginning with Bernard M'Mahon, the key figures included Andre Parmentier, Andrew Jackson Downing, Calvert Vaux, Frederick Law Olmsted, and Charles Eliot.

Bernard M'Mahon was a seedsman, nurseryman, and gardener in Philadelphia. Early in the century, he published the *American Gardener's Calendar*, the first service book in America in the field of horticulture. Considered by some to be the first real American landscape gardener, his book had contained eighteen pages on ornamental design and planting.

One of the most influential amateur landscapers was Dr. Joseph Hosack of New York. A medical doctor, Hosack was also a botanist and horticulturist. In addition to founding the first horticultural society in America, he also founded one of the earliest botanical gardens and was influential in developing the Hudson Valley as a horticultural showplace. By 1828 he had established a 700-acre estate on the Hudson River, which he invited Andre Parmentier to landscape. Parmentier had settled in the United States a few years earlier, but had been trained in Europe. Because of Parmentier's background, Hosack and Parmentier were the first to show the "natural" landscaping style to the New World; this style was begun in England by the famous "Capability Brown" in the previous century.

By the 1850s, there was a twenty-mile stretch of fine country estates on the eastern shore of the Hudson River about 100 miles north of New York City. This is where the skills of Parmentier and Andrew Jackson Downing were especially effective and appreciated. After 1900, this area was one of the first and most important for commercial arboriculture. Both the Davey and Bartlett Companies established their first field offices nearby.

Following Parmentier, Andrew Jackson Downing (1815–50) became the first native American landscape designer. Coming from a family of nurserymen in the Hudson Valley of New York, his influence on professional landscape development was second only to that of Frederick Law Olmsted in a later age. Downing recognized the need for a professionally trained landscape architect, and since there was none available in the United States, he arranged to visit England in 1850. He brought back with him an able, young landscape architect, named Calvert Vaux (1824–95). Downing had been asked to lay out the grounds of new government buildings in Washington, D.C. With Vaux, he designed plantings around the capitol, the White House, and Smithsonian Institute. Carried out after his untimely death, these Washington designs remain as a monument to his memory. He worked extensively on numerous country estates at Newport, Rhode Island, and in the Hudson Valley. Vaux became Downing's able successor. In 1857, in his *Villas and Cottages: A series of designs prepared for execution in the United States,* he urged "the end of ugly, rural houses."

AMERICAN PARKS

Despite the growing interest in urban parks, the American park movement did not really get under way until the city of New York decided to create its massive Central Park in the 1850s. The location was not then central to the main city, being considerably farther north on the Isle of Manhattan. Following several proposals for its design and landscaping, the competition was won in 1857 by Vaux and a young, unknown landscape amateur, Frederick Law Olmsted (1822–1903). Their "Greensward" proposal led to the appointment of Olmsted as superintendent of the proposed park. During the Civil War Olmsted traveled to California, where he designed a cemetery in Oakland and the grounds for the new State University at Berkeley. After advising on the creation of an urban park for San Francisco, he returned to the east for some of his most significant achievements.

His most impressive work is said to be the Boston Parks System, embracing a seven-mile long chain of waterways and parks, extending from Beacon Hill in the central city to Franklin Zoological Park on its southern extremity. Known as the "emerald necklace," this area included both the celebrated Fenway (waterway) and the Arnold Arboretum.

When Central Park was completed after the Civil War, Olmsted became famous as the first American to organize and practice as a landscape architect on a large scale. Continuing the tradition of open naturalistic design established by Downing, his work was so well received that it brought the park-building movement and institutional landscaping to new levels over the following fifty-year period. Moreover, it led to a massive increase in the physical base of urban tree populations essential for an industry of arboriculture.

Working with Vaux, Olmsted designed plans for many different urban parks. In addition to New York City and Boston, he designed parks near Brooklyn, Buffalo, Baltimore, Cincinnati, and Hartford, and other cities too numerous to mention. His design of the Durand-Eastman Park in Rochester is especially noteworthy. In the Chicago suburb of Riverside, he created the first planned garden suburb in North America. Working with Charles S. Sargent, the first director, he helped to design the Arnold Arboretum.

While New York's Central Park was a good model for a large, wealthy metropolitan area, it was too grandiose for smaller cities and towns. Accordingly, the next step in park development occurred at a more modest level in Worcester, Massachusetts. By 1873 Worcester had developed an active tree planting program and was alert to the new opportunities promised by the newly created Arnold Arboretum in Boston. It began a nursery which produced thousands of trees for city streets. Its tree-planting program was aided by the Arnold Arboretum with its "new" trees. Worcester had an early ordinance (1877) against damage to trees by vandals, and established one of the earliest municipal parks in a small city in the United States. It remains today as one of the oldest city parks purchased with public funds.

With the aid of a grant from the Massachusetts Horticulture Society, the first course of landscape design in America was created in 1893 at Harvard University with Olmsted as the first professor. His course evolved into a School of Landscape Design.

The last significant contribution in landscaping before the advent of arboriculture was made by Charles Eliot (1859–97). A student of agriculture and horticulture at Harvard, with a strong interest in public service, he became an apprentice to Olmsted. Following additional landscape study in Virginia and Europe, Eliot returned home in 1891 to create a private organization for preservation of unique and historical sites throughout Massachusetts. Known as "Trustees of Public Reservations," it is the oldest nonforestry conservation organization in the United States. It served as a model for many other such organizations across America and, even in England, in the establishment of the great English "National Trust." It led to the creation of the Metropolitan Park Commission of the Boston area in 1893, embracing other cities and towns around the city.

Thus the development of landscape gardening, which began with landscaping of great private estates, ended in the nineteenth century with the creation of park systems and reservations, both large and small. Begun before conservation was a concept, its ultimate progress and fulfillment owed much to the coincidental development of conservation.

CONSERVATION, THE ROAD TO FORESTRY

The earliest Americans to comment on forest destruction were writers and poets, such as Ralph Waldo Emerson, Henry David Thoreau, Walt Whitman, and John Muir. Except for Muir, a persistent crusader for conservation, their protests were largely offhand and/or sporadic. The first American to gain serious public attention for conservation was George Perkins Marsh (1801–82), U.S. ambassador to Turkey in 1865. A native of Vermont, Marsh began as a farmer and became, successively, editor, attorney, U.S. legislator, diplomat, and conservationist. Sounding the first public alarm, his book in 1864, *Man and Nature*, was a devastating account of the real and theoretical consequences of human disrespect for the balances of nature.

John Muir (1838–1914) became the crusading spirit of the movement. A native of Scotland, Muir grew up in Wisconsin and was, successively, a farmer, wanderer, pacifist, woodworker, inventor, writer, amateur botanist, and conservationist. A prolific writer and legendary outdoorsman from 1875 until his death in 1914, he was a major influence in the establishment of State and National Parks, Forest Reserves, the National Park System, and National Monuments. Although he considered himself a tramp and vagabond, he used his fame as a writer to influence five U.S. presidents from Grover Cleveland to Woodrow Wilson.

While Muir worked to save wild forests from future development, Dr. John A. Warder helped to organize for management of forestry on a scientific plan. He, with others, organized the American Forestry Association (AFA) in 1875 as the first, and now the oldest, conservation association in the United States. Primarily concerned with forest trees, its interest extended to shade and ornamental trees as well.

Coincident with formation of the AFA was a swelling public revulsion of destructive forest practices. This led to a call by the American Association for the

Fig. 2.2 Bernard E. Fernow, a native of Prussia, was the first trained forester in the United States and the first Chief of Division of Forestry in 1886. In 1911 he published *The Care of Shade Trees,* the first book of its kind in North America. Courtesy of the Forest History Society, Durham, North Carolina.

Advancement of Science (AAAS) in 1873 for the U.S. Congress and state legislatures to pass legislation to protect forests. Under public pressure, the federal government responded in 1876 with the appointment of Dr. Franklin B. Hough, who served from 1876 to 1883 as a special agent in the division of agriculture. Hough was a physician who had been stimulated by conservationist George Perkins Marsh. Hough's mission was to study the state of forest conditions at that time. Hough commissioned a study of forest trees in 1880 by Charles Sargent, director of the newly established Arnold Arboretum at Harvard. In his "Report on the Forests of North America" to Hough in 1883, Sargent provided details on 412 tree species. These included taxonomic and biographical references on growth habit, distribution with maps, and notes on uses and characteristics of woods. This was the first technical study in forestry made by the government. It led in time to the production of Sargent's classic, fourteen-volume *Silva of the Trees of North America,* published from 1891 to 1914.

Bernard Eduard Fernow (1851–1923), a native of Posen in Prussia, educated at the Muenden Forestry Academy and University of Koonigsberg, migrated to the United States in 1876. Appointed chief of the newly created division of forestry in the U.S. Department of Agriculture in 1886, he remained for thirteen years. As the first chief forester in the United States, Fernow was responsible for the forest reserve law in 1891 that provided the basis of the National Forest System. Later, Fernow had a long and productive career in forestry at Cornell University, Pennsylvania State College, and as dean of the faculty of forestry at the University of

Fig. 2.3 Gifford Pinchot, first chief of the newly created U.S. Forest Service in 1898, was a crusader for conservation, the philosophical link from forestry to arboriculture. Courtesy of the Forest Historic Society, Durham, North Carolina.

Toronto. Of special interest to arborists was his publication in 1911, *The Care of Shade Trees*, the first of its kind in America.

Gifford Pinchot (1865–1946), scion of a wealthy Pennsylvania family, graduated from Yale and attended the famous National School of Forests and Waters at Nancy in France. Pinchot succeeded Fernow as chief forester in 1898 to begin an outstanding career as conservationist and forester. His crusade for conservation, however, was in conflict with the goal of the preservationists, who wanted to preserve forests as they were, with no thought of using them. But it was Pinchot's goals for wise use under forest management (conservation) that made it politically possible to transform the forest reserves first created in 1891 in the Department of Interior into the national forests in the Department of Agriculture at a later date. Conservation became not only the road to forestry, but also the philosophical link from forestry to arboriculture.

The most powerful protagonist for tree planting in the United States was President Theodore Roosevelt. An ardent man of the great outdoors, Roosevelt knew firsthand the swelling demand for forest protection in the wake of the ruthless despoliation of the forests. A wide traveler and friend of both John Muir, the eminent preservationist, and Gifford Pinchot, the highest conservationist, Roosevelt made conservation his own cause, considered by historians the hallmark of his administration.

Summary

With forestry established early in the twentieth century, the meaning of conservation and the rewards of its application turn to individual trees. This was the period that saw the beginnings of responsible tree care, known then as tree surgery. From this point an arboricultural industry would rise and grow to its present position. It could not have developed as it did, however, without the early explorers and botanists, the early nurserymen and tree planters, the horticulturists and their societies, the landscapers and park planners, the foresters and conservationists. Above all, for arboriculture to become a reality, a whole new urban forest had to be established after the original natural forest had been removed. This was the most significant development in the nineteenth century leading toward the evolution of arboriculture as an industry.

CHAPTER THREE

Introduction of Woody Plants into North America

"Seeds of orange trees came with Columbus" —Richard Campana

With the discovery of the Americas, there began the greatest movement of woody plants across oceans in the history of the world. The exploration of the two immense but underdeveloped continents by the highly cultured nations of Western Europe coincided with a new curiosity and thirst for knowledge stimulated by the Renaissance. The movement of tree species to the Americas, first from Europe and later from Asia, Africa, and Australia, had a significant impact on the development of arboriculture in North America. While the story of introduction into North America is our focus here, introduction of woody species within the continent was also significant for arboriculture, especially in the early development of urban societies in eastern North America when most of the U.S. population lived within 200 miles of the eastern seaboard.

According to Donald Wyman, former horticulturist of the Arnold Arboretum and author of *Trees for American Gardens*, less than fifty percent of amenity trees used in America are native. About fifty percent of these imports are from northern Asia and sixteen percent are from Europe. We are interested in knowing when and how some of the imports and our native trees were introduced to cultivation.

In 1929 Professor Alfred Rehder of Harvard University, author of the classic *Manual of Cultivated Plants,* wrote a paper, "On the History of the Introduction of Woody Plants into North America." The paper was written in English, but no American publication would accept it. His paper was accepted and published as *Mitteilungen der Deutschen Dendrologischen Gesellschaft* in Germany in 1932. Although reissued three times in American publications, it still remains almost hidden.

TABLE 3.1

PERIODS OF INTRODUCTION OF WOODY PLANTS

TIME	PERIOD
1492–97	Columbian voyages
1500–1780	Colonial America
1780–1860	The new United States
1860–1900	The new opening to Asia
1900–40	Organized introductions
1940–	Botanical expeditions

THE COLONIAL PERIOD (1492–1780)

Beginning with Columbus's journeys, many foreign trees were introduced to the islands off the coast of North America over the next forty years. The earliest were probably the citrus fruit trees and the peach. In 1493 the Spaniards planted seeds of orange, lemon, and citron on Haiti, and by 1565 these species had been introduced into Florida. When and where the peach was introduced is uncertain. Known to be present in North America by the early 1500s, and said to have been introduced by Spanish explorers, it was apparently spread more quickly north and west from Florida by the Indians than any other species.

While the Spaniards were influential in making the first tree introductions to California, it was the American Indians who spread the peach tree there from eastern sources. By the early 1500s the Franciscan friars had brought the olive, orange, and pomegranate to their chain of missions from Mediterranean areas. In a later period the California pepper tree and various palms were introduced there from the American tropics. The influence of the missions in extensive tree planting led to early citrus and olive groves in Southern California.

Following the Spaniards in the 1500s, the early English settlers began to introduce trees from Europe beginning in the 1600s. The first period of woody plant introductions was characterized by the introduction of those that were directly useful rather than ornamental. Most of the trees were for fruit production, but there were some ornamental trees and shrubs.

The first trees from England were introduced into northern areas, beginning in the first half of the seventeenth century. The first account of this was from J. Josselyn, the botanist of Charles II in the British Colonies. His *Account of Two Voyages to New England in 1638 and 1663* was published in 1674, and his *New England Rarities* in 1672. He mentioned apple (*Malus*), pear (*Pyrus*), quince (*Cydonia*), cherry (*Prunus*), and barberry (*Berberis*) as thriving in New England.

Among the earliest trees introduced by the English colonists were European littleleaf linden (*Tilia cordata*), crack (*Salix fragilis*) and white (*S. alba*) willow, lilac, and English elm (*Ulmus campestre* and *U. glabra*). Crack willow, introduced into New England, was used principally as charcoal for gunpowder. It was soon naturalized. The white willow was known for its medicinal powers, the salicylic acid in its bark providing the active ingredient in what would become, in a later age, aspirin.

F. G. Meyer of the U.S. National Arboretum has listed 128 kinds of trees, shrubs, and vines introduced into gardens in the southeastern states of Virginia, Georgia, and the Carolinas from 1607 to 1840. These gardens included more introduced than native tree species. Most of the introduced trees had come from Europe. Despite the smaller number of species used, the native trees were also recognized early as valuable assets in landscaping. No introduced tree could equal the southern live oak, and no other flowering shrub could match the beauty of southern magnolia. One Mediterranean shrub that thrived and became popular in the coastal south was oleander (*Nerium oleander*). Other Mediterranean trees less commonly grown were Grecian laurel (*Laurus nobilis*), common myrtle (*Myrtus communis*), laurestinus (*Viburnum tinus*), and Italian cypress (*Cupressus sempervirens*). Asiatic species such as the tea olive, camellia, Chinese and Japanese hollies, and azalea also grew well in those Southern gardens during the colonial period.

Before the Dutch ceded New York to the English in 1640, some of the earliest ornamental woody plant introductions had been made there. Governor Stuyvesant of New Amsterdam (renamed New York) planted a Summer Bonchretien, a grafted pear imported from Holland in 1647. It lived in his garden in the Bowery for more than 200 years. By 1681 common lilac, common snowball (*Viburnium opulus*), and common boxwood were growing in the Van Cortlandt garden at Croton-at-Hudson, as well as in the Peter Stuyvesant garden in New York City.

Meanwhile, the first native American trees were being brought into cultivation. Some of the earliest to be used included American elm, sugar maple, red oak, and in the South, catalpa. One of the earliest native trees to be recorded, which had later ornamental value was sweetgum. The Spaniard, Cabeza de Vaca, saw it in Florida as early as 1528. In his early explorations of the South in the 1700s, Mark Catesby was the first to record, for later cultivation, various native trees including black gum, white fringetree, pawpaw, umbrella magnolia, and rosebay rhododendron. Among the introductions in the early 1700s were the first apricots from Asia by way of Europe into Virginia, the monkey puzzle tree from Chile, Norfolk Island pine from the South Pacific, and avocado from Central America. The latter species mark early introductions of trees from non-European sources, whose numbers were limited up to the middle of the nineteenth century.

While early plant explorers sought ornamental plants in the newly discovered lands of North America to introduce to European gardens and landscapes, European settlers in colonial America were bringing seeds and sprouts of European trees to North America. In the southern colonies from Virginia to Georgia, planting in numerous gardens over a period from 1607 to 1840 showed more than 128 kinds of introduced trees, but only 100 native ones. Crape myrtle from Asia was listed as present as early as 1700, with no record of its earliest introduction. In the north, the English common yew was introduced at Haddonfield, New Jersey, in 1713 by Elizabeth Haddon Estaugh. By 1722 the botanical explorer, Mark Catesby, introduced into cultivation *Catalpa bignonioides*. A few years later in 1726, the barberry, introduced from abroad as an ornamental, became known as the earliest recorded weed. Still valued as an ornamental, and long since escaped into the wild, it is also now a menace in some areas as an alternate host of the black stem wheat rust fungus.

TABLE 3.2

SOME USEFUL TREES INTRODUCED
BY EARLY ENGLISH SETTLERS

TREE	NOTES
Crack willow	Charcoal for gunpowder
English elm	Ornament and shade
Linden	Ornament and shade
White willow	Medicine/salycylic acid (bark extract)

The latter part of the colonial period was aided by the establishment of numerous nurseries and gardens on a much more extensive scale than earlier. Paramount among these were the Bartram Garden near Philadelphia and the Prince Nursery and gardens outside New York City. Another less well-known garden was developed in Savannah, Georgia, following Oglethorpe's landing in 1733. The Savannah garden represented the first organized plant introduction in America. The garden was used to test established plants considered of value for the future economy of the colony. Trees introduced included English fruit trees, mulberries (to develop a silk industry), figs, pomegranates, coffee and cocoa (which failed), tea, crape myrtle and chinaberry. Except for the chinaberry, crape myrtle, and mulberry, none of the other tree species was successful. The effort was abandoned after the American Revolution. In time, however, crape myrtle and chinaberry became two of the most commonly used trees in the arboriculture of the

South. By 1830 the streets and squares of Savannah were heavily populated with them. The garden was a casualty of the American War of Independence.

The Prince Nursery at Flushing, Long Island, had special significance for introduction of foreign trees. Started in 1732, this nursery quickly became a center first for importing fruit trees, and later for receiving ornamental trees and shrubs. The Prince Nursery and gardens also served some of the functions of arboreta and botanical gardens. They were repositories of some of our earliest and oldest introduced trees. Some of the early tree plantings on the Prince Estate contained the oldest specimens in North America of Asiatic magnolias, Paulownia, cedar of Lebanon, European copper beech, and atlas cedar. Other woody species known to have been introduced through the Prince firm were *Populus nigra* var. *italica*; *Cotinus coggygria*; *Viburnum opulus* F.; *Colutea arborescens*; *Hibiscus syriacus*; and *Koelreuteria paniculata*.

In contrast to Robert Prince, who had established a prosperous nursery for procurement and sales of foreign trees, John Bartram had established his garden near Philadelphia to collect, test, and exchange plants with both American and European correspondents. While Bartram was influential in stimulating introductions from abroad, he is best known for his discovery of American trees and their introduction into cultivation. At first a farmer, Bartram was only a part-time plant collector until his reputation grew to the point of a royal commission as the king's botanist. Only then was he able to act independently on a full-time basis as plant explorer, amateur botanist, and arborist par excellence. Bartram was responsible for introducing Norway maple, which he requested from England in 1835. In addition to the Franklinia tree, which he discovered and cultivated for ornamental use, he introduced many other native trees and shrubs into cultivation. Some examples of these are species of *Magnolia, Rhododendron, Kalmia,* and *Halesia.*

Among those active in introducing new trees was John Custis, a wealthy planter in Virginia and future father-in-law to George Washington. In 1734 Custis received seeds of the horse chestnut from Peter Collinson of England and by 1837 had introduced seeds of pistachio, almonds, dates, cedar of Lebanon, Italian evergreen oak, strawberry tree (*Arbutus unedo*), striped box, and Persian lilac.

By the middle of the eighteenth century the record and pace of tree introductions were increasing. By 1752 the following trees were known in the colonial garden at Williamsburg, Virginia: European birch, cedar of Lebanon, English beech, English holly, Scotch pine, and European mountain ash. Also introduced from Japan (through Europe) circa 1750 was an Asian mulberry (*Brousonettia papyrifera*), Austrian pine from Europe circa 1759, and goldenrain tree (*Koelreuteria paniculata*) from Asia by 1763.

Native to China, weeping willow is thought to have come to Europe over the "Silk Road" through central China and Persia to Babylonia during the Middle Ages. It was not known in Western Europe until circa 1700. The date of its introduction to North America is unknown. According to Thomas Willing of Philadelphia, General Cocke of Virginia received a basket of figs from Madeira, threw the basket into a sink in his yard, where a willow stem (presumably from the basket) took root. Thomas Jefferson estimated the date of introduction to be circa 1770. The alternate story also involves figs, in this case a box containing them sent to the English poet Alexander Pope (1688–1744) from Smyrna in Turkey. A twig from his box, planted at Twickenham on Thames, developed into a tree. In the years before the Revolutionary War, a twig from this tree was given to a British officer on his way to America. Said to have been planted in Virginia, a tree developed from this twig. The tree was well established in urban Philadelphia by the 1790s, as described by Abigail Adams, wife of the second president of the United States.

The ginkgo tree was introduced into America in 1774 by William Hamilton of Philadelphia, a cousin of John Bartram. It was introduced into Japan from China probably during the Sung Dynasty. Introduced into Holland early in the 1700s, it was known in England by 1754 and Vienna by 1768.

The mulberry tree (*Morus alba*) was introduced just before the end of the colonial period. Native to China, the white mulberry was highly valued for the production of silk in Asia and Europe. Introduced into Europe some time after 1200, it was brought to America in 1776 by William Kendrick who tried to use it to establish an American silk industry. He was not successful.

EARLY U.S. INTRODUCTIONS (1780–1865)

The second period of tree introductions began with the end of the American Revolution and the development of the new United States. This period saw the new influence of France as the wartime ally of the United States, the results of the Lewis and Clark Expedition, and the origin and development of horticulture as a new profession.

Andre Michaux, a trained botanist, came to America to seek new plants for potential use in France. Working primarily in the South, out of Charleston, South Carolina, he introduced a variety of woody plants in 1786, including the first camellias. Other trees introduced included camphor, English holly, gardenia from China, laurestinus, the strawberry tree (*Arbutus unedo*), tea (*Camellia senensis*) from China, the parasol tree, paper mulberry, the ginkgo tree, the silk tree (*Mimosa*), the tea olive, chinaberry, Indian azalea, and Italian cypress. He sent President George Washington gifts of goldenrain tree, crape myrtle, and the Italian Cypress. In 1787

Michaux or his son discovered a magnolia tree (*M. cordata*) near Augusta, Georgia, which was sent to France.

Thomas Jefferson, in his capacity as ambassador to France, gave to and received from European contacts, all kinds of seeds and plants. In 1784 Jefferson arranged with a French seed trader, Thouin, in Paris, for exchange of seeds of American and foreign plants. President John Quincy Adams formalized this practice in 1827 by executive order instructing federal officials abroad to facilitate introduction of plants of potential value.

In 1827 Henry L. Ellsworth, United States Patent Commissioner, became responsible for introducing new plant materials. In 1839 the U.S. government made its first effort to fund introduction of rare plants and seeds with an appropriation of $1,000 to Ellsworth. Other efforts in the U.S. introduction program before 1860 included bringing in the following trees: cinchona from South America, the date palm from Africa, olive from Europe, cork oak from Spain, and camphor from Asia.

Given the new climate to encourage introductions, many more trees and shrubs were introduced. The Lombardy poplar (*Populus nigra* var. *italica*) originated as a cultivated tree in Europe. Introduced into England in 1758, it was introduced into the United States in 1784 when William Hamilton acquired it for his private "Woodland" arboretum.

Father D'Incarville, a French Catholic missionary, discovered the tree of heaven, native to China, in 1751. Seeds were brought or sent to the Royal Society of London. Its seeds were imported in 1784 by Hamilton of the Philadelphia area for planting in his arboretum. Shortly after Hosack developed his "Elgin" botanical garden in New York City, he had listed the following foreign trees: *Gleditsia sinensis* from Asia, *Malus spectabilis* from Europe, *Magnolia liliflora*, and *Sophora japonica*. By 1818 the new Harvard Botanical Garden listed oriental arborvitae (*Thuja orientalis*) from Asia. By 1828 Chinese elm (*Ulmus parvifolia*) and Chinese wisteria (*W. sinensis*) were listed by the Prince Nursery in its catalog. In 1825 the Minshall and Jacob Painter Brothers began a well-known collection of trees near Lima, Pennsylvania. Still extant by 1929, this arboretum contained the oldest specimen of *Sequoiadendron giganteum* in eastern North America, introduced there from California about 1825.

The pinetum established by H. H. Hunnewell in Wellesley, Massachusetts, in the 1840s was probably unsurpassed in this period in terms of introduction of conifers and rhododendrons. A wealthy merchant and avid horticulturist, he had established numerous connections for plant exchange, importing more than 2,000 trees from England and hundreds of rhododendrons from Europe for his collection.

The Reverend John Grimke Drayton, scion of the famous Draytons of South Carolina, began collecting plants from around the world in 1847. Among the many camellias and azaleas he obtained was the first Belgian Indian azalea. He also brought the first *Azalea indica* to America from Asia.

PLANT EXPLORERS GO WEST

The period 1800–60 was characterized more by transplanting trees from one geographic region to another rather than from abroad. This was accomplished primarily through government and military expeditions, immigration from Mexico and China, development of landscaping, new botanical gardens and nurseries, exploring botanists, and direct efforts by the federal government.

Immigrants from Mexico were responsible for a second introduction of oleander. Native to the Mediterranean area of Europe and Japan, this ornamental shrub is said to have been imported from Jamaica in rum barrel tubs to Galveston, Texas, in 1841. Following the return of the U.S. Army of Occupation from the United States–Mexican War in 1847, other plants were introduced including numerous cacti.

Colonel John C. Fremont of the U.S. Army, in four hazardous journeys throughout the South and the southwest United States, made important gains in the fields of botany and horticulture with his many plant collections in the 1840s. Of special interest to arboriculture was his discovery of flannel bush (*Fremontia californica*) and incense cedar, the latter on the Sacramento River in California. He was the first to see piñon pine (*Pinus monophylla*) and discovered red fir (*Abies magnifica*).

In 1847 Josiah Gregg discovered a new ash tree in Texas that bears his name (*Fraxinus greggii*). Charles Wright in 1851–52 discovered a native acacia (*Acacia greggii*) in Texas and was the first to see the Mexican variety of elderberry (*Sambucus canadensis*) of value for its fruit and ornament. He also discovered the Arizona sycamore in southern Arizona, which was given his name (*Platanus wrightii*). Dr. J. M. Bigelow, at about the same time and place, found as yuccas both the Spanish dagger and the Joshua tree, and first described the fan palm (*Washingtonia filamentosa*).

A British group led by John Jeffrey in the 1840s sent a body of Scotsmen to the United States to collect plants on the Pacific Coast. Of interest to us was their discovery of several pines near Mount Shasta in California, including species of *jeffreyi, balfouriana, murrayana,* and *albicaulis.*

Seeds of the largest tree in the world, the giant sequoia (*Sequoiadendron giganteum*), discovered by unknown botanical explorers earlier in the century, were exported en masse before 1850 to New York and beyond. They were brought to New York by G. H. Woodruff in a snuff box by Pony Express at a cost of twenty-five dollars.

Not so well documented were numerous introductions of exotic plants into the far western United States and Canada after the California Gold Rush (1849). It is said that the first eucalyptus trees that now dominate so much of the California countryside came from Australia about the same time as large numbers of Chinese laborers arrived, circa 1850.

Walker in California is credited with introducing many landscape plants as early as 1849. He brought the first eucalyptus and acacia trees to San Francisco in 1856. The eucalyptus was sought for woodlot plantings, and a craze for them developed all over the state. They were planted for a variety of purposes: ornamental forests, landscaping roads, railroad ties, and furniture. Later they were used for windbreaks, watershed stability, and fuel. Escaping from cultivation, they survive as part of the naturalized flora. Numerous fruit trees from the eastern states were known in California before 1850. By 1860 other exotic trees introduced to California included species of *Sterculia, Shinus, Bauhinia,* and *Pittosporum.*

Some of the nurseries started between 1800 and 1860 became famous for their trees. The Ellwanger and Barry Nursery in Rochester, and that of Samuel and Robert Parsons in Flushing, New York, were both established about 1840. Thomas Meehan opened his nursery in Germantown, Pennsylvania, in 1851. Each of these nurseries carried large numbers of trees and shrubs from European sources.

Prior to 1860, most foreign tree introductions to North America came from Europe. After this period, political developments between the United States and the Orient would open the doors to the trees of eastern Asia.

ASIAN INTRODUCTIONS (1860–1900)

American explorers for trees in Asia were latecomers, having been preceded by botanists from many European countries. By 1860 the growth of American shipping and naval power had opened the way for direct introduction of plants of every type from China and Japan. In 1859, in a paper on the botany of Japan, the American botanist Asa Gray had focused sharply on the strong similarity between the woody flora of northeastern Asia and that of eastern North America.

For the first time it became clear that America and Asia had many woody plant genera in common. Later it would be seen that the Asian species of many genera were more numerous than in the United States. Activity surrounding Asian introductions was often dominated by individual opportunists abroad in Asia for reasons other than collecting plants. Thomas Hogg, American consul to Japan, was instrumental in sending the first katsuratree (*Cercidiphyllum japonicum*) to the

TABLE 3.3

SELECTED SHADE TREES INTRODUCED IN NORTH AMERICA

(Source: Li)

COMMON NAME	SCIENTIFIC NAME	GEOGRAPHIC ORIGIN
Coliseum maple	*Acer cappadocicum*	Western and central Asia
Norway maple	*Acer platanoides*	Caucasia
Sycamore maple	*Acer pseudoplatanus*	Europe, western Asia
Horse chestnut	*Aesculus hippocastanum*	Balkan peninsula
Mimosa	*Albizia julibrissin*	Central Asia
Tree of heaven	*Ailanthus altissimia*	Eastern China, Japan
Speckled alder	*Alnus rugosa*	Europe, northern Africa, Asia
European white birch	*Betula pendula*	Europe, Asia Minor
Paper mulberry	*Broussonetia papyrifera*	China, Japan
Katsuratree	*Cercidiphyllum japonicum*	China, Japan
Dove tree	*Davidia involucrata*	Southern China
European birch	*Fagus sylvatica*	Central and southern Europe
English holly	*Ilex aquifolium*	Southern Europe, northern Africa, Asia
Goldenrain tree	*Koelreuteria paniculata*	Eastern China, Japan
Crape myrtle	*Lagerstroemia indica*	China
Oriental sweet gum	*Liquidambar orientalis*	Western Asia
Chinaberry	*Melia azedarach*	Central and southern China
White mulberry	*Morus alba*	China
Black mulberry	*Morus nigra*	Western Asia
Royal Paulownia	*Pawlonia tomentosa*	China
Oriental plane	*Platanus orientalis*	Western Asia
White poplar	*Populus alba*	Central Europe, Asia
Holm oak	*Quercus ilex*	Southern Europe
Lebanon oak	*Quercus lebanii*	Asia Minor
English oak	*Quercus robur*	Europe, northern Africa, western Asia
White willow	*Salix alba*	Europe, northern Africa, Asia
Weeping willow	*Salix babylonica*	China
Chinese scholar tree	*Sophora japonica*	China, Korea
European mtn. ash	*Sorbus aucuparia*	Europe through western Asia
Littleleaf linden	*Tilia cordata*	Europe
English elm	*Ulmus procera*	England
Siberian elm	*Ulmus pumila*	China, Japan, Korea
Zelkova	*Zelkova carpinifolia*	Caucasia

United States in 1861. Later in this period the plant collectors were trained botanists and educators.

Dr. George R. Hall, a medical missionary, began the new era of direct movement of plants from the Orient to America in 1861. A resident of Newport, Rhode
Island, he made the first significant shipment of live ornamental plants from Japan
to Boston in 1862. Included were several yew species, such as *Taxus cuspidata*.
These were sent to Parsons Nursery in Flushing, New York, as well as to his own
residence. Over a fifteen-year period, Hall collected and sent back to the United
States a variety of woody plants, including *Malus hallania*, a crab apple named for
him; the star magnolia (*Magnolia stellata*); kobus magnolia; peegee hydrangea;
and Japanese walnut. Some of the earliest plants propagated by seed shipped from
China were species of lilacs and rhododendrons. Included were hairy lilac (*Sy-
ringa pubescens*), late lilac (*S. villosa*), and Korean rhododendron (*Rhododendron
dawricum mucronulatum*).

Dr. William S. Clark, botanist and president of Massachusetts Agricultural Col-
lege in Amherst, went to Japan in 1876 to establish an agricultural college in
Sapporo. He was responsible for the introduction of many tree species in America.
In 1877 he sent native seeds of the lilac tree and those of the katsuratree to the
newly established Arnold Arboretum. His collections not only enriched the Arnold
Arboretum, but also added to the collections at the University of Massachusetts.
Some of his collections include Japanese umbrella pine; Sargent's cherry (the first
cultivated beyond the Orient); a choice Japanese maple (*Acer shirasawanum*), at
first classified as the *Acer palmatum*; Japanese elm; painted maple (*A. pictum*);
Manchurian walnut; Japanese larch; silver magnolia; and cork tree.

Another botanist from the University of Massachusetts in 1890 was Professor
William P. Brooks, who extended the introductions begun by Clark. Many of the
tree introductions by Clark and Brooks were established beyond the University of
Massachusetts campus, and remain today to enrich the variety of trees in the town
of Amherst.

About ten years after Hall began sending Asiatic trees directly to America, the
founding of the Arnold Arboretum in 1872 provided a new basis for collecting
more exotic trees directly from Asia. Its director, Charles Sprague Sargent, saw the
similarities among woody plants from northern Asia and eastern North America
as noted earlier by Gray. He saw in these similarities likely new sources for suitable trees for northeastern North America. Introduced from Asia by Sargent were
torch azalea (*Rhododendron obtusum*) and several crab apple species, including
the species named for Sargent himself (*Malus sargentii*).

GOVERNMENT INTRODUCTIONS

Following the enormous success of European plant expeditions to Asia and private plant explorations such as that undertaken by the Arnold Arboretum, the U.S. government became actively engaged in plant introduction. From that beginning, the United States Department of Agriculture (USDA) plant inventories have become probably the single most important historical record of introductions from abroad. In 1898 the USDA established a section of Seed and Plant Introduction under the direction of Dr. David Fairchild. In the same year the first plant introduction garden of the federal government was established at Miami. David Fairchild (1870–1954), trained as a botanical geneticist, became a special agent for the USDA in 1889. By 1898, at the age of twenty-eight, he became head of the new section for plant introduction. During his twenty-nine years as director, there were fifty-four major explorations throughout the world, with more than 27,000 introductions. Even after formal retirement in 1927, he continued to explore for plants. He led seven major explorations, and at least 7,000 introductions were his personal responsibility. Early in the 1900s he introduced the common date palm (*Phoenix dactylifera*) from Egypt, where he collected sprouts from the Nile River and shipped them to Florida packed in the Nile mud. He is also said to have introduced both banyan and mango trees into Florida from Asia by 1910.

It was under his jurisdiction that the famous Japanese cherry trees were first introduced in 1902. A major gift from the city of Tokyo, they were given in recognition of U.S. aid to Japan after a disastrous earthquake. David Fairchild himself brought thirty varieties of Japanese flowering cherry trees to the United States for the first time in 1902. The famous flowering cherry trees now in Washington came in 1912. Fairchild wrote two books that describe his plant hunting career—*Exploring for Plants* and *The World is My Garden.*

One of the most active and productive plant explorers for the USDA was the Dutch-born Frank N. Meyer (1875–1918). Ranging over Manchuria, Mongolia, and northern China, he became the USDA's principal pioneering plant explorer in Asia. In 1905 he began the first of his many plant explorations to the Orient. A prodigious collector, he was responsible for more than 2,500 plant introductions over a thirteen-year period. In 1910 he collected stones of the northern Asian wild peach (*Prunus davideana*) resistant to root knot nematode. Trees developed from this collection became important as stock for grafting apricots, plums, and peaches. In 1912 Meyer astounded the plant world with a telegram disclosing his find of the chestnut blight fungus on Asian chestnuts in China, removing all doubt of the original source of chestnut blight. The achievement for which he may be remembered longest was his finding of the callery pear (*Pyrus calleryana*), some trees of which were resistant to fire blight. Seeds were sent to the United States in 1916, and grown into trees to furnish, through pollen, the gene for resistance to fire blight. Keen observers of this tree in America recognized the tree not only for blight resistance but for ornamental value as well. With further study the wild Chinese pear was shown to withstand street paving, heat, and automobile fumes. A cultivar released for nursery production became the popular and successful Bradford pear.

In the 1870s the Arnold Arboretum received seeds of the now famous *Prunus sargentii* from William S. Bigelow, an American physician in Japan. The director of the arboretum, Charles Sargent, was eager to introduce from Asia, and went there himself in 1892, returning with seeds of many trees and shrubs. Among these were species of rhododendron, apple, maple, and alder.

THE GOLDEN AGE (1900–40)

One of the most colorful plant explorers to influence American introductions from Asia was Dr. Ernest H. Wilson, an Englishman at first employed by the Veitch Nursery in England. He joined the Arnold Arboretum staff in 1909 and was affectionately known as "Chinese Wilson." Between 1899 and 1919 he introduced more than 1,500 plants to England and the United States. His Arnold Arboretum collections included species of maple, euonymus, dogwood, rhododendron, beech, oak, mimosa, yellowwood, mulberry, forsythia, lilac, fir, juniper, spruce, pine, hemlock, cotoneaster, apple, cherry, pear, rose, mountain ash, hydrangea, yew, basswood, elm, walnut, azalea, and chestnut. Of special significance were his introductions of the Chinese dove tree (*Davidia*), beauty bush, and fifty azalea types from Japan. Of interest to arborists was his introduction of Chinese elm (*Ulmus parvifloria*) in 1905 and Siberian elm (*U. pumila*) in 1910.

Subsequent to breaking ground with Asian introductions, the arboretum pressed on to harvest the richness of the Asian woody flora. In 1905 J. G. Jack of the arboretum staff went to China and Korea and returned with many new plants, including Korean rhododendron (*R. yedoensis* var. *poukanense*) and species of Asian oak and willow. The final collector of Asian plants for introduction to the Arnold Arboretum was Joseph Rock. Having first traveled in southwest China, Burma, and Siam, Rock collected in northwest China for the arboretum in 1925 and 1926. During the first thirty years of its Asian program (1902–32), the Arnold Arboretum led the nation in the introduction of foreign trees.

TABLE 3.4

EXAMPLES OF INTRODUCED TREE PESTS AND PATHOGENS

PESTS	PATHOGENS
Birch leaf miner	Beech bark disease fungus
European elm bark beetle	Chestnut blight fungus
Gypsy moth	Dutch elm disease fungus
Japanese beetle	White pine blister rust fungus

SOME INTRODUCTION MISTAKES

Some new discoveries reflected serious problems looming from introductions that would shake the tree world in America as never before. One of the earliest to have unintended results was the semiwoody kudzu vine (*Pueraria lobata*, formerly *P. thunbergiana*). Native to China and Japan, it was introduced into the southern United States as an ornamental in the 1870s. Additional related species (*P. tuberosa* and *phaesioloides*) were introduced by L. H. Bailey in 1911. Considerable assets were seen for this plant beyond ornamentation. As a legume it would add nitrogen to the soil, and it had value for forage, erosion control, and organic matter. Despite this, it became an out-of-control weed because it smothers other plants, including trees.

Between 1900 and 1910, the white pine blister rust disease and chestnut blight were discovered in the northeastern United States at destructive and epidemic levels. Both diseases were caused by fungi infecting imported trees. The result was a new problem for plant collectors. In 1912 Congress passed a new quarantine law to prevent further introductions of new diseases and insect pests.

A new provision of the quarantine law, enacted in 1918, prohibited the routine introduction of woody plants into the United States. Designed to prevent the introduction of new, destructive plant pests and pathogens, such as gypsy moth and the white pine blister rust and chestnut blight fungi, it prohibited all importation of nursery stock. Intensely disliked by nurserymen and plant collectors for botanical gardens and arboreta, it raised a chorus of complaints. Moreover, it discouraged introductions of new trees from abroad.

But the introduction of tree insect pests and causal agents of disease was not over. In this same "golden age" of plant introductions came the worst tree problem for arborists since the gypsy moth. Covered in more detail in the chapter on Dutch elm disease, it is mentioned here only briefly. A European elm bark beetle had been introduced by accident to eastern North America by 1907. Of small consequence by itself, this insect insured rapid spread of the worst shade tree disease in North America. The fungus arrived on elm logs from Europe before 1930. Elms, insects, and fungus made a perfect combination for Dutch elm disease.

Florida was the scene of several pest or weed plant introductions, including the Brazilian coffee tree, Australian pine, and melaleuca. The last of these three may be the worst. Introduced from Australia about 1900, it was widely planted in southern Florida as an ornamental on golf courses, on roadsides, in housing developments, and around agricultural areas. Marching into the Everglades, it crowds out native vegetation, is a haven for mosquitoes and spiders, threatens wildlife habitats, and is a serious fire hazard.

SUMMARY

Tree introductions to North America began with the earliest Spanish explorers and continue to the present time. Earliest introductions were made for survival and health; later introductions were made for ornament and industry, forest productivity, shade, and other amenities. The principal agents of introduction were navigators and settlers; then collectors, importers, diplomats, scholars, missionaries, plant explorers; and finally institutional botanists and horticulturists. The golden age of introduction (1900–40) was flawed by the inadvertent introduction of destructive insects and plant pathogens, requiring quarantines on introductions and plant introduction stations. The postwar period of introduction included new entrance into isolated world areas; the rise of cooperative expedition; and a search for new specific qualities in plants, including a search for new germ plasm in both known and unknown plants.

CHAPTER FOUR

Arbor Day

"Other holidays repose upon the past; Arbor Day proposes for the future"
—J. Sterling Morton

Tree planting ceremonies are probably as old as civilization. The beginning of the Arbor Day movement can be traced to ancient tree planting ceremonies in such diverse areas of the world as Israel, Egypt, India, Switzerland, and Central America. One of the most significant events leading to the development of arboriculture in the United States was the initiation of Arbor Day in 1872 by J. Sterling Morton (1832–1902) in Nebraska.

Tree planting in Nebraska had been well established before the advent of Arbor Day. Following the U.S. Homestead Act of 1862, settlers flocking from well-wooded eastern states into the new lands of the prairie found the lack of trees to be a serious problem. Every farmer needed wood for fuel and housing and fence posts for his fields. Orchards, field crops, and buildings also needed protection from the wind. The settlers had an obvious need for trees for survival alone. Thus, before Arbor Day was initiated a good deal of planting had already begun. But the climate of opinion leading up to the initiation, recognition, and public acceptance of Arbor Day as an institution was stimulated by the writings of a perceptive U.S. diplomat serving President Abraham Lincoln in Europe.

A native of Vermont, George Perkins Marsh was successively a farmer, lawyer, editor, businessman, congressman, and diplomat. Widely traveled and widely read, he championed the scientific approach to natural resources and productivity as reflected by the writings of Thomas Jefferson. This was in sharp contrast to the influence of the growing romanticism about nature offered by artists, philosophers, and wealthy tourists, whose interest was fleeting at best. In 1864 he wrote a powerful book, *Man and Nature; or physical geography as modified by human action.*

Marsh was the first in the United States to call attention to the need for and value of planting trees. In representing the United States at the courts of Italy and Turkey in the 1860s, he noted the active efforts, involving great expense, made in much of Europe to rehabilitate previous timberlands long denuded by reckless and thoughtless exploitation. He noted also how the science of forestry was given serious attention by European governments as one of their most important departments of state. His observations emphasized the critical need for planting of trees to ensure a nation's supply of timber. Marsh was to influence many significant figures of the period in addition to Morton, including Carl Schurz, Secretary of the Interior, and Charles Sargent of the Arnold Arboretum. Despite the fact that the book was well known to scholars, it had no wide public audience.

It would take a dramatic act to rouse the public to the need for conservation by tree planting. This was provided by the action and example of J. Sterling Morton in the creation of Arbor Day in 1872. As the first well-defined act toward conservation and rehabilitation of the environment, Arbor Day would catalyze the movement with its tree planting symbol. Beginning with the initiation of a state Arbor Day in Nebraska, Arbor Day has had and continues to have an enormous impact on arboriculture.

Born in Adams, New York, Morton moved with his family at the age of two to Monroe, Michigan, on the shores of Lake Erie. At the age of fourteen he enrolled at Wesleyan Seminary at Albion, Michigan, for better educational advantages. After three years at Albion, he attended the University of Michigan at Ann Arbor and Union College in New York, obtaining degrees from both institutions. Upon returning to Michigan, he wrote briefly for the *Detroit Free Press* and married Caroline Joy French.

In 1854, with his new bride, Morton headed west to the Nebraska Territory and settled in Bellevue, Nebraska. He became embroiled politically in the battle over location of the territorial capital. Backing Bellevue, he lost out to Omaha (which also lost in the end). He moved to Nebraska City at the age of twenty-three to edit the *Nebraska City News,* the first newspaper in the territory. He settled on a quarter section of government-granted land and became a farmer as well as an editor.

As he began to report the activities of settlers, he noted with interest and care the tree planting by local farmers. Seeing the future Nebraska, then largely treeless, as a great agricultural and horticultural state, he urged the planting of fruit trees. This became both a mission and a hobby, and he named his farm "Arbor Lodge."

Fig. 4.1 J. Sterling Morton. Courtesy of the National Arbor Day Foundation.

Always active in politics, he became secretary of the Nebraska Territory from 1858 to 1861. By 1872, after Nebraska had become a state, he was a member of the State Board of Agriculture. The concept and name of Arbor Day was his own. In January 1872 he addressed the Horticulture Society in Lincoln (the state capital), urgently pressing for extensive planting of fruit trees. Also meeting in Lincoln at the same time was the State Board of Agriculture. He proposed the following resolution on Arbor Day that was passed unanimously:

> Resolved, The Wednesday, the 10th day of April, 1872, and the same is hereby, especially set apart and consecrated for tree planting in the State of Nebraska, and the State Board of Agriculture hereby name it Arbor Day; and to urge upon the people of the State the vital importance of tree planting, hereby offer a special premium of one hundred dollars to the agricultural society of that county in Nebraska which shall, upon that day, plant properly the largest number of trees; and a farm library of twenty-five dollars' worth of books to that person who, on that day, shall plant properly, in Nebraska, the greatest number of trees.

The use of the term *arbor* was chosen over the term *sylvan* by Morton, because he wanted to emphasize the planting of fruit and amenity trees over forest trees. In this he was clearly interested in the tree as an individual (as in arboriculture) rather than one of a massive population.

From the initiation of Arbor Day to the end of his life, Morton was active in promoting tree planting, conservation, and forestry. He held various key positions that would lend great support to these causes. From 1893 to 1897 he served as Secretary of Agriculture in President Grover Cleveland's second cabinet. Morton spent his final years at his mansion on the hill, Arbor Lodge. This home with sixty-five acres of woodlands and gardens is now preserved as a national shrine, named and supported by the Nebraska State Game, Forestation and Parks Commission as Arbor Lodge State Park.

J. Sterling Morton is honored throughout the world as the founder of Arbor Day. He is honored by a statue in the hall of fame in Washington, D.C., and by another statue, the "Nebraskan Tree Planter," in Nebraska City. The latter monument was erected in part by pennies contributed by children for this purpose from all over the world. In 1932 on 22 April (Arbor Day), the United States issued a postage stamp in his honor to commemorate the sixtieth anniversary of Arbor Day. In 1988 Morton was inducted into the U.S. Agricultural Hall of Fame in Kansas City for his "lifetime accomplishments as an agriculturist, U.S. Secretary of Agriculture and as the originator of Arbor Day."

By 1876 the states of Kansas, Tennessee, and Minnesota followed Nebraska in endorsing the Arbor Day concept with legislation. North Dakota and Ohio joined in 1882. Before 1882 Arbor Day celebrations were organized through agricultural associations and town authorities; in 1882 the schools became involved for the first time. Arbor Day in Cincinnati, Ohio, was celebrated during sessions of a national forestry convention in that city, and school children played a prominent part. Under the direction of the school superintendent, John B. Peaslee, 20,000 children paraded through the streets to Eden Park.

TABLE 4.1
GEOGRAPHIC SPREAD OF ARBOR DAY

YEAR	AREA
1872	Nebraska
1876	Kansas, Tennessee, Minnesota
1882	North Dakota, Ohio
1887	Ontario
1895	Spain
1905	Hawaii (*not then a U.S. state*)
1923	Australia, plus various countries in Europe and Asia (11 total)

In 1883 the American Forestry Congress passed a resolution recommending observance of Arbor Day in the schools of every state. A committee was appointed to demonstrate the value of Arbor Day celebrations to school authorities, with N. G. Northrup, author of the resolution, as chairman. In the following year (1884), at the annual meeting of the National Education Association (NEA), Northrup offered a resolution similar to that endorsed by the Forestry Congress.

In 1885 the NEA adopted such a resolution recommending general observance of Arbor Day for schools in all states.

Thus, it was as a school festival that observance of Arbor Day spread not only throughout the United States but also beyond. The Educational Department of Canada's Ontario Province in 1887 set aside the first Friday in May for planting trees and flowers. The plan spread to Spain in 1895 and Hawaii (not then a state) in 1905. By 1923 it was observed in all the dependencies of the United States, and in Canada, Great Britain, Australia, English West Indies, South Africa, New Zealand, France, Norway, Japan, China, and Russia.

Although the tree planting ethic had many influential supporters, by this time, none was more prominent than Theodore Roosevelt, the "Conservation President." On 15 April 1907, he gave special emphasis to tree planting in an "Arbor Day letter to the Children of the United States." Because of his position, both as a sitting president of the United States and a dedicated conservationist, President Roosevelt's letter is cited here in its entirety:

Arbor Day (which means simply "Tree Day") is now observed in every state in our Union—and mainly in the schools. At various times, from January to December, but chiefly in this month of April, you give a day or part of a day to special exercises and perhaps to actual tree planting, in recognition of the importance of trees to us as a Nation, and of what they yield in adornment, comfort, and useful products to the communities in which you live.

It is well that you should celebrate your Arbor Day thoughtfully, for within your lifetime the Nation's need of trees will become serious. We of an older generation can get along with what we have, though with growing hardship; but in your full manhood and womanhood you will want what nature once so bountifully supplied, and man so thoughtlessly destroyed; and because of that want you will reproach us, for not what we have used, but for what we have wasted.

For the nation, as for the man or woman or boy or girl, the road to success is the right use of what we have and the improvement of present opportunity. If you neglect to prepare yourselves now for the duties and responsibilities which fall upon you later, if you do not learn the things which you will need to know when your school days are over, you will suffer the consequences. So any nation which in its youth lives only for the day, reaps without sowing, and consumes without husbanding, must expect the penalty of the prodigal, whose labor could with difficulty find him the bare means of life.

A people without children would face a hopeless future; a country without trees is almost as hopeless; forests which are so used that they cannot renew themselves will soon vanish, and with them all their benefits. A true forest is not merely a storehouse full of wood, but, as it were, a factory of wood, and at the same time a reservoir of water. When you help to preserve our forests or plant new ones you are acting the part of good citizens. The value of forestry deserves, therefore, to be taught in the schools, which aim to make good citizens of you. If your Arbor Day exercises help you to realize what benefits each one of you receives from the forests, and how by your assistance these benefits may continue, they will serve a good end.

The White House, 15 April 1907

On 31 March 1922, a special proclamation was issued by President Warren Harding to commemorate the golden anniversary of Arbor Day, 22 April 1922. In his message he urged all state governors to designate the week of 16–22 April 1922 as forest protection week, and the last day, 22 April, as the golden anniversary of Arbor Day. He also requested that public service officers and those in civic and commercial organizations work together to preserve a common heritage. He urged the planning of educational exercises to emphasize the disastrous results of forest waste by fire, and the need for collective efforts to conserve forests and increase tree growth for ornament and use.

The concept of Arbor Day to stimulate tree planting also stimulated an organization to further the cause. The American Tree Association (ATA) was founded by Charles Lathrop Pack in 1922 to further forest protection and extension and to increase appreciation of forests as natural resources essential to the sound economic future of this country. Pack (1857–1937), a dedicated conservation leader, was a member of President Roosevelt's Conservation Commission in 1908. He was also president of the American Forestry Association (1916–20) and of the National Conservation Congress (1913). He was president of the ATA until his death in 1937.

The ATA was the leading promoter of Arbor Day during the 1920s and 1930s. The ATA sent a certificate to every individual who planted a tree ("The Tree Planting Army"). By 1929 it had enlisted 129,000 troops. Collaborating with the General Federation of Women's Clubs, it promoted highway beautification projects and tree planting as memorials. It stimulated planting of 27,000,000 trees in 1932. Unfortunately, it waned after Pack died and became inactive during the 1950s.

ORGANIZATIONS TO PRESERVE ARBOR DAY

As enthusiasm and activity surrounding Arbor Day waned in the two decades after World War I (1920–40), thoughtful people interested in the Arbor Day ethic began to think of ways to rekindle such interests. Beginning in 1939, various proposals were advanced over the next three decades. Only four of the most significant of these initiatives will be reviewed here. Two were initiated by leaders in arboriculture, and two by business and conservation leaders, some with no previous association with trees. The four initiatives were as follows: (1) Committee for a National Arbor Day (CNAD), which was independent but supported in part by arborist societies such as the National Shade Tree Conference (NSTC) and the National Arborist Association (NAA); (2) a new organization within the NSTC, appropriately called the Arbor Day Association (ADA); (3) an Arbor Day Committee of the International Shade Tree Conference (ISTC); and (4) a new organization, focusing on the home of the founder of Arbor Day, appropriately called the National Arbor Day Foundation (NADF). Each of these organized activities played a role in stimulating interest in the preservation of Arbor Day, but only three survived to be effective over time.

Committee for a National Arbor Day

The first initiative to preserve Arbor Day through legislation originated with Edward Scanlon ("call me Ed"), colorful and dynamic city forester for Santa Monica, California, as well as editor and publisher of *Trees* magazine.

A native of Michigan, trained as a forester at the University of Michigan and at Davey Tree School as an arborist, Ed chose to be a ground arborist after falling out of the one and only tree he climbed. Before he went into the navy in World War II, Ed had initiated a campaign in 1940 to popularize the idea of a National Arbor Day. To get national interest, the idea was first proposed to and approved by the Western Shade Tree Conference (WSTC). At a later date the principle was endorsed by the NSTC.

Ed was a promoter of the first line and soon acquired the support and endorsement of other organizations, including the National Arborist Association, National Association of Nurserymen, American Institute of Park Executives, and other national and local organizations. Because of his efforts more than fifteen states passed laws in the 1950s observing the last Friday in April as Arbor Day.

Keenly perceptive, Scanlon believed in preserving Arbor Day by national recognition of one designated day of the year around which he could push a national public relations program. In order to accomplish his goals, he became chair of a self-organized committee, the Committee for a National Arbor Day; Harry Banker, a private arborist from Orange, New Jersey, became the executive secretary. Through the efforts of Banker and the New Jersey Federation of Shade Tree Commissions, New Jersey and four other states became the first in 1949 to establish by law an

Fig. 4.2 Ed Scanlon (left), chairman of the ISTC Committee for a National Arbor Day, and Harry Banker (with shovel) planting a *Zelkova serrata* on the U.S. Capitol grounds on Arbor Day, 1964. Courtesy of the ISA Archives.

Arbor Day on the last Friday in April. Other states passed similar legislation, so that by 1970, twenty-two states had an Arbor Day law.

In 1962 the first legislation for a national Arbor Day was introduced into Congress by Representative Minisch of New Jersey. It would be one of many introduced by him and by Senator Bradley and others from that state. Although Scanlon remained as honorary chairman from inception of the committee until his death in 1975, the major work in pushing for national recognition of Arbor Day by law was carried out by the dedicated and dynamic Banker.

Following Scanlon's death in 1975, Banker became chairman as the drive continued. Under the direction of Banker, Congress passed a national Arbor Day bill in 1970. It was approved by Congress and President Richard M. Nixon declared the first National Arbor Day since that proclaimed by Warren Harding in 1922. Before the bill was passed, however, the wording had been modified to limit the proclamation to *only* the last Friday in 1970. The amended version was a disappointment to all who favored the legislation to make Arbor Day a permanent national occasion. In 1972 and 1988 similar bills met a similar fate. Thus, despite all the effort expended to urge congressional action, this legislation once again had limited significance.

As chairman of the ISTC Committee on Arbor Day and Beautification as well as secretary and president of the CNAD for many years, Banker received a framed

Fig. 4.3 Harry Banker. Courtesy of the ISA Archives.

copy of President Nixon's Arbor Day Proclamation of 1970. He presented this as a gift to the ISTC officers and members as an expression of his appreciation for the excellent support given him over the years. From its inception in 1924, members of NSTC (precursor of the International Society of Arboriculture [ISA]) were actively committed to support of Arbor Day activities on an informal basis. It was not until after World War II, however, in the late 1940s, that support would be more conscious and deliberate. In addition to Scanlon and Banker, Dewey Wade of New York and George Hood of California were strong regional supporters of CNAD.

The Arbor Day Association

In 1954 Harold Palmer Piser, an insurance executive from Flushing, New York, presented a paper to the NSTC entitled, "The Place and Purpose of an Arbor Day Association," in which he proposed that the NSTC support the organization of such an association. Piser, who had long been interested in nature studies, was concerned that public interest in Arbor Day had lapsed and believed it could be revived.

Piser worked hard and enthusiastically for an organization dedicated to preserving and developing the original concepts and purposes of Arbor Day. He believed that even more good would come from Arbor Day if it were singled out, so as not to be lost in a big conservation movement. Following the report of a special committee of NSTC to explore the proposal, the conference voted to sponsor an Arbor Day Association (ADA). Freeman L. Parr was elected chairman of the board of the association, Clarence E. Lewis became president, Dr. R. R. Hirt was secretary, Dr. D. S. Welch was treasurer. Piser became managing director. In 1955 NSTC voted to give formal approval to the association and to appropriate $250 to defray the legal expenses of this organization.

An Arbor Day Association (ADA) was officially established in 1955 at a meeting in New York City of interested arborists and university professors. The principal article of the charter read: "Arbor Day Association is a non-profit, conservation-educational organization dedicated to fostering and promoting Arbor Day, and a better understanding of trees and forests, and their interrelationships to soil, plants, water, wildlife and recreation." In 1956 it was incorporated completely within the management of the NSTC and held its first meeting in 1957 in New York with Piser as executive director; Joe Dietrich of Greenwich, Connecticut, as president; and Freman Parr of Hicksville, New York, as vice president. Its board of directors included twenty prestigious people prominent in arboriculture and conservation, representing urban foresters, commercial arborists, nurserymen, landscape architects, and research scientists.

Unfortunately, Piser was disappointed in receiving the limited financial support offered by NSTC and he resigned as executive director of the ADA. Reorganized to reflect new direction, the new ADA requested the NSTC to reestablish its Arbor Day Committee so that it could cooperate with the ADA in furthering its activities. The NSTC deferred action.

Meanwhile, a new publication, *Arbor Day Life,* initiated and published personally by Dewhurst W. Wade, was adopted by the ADA as its official organ with Wade as its editor. *Arbor Day Life* ceased publication in 1959 and the ADA failed to survive as an organization beyond that year.

Arbor Day Committee of the ISTC

The objectives of the ISTC committee on Arbor Day were to reemphasize the value of tree planting and to work for adoption of an Arbor Day in states and provinces where it was not designated. For practical purposes this meant involvement in established programs, leadership in establishing new ones, and recognizing worthwhile achievements pertaining to Arbor Day. Harry Banker was chairman of the new committee and set out to bring a new spirit to Arbor Day activity. After evaluating its objectives, the committee recommended that the ISTC allocate $650 for preparation and distribution of 3,500 Arbor Day packets proportionately among the seven regional divisions of the ISTC. This was proposed as a pilot program so that if successful in increasing Arbor Day observance substantially, it could be increased, with ISTC chapters giving financial support.

TABLE 4.2

EFFORTS TO PRESERVE ARBOR DAY

PERIOD	ORGANIZATION	SPONSOR(S)
1922–1937	American Tree	Pack
1940–	National Shade Tree Conference*	Scanlon
	Committee for a National Arbor Day (1949)	
	Arbor Day Association (1956–1959)	Piser
1961–	International Shade Tree Conference	Scanlon and Banker
	Arbor Day Committee	
1972	National Arbor Day Foundation	Conservationists
	Now the International Society of Arboriculture	

After an initial run of 3,500 packets, the committee was distributing 40,000 kits by 1979 throughout North America and abroad. In 1984 the California Association of Nurserymen distributed 1,500 kits along with 80,000 pieces of enclosed materials. The kit included a variety of materials that would appeal to students ranging in age from kindergarten to high school—coloring books, songs, poems, instructions on use of planting tools, and how to plant a tree. By 1985 the International Society of Arboriculture (ISA, formerly ISTC) increased its allocation to support the program for that year to $4,800. Acclaimed nationally and internationally for its merit, the ISA kits program won an award from the National Arbor Day Foundation in 1986.

The ISA Arbor Day and Beautification Committee established a new awards program. A plaque was presented to an individual selected by each ISA chapter that participated. The awards were originally for distinguished service or contributions to promote and support Arbor Day activities. Later known as the Gold Leaf Awards, the program was broadened to recognize outstanding contributions in the field of natural resources and improving the environment. This program was immediately successful in stimulating greater Arbor Day goals and achievement.

The National Arbor Day Foundation

While the ISTC was celebrating its awards program and the second national Arbor Day, a new organization was born in 1972 in Nebraska City, Nebraska, which would come to dominate the observation of Arbor Day in America. Its single-minded dedication to preserve Arbor Day as an institution was well organized, well financed, and appropriately named the National Arbor Day Foundation (NADF). The foundation lost no time in establishing an annual Arbor Day awards program. The foundation recognizes outstanding achievements in conservation and tree planting projects undertaken by organizations, individuals, and the media.

In 1971 a group of interested conservationists and business leaders filed notice of incorporation of the Arbor Day Foundation (ADF) in Nebraska, and in 1972 the foundation became a reality. A nonprofit organization governed by a board of directors listed the following purposes: to create awareness and appreciation of trees; to endorse and support education and understanding of trees; to recognize achievement in the planting of trees and conservation activities; to initiate programs to encourage tree planting; and to establish and maintain a national Arbor Day Center.

In 1980 the ADF filed an amendment to its incorporation with the state of Nebraska. In effect the amendment changed its name to the National Arbor Day Foundation (NADF), enlarged its purposes; restricted activity to remain legally nonprofit; broadened its authority for property distribution on dissolution; limited compensation to officers, trustees, members, and others; and precluded the organization from political involvement or propaganda to influence legislation.

Since its inception the NADF has initiated and sustained a variety of programs of special interest to arborists. The most significant of these include the awards program, Tree City, USA, Conservation Trees: The Arbor Day National Poster Contest, and public service announcements. The awards program initiated in 1972 is a reminder of the early competition fostered by J. S. Morton, Arbor Day founder, for prizes based on individual achievement in tree planting performance. The J. Sterling Morton Award is given to an individual who has done the most to perpetuate Morton's tree planting heritage. Required is demonstration of knowledge and appreciation of wise use, which reflects Morton's ideal that "trees are a joy forever." The Good Steward Award is presented to an individual who best reflects the values of the Arbor Day ethic that one should use his land wisely so that it will be passed on in better condition than it was originally given. The Frederick Law Olmsted Award is presented to an individual who has demonstrated his love for and care of trees over an extended period of time at a state or regional level.

Tree City, USA awards were begun in 1976 because of the clearly recognized need to improve tree management in cities. The foundation noted that tree care programs on public properties in many cities were often poor or nonexistent. The foundation was properly concerned that much time, money, and effort used in planting trees could be wasted without adequate tree care. In addition, it wanted to further the goals of Arbor Day to plant more trees along roads, in front of business establishments and homes, and in parks throughout municipalities. The Tree City project was launched with the cooperation and support of the U.S. Forest

Service and the National Association of State Foresters. The program was designed to use the local expertise of state forestry departments to inventory tree populations, adopt tree ordinances, and design tree management programs.

Standards for any community to be certified as a Tree City by the NADF are basic, conforming to those well established by the ISA and its predecessors, the NSTC and ISTC. In essence they require a legally constituted authority with responsibility to develop and manage a comprehensive tree program; have ordinances or laws providing for tree plantings, maintenance, and removal according to established professional principles; have an active comprehensive community forestry program supported by a minimum of two dollars per capita of public funds; have a formal Arbor Day proclamation by the mayor (or other municipal leader); and have an Arbor Day observance.

The Tree City program was made possible in part through Federal Public Law 92–288 in 1972 which gave foresters authority and responsibility for providing technical services for protection, improvement, and establishment of trees and shrubs in urban areas, communities, and open spaces. In its first three years the program had applications for recognition from 109 communities.

In 1992 the foundation launched the Arbor Day National Poster Contest, described as its largest education effort yet. Designed for fifth-grade students, the contest reached tens of thousands of classrooms annually. The success of such an ambitious educational program would far exceed the relatively simple yet noble goals of Morton when he urged America to plant trees in 1872.

The foundation initiated yet another new public relations program in 1988 with a series of television public service announcements for tree planting and conservation. With the aid of well-known Hollywood actor Eddie Albert, the powerful messages reached millions of Americans.

Summary

The creation of Arbor Day in 1872 by Morton was significant to arboriculture because it was the first formal recognition of the importance of tree planting and the care of trees. Leading to a new popular institution, it played a significant role in boosting the conservation movement and in building a new urban forest throughout North America. Arbor Day was also indirectly responsible for the initiation of many shade tree laws enacted to preserve and protect trees on urban sites. Arbor Day observance has varied from year to year since 1872, but, it is a tribute to a sustained arboriculture that Arbor Day not only continues, but has been reinvigorated as new efforts and organizations have arisen to preserve it.

CHAPTER FIVE

Botanical Gardens and Arboreta

"He plants trees to benefit another generation" —Cicero

Coincident with the introduction of woody plants to North America was the development of botanical gardens and arboreta. While each tended to stimulate the other, introductions of trees to America probably had a greater influence on development of gardens up until 1900, rather than the reverse. Up to this period, the introductions came first and the gardens later. After this period the situation reversed, with more and more gardens seeking greater diversity. Having reviewed the introductions, we now turn to the gardens and retrace the path of chronology.

Botanical gardens were first started by inquiring scholars; then by kings, rulers, and wealthy merchants; later by universities and horticulture societies; and finally by governments. By contrast, arboreta had their earliest origins as pleasure parks for the rich, the powerful, and the nobility. The arboretum, of course, is essentially a special kind of botanical garden where the plants of priority are woody and perennial. Since the term *arboretum* was not coined until 1838, there was no distinction between a botanical garden and an arboretum before that period.

For convenience this review follows the chronological development of botanical gardens over five historical periods: (1) ancient origins and earliest gardens; (2) the first systemic gardens of the Renaissance in Europe; (3) colonial gardens in North America; (4) early American gardens; and (5) modern American gardens and arboreta.

Both botanical gardens and arboreta represent collections of plants systematically arranged for research, education, and demonstration. Where botanical gardens are limited in the number of trees, or in fact may have no trees at all, arboreta are designed especially as collections of trees. Most botanical gardens, however, do contain trees, and most arboreta also cultivate nonwoody plants. Some botanical gardens such as the U.S. National Arboretum have nonwoody-type gardens (e.g., herb gardens) on their grounds.

The earliest real botanical garden, where there is definite knowledge of plant collections used for study, was that of Aristotle. It contained about 450 different species. This garden was inherited by Theophrastus, his pupil and successor. Theophrastus, the first real botanist recognized by historians, began a new type of garden tradition—the botanical garden. This kind of garden differed from all others up to that time (ca. 300 B.C.) because its purpose was not food, ornament, or relaxation, but was essentially for the study of plants as living organisms. This was the only ancient garden, of which we are aware, that was really botanical in this sense. It would be almost 2,000 years before another of a similar nature was recorded.

About a thousand years after Theophrastus, the increasing dependence of the medical field on plants as a source for drugs came more sharply into focus. Some 700 years later in 1447, Pope Nicholas V established a Vatican garden in Rome, essentially for the production of medicines for human use, but also to assist the teaching of botany as a branch of medicine. The Vatican garden is regarded as the oldest botanical garden that exists today. From this beginning the constant association of medicine with botany would persist, even in America, up to the 1850s.

The first real botanical gardens of the Renaissance appeared in Italy—in Padua in 1543 and Pisa in 1544. Both were associated with newly established universities, and medicine was a factor in their creation. Before the close of that period, true botanical gardens had been founded in Leyden, Holland, and Heidelberg, Germany.

By 1700 there were 400 botanical gardens reported in Europe. The number and growth of botanical gardens in Europe expanded greatly in the next century (to 1800), largely as a result of extensive plant exploration associated with European colonization of many different parts of the world. These gardens served to introduce new plants into and within Europe, and were sources of new knowledge, or in some cases rediscovered knowledge from the ancients.

By the 1800s, botanical gardens had become so well respected that at least one was created by a royal order forcing a repressive political decision. Emperor Napoleon Bonaparte of France decreed in 1810 that the Province of Bari in southern Italy must have both an agricultural society and a botanical garden. As a result, the Capuchin friars at Bari were ruthlessly dispossessed of their monastery and lands so that a suitable garden could be created on the site.

While many countries in Europe by 1800 had botanical gardens supported by government funds as national institutions, England did not. But after the defeat of Napoleon at Waterloo in 1815, England became the major world power with a navy unmatched in history. With its many dominions around the world, treasure of all kinds flowed to the British Isles, including plants from around the world. The situation was ripe for the creation of a national treasure house to grow and study this great wealth of plants. Such a place would arise. It is known as the Royal Botanical Gardens at Kew, or more commonly, Kew Gardens.

Kew grew to be first in the world in importance, especially for its magnificent collection of woody plants from around the world. Even today, more than 150 years after its founding as a public garden, it is still ranked as the best. Of special interest to arboriculture, its primary importance is its arboretum, considered to be the largest, most complete, and of the highest quality known. Although not called an arboretum, it contains probably the finest arboretum in the world.

Kew Gardens began privately in 1759 on nine acres of the estate of Princess Augusta, wife of Prince Frederick Louis. The prince and his bride were great garden lovers. Frederick Louis, heir to the throne, died unexpectedly in 1751 from a cold caught at a tree planting. His son, George III, who became king in his place, was the same king who lost his thirteen colonies to the Americans. One can only speculate on the possible influence of arboriculture on the course of English and American history.

Following the death of her husband, Princess Augusta continued to expand Kew as a private botanical garden. Some of John Bartram's seeds of various American trees were given to the Princess by Peter Collinson, an English collector. By 1802 the garden was enlarged by merger of the adjoining garden of Richmond Lodge owned by her son, George III. In 1841 the gardens were given to the nation and increased first to 75 acres and later to 270 acres. The arboretum forms the largest part of the garden and now contains more than 16,000 species of various woody plants from around the world. The first director of the garden was Sir William Hooker, a renowned botanist, to whom Charles Sargent would turn for advice in 1872 in building the Arnold Arboretum in America in the old "lost colony" of Massachusetts.

Possibly the first true arboretum was established in 1750 by another Frenchman, Duhamel du Monceau, who assembled 1,000 different tree species for observation and study. Taking advantage of new discoveries in North America, he used both European and North American species to create perhaps the first real arboretum for scientific study. This led to the extensive introduction of many American trees into French parks and cities. His collection was arranged systematically. Monceau also wrote a book on the character and cultivation of trees and shrubs. His work is said to have influenced the study and early distribution of woody plants.

After Monceau, Pierre Phillippe Andre de Vilmorin established a large arboretum at Les Barres in France in 1825 with European and exotic trees of different geographic origin. One of the most important collections in Europe, it was noted for its different forms and races. This may have been the first arboretum to emphasize such differences. Its importance was underlined when it was purchased by the French government in 1856. Two more arboreta in France were established in 1857 and 1858. The arboretum established by Alphonse Lavallee at Segrez, became one of the largest collections of woody plants in Europe by 1875; the other, by G. Allard near Augers, represented one of the most interesting collections of oaks known.

AMERICAN GARDENS AND ARBORETA

John Bartram established the first botanical garden in the colonies beginning in 1728 after he began collecting trees and other plants for study. Bartram's garden was a way station for the raising and acclimatization of European plants and the propagation of American seeds for European clientele. His garden was unsurpassed in the colonies, with the possible exception of the garden of John Clayton, an early native botanist in Virginia. With more than 2,000 different plant species, including many trees and shrubs, Bartram's garden in Philadelphia became famous. Now located at the south end of Fifty-fourth Street, it is restored and maintained as a public garden.

Among his many accomplishments, Thomas Jefferson wanted his entire plantation to be a botanical garden. Begun in 1766, his gardens had become by 1790 a huge experiment station for new and unusual plants, including trees introduced from abroad. Perhaps the most significant garden development for arboriculture, however, during the close of the colonial period occurred because of the efforts of Bartram's cousin, Humphrey Marshall. He established another true botanical garden in 1773 at West Bradford (now Marshalltown), Pennsylvania, which became in effect the first arboretum developed by an American, using native trees and shrubs.

The first public botanical garden in America was created in 1801 by Dr. Joseph Hosack in New York City. It would be short-lived, however, as it was transferred to the state in 1810 for a College of Surgery. Later given to Columbia University, it was abandoned as a garden in 1821. Dr. Hosack's far-sighted dream would not be realized until 1889 when the Torrey Botanical Club pressed for creation of the New York Botanical Garden, which was finally established in 1896 on a completely different site.

TABLE 5.1

BOTANICAL GARDENS AND ARBORETA
IN THE UNITED STATES

NAME	FOUNDED	LOCATION
Missouri Botanical Garden	1859	St. Louis, MO
Arnold Arboretum	1872	Boston, MA
New York Botanical Gardens	1896	Bronx, NY
Marsh Botanical Gardens (Yale University)	1900	New Haven, CT
Huntington Botanical Gardens	1905	San Marino, CA
Brooklyn Botanical Gardens	1910	Brooklyn, NY
The Morton Arboretum	1922	Lisle, IL
Boyce Thompson Desert Arboretum	1924	Superior, AZ
Institute of Forest Genetics	1925	Placerville, CA
National Arboretum	1927	Washington, DC
Morris Arboretum	1931	Philadelphia, PA
Huntington Botanical Gardens & Arboretum	1935	Huntington, IN
Strybing Arboretum & Botanical Gardens	1939	San Francisco, CA
Longwood Gardens	1955	Kennett Square, PA
National Tropical Botanical Garden	1964	Maui, HI

Coincident with the development of the Hosack garden, another private botanical garden was created by Harvard College in Cambridge, Massachusetts, in 1805. This was the first in America to be established by a college or university. As with the Hosack garden, it was begun for teaching and medical purposes and so the primary interest was not trees; it was known as the Botanic Garden of Harvard University. This garden is of interest to arboriculture because of its influence in the creation of the Massachusetts Horticultural Society and its tie in the early years with the Arnold Arboretum.

William Penn had given a grant of 400 acres near what is now Kennett Square, Pennsylvania (southeast of Philadelphia), to one of his Quaker settlers. Family heirs to the land, Joshua and Samuel Pierce began to create an arboretum in 1798 that would become outstanding in the early 1800s. The Pierces imported large trees from England, which could be obtained only at great expense. The trip across the Atlantic was long, and for the trees, dry. To avoid losing the trees, both passengers and crew gave some of their drinking water to keep the trees alive.

The Pierce brothers ranged the countryside on horseback for many miles to bring new plants to the garden. When making extensive forages into the South, they rode only at night on the return trips and rested in the daytime so that the seedlings and shrubs in their saddle bags would not dry out. They took additional precautions to prevent drying by stopping at water holes to rewet or repack the roots. The Pierce arboretum (Pierce's Park) became famous locally, attracting visitors for miles around and influencing the landscaping of many local country estates.

In 1906 the Pierce property was up for sale. Pierre Samuel Dupont, scion of the wealthy Dupont family, decided to buy it to save the beautiful arboretum from destruction. He looked for someone to trim trees of their dead branches and treat them. He said "I want a good man who will work absolutely under my direction, removing no branch dead or alive unless I specify it to be done." With this kind of personal devotion, it is not hard to see how Dupont's garden could become in time the famous Longwood Gardens of today.

The Longwood Gardens were formally founded in 1921, became public in 1937, and have been maintained and improved on since by the Dupont heirs. Now heavily endowed and privately operated, the gardens have the aura of a public garden whose primary purpose is exhibition and display. Despite this impression, the gardens have active research and education programs, and host scientific meetings as well. Some of the original trees planted by the Pierce brothers are still in existence.

In 1833, only four years after its founding, the Massachusetts Horticultural Society established an experimental garden, which became a part of the famous Mount Auburn Cemetery in Cambridge. Consisting of thirty-two acres, it was used to exchange plants with other botanical gardens.

H. H. Hunnewell, banker and eminent horticulturist, began to build an arboretum in Wellesley, Massachusetts, in 1851. An ambitious collector of evergreen trees, he was among the first in 1857 to import and try to grow the California redwood tree in the Northeast. Hunnewell's private arboretum grew from three acres in 1851 to forty by the end of the century. On land adjacent to where Wellesley College would rise, it represented the largest collection of conifers and oriental ornamental trees in America, including one of the finest collections of rhododendrons in the eastern United States. The source of many exotics distributed over much of North America, it would also be the source for many plantings for the Arnold Arboretum. Some of the finest remnants of his collection still exist on the Hunnewell Estate in Wellesley overlooking the college nearby.

Modern botanical gardens and arboreta in North America began with three great gardens in the second half of the nineteenth century. The Missouri Botanical Garden and the Arnold Arboretum were in the United States and the Queen Victoria Niagara Falls Park was in Canada. The following sections discuss these as well as other gardens begun in the twentieth century.

The Missouri Botanical Garden

The first of its kind in North America, the Missouri Botanical Garden was begun in 1859 by Henry Shaw of St. Louis. An English-born merchant who came to America as a young man of nineteen, Shaw was highly successful in St. Louis and had made a handsome fortune by 1840. Disdaining money for its own sake, he retired in 1840 and purchased a tract of prairie land over a square mile west of the city. Traveling extensively in Europe to enhance his education, he went to London's World Fair (apparently the first of its kind) in 1851 to see the Horticultural Display in the famous Crystal Palace built by Prince Albert, husband of Queen Victoria.

Returning to America he became absorbed with botanical literature and consulted Sir William Hooker, director of Kew, about founding a botanical garden. The link with Hooker was significant, as it led him to Dr. George Englemann, recent founder of the new Academy of Science in St. Louis. Englemann became his science advisor, pressing for a library, museum, and research program despite Shaw's reluctance. He also sought the aid of Professor Asa Gray at Harvard, by then the most eminent botanist in America. With urging from Gray and Hooker, Shaw was finally persuaded to do what Englemann's direct appeal to science could not. Englemann had advised him in the beginning "to develop his garden not only as a pleasure park, but as a complete botanical garden of scientific distinction." Thus from its beginning, this garden was designed for research and study as well as for show, and included an excellent library. Shaw began in 1857 by purchasing the extensive herbarium collection from the estate of the German scientist, Johann Bernhardi.

The English woodland garden on the St. Louis site contains a wide range of tree species with varying degrees of shade. The same can be said of the tree populations in Tower Grove Park adjacent to the gardens. Together these populations constitute a substantial urban arboretum. The main arboretum of the institution is on a larger, 2,200-acre site forty miles west of St. Louis. Known as the Shaw Arboretum at Gray Summit, this development was begun in the 1930s because of air pollution. In the 1920s large numbers of plants, including coniferous trees, were being killed by the pollution from St. Louis and Illinois factories nearby. The new arboretum contains large sections of conifers that are highly sensitive to certain air pollutants. After this development, trees became a more significant aspect of the garden program. In the past several decades the garden has become deeply involved with the tropical flora of Central and South America and Africa. Since 1970 it has been the designated center for study of African botany in the United States.

The Arnold Arboretum

The most famous arboretum in North America is the Arnold Arboretum of Harvard University established in 1872. It was designated specifically as an arboretum for the primary purpose of research on trees. The original 125 acres of the arboretum at Bussey Farm near Boston were purchased by Harvard University in 1850. The area was expanded by additional purchases so that now there are 265 acres at Jamaica Plain on the western edge of Boston. By mutual agreement between the city of Boston and Harvard College in 1882, Boston assumed legal title to the land, and immediately leased it back to Harvard for 1,000 years at $1.00 per year.

The arboretum is not only endowed with seven million dollars, but has a library of books on woody plants unsurpassed in North America, and second in the world only to that of the British Museum in London. The first director, Charles Sprague Sargent, expressed the hope that the arboretum might become a museum founded and carried on to increase the knowledge of trees. As with mighty oaks grown from tiny acorns, however, the Arnold Arboretum had a modest beginning. The arboretum that bears his name was established in 1827 from a fund willed to the Harvard Corporation by James Arnold, a wealthy merchant in New Bedford, Massachusetts. Arnold's fortune came from lumbering in Michigan and his fund was to be applied for the promotion of agriculture or horticulture improvement. Two of the three trustees of his will had strong interests in horticulture in general and in trees in particular. George B. Emerson was the author of the first published book on the native trees of a state (Massachusetts). The other trustee, James J. Dixwell, was an amateur horticulturist in Jamaica Plain, where the arboretum came to be established. The trustees requested that the Harvard Corporation accept the bequest and create an arboretum comparable to the Harvard Botanic Garden in Cambridge. Acceptance was granted in 1872 and land was chosen from part of the Bussey Estate in Jamaica Plain already owned by Harvard.

Charles S. Sargent (1841–1927) was appointed as the first director of the arboretum and also director of the Harvard Botanic Garden in Cambridge. Widely read and possessing a personal fortune, Sargent amassed an outstanding collection of books and manuscripts that became the core of the impressive arboretum library. Over a fifty-year period he raised more than a million dollars from outside sources, and stimulated substantial gifts well in excess of that figure. The arboretum is truly a living monument to his dedication, industry, and generosity.

Sargent had a Harvard appointment as professor of arboriculture. This was the first, and as far as I can determine, the only such professorship in the world at that time, although the term *arboriculture* had been known for more than 200 years. The term *arboriculture* then was still comparable to that of *forestry*. The close association of Sargent with Asa Gray, however, ensured that Sargent's emphasis on the arboretum would be more basic than applied, even though Sargent was later called by the U.S. government to aid in its search for reliable information to justify a national forestry program.

As with Shaw of the Missouri Botanical Garden, Sargent consulted the director at Kew (by now Sir Joseph Hooker, son of Sir William), and he himself went to Asia, South America, and Europe for new tree species, initiating the many tree-hunting expeditions. With the help of Frederick Law Olmsted, then designing the park system for Boston, he succeeded in having the arboretum included in Olmsted's "emerald necklace of parks" for Boston. He thus gained the expertise of Olmsted in designing the arboretum, he acquired more land for it, and he secured the added advantage of having the city of Boston build and maintain park roads. In return Boston received more than 100 acres of new parkland, whose plantings would become a monument to the city and be managed by Harvard College.

The arboretum began on a shoestring and has since operated on a limited budget despite many gifts and endowments. From the outset it provided the first sound model in America for a lasting arboretum that others could emulate. With a small grant, Alfred Rehder compiled a bibliography on the world's recorded literature in arboriculture and forestry up to 1900. Known as the "Bradley Bibliography," it is a library treasure of immense value. Many other publications of value have come from its staff over the years, including Donald Wyman's *Garden Encyclopedia.*

Of all the botanical gardens and arboreta developed in America, probably none has been more significant to the development of arboriculture than the Arnold Arboretum. Preoccupied with woody plants over all other considerations, it has played a major role in dendrological science, having no equal in America as a dendrological research station. Its influence has been significant in support of American trees, creation of a national forestry program, creation of a forest library research center, introduction of exotic woody plants, and publication of prestigious books and journals stemming from a productive staff and their research. Like its predecessor the Missouri Botanical Garden, it became a worthy follower in the wake of the distinguished program at Kew, and became in itself a model for new American arboreta.

The Morton Arboretum

Charles Sargent received a letter in January 1921 from Joy Morton, founder of the Morton Salt Company, who sought information on the establishment of a new arboretum outside of Chicago. Morton was concerned that the site—twenty-five miles outside of Chicago—would be too far from the city for an arboretum. Chicago was growing rapidly and before much longer the arboretum would be in a suburb.

Joy Morton was one of four sons of the Arbor Day founder J. Sterling Morton. A true son of his father, whose tree planting goals were essentially practical, Joy Morton would not establish a botanical garden, but a hard core arboretum at the outset. By the 1950s Sargent's prophecy was fulfilled as the new plantings matured, first on an original 50 acres with 70 native woody species, and later to include 1,425 acres with more than 4,800 species, varieties, and hybrids. Located amid gently rolling hills, its size is surpassed in the United States only by the Boyce Thompson Desert Arboretum in Arizona and the Shaw Arboretum in Missouri. After almost eighty years, the record of this arboretum has fulfilled every expectation with a sound reputation as another of America's great arboreta.

The National Arboretum

Not long after The Morton Arboretum began, Congress moved to create a "National Arboretum" that would be the first federally supported institution of its kind. In 1901 the U.S. Congress created the McMillan Commission (later to be the Commission of Fine Arts), which recommended federal action in creating an institution that would combine an arboretum with a botanical garden in Washington, D.C. Congress passed a bill in 1927 directing the secretary of agriculture to establish and maintain a national arboretum for research and education concerning trees and plant life.

The first director of the new arboretum was appropriately B. Y. Morrison. Morrison, though a native American, spent a traveling fellowship in English gardens. His successor, Henry Skinner, was English-born, and the third director, John Creech, though American, had English roots. Thus the English influence had extended well into our modern era. The arboretum development was guided by an advisory council appointed by the Secretary of Agriculture. Its first priority would be plant breeding. Other priorities were evaluation and classification of cultivars developed elsewhere, and introduction of new plants. Comprising about 440 acres in northeast Washington, D.C., the site has some high ground that overlooks the capitol. In the first major planting, masses of azaleas were established in 1946, followed in 1949 by major plantings of camellias. These two collections now number 70,000 for azaleas and 400 for camellias.

One of the new arboretum's early projects was devising a new hardiness zone map. The first hardiness zones, mapped from data from the USDA and the *Atlas of American Agriculture* in 1928, needed revision in light of new data. The

Fig. 5.1 The U.S. National Arboretum in Washington D.C. Courtesy of Frank Santamour, National Arboretum.

arboretum has updated the National Arboretum Zone Map, first published in 1952, several times.

Every botanical garden looks forward to having a unique plant collection distinctive from any other garden. In 1962 William T. Gotelli gave such a collection to the National Arboretum. It is made up of a comprehensive group of slow-growing conifers, located on a five-acre hillside. A collection of bonsai trees was received in 1976, as a gift to the United States from Japan in the U.S. Bicentennial year of independence from England.

The U.S. National Arboretum is now one of the world's most noted botanical gardens with a primary emphasis on trees. In addition to its extensive tree collections and other plantings and its extensive herbarium holdings and library, it is well equipped for its primary missions of research and education. As a unit of the Department of Agriculture, its library is also a branch of the extended, massive National Agriculture Library. In addition, it has valuable ties to the plant-exploring section of the USDA, with its several Plant Introduction Stations. Such an institution is a significant asset to the development of arboriculture and will continue to influence its future.

THE FIRST AMERICAN TROPICAL GARDENS

Until 1938 there was no tropical botanical garden in the United States for research and education to match the extensive gardens and arboreta rising in universities and around large population centers. None of the many display gardens or tree collections featuring tropical flora in parks and other public grounds in southern states could meet the new criteria of research and education now routine in such respected institutions.

The first tropical botanical garden was established in the United States in 1938, the second in 1964. The first, named in honor of America's first plant explorer, was founded in 1938 as the David Fairchild Botanical Garden outside Miami, Florida. Fairchild had distinguished himself as head of the USDA Seed and Plant Introduction Program for almost thirty years, and had an international reputation as a plant explorer. The second, the National Tropical Botanical Garden, was established in Hawaii.

Developed through private funding, the Fairchild tropical garden contains a variety of 4,000 native and exotic plants on 83 acres, including at least 10 species collections such as cycads and palms and 5,000 orchid species and hybrids. The largest tropical garden in the continental United States, it contains 400 species of palm and the largest world collection of cycads, the ancient progenitors of pines. While spectacular for its variety of nonwoody plants, its chief value is the collection of tropical trees, and especially the palms and cycads increasingly used in southern arboriculture.

The National Tropical Botanical Garden (NTBG) was chartered in 1964 by Congress to form a private nonprofit organization to serve the following purposes: (1) establish, develop, operate, and maintain for the benefit of the people of the United States an educational and scientific center in the form of a tropical botanical garden or gardens, together with such facilities as libraries, herbaria, laboratories, and museums which are appropriate and necessary for encouraging and conducting research in basic and applied tropical botany; (2) foster and encourage fundamental research with respect to tropical plant life and to encourage research and study of the uses of tropical flora in agriculture, horticulture, medicine, and other sciences; (3) disseminate through publication and other media the knowledge acquired at the gardens relative to basic and applied tropical botany; (4) collect and cultivate tropical flora of every nature and origin and to preserve for the people of the United States species of tropical plant life threatened with extinction; and (5) provide a beneficial facility which will contribute to the education, instruction, and recreation of the people of the United States. The NTBG headquarters are at Lawai on Kauai in Hawaii, with a mainland office in New York.

The main garden (the flagship) located on Kauai consists of 180 acres and is developed for research, education, and living collections. One satellite garden of 120 acres, near Hanaon on Maui, is the center of ethnobotanical plants and breadfruit, coconut, and laulu palm collections. A second satellite garden of 1,000 acres in the Limahuli Valley on the northern coast of Kauai contains many rare, newly discovered plants. The garden also has an office and laboratory in the Department of Botany at the University of Hawaii on Oahu.

CURRENT GARDENS IN THE UNITED STATES

Currently, there are more than 800 botanical gardens and arboreta in the United States, and new, small ones are being created with increasing urbanization. It is not known how many meet the "reality" test for research, but most if not all offer opportunities for education and display. With the exception of the Missouri Botanical Garden and The Morton Arboretum, most were in the Northeast or Far West until 1925. With the exception of the Boyce-Thompson Desert Arboretum and the Institute of Forest Genetics, all were in or near densely populated urban areas. Many were of private origin, and some are now great gardens.

There is diversity of origin and geography. Both private and public sources are reflected, such as the Morris Arboretum in Philadelphia supported by private funding, and the National Arboretum in Washington supported by federal funds. Most gardens listed were created and are supported by municipalities or universities, such as the Strybing Arboretum of San Francisco or the University of Washington botanical garden in Seattle. With the exception of Alaska, all major regions of the United States are represented, including the extremes of Florida in the Southeast and Hawaii in the Pacific Ocean.

CANADIAN BOTANICAL GARDENS AND ARBORETA

Coincident with the development of the Arnold Arboretum was the founding and development of the "Queen Victoria Niagara Falls Park" in 1887 at Niagara Falls, Ontario. Not known as either a botanical garden or arboretum, this park is included here because it functions as both. In cooperation with the state of New York, the Canadian province of Ontario created a park of the extensive lands surrounding Niagara Falls and its contiguous waterways. Designed to preserve the falls and its environment from commercial development, the park included extensive areas of natural flora. Roads, paths, walkways, shelters, stairways, and trails were designed to make the natural beauty of the park accessible to the public. In addition to developing the land and making other improvements, collecting and cataloging the flora was also pursued. By 1908 the park commissioners urged that the park system form a provincial school of forestry, horticulture, and arboriculture. Planting of shade and ornamental trees had been initiated as early as 1895, and preservation of the existing native trees was itself a challenge. Beds of ornamental

TABLE 5.2

SELECTED CANADIAN BOTANICAL GARDENS AND ARBORETA
WITH EMPHASIS ON WOODY PLANTS

NAME	FOUNDED	LOCATION	WOODY FLORA EMPHASIZED
Dominion Arboretum & Botanical Garden	1887	Ottawa, ON	Native trees
Niagara Park Gardens*	1890	Niagara, ON	Native flora
University of British Columbia Botanical Garden	1916	Vancouver, BC	Ornamentals
Morden Arboretum	1930	Morden, MB	Cold-hardy trees and shrubs
Montreal Botanical Garden	1931	Montreal, QC	Cold-hardy trees and shrubs
Royal Botanical Gardens	1941	Hamilton, ON	Ornamentals
Ross Arboretum	1946	Indian Head, SK	Hardy prairie trees
Morgan Arboretum (McGill University)	1948	Montreal, QC	Native trees
Devonian Botanical Gardens (University of Alberta)	1959	Edmonton, AB	Ornamental woody plants
Guelph University Arboretum	1970	Guelph, ON	Ornamental woody plants
Erindale College Arboretum	1972	Mississauga, ON	Woody plants for urban use
Lakehead University Arboretum	1975	Thunder Bay, ON	Woody plants

*Not designated as a botanical garden or arboretum; however, in use and function it is both.

shrubs were established in 1896. Extensive rearrangement of trees from 1912–13 facilitated regrouping of specimens in a natural and logical sequence. Although activity lapsed during the war years (1914–18), extensive plantings were made throughout the 1920s and 1930s. By 1935 an expert in arboriculture was added to the staff and an arboretum was created. The new arboricultural development was centered on a Training School of Apprentice Gardeners founded in 1936. The only institution of its kind in North America, its graduates were and are well grounded for future park work, including the care of trees.

The development of botanical gardens and arboreta in Canada was concurrent with development in the United States. The development of Canadian botanical gardens was described by Dr. Roy L. Taylor, former director of the Chicago Botanical Garden. Shortly after the founding of the Missouri Botanical Garden in the United States in 1859, the eminent Canadian botanist, George Lawson, established the first Canadian Botanical Garden at Queens College (now, University) at Kingston (in Ontario) in 1861. It was the first Canadian garden established at a university, and for more than a decade it was the only botanical garden in Canada, but it lasted only into the early 1870s.

Following enactment of the Federal Experimental Farms Act in 1886, the Dominion Arboretum and Botanical Garden was established in 1887 at the Experimental Farm in Ottawa. Essentially a national institution, named both an arboretum and botanical garden, it preceded the U.S. National Arboretum by more than half a century. Located outside the federal capital of Ottawa, it initially included twenty-six hectares. Later it included an additional twenty hectares adjacent to Carleton University. North of forty-five degrees latitude, the Dominion Arboretum was the most northerly one in North America, and thus of special significance for testing the cold hardiness of woody plants.

The first botanical garden in Canada to survive at a university was established at the University of British Columbia in Vancouver in 1916 and continues as a separate academic service department. With about forty-five hectares, this garden operates a plant introduction program of special interest to nurseries. It was not until 1930 that another garden was established as an arboretum. The Morden Research Station Arboretum of 254 hectares in Morden, Manitoba, was the first arboretum to be established in Canada since the Dominion Arboretum in 1887, a span of almost fifty years. Its primary function involved selection and introduction of cold-hardy ornamental cultivars of herbaceous perennials, trees, and shrubs.

Although relatively recent in establishment (1931), the Montreal Botanical Garden was the first large public botanical garden created in Canada by one of its great cities. Located in one of Canada's largest and oldest cities, it was founded by Brother Marie Victorin with the help of the Institut Botanique de l'Universite de Montreal. With emphasis on four major themes of horticulture, botany, ethnobotany, and landscaping, its scope includes a wide diversity of plant collections in thirty special gardens. With emphasis on local flora as well as plants from around the world, it has 20,000 plant varieties with special collections from Mexico, Asia, and Australia.

Of interest to arboriculture is its arboretum with more than 3,000 species of woody plants including trees, shrubs, and vines. With emphasis on native trees and shrubs, it includes collections by genera, such as ash, maple, and oak. Also of interest are its tree and shrub collections not suited to the Montreal climate, such as Japanese cherries, magnolias, and metasequoia.

As with both the Kew Gardens in England and the National Arboretum in Washington, its more recent origin probably enhanced its potential for excellence. Owned and operated by the city of Montreal, the garden is now a national treasure of international status and among the best in North America. On 180 acres within the city, it now claims the world's most beautiful flowers and the third most important garden of its kind in the world, after those in London and Berlin. The Montreal garden is unique for Canada as the first large public botanical garden designed primarily for education and display in a large urban area.

The next great botanical garden to rise in Canada was the Royal Botanical Gardens created in 1941 at Hamilton, Ontario. The largest of all Canadian gardens and arboreta, it includes 809 hectares on a site with large natural woodlands. The Royal Botanical Gardens brought the total in Canada to five botanical gardens. Although trees and woody plants were substantial features of each of these gardens, only two were designated as arboreta. Following World War II additional botanical gardens were established in Canada, from Quebec in the east to Saskatchewan in the west.

The first, an old tree planting site at Indian Head, Saskatchewan, as early as 1902, was created as the Ross Arboretum in 1946. Operated by Agriculture Canada, this arboretum specializes in developing cold-hardy trees for the prairie. Morgan Arboretum of MacDonald College (McGill University) was established at Montreal in 1948. Stressing collections of native Canadian trees, it specializes in birch. The Devonian Botanical Gardens at Edmonton, created in 1959, are at the University of Alberta. With a primary interest in native and alpine flora, its research focuses on the hardiness of ornamental perennial and woody plants.

Three additional arboreta were established in Ontario from 1970 to 1975. The first of these was the University of Guelph Arboretum on 135 hectares, with collections of conifers and hardwoods for evaluation and research. The Erindale College Arboretum at Mississauga, established in 1972, emphasizes trees and other woody ornamentals for urban use. The last of the postwar Ontario arboreta to be established was the Lakehead University Arboretum at Thunder Bay in 1975.

A NATIONAL CANADIAN BOTANICAL GARDEN SYSTEM

In 1971 a symposium to explore a national botanical garden system for Canada was held at the Royal Botanical Gardens at Hamilton, Ontario. More than one proposal for a single national botanical garden had been made since 1926. A Royal Commission on National Development of the Arts, Letters and Sciences recommended that there be established a National Botanical Garden in the Ottawa area under the Department of Agriculture and the federal government assist in the establishment of or support for other botanical gardens in various climatic regions of Canada.

No action had been taken by 1969, and Canadian directors of botanical gardens sensed the need for a national policy to guide development of botanical gardens. In that year, Dr. Roy L. Taylor, then director of the University of British

Columbia Botanical Garden, proposed that a network or consortium of botanical gardens be created. A resolution was adopted to formulate and implement a federal policy to establish such a network, but the consortium was not finalized.

SUMMARY

Since their inception as centers for plant study during the Renaissance, botanical gardens have become increasingly significant in many ways. From the beginning they were essentially resource centers for a wide variety of plant materials and practical knowledge in the growth and care of plants. Later they became sources of new research findings as well as sources of books and publications for documentation of knowledge.

Both botanical gardens and arboreta are important testing grounds for demonstrating the potential growth of local and exotic species under local conditions. They are, of course, an educational resource at all levels, amateur to professional, children to senior citizens. Above all they are living collections and sources for continued research leading toward new knowledge of plants.

CHAPTER SIX

The Gypsy Moth

"The worms are a public nuisance—and they kill trees"
—Massachusetts housewife, 1869

About twenty years after the first Arbor Day and the founding of the Arnold Arboretum (1872), a new problem destined to have a significant impact on the development of arboriculture became apparent for the first time. The first major insect problem for North America—the gypsy moth—is one of the most damaging, persistent, and expensive pests in the history of arboriculture.

The gypsy moth (*Lymantria dispar*) is of European origin and earlier was known as *Porthetria dispar* L. It was brought to the United States in 1868 or 1869 by Leopold Trouvelot. Trouvelot was a noted French artist, naturalist, and astronomer, interested in experiments with silkworms. Trouvelot was then living in Medford, Massachusetts, a suburb of Boston, where he was trying to produce silk from native American silkworms, and had introduced European species for the same purpose. He brought gypsy moth eggs in egg masses from Europe to use in crossing the gypsy moth with the silkworm to produce hybrids. It was hoped that such hybrids would enhance the production of silk, or at least, provide a new fiber source. Interest in this subject had been stimulated by the unavailability of cotton in the northern United States during the Civil War.

During a violent, evening windstorm, a cage housing a small number of larvae (described as a "handful") was smashed, allowing the larvae to escape into the nearby woods of a vacant lot. After the moths had gotten away, Trouvelot became deeply concerned about the possible consequences and tried to alert the local authorities to the danger. His prophetic warnings fell on deaf ears, however, as he could find no officials willing to help search for and destroy the liberated gypsy moths. After giving public notice of its escape, but failing to eradicate the insect locally, he retired from history by returning to Paris.

By the time the gypsy moth was introduced into North America, it had a wide distribution in Europe, Africa, and Asia. Occurring in both lowlands and highlands, it extended from Stockholm, Sweden, in the north to Algiers in Africa in the south, England in the west, and the Atlas Mountains and Caspian Sea of western Asia in the east. Also known in eastern Asia, it was reported in China, southern Siberia, Japan, Ceylon, and the southern Asian tropics.

Gypsy Moth Life History

The gypsy moth has only one generation each year. It overwinters in the egg stage in brown masses of eggs. In the spring (early May in New England), eggs hatch into tiny wormlike larvae. Crawling from egg masses, or spinning down on silken threads, the young larvae seek foliage on which to feed. Larvae suspended from threads may be windblown for long distances in this first larval instar stage. The windblown larvae are the reason for the name "gypsy" moth.

Larval feeding is usually completed by late June or early July. Molting occurs during this period, four times for males and five for females. Larvae may migrate considerable distances in search of new foliage, before changing into pupae. The mature larva is a colorful, hairy caterpillar about 1.5 to 2.5 inches in length. While the head has yellow markings, the body is slate colored, with a double row of five pairs of blue spots, followed by a double row of six pairs of red spots. The pupa is short-lived and less conspicuous, being reddish brown with sparse red hairs. The adult moths are of two distinct types—the male is dark brown with black-banded forewings and distinctly triangular in shape; the female is nearly white with navy and black bands on its forewings, and more ovate in form. The wing expanse of adult moths is about two inches. Egg laying occurs in late summer and early fall on a wide variety of natural and artificial surfaces, such as tree trunks, rocks, inside tree cavities, fences, sides of barns, and wooden houses. While severe winters may cause some egg mortality, survival has been recorded down to twenty-three degrees Fahrenheit below zero in New England.

Spread of the Gypsy Moth

The moth was unnoticed and largely unseen from 1869 to 1881. When first noticed near the Trouvelot house at 27 Myrtle Street in Medford in 1881, it was

Fig. 6.1 Adults (white female, dark male) of the gypsy moth, *Porthetria dispar L.* Courtesy of the Forest History Society, Durham, North Carolina.

Fig. 6.2 Gypsy moth larvae on an oak leaf. Courtesy of the U.S. Department of Agriculture Bureau of Entomology and Plant Quarantine.

Fig. 6.3 Female gypsy moths and egg masses. Courtesy of Forest History Society, Durham, North Carolina.

SPREAD OF GYPSY MOTH

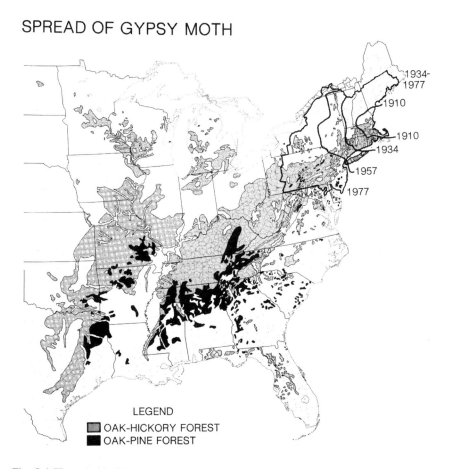

LEGEND
■ OAK-HICKORY FOREST
■ OAK-PINE FOREST

Fig. 6.4 The spread of the gypsy moth. Courtesy of the ISA Archives.

regarded only as a caterpillar of troublesome nuisance, and was believed to be native by lay observers. Even though it had spread into thirty townships of eastern Massachusetts during this period, it failed to attract wide public attention until twenty years after its introduction. The earliest recorded outbreak of gypsy moth infestation occurred in 1889 in Medford.

From its earliest inception the gypsy moth has been a problem in North America. The first outbreaks included both forested and residential lands in the suburbs of Boston. It was seen as a nuisance, as a living menace to health, and especially destructive to trees.

The moths were destructive to a wide variety of plants. Trees were killed. Fruit, garden crops, and other plants were destroyed. The people fought them in a variety of ways: scraped, raked, piled, burned, and scalded them. It soon became clear to local authorities, however, that they had a serious problem that required immediate attention. The combined wrath of the people, plus the obvious damage to trees in both towns and forests, would begin a movement of great significance to arboriculture.

Following the outbreak, the Medford road commission voted $300 for control action. Hired men were set to scraping moth egg masses from tree trunks and sides of buildings. These masses were then burned in kerosene.

Meanwhile, the town selectmen were urged to petition the Massachusetts legislature for funds to fight the moth. Professor Charles H. Fernald, entomologist with the Massachusetts Agricultural College in Amherst, urged the town to press its petition. He prepared a bulletin on the moth from the Experiment Station for use in educating the public. With cooperative aid from the State Board of Agriculture and the Massachusetts Society for the Promotion of Agriculture, 45,000 copies were mailed to homeowners in Medford and the surrounding area. By January 1890, numerous towns in eastern Massachusetts supported the Medford petition.

In 1890 the gypsy moth was known in thirty townships east, north, and west of Boston. A massive and intensive control program begun in 1891 initially slowed the spread. After control efforts were abandoned in 1901, however, populations increased significantly. New infestations occurred in Rhode Island in 1901, New Hampshire in 1905, Connecticut in 1906, and Vermont in 1912. Over the fifteen-year period from 1906 to 1920, the moth spread westward at about six miles per year. By 1914 isolated infestations were found hundreds of miles west of Boston, at Geneva, New York, and in Cleveland, Ohio. Meanwhile, massive infestations had become prevalent in the southern half of New Hampshire, throughout Rhode Island, in all of Massachusetts to the Connecticut River, in southern Vermont, and in eastern Connecticut.

A new infestation discovered in 1920 in Somerville, New Jersey, was not spread from Massachusetts, but from a new introduction from Holland. This separate introduction on blue spruce, unlike the Massachusetts introduction, was truly accidental. Since the moth in New Jersey was discovered infesting an area about six square miles, this new introduction probably occurred several years before 1920. After a ten-year battle, this New Jersey infestation was eradicated by 1931 at a total cost of $2,500,000.

When the moth reached the Massachusetts-New York border in 1922, agricultural representatives from Canada and the United States decided to prevent further westward spread by creating a barrier zone in 1923 embracing about 400 square miles. New spot infestations occurred each year in the barrier zone despite successive reduction or elimination of old ones. By 1939 the barrier zone was largely infested and federal funds to maintain it were significantly reduced in 1941. The eradication program within the barrier zone had been conducted by the states involved and supplemented by release of parasites and other enemies of the gypsy moth provided by the U.S. Bureau of Entomology.

Following a respite from 1920 to 1925, a heavy defoliation occurred on Cape Cod in 1926. This was the second time in thirty years that the gypsy moth infestation in Massachusetts first exploded and then collapsed, a phenomenon that would become characteristic of gypsy moth populations in any one area. By 1934 the moth had entered the New York City area, spotted in the New York Botanical Garden in the Bronx. By 1932 a new, serious infestation was found far west of the barrier zone in the area of Wilkes Barre-Scranton, Pennsylvania. The main infestation in this new area included about twenty-five square miles in five counties.

Dr. Ephraim Porter Felt, past New York state entomologist, warned in a 1942 position paper that allowing the gypsy moth to spread unchecked throughout the native range of white oak might result in annual costs of $90 million for ornamental tree maintenance. With a major world war looming, however, federal funds for gypsy moth control were not appropriated.

Following the war, dichloro-diphenol-trichloroethane (DDT) was sprayed by air to eradicate the newly expanded Pennsylvania infestations. Despite reported "eradication," at least two undetected infestations remained. A new appraisal in 1952 was the basis for a new coordinated plan for eradication of the gypsy moth in the United States. The plan was based on reinforcing the natural ecological barriers of the mountain ranges in western New York and Pennsylvania, and those in West Virginia, to prevent spread to the west and south. A seven-point plan included creation of a new barrier zone. It was approved in 1953 by a regional coordinating committee on the gypsy moth. By 1952 a new infestation was found near Lansing, Michigan, hundreds of miles west of the new barrier zone; and by 1956 the moth had spread to Clinton County in New York near the Canadian border.

In 1956, Congress appropriated funds to initiate a new eradication program. This was the first in a scheduled long-range program to eradicate the gypsy moth from the United States, and a massive spray program was launched in New York, New Jersey, and Pennsylvania. More than three million acres of trees were sprayed aerially with DDT. By 1958, with the program considered an immense success, only 120 acres were known to remain infested.

The elimination, however, was not total, and the gypsy moth lived on to spread again. By 1959 the moth was prevalent over most of New England, apparently limited in the northern areas of Maine, New Hampshire, and Vermont only by the boreal forests of spruce and fir. Defoliation increased steadily in New England and

New York. After another pause between 1966 and 1968, populations again exploded in 1969 in the Northeast. The first defoliation was heavy in both New Jersey and Pennsylvania. By 1970, the hope of eradication was fading, and efforts turned to more intensive research in biological control. The moth spread dramatically at this time, defoliating more than one million acres per year from 1971 to 1973; two million acres in 1971 was the largest area ever affected. Oak mortality was especially severe in New Jersey following repeated defoliations.

In Canada by 1959 the gypsy moth had been found south of Montreal in Quebec. About ten years later it appeared on Wolfe and Howe Islands, near Kingston, Ontario. Isolated infestations occurred in British Columbia as early as 1976, in Vancouver by 1978, and in greater Toronto by 1980. Infestations in Canada are now assumed to be continuous in southeastern Canada from near Quebec City in the east to Belleville, Ontario, in the west.

Following the end of the 1968 control season, the U.S. Department of Agriculture altered the federal gypsy moth quarantine. Pennsylvania was placed under quarantine for the first time, and quarantine areas in New York and New Jersey were increased. In 1971 gypsy moths were trapped in nine new states, within the area between Washington, D.C., Florida, Alabama, and Wisconsin. This confirmed their distribution over the eastern third of the United States.

By 1979, through insect traps baited with a sex attractant, it became clear that the gypsy moth was present in most areas of the northeast United States and was detected in thirty-nine states. With isolated infestations of gypsy moths discovered in California, Oregon, Nebraska, Michigan, and Florida, the moth had been reported in most states of the continental United States. By 1988 the gypsy moth was reported to be established in Nova Scotia, New Brunswick, Quebec, Ontario, and British Columbia.

To make matters worse, the severity of infestation in the Northeast had reached new levels in the 1980s. In Massachusetts alone, where it had all begun more than a hundred years ago, tiny caterpillars fell from the trees constantly and could be heard chomping leaves day and night.

From thirty townships in Massachusetts, over the span of little more than a hundred years, the gypsy moth has spread from coast to coast in North America and continues to be a serious problem in both arboriculture and forestry.

Damage and Cost

Before the first ten-year Massachusetts control project ended in 1899, the program had cost about $1,200,000. One can only speculate on the total losses by the state and its citizens during this decade. These early losses, however, were just the beginning of a regionwide, and then a nationwide crisis. By 1923 the gypsy moth problem had cost the state of Massachusetts and the U.S. government more than $15,000,000 for moth control, and by 1929, the figure had risen to $25,000,000. By the 1940s it was estimated that it might cost $90,000,000 annually to maintain ornamental trees alone. The ultimate cost of the gypsy moth problem was staggering, reaching into the hundreds of millions of dollars every year, including forestry and urban programs.

From early observations by foresters, it was clear that the gypsy moth preferred oak species over others. A twenty-year study in eastern Massachusetts from 1911 to 1931 showed that fifty percent of an infested oak stand died after five years of exposure. The decade from 1911–21 was particularly severe for gypsy moth infestation and defoliation. Mortality of defoliated trees was associated with poor condition of trees before defoliation, and two or more successive defoliations. By 1941 mortality from the gypsy moth was clearly associated with white root rot caused by the fungus *Armillaria mellea*. By then it was recognized as the number one tree problem in the Northeast.

While many deciduous trees, such as oaks, did not die with a single defoliation, growth was reduced in successive years, and growth reduction persisted for several years. While severe defoliation of pines killed some trees in a single year, more often they died over two or three years from a single defoliation.

By 1972 studies on the gypsy moth host preference and consequent damage confirmed by data what had been generally observed. The preferred trees included apple, speckled alder, basswood, gray and river birch, hawthorn, oak, and willow. By all measures, oak was preferred above all. Less sought after but often devoured was the foliage of black, yellow, and paper birch; cherry; chestnut; elm; black gum; hickory; hornbeam; larch; maple; and sassafras. Age-preference studies indicated that mature caterpillars (but not young ones) fed on the foliage of hemlock, southern white cedar, and native pines and spruces. Generally avoided was the foliage of ash, balsam fir, butternut, black walnut, catalpa, red cedar, flowering dogwood, American holly, locust, sycamore, and tulip poplar.

The year 1976, believed to be the worst year yet for serious defoliation in the eastern United States, was a mere prelude to what would occur in 1980 and 1981—the worst years yet for both extent and severity of infestations and defoliation. Whole mountainsides of forests were denuded. In 1980 in Massachusetts alone, almost one million acres were affected. In some places there were up to 30,000 larvae per tree. In 1980, 5.1 million acres were severely defoliated in North America. Then considered a national disaster, the gypsy moth was so bad that arborists and foresters worked constantly to respond to public calls for help.

By all accounts, the year 1981 was the worst in North America for gypsy moth infestation. Nearly thirteen million acres were defoliated, 2.5 times the record damage of 5.1 million acres in 1980. From Maine to Delaware to mid-Pennsylvania, the area was "blanketed" with moth larvae, pupae, adults, and/or larvae, and the arborist industry in those areas was besieged by those seeking help. The fight to control the gypsy moth, which began in Massachusetts more than a hundred years ago, has a long and complex history. Time and space limitations allow for little more than a superficial review here.

CONTROL BEFORE DDT

The earliest efforts in 1891 to control the moth by the residents of Medford, Massachusetts, were essentially both amateur and mechanical, involving physical destruction of the caterpillars in one way or another. Many methods were tried. Some people flushed the caterpillars out of the trees with water hoses. Others banded their trees with tarpaper, to which they applied printer's ink. People fought the insects with fire, water, and coal oil to keep the numbers down. Moths were scalded with boiling water, scraped into cans, brushed by brooms, and treated with whale oil, soapsuds, kerosene, and ammonia.

Early trials to control the gypsy moth with chemicals began in 1891 with Paris green. The active ingredient for toxicity in Paris green was copper arsenite, a stomach poison. Other methods included application of creosote to egg masses, banding trees with burlap or stickum to interdict and prevent larval ascent into the upper tree, and pruning and burning infested trees and shrubs. By the end of the 1891 control season in Massachusetts, it was clear that Paris green would fail to eradicate the moth. It not only failed to kill all exposed moths, but also was toxic to foliage and easily washed away in rain. Paris green was unpopular. In their classic accounts of those early years, E. H. Forbush and C. H. Fernald wrote: "Considerable opposition to the use of Paris green for spraying was manifested by many people living in the infested towns. A mass meeting of opponents of the spraying was held in Medford. One citizen, who attempted to cut the hose attached to one of the spraying tanks, and threatened with violence the employees of the Board who had entered upon his land, was arrested and fined. Others neutralized the effects of the spraying by turning the garden hose upon trees and shrubs that had been sprayed, and washing off the solution. The opposition to the spraying affected the results of the work unfavorably to a considerable extent."

Despite entomologists' assurances about human safety, popular prejudice against spraying persisted. But, the spraying also continued. This was probably the first use of chemical control for an arboricultural problem. At the end of the season, it was clear that spraying alone could not exterminate all the moths, as many survived the treatment.

Beginning in 1905 parasites and predators of the gypsy moth were used to control them for the first time. Many were brought to the United States from Europe and Asia. This was the beginning of a long period of introduction of other insects for gypsy moth control extending over almost eighty years.

By 1910 it was clear to gypsy moth entomologists that unusually severe infestations were often followed by sudden and precipitous population declines. This cycle was attributed to diseases of gypsy moth. Now known to be caused by a nucleopolyhedrosis virus (NPV), its effect was noted in 1911 by Professor W. Reiff of Harvard University: "I am quite convinced, we can apply the wilt in a systematic manner to the benefit of our forests, and—we shall come considerably nearer—to destroying the gypsy moth." Note that even as late as 1911 it was generally believed that the gypsy moth could be "destroyed," or in other words, exterminated or eradicated.

By 1912 the alarming devastation caused not only by the gypsy moth, but also by unfortunate introductions of parasitic fungi, led to a U.S. federal quarantine law. Established in 1912, the quarantine was designed to prevent additional, harmful introductions from abroad. The quarantine is credited with reducing long-range accidental transport of pests and parasites, but as we have seen, it did not prevent the introduction of the gypsy moth from Holland to New Jersey in 1920.

From 1905 to 1942, chemical control was pushed with great intensity at both state and federal levels. Lead paste and arsenate of lead were the principal chemicals used. Lead paste in barrels, sprayed successfully only with great physical effort at low tree levels, was used up to 1909, when lead arsenate became available. Lead arsenate then became the principal chemical used for control up to 1945, when DDT first became available.

By the early 1940s, lead arsenate proved to be inadequate, and its toxicity to grazing animals was causing some concern. Eradication efforts were largely abandoned, too, because of the war. This era ended in 1945 with the advent of a powerful new insecticide called DDT. The new era was one of broad insect control, of which the gypsy moth program was only a part.

THE ERA OF DDT

Although synthesized many years earlier, the broad insecticidal properties of DDT did not become apparent until 1939, and it became available for civilian use only at the end of the war. The use of DDT as an insecticide began on a large scale during World War II against a variety of insects around the world. It was especially helpful in preventing epidemics of destructive human diseases spread by insects. Credited with preventing many diseases, it was said to have saved millions of lives in war-torn Europe from typhus alone by 1945.

Its first test as a potential agent to control the gypsy moth came in 1944 when the U.S. War Department allotted 100 pounds as a trial sample. After the war extensive research showed its efficacy against the gypsy moth, as well as against many other insects, targeted and nontargeted. Seen as a panacea to eradicate or suppress a wide variety of pests, the use of DDT initiated a golden era of chemical control of insect pests. DDT was used for the gypsy moth until about 1960; it was used for other pests up to the early 1970s.

By 1948 DDT in emulsion, solution, and powder became the chosen insecticide against the gypsy moth and many other insect pests. In the following decade millions of gallons of it were used against the gypsy moth alone. Coincident with DDT emergence after the war was the development of modern methods and equipment for aerial and mist-blower application of chemicals

From 1945 to 1958, it was generally believed that DDT could eradicate the gypsy moth, and aerial spraying toward that end involved this single chemical almost exclusively. At the height of its use in 1957, 2.5 million acres of forest and community lands were sprayed in the control programs in New England, New York, New Jersey, Pennsylvania, and Michigan. During this period 12.5 million acres were sprayed aerially in the nine northeastern states and Michigan.

Available in many forms, its use for most gypsy moth suppression was in oil emulsion, the solvent being xylene or kerosene to prevent crystallization of the DDT at temperatures below freezing of water. Aerial application of one pound per acre was said to kill all gypsy moth larvae with a single spray. Acting both as a contact and stomach poison, it killed quickly.

Beginning in the late 1950s, the public reacted against aerial spraying on many fronts. In 1957 DDT residues were found on forage crops and in the milk of cows grazing on such crops in New York state. When such residues were found to persist for as long as a year, the state suspended DDT applications. Thus, for gypsy moth control, the DDT era was over even before publication of Rachel Carson's *Silent Spring* in 1962.

As DDT was beginning to be phased out in 1958, a new chemical, carbaryl (Sevin), became the primary replacement for it until the 1970s. This substance, however, was toxic to honeybees. By the late 1960s trichlorfon (Dylox), a broad-spectrum organophosphate, was found to be an effective alternative to Sevin. With low levels of toxicity for honeybees, it was used successfully for many years. Some time after DDT was phased out, in the early 1960s, all hope to eradicate the gypsy moth was abandoned. Although other chemical sprays were still used, research on alternatives to chemicals turned toward biological methods for control.

BIOLOGICAL CONTROLS

The publication of *Silent Spring* in 1962 had serious implications for toxicity of chemicals to nontarget biota in the environment. It caused strong public outcry against the use of chemical pesticides, which led to a search for alternative methods of control.

Importation of gypsy moth parasites and predators was not resumed until the end of large-scale applications of DDT against the gypsy moth. Beginning in the late 1950s, however, foreign studies and explorations were sponsored by various federal and state agencies, including the Forest Service, the Plant Protection Division of the New Jersey Department of Agriculture, and the Agricultural Research Service (ARS).

Beginning in 1960, based on Forest Service projects in Spain, Yugoslavia, and India, a number of natural enemies of the gypsy moth were imported for study and release. Beginning in 1967, the ARS project in Spain obtained large quantities of parasites, and substantial numbers of the gypsy moth's natural enemies came from the ARS project in New Jersey.

Native predators were not overlooked. Apparently, in addition to birds, several mammals consume the gypsy moth. The predator/prey system involving the gypsy moth is complex, comprising many species with varied food habits. All predators are opportunistic, using food that is available and abundant. Examples of mammal predators affecting gypsy moth populations are the white-footed mouse and the shrew. Although bird predation was mentioned as early as 1896, it was not until the 1940s that mammal predation was considered significant in gypsy moth population dynamics, and data on predator potential became available. The role of predators in suppressing gypsy moth populations is another factor in the complex system of control through integrated pest management.

CONTROL AFTER DDT

By 1971 federal restriction of DDT use and public concern over its environmental impact resulted in postponement or cancellation of many government-sponsored DDT spray programs. As new massive increases in gypsy moth populations became a reality, however, authorities began to seek natural controls, and to concentrate on research for new biological controls. In 1967 a new effort known as the National Gypsy Moth Advisory Committee sought and received new funds for research and control for a five-year accelerated research and development program. The program was initiated in 1971 with funding of $1,000,000 for research from the U.S. Department of Agriculture (USDA), and additional funds from the ARS and the Forest Service.

New agents were introduced periodically in the chemical programs to fight the gypsy moth, especially in the face of the severity of new infestations in 1970 and 1971. In the early 1970s two new chemicals were tested and registered for gypsy moth control: acephate (Orthene), an organophosphate; and diflubenzuron (Demilin), an insect growth regulator. In 1973, Imidan joined carbaryl, Gardona, and *Bacillus thuringiensis*, a bacterium, as recommended by the Environmental Protection Agency for control of gypsy moth through ground applications.

Since the 1950s, commercial preparations of the microbial insecticide *Bacillus thuringiensis* var. *thuringiensis* Berliner (*Bt*) had been available for control of leaf-feeding beetles. Extensive testing showed that *Bt* could be used to reduce gypsy moth populations. While it was most effective against juvenile larvae, however, it had no significant effect on mature caterpillars.

By the early 1960s, *Bt* had been shown to be as effective in controlling the gypsy moth as some pesticides. It had many attractive features, being selectively pathogenic against leaf-chewing insects. Up to that point, it had not stimulated or acquired resistance, as had chemical pesticides. Once established, it multiplied in its host, synthesizing increased amounts of toxins. It was easily produced by mass fermentation and was available at low cost. It also came with some limitations. Its viability and pesticidal capacity varied with climate and host changes, and staggered development of the gypsy moth often required multiple applications. Nevertheless, it was an effective alternative to chemical pesticides, could be used alone or in integrated pest management control programs, and was environmentally safe.

By 1970 more than fifty million parasites of the gypsy moth had been released for gypsy moth control. Beginning in 1972 the USDA-ARS project involved further exploration and studies seeking additional exotic species of natural enemies in areas of the world not completely explored. Although satisfactory regulation of gypsy moth populations in the northeastern United States was not achieved, at least one of the insect parasites used in combination with the *Bt* bacterium reduced populations more than when it was used alone.

By 1981 the most common parasite of gypsy moth was another insect—a small, black wasp (*Ooencyrtus kuwanai*), which destroys the surface eggs of a mass. In addition, two effective predators were species of large ground beetles that prey on both larvae and pupae. Other effective predators include a large number of bird species, medium-sized mammals, and smaller animals such as shrews and white-footed mice.

The wilt disease noted by Professor W. Reiff in 1911 is characterized by infection in the larval stage by a nucleopolyhedrosis virus, known as NPV. Early trials to identify the causal agent for use against the gypsy moth were unsuccessful until 1947, when the true nature of NPV was discovered. With the development of the new field of insect pathology by 1970, research on gypsy moth wilt disease had intensified. NPV was selected, along with *Bt,* as one of the most promising disease agents to control the gypsy moth because it is naturally occurring, has been associated with collapse of gypsy moth populations, is environmentally safe, gives evidence of long-term carryover, and is insect selective. Studies with NPV indicate that it is probably the most effective agent in causing disease of gypsy moth populations.

RECENT GYPSY MOTH CONTROL

The severity and scope of the gypsy moth disaster in the 1970s, combined with other critical insect problems, led to an expanded gypsy moth control program as part of a combined Forest Pest Research and Development Program for the years 1975–78. New goals for gypsy moth control included the following: prediction of population trends; improved methods for relating defoliation to tree mortality; evaluation for registration of NPV; improved formulations of *Bt* and NPV; demonstration of disparlure against gypsy moth; evaluation of new chemical insecticides and newly introduced parasites; evaluation of the sterile male technique; and development of a mass moth rearing for research. By 1981 the following materials were used against the gypsy moth: Gypcheck, Demilin, Orthene, Sevin (carbaryl), Midan, Dylox (trichlorfon), *Bt,* Bidrin (dicrotophos), and disparlure.

By 1988 it was generally believed that widespread use of chemical pesticides was less effective than the bacterial pesticide, *Bt.* Where possible, however, the use of integrated pest management (IPM) is considered to be the most effective of all direct methods to reduce or maintain populations at minimum levels.

PHEROMONES

It had been known since 1896 that adult female moths had an odor that attracted male moths. Since then thousands of males were captured and destroyed using this attraction, but only small numbers of egg masses remained infertile. By 1953 the isolated chemical attractant was known as "gyptol," and was identified by 1960 as (+)-10 acetyoxy-1-hydroxy-cis-7-hexadene. Field tests with gyptol and a homologue "gyplure" were unsuccessful. By 1970 the chemical identification was challenged and withdrawn. New research found the chemical to be cis-7,8-epoxy-

2-methyloctadecane, known as disparlure. This chemical, now known as a sex pheromone, was the first to be used in arboriculture to bait moths for population studies. Pheromones were particularly useful to monitor insect spread into new infested areas.

IMPACT OF THE GYPSY MOTH

Despite its damage, cost, and continuing threat, the gypsy moth was a direct stimulus to the development and institutionalization of arboriculture as an accepted professional practice. It led to advances in new chemicals for insect control; new machines for spraying; new laws for shade tree care; quarantine of dangerous insect pests and tree disease fungi; and new organizations in entomology, plant pathology, forestry, and arboriculture. The early powerful insecticide, arsenate of lead, was developed specifically in 1893 to control the gypsy moth; and the first gas-powered spray machines with power to reach shade tree tops were developed in 1907 for moth control. The first state law creating town tree wardens to care for trees came as a direct result of the need to control the moth, and this in turn led to the first professional association of arborists. Finally, the first U.S. quarantine law stemmed from the combined impact of the gypsy moth, the white pine blister rust, and finally the devastating chestnut blight. The rust has abated and the chestnut blight now has little to destroy, but the gypsy moth lives on, providing work for arborists on an annual basis.

SUMMARY

As the first serious insect problem for arboriculture in North America, the gypsy moth has had a far-reaching impact. With 350 known woody host species, it has been a most formidable, destructive, and costly insect pest on forest, shade, and ornamental trees in North America for more than 100 years. It led to the first tree protection laws, the first town tree wardens, and the first arborist societies. It continues today as a major tree insect problem through much of the United States and Canada and looms as a constant threat to woody plants in both countries.

CHAPTER SEVEN

The Davey Tree Expert Company

"Do it right—or not at all" —John Davey

Although commercial tree work was under way in the United States and Canada before 1900, it was not until after John Davey's book, *The Tree Doctor,* in 1901 that arboriculture would become a recognizable institution, accepted by the public as a legitimate practice. The extensive tree care industry that arose during the current century had its basis in two distinct periods. The first period—with early, primary interest in care of individual trees—began with John Davey, Harold Frost, and others, even before 1900. It was reinforced by the rise of both the Davey and Bartlett Companies as national organizations over the same period to about 1930. The second period—with primary attention focused on line clearing for utility companies—started in the early 1920s, but did not emerge as a major practice until about 1930. Both the Davey and Bartlett Companies moved into line clearing in the early twenties and expanded that aspect of their business during the 1930s and 1940s.

JOHN DAVEY

Founded by John Davey, the Davey Company remained in the family as a private company for nearly 100 years, 70 of those as an incorporated company (1909–79). During much of that time it was managed by Martin L. Davey, son of John Davey, and his son, Martin L. Davey Jr. The beginnings and major growth of the company occurred over four periods of Davey family direction: John Davey, the

Fig. 7.1 John Davey, considered the "Father of Tree Surgery" in North America, wrote *The Tree Doctor.* Courtesy of the Davey Tree Expert Company

founder (1880–1909); Martin Davey, the builder (1909–46); Martin Davey Jr., the manager (1946–61); and other Davey family presidents, the transition period (1961–79). The final period of the Davey story began when the Davey family sold the company to its employees (1979–present).

John Davey, the founder, was an English immigrant who came to the United States in 1873 with little cash but great ambition. When he died in 1923 at the age of 77, he left a dynamic and growing tree care company, the first and, at that time, the largest national tree company in North America. A history of the company, *Green Leaves,* by Robert E. Pfleger was a valuable source for this chapter. Since the Davey Company was the first in its field, it pioneered organized tree care in America with many unprecedented activities.

John Davey was born in 1846 in Stawley, Somersetshire, in England where his father was a farm manager. At the early age of four, by his own word, John not only began to plant potatoes, but was cautioned by his father to "do it right or not at all." From this early lesson Davey developed such a healthy respect for "doing it right" that it became a hallmark of his reputation and the motto of the company he would found. His biographers say that two principal characteristics that helped him to succeed were apparent in his early youth—a love of nature and a natural curiosity that sustained him throughout his entire life. The Davey family was not affluent. John spent his youth working on the farm without knowing how to read and write until he was twenty-one.

At twenty-one he began an apprenticeship in horticulture and landscape gardening that shaped his future. For this he went to Torquay in southern England, famous for its greenhouses and gardens, and served for seven years. It was here that he acquired an extensive knowledge and hands-on know-how of plants and planting. Making acquaintance with an educated man who helped him, he also learned to read at this time. Eventually, however, it was "growing things" and the call of America that decided his future. At the age of twenty-seven, still single, he sailed from England to seek his fortune in the New World.

Landing at Castle Garden, New York, Davey went directly to Warren, Ohio, to work as a janitor in a private school. After only five years in America, John bought a greenhouse in order to grow and sell plants and flowers. He also launched a monthly publication, *Davey's Floral and Landscape Educator*, a small sheet that began in 1878. About this time he became concerned about the disregard for trees wherever land clearance or construction left them injured in the wake of development. He began to think more strongly of tree preservation and so moved to Kent, Ohio, in 1880 to become caretaker of Standing Rock Cemetery. The cemetery had been long neglected, was overgrown, and the trees needed intensive care to survive and prosper. Using his apprentice training he "cleaned house," and carefully organized new plantings. Davey's success here with the trees was not based on the tree care expertise for which Davey later became famous (i.e., surgery). Instead, it was due primarily to his knowledge of soils, fertilization and aeration of tree roots, mulching, watering, and basic root needs.

By 1890 Davey had become known as the "treeman of the town" (Kent). He and his eldest son, Wellington, had become well known for planting and caring for hundreds of trees in the community. By 1900 Davey had been able to demonstrate his success in tree preservation around Kent and Warren, Ohio. As his work became recognized, demand for his services increased gradually to make enough work for himself and his two older sons. Above all, Davey wanted his work to be recognized because he wanted to preserve trees; this led him to write his book.

The Tree Doctor was the opening to the foundation of commercial arboriculture as an institution. Working twelve hours a day to support his family, he prepared copy for the book at night. Determined to tell the public what should and should not be done, he decided to illustrate his points with photographs. He took hundreds of photographs to illustrate his text. To his dismay he could find no one to finance his book. He assumed a personal debt of $7,000 in 1901 dollars to do so himself.

Although he claimed to cover practically all that has ever been written on tree culture, the introduction recognized no past work. He took pains to note that his book avoided scientific terminology, was written in plain language for easy understanding, and was prepared at low cost to promote wide distribution. Of the seventy pages of text and photographs, in three sections, seventy percent was devoted

Fig. 7.2 John Davey (second from left bottom row), with his first crew to do tree work in 1902. Wellington Davey is second from the right. Courtesy of the Davey Tree Expert Company.

to tree surgery, six percent to ornamentals, and twenty-four percent to landscaping and floriculture. His observations on cavity filling follow those of Forsythe a hundred years earlier, with the notable exception of using concrete (used in England even earlier than Forsythe). His recommendations stressed care to avoid unnecessary injury to living cambium, and shaping the opening lengthwise to facilitate translocation of water, nutrients, and sugars around the wound. His recommendation for cavity filling required not only removal of decay, but also, tracing the wound back to living tissue. He believed that the filling would destroy residual microorganisms, and that the seal over the wound would prevent further exposure to decay fungi. Watershed grooves were recommended for the filling surface and copper drain tubes installed to remove water. Part of his method was the use of a steel brace for mechanical support of the tissues around the wound. He also believed that wound dressings were essential to prevent premature death of the tree.

Davey's second priority concerned pruning of limbs from trees. Noting that the best time to prune is when the sap does not flow, he mistakenly believed this time to be in summer. Noting the vigor of the "shoulder" attachment of the branch at the stem, he recommended it be cut off so that it would not take a long time to close over. He recommended that all pruning wounds be painted to protect them from moisture and to promote healing. He favored painting all pruning wounds down to 0.5 inch in diameter and painting of large wounds twice a year.

Noting the narrow tree crotches and acute angle attachment of branches, he was tolerant of topping elms to prevent wind splitting. In his view, the worst offenders in the mutilation and slaughter of trees were the early line clearers for the telephone and telegraph companies. As with cavity treatment, his views on pruning had a significant impact on tree care practices.

Another new art was chaining and bracing, later known as cabling and bracing. The use of structural metal in tree work was probably not well known or much practiced before it was publicized in Davey's book. He favored structural support for weakened trees, noting success in tree survival for a hundred years with such support. He believed that chains could be damaging to trees, causing girdling and death when used improperly. Where trees had crotches with narrow angled branches, he urged use of bolts instead of chains.

Davey took pains in his book to discuss the "Calamity of Cleveland," by which he meant the disaster that occurred there in terms of low survival of planted trees. Disagreeing strongly with excuses offered to explain the inability of planted trees to survive, he offered his own version, which was correct. Brushing aside claims by city apologists of gas leakage, electric currents, and smoke as probable causes of decline, he minced no words in pointing out the lack of good soils and the need for site preparation and additional care. Because of his reputation and knowledge, the city petitioned the legislature to authorize a city department of forestry for shade tree care. He can thus be said to have had a hand in creating the seeds of urban forestry seventy years before the concept was recognized.

The Tree Doctor is considered to be the first serious work in North America concerned with the care of shade and ornamental trees. In his book Davey demonstrated that his approach was based on methods and observations considered sound at that time. Before Davey, there was little or no informed experience or training, there were no recognized standards, no guarantees, and little responsibility for the end result. His guiding motto, "do it right or not at all," struck a responsive chord from a public looking for integrity. He was the first in this country to establish a leading company skilled in tree surgery practices. His example set the tone for many other dependable commercial arborists whose enterprise and success led to the development of a new industry of tree care. His views on what is called tree surgery, cavity treatment, or wound dressing would become the basis for most tree care in the first two decades of the twentieth century. The practice of tree surgery as such would dominate every other tree care practice up to 1930 as the cornerstone of the new tree care industry.

When Davey wrote his book, there was little individual tree care in North America, and little if any organized effort toward shade tree care. To meet the demand for his services that were created by the book, Davey literally had to draft his sons to handle the load. The book was also the basis for municipal controversy over the care of public trees. While cities took note of the Davey message, the most significant reception came from large landowners with landscaped estates. Such estates provided the basis for large-scale tree care work where there were ample funds to support commercial arboriculture. It was not by accident, then, that in addition to northern Ohio where Davey lived, the metropolitan areas of New York, Philadelphia, and Boston would become the early proving grounds for the rise of commercial arboriculture on a large scale in North America.

The development of tree surgery in Europe had preceded Davey by more than 100 years with the definitive work of Forsythe. Davey's work, however, resurrected tree surgery in the United States along a more scientific line than Forsythe. Thus, rather than being known as the father of tree surgery, he is more accurately described as the father of arboriculture in North America.

When John Davey died in 1923, he had truly become a national figure who inspired more than twenty eulogies throughout the nation. These included scores of prayers, poems, obituaries, editorials, and laudatory articles from newspapers, state and local elected officials, presidents of civic associations, colleges, horticultural and conservation societies, botanists, and many others. He was honored in 1924 when his name was included in a historical review of fifty famous farmers, and again in 1942 when the national government gave his name to one of its Liberty ships in World War II.

MARTIN LUTHER DAVEY

Of John Davey's five surviving children, four were sons, all of whom were bright and able. Martin Luther Davey, the second son, was born in Kent, Ohio, in 1884. He was probably the most imaginative and energetic son. Although the Davey family was rich in ability and spirit, father John was never wealthy until late in life. Since he was poor when his family was growing, each of his children worked as youths. Martin worked hard in the fields raising food, but distinguished himself in the selling of produce.

After his father's book appeared, Martin sold it in the Ohio area. After graduation from Kent High School in 1900, he completed studies at Oberlin Academy and entered Oberlin College. When asked by his father to go east in 1906 to develop the Davey tree business rising in the Hudson Valley above New York City, he was offered a full partnership and given a free hand. For this he sacrificed the remainder of his formal education. Because there were almost no funds, his first goal was to raise $10,000 as venture capital, the only "outside" money ever invested in the company. He became both treasurer and manager of the Davey Company when it was incorporated in 1909. He held one or both of these offices until his death in 1946. In every true sense he built the Davey Company from the ground up, seeing it through two world wars and the severe national economic collapse during the Great Depression.

With Martin providing company leadership, father John pursued his widespread ideological interests, and continued lecturing and pamphleteering on birds, trees, and other plants. Many affluent and influential men, including J. Horace McFarland of the American Civic Association and George Eastman, founder of the Eastman Kodak Company, were profoundly influenced by his book and were eager to support his goals. Demand for his work was increasing in Ohio, Pennsylvania, and New York, as well as in Toronto and Ottawa, Canada.

INCORPORATION

The company was incorporated in 1909 in the state of Ohio as the "Davey Tree Expert Company." Those signing the articles of incorporation included John; his son, Martin L. Davey, and a son-in-law, Harmon L. Carson. In addition were two Kent businessmen, Fred L. Allen and Charles W. Bishop. The original stock was divided among father John and his children, Belle, Martin, and Jim. A block was set aside for Paul who was then in school. Another block was held as treasury stock for future financing. Father John immediately signed his shares over to his wife, who was a prudent money manager. For all practical purposes, Martin was the sole leader of the company.

Omitted from original stock shareholders was John Davey's oldest son, Wellington, but company records of 1910 indicate that he had at least thirty shares and was elected a director of the board. Wellington had joined his father in early tree work in 1900, and had helped him to organize the Davey School of Practical Forestry in 1905. At some point after that, he left Kent with his family's blessing to operate his own tree surgery business, first in Pittsburgh and Cleveland, and later in Michigan. In 1928 when the Davey Company at Kent had a commitment for work in California, Wellington's help was sought. He accepted a proposal that he move west to meet the challenge.

Fig. 7.3 The Davey School of Practical Forestry. Courtesy of the Davey Tree Expert Company.

THE DAVEY SCHOOL OF PRACTICAL FORESTRY

The Davey School of Practical Forestry was designed to teach men how to treat sick trees. At first the school was for field training only, but, because of the seasonal nature of the work (no work in winter), there was a high turnover rate, which in turn required constant retraining. To meet this problem the school curriculum was upgraded in 1909 to include formal classroom study and was renamed the Davey Institute of Tree Surgery (DITS). Later, it was again renamed as the Davey Institute of Tree Sciences.

In order to hold trained employees, a winter program of instruction was offered to provide knowledge that would supplement their technical skills. With an added dimension to their work, trainees became more valuable to the company, and their jobs became more interesting. When at first there was little enthusiasm for this program, Martin offered a dollar a day pay raise for those who enrolled, effective at the beginning of the next working season. Twenty enrolled for the first class of three months.

Once established, the schedule was like a college semester and was expanded to four-month terms in three consecutive winters. Faculty members were recruited from leading colleges and universities. Course content included botany, entomology, plant pathology with the accent on disease and insect control, soils, fertilization, tree surgery, accounting, business, English, and ethics.

This early training of arborists for professional tree care was the first of its kind in North America. While giving paternal advice and support to his new company, John's initiation of early employee training appears to have been his most significant management innovation.

As early as 1910 Professors Rankin and Illingworth of Cornell University were recruited to teach at DITS. In addition, they were given fellowship grants to do research in tree-oriented projects at Cornell. This marked the earliest direct involvement of university personnel in a commercial arboriculture program. It also represented the first instance of grant funds from commercial arboriculture to a university for research.

By 1913 the company had developed a winter field program in the South, and there were able field men working there who could not attend the DITS in Kent. To solve this problem, a correspondence course was created. Patterned on the institute's curriculum, $2,000 was allocated for its support. It was promoted aggressively and with success. By 1916 the budget to advertise it was increased to $8,500. This is probably the earliest course of its type in arboriculture, and the forerunner of many more.

By 1923, DITS was so popular and successful that the company was forced to be more selective. This selectivity made the institute more popular as well as more prestigious. By 1925 it had 280 students, 28 faculty members, was costing the company about $25,000 annually, and was considered a good investment. National recognition came when a newsreel movie was made of one of the Davey crews working in Central Park in New York. Shown in movie theaters all over the United States, this gave the company and the field of arboriculture their first national publicity.

By 1932 there was a precipitous drop in company business and overwhelming debt, and the institute had to be discontinued. It resumed on a limited basis after the war. The school term was reduced to six weeks and the subject matter was limited to tree surgery. Utility companies did more winter work by this time, and so there was no reason to hold men over winter. The new school was under the direction of Red Jacobs, a proven Davey professional, and faculty members were now professional Davey tree surgeons.

The postwar advent of new machines and new chemicals (1946–50) created the need for new training. By 1948, before assignment to a field squad, each Davey employee was required to complete a three-week field training period. Some of this training was done away from Kent at training centers, such as one in Savannah, Georgia. Selection of new candidates for DITS became more demanding than ever. The preschool extension course involved a 10-lesson, 225-page program on tree surgery. A new requirement was safety training. Uniformity in field training was extended to uniformity in dress and equipment. Davey men were required to dress in forest green, with breeches and high-top boots, and all Davey vehicles were painted a standard green.

THE EARLY YEARS

One of the earliest publications by a commercial tree company was the *Davey Tree Surgeons Bulletin*, later renamed the *Davey Bulletin*. First issued 19 February 1910, the bulletin has been published continuously since then with two exceptions: in 1913 it was published only when convenient and in 1934 publication was suspended for financial reasons. Originally published as a weekly, sometimes published as a quarterly, or even sporadically, it has been published over the years mostly as a monthly. In 1998 it was still published for all employees of the company, including its subsidiaries and divisions.

Special editions have appeared for special occasions. On the death of John Davey in 1923, there was a twenty-page memorial issue. For a national advertising campaign in 1928, a special edition was issued. The *John Davey Centennial* issue in 1946 (his 100th birthday) was a memorial issue in honor of Martin L. Davey who died in that year. Two issues were also prepared as memorials after both world wars to list employees who had served, noting those who died, were captured, or were missing.

By 1909 when the Davey Company incorporated, it had two main centers of activity—northern Ohio and the lower Hudson Valley of New York. By 1910 the New York operation had spread a hundred miles north up the Hudson River to Poughkeepsie, east into western Connecticut, and south into New Jersey. By this time Martin had acquired three additional salesmen for this region, including his brother Jim. Davey work in Ohio had expanded east to Pittsburgh, north to Detroit, and south to Cincinnati.

In 1910, in order to get business for winter employment, Martin sent some of his best salesmen throughout the southern states, initiating what would become almost a thirty-year period of barnstorming with assorted crews, moving south in winter and back north again in summer. In this same year, Martin began to develop his management plans around organized territories run by salesmen who obtained sufficient business to keep tree crews operating. Each crew was headed by a foreman who scheduled work, estimated costs, supervised work, and reported to a salesman.

To enhance the prestige of the company, Martin tried to get work on the White House grounds in Washington, D.C. At first denied, he succeeded in 1911 with a hands-on demonstration of insect-infested maple branches right under the nose of the grounds superintendent. Seeing the need for care, the superintendent yielded. This led to more government orders. A request for services was later received for care of trees on the Parliament grounds in Ottawa, Canada. Early in its history, therefore, the Davey Company was known in Canada as well as the United States.

In the 1920s the Davey Company continued to grow and prosper partly because of Martin's public relations skills. He was successful in obtaining much-publicized work in New York's Central Park; in getting the famous cowboy-comedian, Will Rogers, to plug his line and preside at Davey ceremonies in Philadelphia; and in sponsoring the weekly radio program, *Davey Hour,* in 1930.

In 1921, somewhat by accident, the Davey Company became involved in its first line-clearing operation. When Wesley Hollister, a professor in the Davey Tree Institute, was elected mayor of Kent for 1921–22, he appointed Paul Davey to be the tree commissioner for Kent. Approached by the Northern Ohio Power and Light Company for permission to clear trees for new power lines in Kent, Paul found himself in a tight spot. If he gave permission, he invited public abuse for allowing unskilled clearing of local trees and embarrassment for the Davey Company, with its reputation for skilled tree care. Denying permission meant losing power development that the city needed. Against the wishes of all his family, he arranged to have the Davey Company do the work itself. The power company and the city were pleased with the results, but the Davey Company was not. Subsequent requests for line clearance, however, justified Paul's judgment. Line clearance had far-reaching consequences for the survival of the company, and also marked the beginning of unprecedented expansion of skilled tree care work for utilities, where before there had been little or none. The Bartlett Company followed on the heels of the Davey Company, but in 1928 Asplundh rose to dominate this aspect of arboriculture to the present time.

By 1925 the company had established offices in seventeen cities in twelve states, in Washington, D.C., and in Montreal. The first large company in organized tree work, it was the first to train its own workers and the first in line clearing (1921). In 1925 its operations extended from Minneapolis and Montreal in the north; Boston in the east; Louisville, Kentucky, in the south; and Kansas City, Missouri, in the west. In 1928 it had offices in thirty-one cities in sixteen states and two Canadian provinces. A year later it had spread to Des Moines, Iowa; New Orleans; and Tulsa, Oklahoma, with more than 21,000 clients.

Fig. 7.4 Reo Spray outfit powered by a twenty-two horse power standard Ford engine with a 300-gallon tank, Kent, Ohio, 1925. Courtesy of the ISA Archives.

As the twenties drew to a close, the company decided to memorialize John Davey, its founding father, in a most unique way. It secured a native, wild American elm from a farm west of Kent, as a memorial gift to be given to the town. The "John Davey Elm" was fifteen inches in diameter and fifty feet in height. It was dug up, moved, and planted on the grounds of Roosevelt High School in March of 1930 to celebrate the company's fiftieth anniversary. Encased in lead was a copy of Davey's book, *The Tree Doctor,* sealed within the trunk of the tree at about breast height. Although intended to remain in the tree into a distant age, it stayed but forty years. A victim of Dutch elm disease in 1971, the tree yielded the treasure to the company when it was cut down.

Geographic expansion slowed down and even stopped in the 1930s and 1940s, but increased again after the war. Wellington's independent Davey Tree Surgery, Ltd., based in California, was another Davey empire. Upon the death of Wellington in 1969, the parent company acquired the California company, thereby increasing its size significantly, and bringing seven additional western states into the company. When the company obtained utility work in Hawaii and the Virgin Islands in the mid-1970s, it had literally spanned the North American continent and beyond. By 1984 the company was operating in thirty-five states and the province of Ontario, and by 1988 had expanded into British Columbia.

The Role of Family and Employees

Martin Davey had a parallel career in politics for almost thirty years. He was elected mayor of Kent at age twenty-nine, one of the youngest mayors at that time. He was reelected twice more. Elected to the U.S. House of Representatives in 1918 from the Fourteenth Ohio District to serve an unexpired term, he was elected again the following term. After a gap of two years, he served three additional two-year terms in Congress. In 1934 he was elected governor of Ohio. He was re-elected in 1936. From 1940 until an early death in 1946, he directed the company full time. He had spent eighteen years in elected office, twelve years away from Davey headquarters in Kent, and eight in Washington away from Ohio. This was the period of the most dynamic growth in the history of the company until after the employee purchase in 1979.

His dual role as manager and politician, however, involved sacrifice, near disaster, and ultimately his early demise. Although defeated for Congress in the Republican landslide of 1928, his popularity was high. His vote count in Ohio exceeded that of the Democratic presidential candidate, Al Smith, by more than 500,000. Pressed to run for governor in 1930, he had to forego the opportunity until 1934. And even then, during his first campaign for governor, the real possibility of imminent financial collapse of the company threatened to be his ruin in both business and politics. Finally, less than a year after his final political defeat in 1940, he suffered a severe heart attack, which would be the prelude to a fatal one in 1946.

Martin's dual role as company manager of the largest tree company in America and political leader over almost thirty years is a remarkable achievement in the history of arboriculture. The news attending his political campaigns, plus his tenure in the limelight of publicity as mayor, congressman, and governor, must have given his company, as well as the field of arboriculture, a favorable reputation. Political partisan considerations aside, his role as a public leader provided an excellent image for the tree industry, then more popularly known perhaps as "tree surgery."

The third oldest of John Davey's sons, James (Jim), had begun working with his father in 1904, shortly after publication of *The Tree Doctor*. With Martin he went east to New York from 1906 to 1908 (summers) and was in charge of field crews. His role there was significant. First in charge of field crews, and later as a salesman, he played a key role, beginning in 1910, in leading Davey crews to southern states for winter work. When, in 1913, key Davey workers deserted, lured away clients, and infringed on Davey patent rights, he took to the field to salvage the

Davey position. Moving from one area to another, by sheer determination, he outsold the competition and obtained the necessary evidence for Davey to win its legal battle. This incident and others taught the Davey Company about the costs of litigation; it learned to ignore fraudulent competition, warn the public about frauds, and to outperform the competition in quality service. The need for such a policy reflects strongly on the low order of tree care business ethics and practices at that time. Jim Davey retired early from the company after World War II for health reasons.

The youngest son of John Davey, Paul, had joined the company at an early age but did not become active until he returned from World War I. In 1919 he became head of both the field forces and the research department. A born engineer with imagination and a strong inventive capacity, he was instrumental in improving many tree care operations by development of new equipment over the next forty years. He would have fifty patents for inventions to his name. Paul initiated a program to mechanize tree care equipment, focusing initially on spray apparatus and power sources. Among his inventions was an actuated power tool for cleaning out decay in tree cavities in 1926. Though successful, it was little used because it was expensive and difficult to activate at long distances from a power source.

Paul was instrumental in steering the company to utility line clearing and large tree moving. Line clearing was a major step in the development of the company, because in time it became a major source of work volume and has remained the most significant segment of total business to date.

The rapid development of power spraying in the 1920s stimulated a search for larger and more powerful equipment. In 1926 the large capacity machines made of cast iron and cooled by water were heavy and cumbersome. Seeking in vain for a lighter, air-cooled model, Paul was told there had never been a satisfactory one produced. This led him to develop his own air-cooled compressor, which used a finned aluminum head that conducted heat away from the engine without the need for water cooling. Smaller and lighter, yet high powered, it required less maintenance, started easily in cold weather, and used little fuel. The three Davey brothers founded a new organization, the Davey Compressor Company, in 1930. Although most active in the new compressor company, Paul continued his association with the Davey Tree Company over fifty years, serving in diverse managerial capacities. He was a member of its board of directors until 1961 and served as vice president of the Davey Investment Company. When Martin was serving as governor of Ohio in the 1930s, Paul became acting manager of the parent company. Paul also perfected the Davey Power Take-Off, making it possible to power auxiliary equipment from the truck engine. Paul retired in 1961 for health reasons.

Fig. 7.5 Whitey Meyers operating a cavity machine from the comfort of a bosun's chair and ladder (ca. 1931). Courtesy of the ISA Archives.

In 1922 Homer L. ("Red") Jacobs was assigned to do studies on shade tree fertilization for the research department. The only information on tree fertilization to that time had come from orchard trees. The prevailing view in horticulture then was that early fall application of fertilizer for trees was detrimental, ineffective, or both. In a massive three-year study with three tree species and 378 trees, Jacobs showed that fall fertilization was significantly better than no fertilization and as effective as that done in spring. Research of this kind, including other investigations, was collated by Jacobs and published in 1946 in a 211-page book called the *Arboriculturist*, somewhat of an encyclopedia of shade tree care.

The Depression and World War II

The Depression brought hardships to many. With unemployment in the millions the government moved to create jobs to help the unemployed. One of the federal programs known as the Works Progress Administration (WPA) had a project of trimming trees in public parks. To attract skilled workers, wages were set at $1.20 per hour, about fifty cents more than tree companies could afford. When the Davey and Bartlett Companies began losing men, Martin Davey and F. A. Bartlett, normally competitors, became allies. Both Davey and Bartlett went to Washington. The two arborists explained to President Roosevelt that his errand of mercy for the unemployed had dealt the arborists a blow that could be fatal. The WPA wage rate was adjusted so that the wage discrepancy was reduced from $1.20 per hour to 80 cents against the company's rate of 70 cents. While the difference still was attractive enough to get good men, it was not enough for those with permanent jobs to give them up for a small, temporary advantage. In this way the threat of labor loss to the tree companies was resolved so they were able to survive the serious crisis.

Despite the resolution to the wage crisis, the Davey Company faced a grim future as the Depression brought on an even more menacing financial crisis. This was probably the darkest period in Davey Company history. Company sales volume had fallen from $3 million in 1930 to $700,000 in 1932. The radio advertising and the resident tree surgery school were discontinued, and the bank creditors closed in. The company was unable to repay bank loans, and the banks assumed fiscal control of the company. Then the banks were closed by the federal government. Payrolls went unmet, Davey family members loaned cash to the company, and layoffs were essential. The Davey Company faced financial ruin. Martin's wife and other family members loaned their personal savings to the company. Despite these financial problems, Martin decided to run for governor at this time and was elected. Within three years he had repaid his creditors in full, refusing to make a deal to repay at a discount. And his wife got her personal savings back in full.

World War II affected every economic activity in the United States. There were shortages of all kinds, but the most critical to Davey was labor for tree work. The company lost more than 700 employees to the armed forces. Gasoline was rationed, travel was curtailed, and new tools and equipment were unavailable. With labor in short supply, many blue-collar industries turned to women to meet their needs. In the words of one of the Davey managers, "We operated the Company during the war years with old men and very young men, the rest were in the service or in war industries." Not mentioned was the fact that Davey hired two young women in 1944 for tree work.

With two years of college course work in horticulture, the women may have been better prepared than most young men first working as "rabble" in tree work (rabble was a term used for tree workers at the very bottom of the employment ladder for whom all the dirtiest and toughest work was often reserved). The women were described as professional and competent. This is the earliest record found by the author of women in this area of arboriculture.

The end of the war was in many ways a watershed period in American history. For the Davey Company it was the end of an era, as the life of its leader for almost forty years came to an end in 1946. The passing of Martin Davey at the early age of sixty-two is seen as a casualty of his parallel careers. In his thirty years as mayor, congressman, and governor, he had continued as an active officer (manager or president) of the Davey Company. In reality he had shouldered the company burden from 1909 to 1946, because father John, though nominally president, had ceased to be a dominant figure when Martin became manager in 1909.

Just before his death, Martin wrote a letter to his son, expressing his philosophy on business as well as life. The letter reflected sound advice in upholding a good reputation, being humane to employees, acting responsibly to clients, offering decent wages, and practicing careful economics and personal humility. Such a letter reveals Martin's honor as a leader of men and one who had great influence on arboriculture during a critical period. It would be an inspiration and guide to his son to "keep going forward" in the same spirit. At a later time the humane and caring management record of the two Daveys would provide the opportunity for company management by employees.

THE MIDDLE YEARS

The death of Martin Davey in 1946 represented the end of an era in the Davey Company. The ensuing period, considered by the company as "the Middle Years" (1946–77), included two distinct periods of management: the first (1946–61) was under the leadership of Martin Davey Jr. and the second (1961–77) was marked by a series of short-term company presidents, divided between secondary family and nonfamily executives.

Martin L. Davey Jr. was a 1940 graduate of Yale with a major in botany and a minor in business administration. Before his years in the army, he had worked summers in the field in the Chicago area, as well as in the company personnel department. He also completed the Davey Institute of Tree Surgery in his early years. At the age of twenty-eight and surrounded by a brain trust of Davey veterans, Martin Jr. began as president in April of 1946. His election to the Davey presidency did not sit well with some of the senior management, and some gave serious thought to leaving the company. Those who remained saw his leadership bring fifteen years of progress before poor health ended his reign.

Known affectionately for most of his life as "Brub," a childhood nickname, Martin Jr. set about to "keep going forward." In his first two years as president he adjusted to the aftermath of the war by reopening the DITS and improving employee benefits. He also revived the annual sales convention and increased sales volume. Most significantly, he started a new profitable service in chemical brush control.

Conceived by Red Jacobs, the era of brush control by chemicals was about to begin. Prior to this time, line-clearance utilities had crews of men removing brush by hand. In 1946 Jacobs demonstrated the ability of ammate, a new chemical produced by Dupont, to kill hardwood brush by spray application. In 1951 Jacobs was principal speaker at the Fifth Northeastern Weed Conference. Considered by many as the "dean" of chemical weed control, he lectured to a large audience in New York City, where foresters, utility arborists, federal and state research scientists, and chemical company representatives came from all over the Northeast to learn about the effectiveness of the new weed killing chemicals.

After two years at the helm, Brub became concerned about what he called the company service mix. Starting out in 1909 as a tree surgery organization, the Davey Company meant to "care" for individual trees. In order to survive during the Depression and the war, however, the company had become excessively involved in line clearing. During the war eighty percent of its sales volume and two-thirds of its field crews had been so occupied. This disturbed Brub and others who felt uneasy with such a major change in the company's workload. In 1948 he began a concerted effort to focus more on individual tree care. The Davey Institute of Tree Surgery reopened for its first sessions since the prewar years. A special program with an emphasis on safety was initiated. The company prospered during the 1950s, aided by new mechanization and equipment. The chemical brush sprayers that were available by 1947 were followed by chippers in 1949. The chainsaw developed during the war was cumbersome to use. Heavy and requiring two men, it was soon supplanted by one-man, lightweight models. The aerial bucket as well as brush hogs came into use in 1953.

Since technological innovations in machines and chemicals became more important in arboriculture, the Davey Company built a Technical Service Center in Kent in 1954. Serving not only as a center for diagnosis and research, the new building was able to house the offices, laboratory, and library of the technical staff. In addition, it provided classrooms for the Davey Institute and space for the photographic department and its extensive files of negatives in one location. On the grounds were facilities for equipment storage and experimental plantings. From its inception, the service center became a center for conferences, training, and exhibits for visiting clients.

In 1961 Brub took a six-month leave because of a serious heart condition and never returned as president. In his place Alexander M. Smith, who had been chairman of the board of directors, became president. As the son-in-law of Martin Davey Sr., Smith continued the Davey family direction, but did not leave another executive position with a nontree company. Thus, he served Davey as president in absentia from 1961–65, delegating responsibility to Paul Hershey, previously vice president of field operations, who then became executive vice president in name, but president in fact.

Brub's retirement in 1961 marked the end of direct, sustained family control of the company. In retrospect it can now be seen as the prelude to a transition period of eighteen years, from family to employee ownership. Such a transition became possible largely through the enlightened leadership Martin and his father before him had provided, thereby shaping the loyalty and morale of the employees. The transition period from 1961–79 was characterized by a series of short-term presidents.

In 1965 Hershey became the first president that was not from the Davey family. With Smith serving as chairman of the board, however, and the bulk of stock still in Davey family hands, it was still a family company. Facing retirement himself, Hershey was especially conscious of the role of his successor. Thus, his short tenure was essentially preoccupied with restructuring management. His leadership was productive, with annual sales reaching a new high of $20.8 million in his final year (1969).

Upon the retirement of Hershey, Smith returned as president on a full-time basis. In his new term the company developed a tree farm at Wooster on land acquired in 1963. By 1984 this farm had an inventory of 45,000 trees. The company also developed an infrared inspection service to detect underground problems for line-clearing utilities, and a striping machine for marking highways.

Smith retired as president in 1972 to become chairman of the board. He was succeeded by Joseph T. Myers, another family member. A successful business executive with wide management experience, he was new to the tree care business, but perceptive enough to reemphasize residential tree care and landscaping. From 1972–76 the company introduced a lawnscape service involving lawn fertilization and pest control, destined for annual sales of $12,000,000 by 1990. Another successful development was Arbor Green, a tree-shrub fertilizer developed by Dr. Roger C. Funk of the research department.

In the 1970s the national recession and ensuing inflation had a negative financial impact on Davey and the other tree companies. By 1976, with company finances and morale at a low point, Smith was returned by the board to be president for the third time. He was the last of the Davey family presidents. His immediate goal was reorganization by restructuring along service lines. This was beneficial for the tree care and utility services. Their vice presidents were represented again in the managing group. Overall results of the reorganization were positive and the serious financial problem was eased.

EMPLOYEE PURCHASE

In November of 1977, the company made two significant decisions that would have a major impact on its future. A nonfamily member, John W. (Jack) Joy, was elected as president, and the Davey family decided to sell the company. An employee ownership committee of J. W. Joy, James H. Pohl, and R. D. Cowan, all company executives, made it known that a group of employees wanted to buy the company. The Davey family agreed that the employees might be the preferred buyers, but doubted their ability to finance the sale. At least four other companies or investment groups were very interested in acquiring the company. Four purchase plans were put forward by the employee committee before a final settlement was made. On 4 February 1979, the company passed to a group of its employees after seventy years in the Davey family.

During the next five years, Davey management and employees achieved increased revenues and profitability, which proved that the employee investment in themselves was sound. Sales from 1979 to 1984 essentially doubled and profitability increased fourfold. Earnings per share and dividends increased 300 percent. In 1982 a new stock purchase plan for employees was initiated.

In 1985 a new corporate office and technical research center, located on the outskirts of Kent, was built and occupied. Seventy-seven years after company incorporation, the employee group had accomplished a corporate renewal. The impressive new facilities were a tribute to past employees and a testimonial to the confidence of the employees in the future. In 1985 R. Douglas Cowan was elected president and J. W. Joy continued as CEO and chairman. Cowan was elected CEO in 1988 and later assumed the responsibilities of chairman in 1997.

SUMMARY

The Davey Company was the first to offer arborist training, surgery schools, and arborist publications, and was also first into line clearing, the mainstay of the industry. Still growing and expanding, it continues as a leader in the tree care industry. As the first national tree care company, Davey probably had a greater influence on the tree care industry than any of the national companies to follow. Because of its size and early schools, it may have trained more men who would establish their own successful companies than any other company. The records of the National Shade Tree Conference, the International Shade Tree Conference, the International Society of Arboriculture, the American Society of Consulting Arborists, and the National Arborist Association are replete with leaders of private companies who were early alumni of the Davey schools.

CHAPTER EIGHT

The F. A. Bartlett Tree Expert Company

"The Scientific Way" —Bartlett Company motto

In 1907 a young teacher and tree specialist, Francis A. Bartlett, arrived in New York City to begin commercial tree work. Although financed by the Frost Insecticide Company in its earliest years, over the next thirty years Bartlett built a major tree care company to rival the Davey concern. During that time (1907–37), Davey and Bartlett were the only really large tree companies in North America. Though competitors and rivals, sometimes in disagreement and at times cooperative, together they established the foundation of commercial arboriculture in America.

Francis Alonzo Bartlett, founder of the tree company with his name, was born on a farm in Belchertown, Massachusetts, on 12 November 1882. He was one of five children. After graduating from Belchertown High School in 1901, he enrolled at Massachusetts Agricultural College (MAC, now University of Massachusetts). Coming under the influence of the inspiring professor of botany and plant pathology, Dr. George E. Stone, a keen student of trees, he changed his major from chemistry to horticulture. Stone, head of the botany department, had recently returned from Europe (1895), having had contact with Dr. Robert Hartig of Germany, then the world's foremost authority on tree disease. Stone was also a productive researcher and the founder of the Massachusetts Tree Wardens' and Foresters' Association, now the oldest arborist society in North America. Bartlett's college training, with an emphasis on tree care, gave him a perspective that was quite different from that of either John or Martin Davey. Bartlett graduated in 1905 with a bachelor of science degree in agriculture.

Fig. 8.1 F. A. Bartlett with Dr. J. Went, in Holland in 1951. Courtesy of the F. A. Bartlett Tree Expert Company.

Following graduation, Bartlett became an instructor in horticulture at Hampton Institute in Virginia. He taught horticulture to advanced students and supervised the institution's nursery and orchards. He worked as a consultant to the Oasis Farm and Orchard Company in Roswell, New Mexico, during summers and breaks in his teaching schedule.

After two years at Hampton Institute, Bartlett decided to work on shade trees and sought out Harold L. Frost, who had graduated from MAC before him. Frost had acquired a reputation for lending financial support to beginning arborists. As head of Frost Insecticide Company, he had an interest in promoting users of his products, and over the years backed eleven tree companies. Financed by Frost, Bartlett became part owner and sole manager of the firm of Frost and Bartlett. In 1907 Francis A. Bartlett saw his greatest opportunity in the need to apply scientific methods to tree care and the need for intelligent service to clients. The Bartlett way became "the scientific way," and he used this as his motto.

In 1909 Bartlett offered to buy out Frost for $5,000, which Frost accepted. Bartlett became sole owner of the company in 1916 when he completed payments to Frost. Based in Stamford, Connecticut, the company name was changed officially to the F. A. Bartlett Company. In 1920, when it became incorporated under the laws of Connecticut, the company assumed its official name, the F. A. Bartlett Tree Expert Company, by which we know it today.

After receiving initial backing from Frost, Bartlett moved to White Plains in Westchester County, New York, a land of old and large shade trees, wealthy men, and big estates. Without an automobile, he rode the train to nearby towns, and walked up and down the tree-shaded streets and estate roads to sell tree services. His first job was on the Jacob Gould Schurman estate in Bedford, New York. He hired a crew of men nearby and completed the job on 6 June 1907. His primary clientele were wealthy estate owners, municipalities, churches, and even modest homes. Job sizes reported by Bartlett in that first year ranged from $1 for spraying, to $2,444 for pruning (a king's ransom at that time).

From its inception in 1907 in White Plains, New York, the Bartlett Company began to grow and expand. By 1908 he had clients in the Hudson Valley of southern New York, nearby Connecticut towns, the Berkshire hills of western Massachusetts, upstate New York, Philadelphia and suburbs, New Jersey, and Long Island.

In 1909 Bartlett moved his office to Stamford, Connecticut, to be on a main railroad line on the Long Island Sound. He rented a store with adequate storage space. He purchased a new, bright red Buick to ease his sales walking. He also sold farm implements and tree tools for eight years before giving full time to the tree business. In 1910 he increased his permanent staff to three by adding two more men—one to sell, the other to produce. In 1913 he bought a farm in North Stamford, which included 60 acres and a house. That farm changed the whole outlook of his company; from it would come a training ground, school, laboratory, experiment station, and arboretum.

For his growing organization Bartlett sought young men with promise. Clinton C. Lawrence was only sixteen when he went to work for Bartlett in 1909 during his high school days. Later, he would attend Cornell University to major in plant pathology while working for Bartlett. He became a full-time Bartlett associate in 1914. A second man, Lem Strout, drifted into the Bartlett organization in 1910 as an ordinary handyman. He proved to have extraordinary mechanical ability and insight. A third key individual in those early years was Orville Spicer, who joined Bartlett in 1916. Lawrence and Spicer would become the core of the "Bartlett Associates" in 1924, and Strout from 1911 to his death in 1968 was chief troubleshooter, engineer, and innovator in the mechanics of operational arboriculture. By 1915, the company had six permanent staff members, one secretary, and, at the peak of the spray season, between 35 and 40 production men.

World War I interrupted growth when most of the production men left for military service. When the staff returned in 1918, the company began its greatest expansion. Permanent field organizations were established where business seemed most promising. The first field office was opened in Mt. Vernon, New York, in 1919, not far from where the company had been founded twelve years earlier.

Fig. 8.2 F. A. Bartlett in his Buick. Courtesy of the F. A. Bartlett Tree Expert Company.

Beginning in 1920 with the purchase of Vick and Company in Philadelphia, the Bartlett Company grew in part by acquiring other tree care companies. Other field offices followed: Boston in 1921; Westbury (N.Y.) in 1923; Albany (N.Y.) in 1924; Danbury (Conn.) in 1924; and New Jersey in 1924. By 1928 field offices had been established in Charlotte, North Carolina; Syracuse, Rochester, and Poughkeepsie, New York; and Chicago. By the end of that year, the company operated in seven states from Boston to Charlotte to Chicago.

By 1930 the company claimed to have a larger fleet of motorized power sprayers than any other commercial organization at that time. Within that calendar year it sprayed 1.5 million gallons of liquid, increasing its volume over a nine-year period by 2,000 percent. The increase over the previous year was 50 percent, with 80 trucks consuming 47,000 gallons of gas.

Following the crash of the stock market and the ensuing Depression, the Bartlett Company had to reduce its number of employees and the pay for those who were retained. Despite the enormous decline in business, however, the need for electricity and power kept expanding, giving arborists an opportunity to survive. Without the new line-clearing work, the Bartlett Company does not believe it could have survived as a large company. By 1941 there were eighteen new offices in six more states, so that the company then had thirty branch offices, with one in Maine extending its range in the Northeast.

In 1963 there were sixty offices in the East, South, and Midwest, and by 1978 there were operations in twenty states. In 1978 the company purchased Utility Tree Service, Inc. of Eureka, California, extending its operations for the first time west of the Mississippi River and over to the West Coast. In 1982 it had expanded into Oregon, and by 1985, after acquiring the Horti-Care Corporation in San

Antonio, Texas, it had tree care and utility clients in twenty-six states from coast to coast. Still expanding, Bartlett established a new office in the San Francisco Bay area in 1987 with purchase of the long-established Sohner Tree Service, and later expanded to other California markets. Bartlett went international in 1994 with the acquisition of the largest European tree company, Southern Tree Surgeons, Ltd. Bartlett expanded into Canada in 1996.

INNOVATIONS

During the early years when F. A. Bartlett was president of the company, there were several innovations in tree care, and Strout was responsible for many of them. The earliest occurred in 1910, when the company was the first to use steel cables anchored with eyebolts to support weak crotches. Bartlett was the first commercial tree company to use cables. One of Strout's early jobs, and one that he disliked intensely, was the manual pumping of insecticide barrels to build pressure for aerial spraying. In 1911 he devised an effective gasoline powered spray pump to get the "barrel off his back." Bartlett was one of the first companies to use a climbing rope. This small innovation would save many lives and injuries, and avoided the need for climbing spurs, known even then to be harmful to the tree.

In 1920 fertilization of trees was still somewhat of a mystery. Even then, however, based on work with fruit trees, it was widely believed that they needed more nitrogen than either phosphorus or potassium. In that year George M. Codding and F. A. Bartlett formulated the first fertilizer designed specifically for trees, known as "Bartlett Green Tree Food."

When Bartlett acquired Vick and Company of Philadelphia in 1920, it also acquired patented rights to a new product called Nuwud, for cavity filling. Patterned after a filler for decks of wooden ships, Nuwud cavity filler was soon found to damage the cambium of trees and to inhibit "healing." In 1924, following experimentation, the toxic salts were removed from Nuwud and it became an important part of a new healing method, and could be cut by saw, unlike concrete fillers.

In 1920, F. A. Bartlett and Lem Strout devised what became known as the "Bartlett Heal Collar." A collar was stimulated to form from callus in a vertically oriented oval around a cavity at first filled with Nuwud or later with Flexifil. Unlike concrete filling that was stiff and often cracked, the new Flexifil formed the inner circle over which the living callus developed as a ring from the vascular cambium. When skillfully made, the heal collar was considered a safeguard that would not allow water and decay fungi to enter the cavity, and would stimulate rapid growth for closing of the wound. Early trials were so successful that in time they led to a "guarantee" for future success.

In 1922, at the request of electric utility companies, the Bartlett Company entered the field of line clearing. In the early days of line clearing, all agreements for work were made on the "honor system," sanctioned only by a "handshake." The Bartlett Company initiated the written contract for tree care industry utility work.

For many years lightning damage had been a serious problem in maintaining old, tall, specimen trees of great value, often standing alone or in small groves, isolated from buildings or other trees. With their unusual height and splendid isolation, they were often struck by lightning. The company devised practical methods for installing lightning rods in trees in 1924.

According to company history, it was responsible for other "firsts" in the industry in the 1930s: the use of power tools for installing cabling and bracing in 1933, and a system of forced feeding using liquid fertilizer under pressure in 1934. Finally, in 1935, Lem Strout invented a hydraulic device for spraying called the Strout gun. Advised by manufacturers that it was not possible to get a nozzle to produce both a strong stream and mistlike fog, Strout did it anyway. It was licensed by the John Bean Company for its sprayers. This led in time to the Bar-Way Manufacturing Company, a Bartlett subsidiary that made Strout guns and hydraulic fittings.

BARTLETT PUBLICATIONS

The Bartlett Tree Company initiated its first publication, entitled *Tree Talk,* in 1913. *Tree Talk* was designed to educate the public, as well as its own staff. It would be only the first of several Bartlett publications, including *Tree News, Tree Topics, Scientific Tree Topics, Radio Tree Talks, Bartlett Tree Research Laboratory Bulletins,* and *Tree Tips.* Aimed at a large audience beyond the company, *Tree Talk* was sent to a list of subscribers at 25 cents per copy, and carried a variety of articles written by various authors. Originally edited by Bartlett himself, it was edited next by Frank L. Brace. By 1933 the new editor of *Tree Talk* was Dr. E. Porter Felt, a prominent scientist in the field of shade tree care. Dr. Felt had been state entomologist for New York for more than 30 years, a professor at Cornell University, and coauthor with Dr. W. H. Rankin of a recent book on shade tree care. As editor of the *Journal of Economic Entomology* for more than twenty-five years, Felt was unusually well qualified to edit the Bartlett magazine.

More comparable to the *Davey Bulletin* designed for employees was the Bartlett *Tree News* started in 1924. Its purpose was to exchange ideas and to give each other helpful suggestions. *Tree Topics,* begun in 1932, contained many educational and informative articles on tree care, as did the "Radio Tree Talks" issued

Fig. 8.3 Dr. E. P. Felt, Bartlett Laboratories. Courtesy of the F. A. Bartlett Tree Expert Company.

over WEAF in New York City. *Scientific Tree Topics*, written by the staff and published by the laboratories, contained research information distributed to universities. Another Bartlett publication, a four-page newsletter called *Tree Tips*, was designed for Bartlett clientele.

THE BARTLETT SCHOOL

As early as 1913 the Bartlett Company was training its men at the North Stamford farm. The Bartlett School of Tree Surgery was formally established in 1923 and areas on the farm were reserved for field practices by students. Later, when the Forsythe Building of the Bartlett Laboratory was constructed in 1927, there were also classrooms on the farm. The Bartlett School had a three-year course that combined tree science with practical field work in climbing, equipment, and surgery. The Bartlett School survives today as a correspondence course.

"Dendrician" was a name used to designate Bartlett-trained tree workers. Derived from *dendro*, the Greek word for tree, the new name was designed to upgrade the image of professional tree workers, and was used within the company with dignity and pride. It continues in use to this day. To lend further dignity and honor to the term, in 1928 a Dendrician Award was created to honor conspicuous service. The award was known as the Bartlett Medal for service to the company beyond that expected of every member of the organization. Only issued when such service was truly outstanding, it became a coveted goal. The first award went to Nelson R. Minch of the Boston territory for his knowledge and application of first aid to an injured worker in shock, who otherwise may have died.

Fig. 8.4 The Bartlett School of Tree Surgery. Photo by the F. A. Bartlett Tree Expert Company, courtesy of the ISA Archives.

In addition to the Bartlett Medal, the company also gave awards in 1928 for achievement in the School of Tree Surgery in such categories as scholarship, outstanding foreman qualifications, improvement, effort expended, and personal neatness. Each of these awards was designed to motivate students to achieve high standards. In 1930 the graduating class of dendricians established a "dendrician fund," an emergency fund to help sick or needy company employees, which is still active today.

THE BARTLETT ASSOCIATES

By 1926 Bartlett had surrounded himself with a group of college-trained men at the top of his organization. These and others who followed were named the "Bartlett Associates" to distinguish the company as the most attentive to scientific training. These men were graduates of colleges of agriculture or schools of forestry and had years of study and practical experience in tree care. Each was either in charge of a geographic unit of the company or in charge of another organization of tree experts, closely affiliated with Bartlett. Following is a list of some of the associates: Clinton C. Lawrence, the first vice president and a company director, with a degree in plant pathology from Cornell University; Orville Spicer, vice president and staff entomologist, with a forestry degree from Syracuse College of Forestry; George

Fig. 8.5 Training in climbing techniques and the use of ropes. Photo by the F. A. Bartlett Tree Expert Company, courtesy of the ISA Archives.

Fig. 8.6 Sometimes workers had to climb off the top of the platform ladder to access the tree (1940). Courtesy of the F. A. Bartlett Tree Expert Company.

M. Codding, company board member, with a degree in entomology from Massachusetts Agricultural College and insect control experience with the USDA and state of Connecticut; and A. W. Dodge Jr., Bartlett manager in Boston and tree disease specialist, with a horticulture degree from Michigan Agricultural College.

THE BARTLETT TREE RESEARCH LABORATORIES

Bartlett wanted to develop his own laboratory and experimental grounds for study of the practices and principles involved in shade tree care because government activities of this type were then, as now, largely designed for fruit and forest trees, with limited application for amenity trees. In addition, because of his interest in a scientific approach to solving shade tree problems, he was anxious to get new information quickly for rapid application. His primary interest was in disease and cultural and insect problems.

Bartlett was interested primarily in ideas and preferred to delegate routine management and selling to others. With the purchase of a run-down pig farm in North Stamford in 1913, he foresaw many possibilities to aid development of the company. In that first year Arthur O'Brien, senior foreman of the company, had new recruits "in the trees" on the farm learning to be "tree skinners," learning the hands-on aspects of tree surgery skills. Many of the trees were soon full of cables, rods, bolts, hooks, and cement.

Bartlett himself began experiments with grafting, and collected new tree species to add to the thirty native varieties then present. He added many new varieties of nut trees. The federal government in 1916 sent him seedlings of rare, exotic, and introduced trees for hardiness and disease resistance testing.

By 1920, through purchase of adjacent properties, he had increased the laboratory acreage to 200, started an arboretum, and constructed an insectary to experiment with insecticides. In 1921 he began planting conifers, laid out test plots for new experiments on trees, and began a nursery. By this time his "farm" began to look like the grounds of an experiment station, and was open for such purposes to scientists at Yale University and the Connecticut Agricultural Experiment Station.

As a charter member of the Connecticut Tree Protective Association in 1922, F. A. Bartlett saw the need for a broader forum where arborists could meet to discuss tree science and tree problems. In 1924 he invited scientists and arborists to a meeting at the first Shade Tree Conference (later to become the National Shade Tree Conference, the International Shade Tree Conference, and the International Society of Arboriculture) at the Bartlett Experimental Grounds in Stamford, Connecticut.

In 1926 he formally initiated the Bartlett Tree Research Laboratories. The first laboratory building, designed for research in tree pathology, was erected that year and the entomological building was built in 1928. This was the first laboratory designed specifically for shade tree research in North America. F. A. Bartlett himself became the first director.

The research department was established and staffed. Dr. W. Howard Rankin, a plant pathologist from Cornell University, became department head, assisted by Dr. Rush P. Marshall, a doctoral candidate at Yale, then working on the wound aspects of what would become the famous Bartlett heal collar for tree surgery. At first these men were consultants, retaining their university positions; later the company employed them. Rankin previously had been an instructor at the Davey Institute of Tree Surgery.

In 1928, newly retired as state entomologist of New York, Dr. Ephraim Porter Felt was named director of research. Felt served here until his death in 1941, when Rush Marshall succeeded him, then at Yale University and the USDA nearby. In 1928 Dr. Carl Deuber, plant physiologist and plant nutrition specialist at Yale, was appointed as staff physiologist. Dr. John Shaw Boyce succeeded Rush Marshall as director. Following Boyce as director of research in 1960 was Edward Duda, who served until the laboratory was moved to North Carolina.

An early feature of the laboratory was its research bulletins, comparable in substance and quality to those of State Experiment Stations. The *Bartlett Tree Research Laboratory Bulletins* were scholarly articles or reports by serious scholars. Of much interest is the first one issued by F. A. Bartlett himself. Alarmed by the destruction of the so-called "European Elm Disease" (Dutch elm disease) in Europe, he had the perception and insight to see before almost anyone else in arboriculture what a menace it could be if introduced to North America. In the fall of 1927 he went to Europe to see it for himself. After interviewing the principal scientists and authorities in Holland, France, Germany, and Belgium, and touring these countries to see the disease in the field, he returned to Connecticut and wrote a scholarly paper on the nature, spread, and significance of the disease. His 1928 *Bartlett Tree Research Laboratories Bulletin #1*, "The European Elm Disease," was a comprehensive report on the disease as then known. A scholarly work of much credit to both Bartlett personally and his company, it remains a valued historic reference.

THE RESEARCH FELLOWSHIPS

In keeping with the establishment of the Bartlett laboratory in 1926, the company began to award graduate research fellowships at various universities in the

Northeast and Virginia. Such grants were not awarded routinely, but to support research to obtain specific, significant information of practical value to arboriculture. Over a period of thirty-three years the Bartlett Tree Research Laboratories supported the graduate research of nineteen men in seven institutions for master's or doctorate degrees. With the exception of Yale University's nearby forestry school, all grants went to state universities. Of special interest is that 42 percent were for tree disease research, 32 percent were for growth studies and 26 percent were for insect studies. Three of the nineteen grants were for study of Dutch elm disease.

THE MOVE TO NORTH CAROLINA

In 1965 the laboratory grounds in Connecticut were sold and a new laboratory site was created in North Carolina. The original sixty acres near Stamford were sold to the state of Connecticut with the provision that the land would remain undeveloped and be called the State of Connecticut Bartlett Arboretum. A tract of 300 acres south of Charlotte, North Carolina—an old horse farm—was developed into a new experiment station, research laboratory, and arboretum. Robert A. Bartlett Sr., son of F. A. Bartlett, supervised the move to North Carolina. He chose the site and supervised the planning. Bartlett arborist H. S. Porter planned the nursery and arboretum. More than 11,000 trees and shrubs, including more than 2,000 species, were established in the arboretum. The first director was a trained forester, H. C. Haines. The laboratory building was constructed in 1969, and early consultation on diagnosis was handled by nearby university tree scientists, including Dr. John S. Boyce Jr., son of the previous Bartlett laboratory director at Stamford.

PUBLIC RELATIONS

Beginning in 1929 the Bartlett Company initiated a series of educational radio talks for public relations and advertising. These were presented in fifteen-minute sessions over WEAF and affiliated stations of the National Broadcasting Company in New York City in 1929–30. The programs featured F. A. Bartlett, one of the Bartlett Associates, or distinguished university personnel cooperating with the company. These talks were carefully prepared over a wide range of tree topics.

By 1931 the Bartlett Company had established a series of departments to handle the new complexities of its growth and expansion, including municipal, institutional, public relations, financial, purchasing, educational, advertising, and sales. The institutional department was unique in being concerned expressly with special problems in the care of trees on grounds of schools, colleges, golf courses, hospitals, and so on. Trees used for memorials were considered valuable enough to attract a higher degree of attention than most specimen trees.

THE SPICER YEARS

In 1937 F. A. Bartlett chose to be relieved of direct management of the company and resigned as president to become chairman of the board of directors. He was succeeded by Orville W. Spicer who presided until his own retirement in 1961. A trained forester, Spicer had joined the company in 1915 after graduating from Syracuse University. He would be the only nonfamily president in the history of the company.

Entering his position as president during the Depression, with World War II and its aftermath to follow, he had a tenure that extended over turbulent times. The company was forced to cut expenses at all levels. Employees had to take cuts, and the publication *Tree Talk* was eliminated in 1930. During the Depression and World War II, the company not only ceased to grow, but had to cut back. With its well-trained personnel, however, it was in a good position to handle line-clearance work during the period of rural electrification. Since line-clearing work was a war priority, men so engaged were exempt from the draft. On the positive side, Bartlett offered its equipment for local use in fire control. In addition, it became engaged in camouflage work under a war defense contract to conceal critical military, industrial, and defense installations from enemy aerial surveillance.

The postwar world was a new ball game in arboriculture, as in almost everything. Gone were the big estates and low-cost labor. In place of the estates would come thousands of small new homes in massive housing developments with a few trees to each plot. Instead of barnstorming for business in faraway places, young married men wanted permanent homes.

Under the provisions for education and training, the Bartlett School of Tree Surgery was qualified to accept returning veterans, with tuition paid by the government under the GI Bill. Thus, the school was active again for a few years until the demand was filled. Following this postwar period, the school still functioned but lessons were handled by correspondence.

In the aftermath of the war Bartlett was involved in several new developments. Chemotherapy research for control of Dutch elm disease, pioneered in 1940 by the Connecticut Agriculture Experiment Station, was continued by Bartlett after the war. Through its pathologist, Dr. Nestor Caroselli, a chemical called carolate was developed in 1948 for chemotherapy against Dutch elm disease. The company was among the earliest to test such chemicals for control of this disease with some early success. Later results with carolate were not as successful as the early trials had promised, and were somewhat controversial. A second chemical, carolate II, developed in 1952, was no more successful.

Spraying flowered into a massive business in the 1950s, and Bartlett was the first tree company to use helicopters for aerial insecticidal sprays and brush control in 1953. As utility aerial spraying increased, the company developed its own helicopter capacity at Charlotte, North Carolina.

ROBERT A. BARTLETT SR.

Spicer retired in 1961 and was succeeded by Robert A. Bartlett Sr., son of the company founder. Bob had seen the company grow from childhood, and had been active in a wide variety of field and managerial areas within the company. During his tenure (1961–74) there were significant challenges and developments, beginning with the first challenge in 1962. In her polemic book *Silent Spring,* Rachel Carson indicted poisonous chemicals as a menace to all the biota of the earth, including humans. Her book had a significant impact on tree companies, then heavily involved in spraying.

A second challenge came in 1965 with the testing of a powerful new insecticide, bidrin, for control of Dutch elm disease. Developed by the Shell Oil Company and extremely toxic to bark beetles, bidrin was also phytotoxic to elms at certain levels and toxic to mammals including humans. The Bartlett Company performed most of the field testing under a special arrangement with the Shell Company. The chemical was quite successful in preventing infection by killing the insect vectors. Because of its mammalian toxicity, however, it could not pass required standards for safety and was withdrawn. Nonetheless it foreshadowed new chemicals and new techniques to come, as it was the first truly systemic chemical injected into trees from an external contained source.

ROBERT A. BARTLETT JR.

In 1974 Robert A. Bartlett Sr. became chairman of the board and his son, Robert A. Bartlett Jr., became the fourth company president. He had served the company as an assistant to his father for many years in many capacities. The purchase of Utility Tree Service of Eureka, California, in 1978 was symbolic of acquisitions to come. It was also significant in giving Bartlett its first presence west of the Mississippi River, making the company truly national in operations from coast to coast.

By 1982, the date of its seventy-fifth anniversary, about sixty-five percent of company revenues came from contracts for line clearing and thirty-five percent

Fig. 8.7 Robert A. Bartlett Sr. Courtesy of the F. A. Bartlett Tree Expert Company.

came from general tree care. By 1998, although both lines of service had grown substantially, these percentages had reversed, with general tree care bringing in sixty-five percent of revenues. This does not reflect a reduction in line clearing, but a major expansion in the general category.

In 1982 the company was pleased to note its continued preoccupation with leadership in tree science, citing a 1982 National Arborist Association (NAA) Award of Merit for outstanding contributions to the tree care industry. It also considered itself to be the safest large company in the industry, citing a Safety Award for Merit, again from the NAA.

In 1987 the company established the Bartlett Tree Foundation for the purpose of establishing scholarships in arboriculture. Unlike the earlier fellowship awards designed to advance research on specific tree phenomena at the graduate level, these scholarships are designed to aid worthy students in arboriculture and related disciplines at the undergraduate level.

SUMMARY

The Bartlett Company grew and expanded almost in tandem with the Davey Company. It had a unique impact on arboriculture. Over the years it trained many men, who in turn would establish their own successful tree companies. It was organized and built from the beginning by leaders trained in forestry. Preoccupied with science and research, it was the first commercial tree company to lead in organizing a conference of scientists and arborists, the first to establish research laboratories, and the first to maintain a university research support program in arboriculture. Still growing and expanding, it continues as a leader in the tree care industry, with a strong commitment to scientific care of landscape plantings.

CHAPTER NINE

The World Wars

"Use older men, and limit vehicles used" —E. Higgins, 1942

WORLD WAR I

World War I was the first of three national crises that affected arboriculture in North America over three decades from 1914 to 1945. The others were the Depression and World War II. Although there was a twenty-year interval between the wars, in some respects the wars were related, and will be reviewed here together. The ten years of dynamic economic upheaval from 1930 to 1940, leading to World War II, is reviewed separately.

The tree care industry was just getting established when World War I began in 1914. The only large tree companies at that time were Davey and Bartlett, municipal arboriculture was just beginning, and utility arboriculture had not yet begun. Arborists benefited from increased consumer earnings early in the war. This was short-lived, however, as inflation began to take its toll. Above all, a manpower shortage affected arboriculture directly, as key personnel went off to war. Arborist firms had to pay higher wages to workers in addition to higher prices for materials and supplies, but were unable to raise prices.

The onset of the war in Europe was not profitable for an arborist company such as Davey. By 1915 the economy was strongly stimulated because of buying in preparation for war this increased Davey volume, but also pushed up both prices and wages in a cost-wage squeeze. This led to a general business boom prior to the entrance of the United States into war in 1917.

Direct U.S. involvement in the war at first accelerated the pace of business, and for some arborists, profits were the best they had seen. With both prices and wages up, however, and with labor already short, the draft of men for war service made the labor shortage critical. Active, production tree men were prime targets for service with their youth, health, vigor, and athletic ability. Since there was no basis for draft deferment, it was impossible to find or replace able workers, and so the Bartlett and Davey Companies, and probably others, had to retrench.

The war influenced other aspects of arboriculture beyond the tree care industry such as operations of arboreta and botanical gardens, control of the gypsy moth, and public park development. Not only were funds curtailed for support at home, but a shortage of lead for tree tags became a problem. There were no suitable substitutes for it at the time. Also affected were the successful and ambitious tree introduction programs then in full swing by the Arnold Arboretum and the USDA. The tree exploration programs in the Far East had to be curtailed. Unfortunately, there were also strained personal relations between Arnold Arboretum staff members, such as the eminent, German-born botanist Reineke and the equally eminent, British-born "Chinese" Wilson. The war prevented continuation of studies under way by the USDA on the gypsy moth. Especially affected was the collection of insect parasites of potential value for moth control in the United States. Budget limitations, plus a severe shortage of skilled labor, stopped arboricultural development in parks and other public places.

By 1918 arborist work forces were seriously depleted, growth of tree companies was interrupted, and business activity had gone into a period of retrenchment. The Davey Company was down to eighteen salesmen and seventeen field men. Bartlett growth was interrupted, but its history is less explicit. Not only did it lose most of its production men to the service, most of its key office personnel left for the service also, with two of its most promising young men (Lawrence and Spicer) serving as pilots. Not only were planned plantings of trees and expansion of park areas affected, both in-service instruction and extended courses for new students had to be held in abeyance or even terminated.

Both the Davey and Bartlett Companies emerged in good financial condition after the war. At this time, many civic organizations and communities decided to commemorate the supreme sacrifice made by those of its group who did not return by planting living memorials in the form of groves or avenues of attractive ornamental trees. The American Forestry Association took the lead in this area in 1920, initiating a movement for planting memorial trees and parks. With the help of government support and popular enthusiasm, many such plantings were established and continue to serve today.

The only noncommercial tree care organization existing at the time of World War I was the Massachusetts Tree Wardens and Forestry Association (MTWFA), which is still functioning. During the war the MTWFA initiated a program designed to conserve trees. Cooperating with the State Public Safety Committee, it addressed the matter of fuel shortage and the need to increase supplies of wood. After the war the association was active in encouraging the planting of trees as war memorials. Along the same line, postwar memorial plantings were urged by arborists in New Jersey. Disturbed by the neglect and lack of maintenance of street and highway trees there, a campaign was initiated in 1924 to popularize such tree plantings with special emphasis on continued maintenance.

With food supply a major concern during the war, the USDA originated a plant disease survey for the first time. Still in use today, the survey, originally designed for food plants, was extended in time to all economically important plants including amenity plants.

WORLD WAR II

The impact of World War II was significant and far reaching in almost every aspect of life in North America. Its impact on arboriculture was no less significant. It affected arboricultural organizations, availability of supplies and materials, and the role of arboriculture in the postwar period.

When the war began in 1939, Canada was involved immediately as a member of the British Commonwealth of Nations. F. E. Martin, a prominent arborist in the Toronto area, reported business as usual when Germany invaded Poland in 1939. Later, business declined when Germany overran Norway, Denmark, and Holland, and invaded Belgium and France in 1940. Canadian arborists were hampered in their operations by two restrictive, wartime regulations—a permit was required to leave the country, and another to purchase U.S. currency. Faced with rationing and shortages, it became difficult to seek needed materials and supplies from the United States for tree care practices. There was a greater demand for line clearing than before. This was probably a reflection of the fact that electric power was a war priority.

After Pearl Harbor, arborist companies lost hundreds of employees to the armed forces. Gasoline was rationed, travel was curtailed, new tools and equipment were unavailable. Arborists were advised by the leaders of the NSTC and NAA to prepare for the problems expected. They were cautioned to plan well ahead by laying in adequate supplies, such as fertilizers, fungicides, and insecticides. Waste from spraying had to be reduced to a minimum or eliminated; care and efficiency in every arborist practice had to be reviewed. Arborist firms were urged to contact customers early for lining up essential work on a priority basis. They were also advised early to make their tree spraying machinery available for national defense, recommending that such availability be reported to local police.

Responding to the emergency of war, F. A. Bartlett submitted a plan for arborist aid to national defense authorities in Washington. The plan involved registration with local fire departments and air raid wardens. Crews and equipment were to be available on a voluntary basis. The plan had merit and equipment was registered, but fortunately never had to be tested by use.

As public servants, municipal arborists had a larger role in community activity than commercial arborists and were involved in preparation for emergencies in defense and in public safety. They assisted the armed services in civilian area defense and camouflage of important installations. They provided equipment and manpower for emergency home defense, and helped train men for defense industries as well as for the armed services. In addition, they carried on in their primary capacities of trimming and removing trees for public safety.

With war priorities established, there were shortages of labor, materials, supplies, and equipment. Companies such as Davey had their men spending valuable time scrounging for tools, supplies, and equipment. Biff Staples of the Davey Company was hired full-time to find ropes, saws, ladders, chains, and axes. Junk saws were reconditioned or remade. Saw handles were in short supply, as were the woods of pear, apple, and birch from which they were made. Innovative substitute handles were made of plywood. Employers also had to deal with price controls and rationing. From 1942 to 1945 the net results of these shortages included severe retrenchment in business operations, depletion of field crews, sales force reduction, merging or closing of work territories by large companies, and employment of untrained and unskilled labor.

The drafting of all able men between twenty-one and thirty-five years of age commenced in 1940, even though the United States was not officially at war. After 1941 the draft was extended to ages eighteen to forty. Critical shortages in labor arose not only from the draft but also because many men left to work for war material manufacturers. Despite control of both prices and wages by the U.S. Office of Price Administration, manufacturers were able to offer wages to unskilled labor that greatly exceeded those paid to skilled arborists.

The labor crisis for arboriculture was worse in World War II than in World War I. To hold foremen, tree care companies increased their salaries, allowed overtime work, and showed them an unusual personal interest. Enlistees and those drafted were promised jobs on their return. Companies had to use teenaged boys and older men beyond draft age. The Davey Company hired two women for field operations during this period, and both became productive workers.

There was one bright spot for arboriculture. Line clearing was declared to be essential for national defense. Power for war industries was essential; telegraph and telephone communications were vital, as were railroad and vehicular transportation for rapid supply and transport. More than two-thirds of the remaining personnel in arboriculture would be in line-clearing work before the war ended. This line of work allowed tree companies to survive. Since its inception the Asplundh Company had depended on line clearing, and Davey and Bartlett depended on it for seventy to eighty percent of their total business volume.

The arborist was soon caught in a vicious wage-price squeeze. While both wages and prices were frozen, taxes were not. With taxes increasing, potential clients were reluctant to spend money on anything unnecessary, and most tree work was seen to be so. With gas and tires rationed, tree companies had to be more economical in their use of vehicles for work. The free inspections of the past were out, and many arborists restricted work to a fifteen-mile radius. Arborists working alone had to turn business away; safety work to reduce hazards was given priority; routine work such as scheduled pruning had to be ignored; and men were placed on a monthly salary basis in order to retain them.

Equipment and Chemical Shortages

All ceiling prices were posted on fertilizer, seeds, spray materials, soil, and axes. Even though arborists' services such as disinfection, dusting, spraying, fumigation, planting, cultivating, harvesting, and tree surgery were exempted from regulation, it was illegal to increase rates over previous charges.

Most new rules and regulations governing a wartime economy became effective in early 1942. The newly created War Production Board issued priority regulations on tools, equipment, and materials. As with all other regulations, they were designed to conserve national resources for best use in the war effort. Under maximum price regulation were tree bracing materials, including rods, cables, and screws.

The war reduced both the quantity and quality of rope available to arborists. The U.S. Office of Production Management in 1941 had placed 100 percent manila rope on a war priority basis. This prevented its procurement for tree work, with the exception of use in line clearing. Manufacturers were allowed to fabricate "C" class material using fifty percent manila fiber with fifty percent sisal. The substitute "war rope" available in half-inch size was found lacking in strength. The safety loading of the new war rope was significantly lower. Since it was considered unsafe for climbing arborists, a warning was issued through *Arborist's News*.

Chemical supplies such as fertilizers, insecticides, and fungicides were in short supply. To conserve essential resources for food production, the War Food Administration (WFA) began regulation of fertilizer distribution as soon as war was declared on 8 December 1941, but most regulations did not become effective until 1942.

In 1942 the Office of Defense Transportation issued Order No. 21, which restricted motor transport by trucks, striking at the heart of the arborists' mobility. Use of trucks could be authorized only with a Certificate of War Necessity. The War Production Board issued regulations for priorities on the procurement and use of tools and equipment. One of the largest arborist suppliers, the Bartlett Company, was unable to obtain steel except for the purpose of manufacturing cutting tools for the War Department. The shortage of tree trimming and pruning tools created a genuine hardship for many working arborists.

By 1944, despite shortages and the relatively low priority rating for arborists, they were able to obtain some bracing equipment and repair materials, pruners, and saws. Although most heavy equipment was unavailable, the new "electric saw" was available. This may have been the first reference to the chain saw, which would revolutionize the arborist industry.

Of all the fertilizer requirements, the conservation of inorganic nitrogen had the highest priority, probably because of limited availability and dependence on overseas sources, such as Chile. This helps to explain War Production Board Conservation Order No. M-131, Part 3080, Chemical Fertilizer F, effective in September 1942. This restricted use of all nitrogen fertilizer, and especially inorganic nitrogen for use only on plants producing food. Despite this, an exemption permitted commercial nurseries to use organic nitrogen.

The WFA began regulation of fertilizer distribution as soon as war was declared. Temporary price regulation #1 of 1942 allowed the maximum price on mixed fertilizer and required that manufacturers produce a record of past sales. Manufacture of chemical nitrogen for fertilizer was prohibited in seventeen states, including an area from Maine to Minnesota and Kansas to Virginia. Nitrogen fertilizer was not to be used on lawns, golf courses, parks, or roadsides. Despite this, organic nitrogen was available in considerable quantity.

Regulations limited the quantity of fertilizer that could be produced, limited their organic nitrogen content, prescribed ratios of nitrogen, phosphorus, and potassium for food production, and limited fertilizer supply for amenity plants. In addition they required commercial growers of ornamentals to apply for fertilizer in advance, based on two six-month periods before delivery. Nurseries were allowed up to seventy-five percent of previous use of approved grades. Landscape gardeners, however, could get only fifty percent of nitrogen and potassium with organic nitrogen not to exceed twenty-five percent of total nitrogen content.

In 1942 lime sulfur was available for use as an insecticide and dormant oils were not scarce; rotenone and pyrethrum were not available at all, however, and arsenical supplies in particular were limited. Also in short supply was yellow insecticide paint used by arborists for control of Japanese beetles. Wartime regulations stressed that the best use of insecticides was in dormant sprays. Arborists were advised to use sticky banding materials on tree trunks in the absence of insecticides.

There was no shortage of fungicides up to 1942, but users were cautioned that labor shortages in productivity could result in shortages by 1943. (Fixed copper was rapidly replacing bordeaux mixture, for reasons of safety and efficacy. There was a shortage of bordeaux mixture for those who wanted it due to a serious shortage of copper.) The War Production Board allocated sufficient copper for fungicide use in 1942, but warned of uncertainty regarding future availability. Accordingly, arborists were advised by their leaders to use it only when essential, to apply it only where it would be most effective, and to use sulfur in its place when possible. With all fungicides, arborists were cautioned to be frugal, and use of stickers and spreaders was urged to increase spraying efficiency.

Because of the critical need for agricultural chemicals, the Agriculture Insecticide and Fungicide Association monitored the availability of these chemicals. Its reports provided the basis for most of the information given arborists in the "Tilcha Chats" column of *Arborist's News*. This column was initiated specifically to keep arborists abreast of government regulations and policy affecting arboriculture. The title for this column was derived from the names of the two authors, Dr. Paul Tilford, NSTC editor of *Arborist's News* and executive secretary of NAA, and Dr. L. C. Chadwick, executive director of NSTC.

In 1943 Tilford and Chadwick predicted a sufficient supply of insecticides and fungicides for that year, but warned of severe shortages of imported insecticides and some problems with containers and transportation. One bright spot on the horizon during the war was the earliest mention of a new chemical called DDT. Its first mention for use was in Connecticut in 1943, possibly against the gypsy moth. In 1945 its use in control of the gypsy moth by aerial spray in Massachusetts had dramatic results.

Effect on Organizations

The war had an adverse effect on several arborist organizations. In preparation for wartime conditions, the National Shade Tree Conference urged arborists to stockpile early, increase spraying efficiency with use of spreaders and stickers, and assume personal supervision of work. They were also advised to apprise clientele on limitations to essential work, list trucks and sprayers for emergency fire use, convert tree climbers to auxiliary linemen and spray men to auxiliary firemen, support all government agencies, and lend aid to the Office of Civilian Defense.

TABLE 9.1

NEGATIVE AND POSITIVE IMPACTS OF WORLD WARS ON
DEVELOPMENT OF ARBORICULTURE IN NORTH AMERICA

PERIOD	FACTOR	INFLUENCE ON ARBORICULTURE
World War I (1914–18)	Inflation	Prices and wages increase
	No draft deferment	Shortage of workers
	Military's need for equipment and materials; public's hoarding of supplies	Shortage of equipment and goods
	Public spending curtailed	Parks and trees neglected
	Tree introductions ceased	Arboreta affected
	Pest control abandoned	Gypsy moth not controlled

In short, the growth of tree care companies was curtailed and business decreased.

Postwar recovery (1920–30)	Business recovery	Tree company growth
	Memorial plantings	Planting without maintenance
World War II (1941–45)	Inflation	Prices and wages increase
	Rationing and hoarding	Shortages of equipment/supplies
	Wage and price freeze	Reduction in business
	Public spending curtailed	Parks and trees neglected
	Draft	Shortage of workers

As with World War I, World War II had a negative overall impact on tree businesses; many small companies went out of business. However, this war had some positive influences:

	Line clearing became a war priority	Draft deferments given to tree workers; major tree companies recover
	Civil defense became a priority	Spray machines available for fire control; tree plantings used for camouflage
	No labor shortage	Women and older men are trained in arboriculture

Postwar recovery (1945–50)	Economic boom	Increase in construction of housing, hospitals, businesses, and municipal buildings brings an increase in demand for tree workers
	Federal support for veterans' education	Arborist company schools reopen
	Policy on landscaping federal buildings	More work for tree companies
	Advances in technology	Chain saws; powerful insecticides

In general, this postwar recovery period was beneficial to the advancement of arboriculture.

At the annual meeting of the NSTC in Chicago, in 1942, the hotel scheduled for the conference was taken over at the last minute by the army and new facilities had to be hurriedly secured. At this critical meeting the NSTC decided to keep membership open for the war's duration for all those serving in the armed forces, eliminated program booklets, recommended purchase of Series G war bond funds with its modest reserves, and resolved to give full support to the war effort. Also at this time the NAA sponsored its first session at an NSTC meeting. It was highlighted by an address from NAA president, Captain Karl Amalia, on furlough from the army. In a discussion on priorities and federal regulations affecting arborists, he focused on priority specifications issued by the War Production Board.

The 1942 NSTC meeting was very much attuned to the new circumstances of the war climate. Gone were the papers on insects, diseases, cabling, tree cavities, and spraying. Arborists were advised by Major R. P. Breckinridge of their ability to help by using trees to conceal weapons and military installations. A speaker from the War Production Board discussed "Priority Regulations on Tools, Equipment and Materials." An agent from the Office of Price Administration spoke on consumer services. The arborists' presenter, Dr. L. C. Chadwick, discussed the new restrictive uses of inorganic nitrogen dictated by the War Production Board.

The sessions concluded with an extensive panel discussion, "Arborists and National Defense." Ed Higgins of Boston advised arborists on the subject of raising salaries to hold foremen, using older men, and limiting numbers of vehicles used. S. W. Parmenter of Ohio advised small operators to do most of the work close to home, accept no new work beyond fifteen miles, and make no free inspections. P. L. Sandahl of Iowa stressed safety above all other considerations and suggested placing men on monthly salary to reduce paperwork. M. Weakley of Florida wanted arborists to conserve resources, use material most carefully and sparingly, give more advice by phone, and restrict site visits to a minimum.

In 1942 in a patriotic gesture to aid the war effort, the NSTC and NAA cooperated in a nationwide survey of arborist equipment of potential value in national defense. In that same year, A. R. Thompson, active member of the NSTC and landscape director of the Department of Interior, was appointed NSTC liaison representative to the War Department and Office of Civilian Defense on Camouflage. These agencies were interested in using trees and shrubs to prevent aerial identification of critical equipment and facilities, especially defense weapons and installations. A committee prepared lists of suitable plant materials for use in concealment.

The NSTC canceled its annual convention in 1943, and again in 1945 at the request of the Office of Defense Travel. Instead it encouraged its members to hold state or regional meetings of short duration. Arborists in eastern areas met with members of the New Jersey Federation of Shade Tree Commissions. New England arborists met with the Massachusetts Arborist Association and Massachusetts Tree Wardens and Foresters, and Midwestern arborists met with the Ohio Chapter of the NSTC.

In response to a request from the army in 1943, a joint committee of the NSTC and NAA, under the chairmanship of E. W. Higgins of Massachusetts, prepared a publication on transplanting and maintenance of trees and shrubs. This was prepared for the Camouflage Branch of the Army Corps of Engineers. Entitled "Procedure for Camouflage," it was published in *Arborist's News*. This was the first publication for both organizations, and it was later revised and reprinted as the *Transplanting Manual for Trees and Shrubs*.

In Canada, the Canadian National Parks development was a civilian casualty of the war, as was arboricultural development of the Niagara Parks System. The combination of reduced funds and acute labor shortages sharply restricted long-range plans for planting additional trees and initiating professional instruction in horticulture.

In 1943 Ed Scanlon, editor and publisher of *Trees* magazine and an active member of the NSTC, discontinued publication when he went into the navy for war service. Sometimes known as "crazy Eddie," he continued to write in the service, but not on trees. No sooner was he settled at the San Pedro Naval Base, than he became editor of the station newspaper, the *Nob News*, and wrote his own column, "Along the Quay." When the war was over, Ed resumed publishing *Trees* until he died in 1975.

Important research toward control of Dutch elm disease was curtailed at this time. In pioneering work at the Connecticut Agriculture Experiment Station, Dr. George Zentmeyer had begun to infuse trees with antifungal chemicals. Known as chemotherapy, this early work came to a stop until after the war.

In addition to the NSTC and NAA, other arborist organizations were affected by the war. Both the Connecticut Tree Protection Association, one of the oldest state arborist associations, and the relatively new Maine Arborist Association ceased activity until the war ended

As the end of the war grew near, there was again interest in planting trees for war memorials, which made both arborists and nurserymen apprehensive. The rash of plantings of memorial trees in the 1920s had not fared well. Many perished for lack of maintenance or were in poor condition.

The war structures that arose in great numbers following World War II were not tree memorials but veterans hospitals. When an ordinance appeared in 1944 prohibiting planting of greenery around hospitals for veterans, both the NSTC and the NAA reacted with dismay. They urged both planting and maintenance of trees around these newly constructed institutions. In response, the army prepared a directive to the chief of army engineers to proceed with landscaping programs.

Despite the directive, it became apparent that the army was failing to do what had been assured, and so Dr. L. C. Chadwick went to Washington in 1945 to urge action on hospital landscaping. A paper that he wrote on this experience, "Rehabilitation Rights of Veterans," and an NAA brochure on trees as living memorials, urged the use of trees in plantings, but with a stipulation for maintenance after planting.

With the postwar housing boom came a need to incorporate trees into landscaping plans. Both the Veterans Administration and the Federal Housing Administration were urged by NSTC and NAA to plant trees to convey a sense of the open countryside. It would take many years, but ultimately minimum requirements, for tree planting would be written into laws governing new home loans.

POSTWAR YEARS

After the clouds of war had lifted in 1945, the tree care industry emerged as a completely different entity compared to prewar days. In came new and sophisticated kinds of equipment, much of which had been developed or used by the military during the war. The revolutionary chain saw was available almost at once. On the near horizon were aerial lifts and chippers. Especially new were the chemicals developed during the war. DDT was effective against many insects, and the new weed killer, 2,4-D, opened new vistas for control of vegetation by spraying.

One of the most dramatic and far-reaching effects of the war was the passage of the GI Bill. The educational aspects of the bill were of special interest to veterans seeking to learn the tree care business, either on the job or by attending school or college. The GI Bill enabled the large tree companies to reopen training

Fig. 9.1 An early two-man chain saw displayed at the National Shade Tree Conference. Courtesy of the ISA Archives.

schools closed by the war. The Bartlett Company used its university fellowship program and the GI Bill to support students in graduate programs at the highest level of education and research.

In the aftermath of World War II it was clear that both the United States and Canada would soon be facing building booms of national scope and significance. Only a few far-sighted prophets warned of the stresses to which many urban trees would be exposed through wide ranging bulldozers, uprooting and undermining soil horizons in underground construction, and increasing severity of diseases and insect pests due to weakened trees.

Following the war massive housing construction was needed to satisfy the pent-up demand occasioned by the war, when little or no new housing was allowed. One of the largest builders, a man named Leavitt, produced whole communities of new homes sold largely through federal home loans. One of the conditions of these loans was the planting of a tree, either for every 28 linear feet of residence, or 2.5 trees per residence, where the distance from tree trunk to tree trunk was precise. This pleasant innovation proved to be only the first step in a massive new landscaping movement that would surpass even the massive housing boom that set it off. In time the new plantings would become a significant addition to the new urban forest that continued to develop.

Finally, in the aftermath of the war, the NSTC provided a noble public service that is little known. Before the war the Science Library of the Department of Agriculture of the Commonwealth of the Philippine Islands in Manila had the largest and best-known collection of technical and scientific publications in the Orient. This collection was totally destroyed in the war. At the request of Jose S. Camus of the Philippine Commonwealth, the NSTC donated a complete collection of all its proceedings and publications to this library.

SUMMARY

Despite the negative influence of the war on the development and practice of arboriculture, it was responsible for several positive developments ranging from the discovery of new chemicals to discovery of a new tree. The stories of DDT, 2,4-D, and a newly discovered metasequoia tree are discussed elsewhere in the book.

Among the positive aspects of the war was the creation of an Emergency Plant Disease Prevention Program. Wartime food supplies were considered vulnerable to enemy attempts at crop destruction through plant disease. Created by President Roosevelt in 1943 with emergency funds, the plant disease project was designed to ensure immediate detection of any enemy-stimulated disease. Following the war, the core of the program was maintained by the USDA for continued monitoring of plant disease.

Perhaps the most significant development in World War II affecting arboriculture was the need for increased tree trimming along power lines. This kept many tree companies in business that otherwise might have failed. The high priority of line-clearing work in the war effort gave the field work a boost that would have far-reaching results.

CHAPTER TEN

International Society of Arboriculture

"Mighty oaks from little acorns grow" —David Everett

The history of modern arboriculture is largely the story of its development in the twentieth century. While such a history is not exclusively that of the National Shade Tree Conference (NSTC) and its successor organizations, the International Shade Tree Conference (ISTC) and the International Society of Arboriculture (ISA), there is little of significance in North American arboriculture that is not reflected in NSTC publications since its inception in 1924.

The NSTC began as a marriage of convenience between forward-looking commercial arborists and scientists whose research concerned trees. Each group needed the other for different reasons. Although tree care had been practiced by commercial companies and individuals in North America for at least fifty years prior to this time, the industry was largely unregulated and uninformed. The conscientious tree men in the field in the early 1920s were outnumbered by hundreds of others without rudimentary knowledge or training.

For scientists, their knowledge of trees and tree care was also in an embryonic stage. There were many demanding tree questions in horticulture, forestry, entomology, and pathology that required research for answers. Many of these questions were just barely being addressed in the early 1900s following the devastating epidemics of gypsy moths, chestnut blight, and white pine blister rust. Thus, the tree men needed sound information to improve their work, and the scientists needed support from a clientele beyond the Forest Service to justify research on amenity trees.

The Shade Tree Conference (STC), from which the National Shade Tree Conference traces its origins, first met in 1924. Perhaps the best insight came from Dr. Wilton E. Britton, Connecticut State Entomologist and STC chairman: "Since Connecticut was the first state to enact laws providing for the examination and certification of tree surgeons, it was fitting that this board should sponsor a conference of this sort." Thus the credit for the origin of the STC belongs to Connecticut, and the conference was called at the invitation of the executive board of the Connecticut Tree Protective Association for 25–26 August 1924, in Stamford. Britton and Francis A. Bartlett, president of the F. A. Bartlett Tree Expert Company in Stamford, were the two principal figures in organizing the conference.

Britton chaired the sessions and Bartlett was the local arrangements chairman. At the invitation of Bartlett, some of the meetings were held on his experimental farm north of Stamford. The conference opened with about thirty-six participants—commercial tree men and scientific specialists in areas related to the care of trees—from seven states and Washington, D.C., two-thirds of whom were from Connecticut and Massachusetts. Bartlett established a precedent of combining paper presentations with field observations and/or trials. This became a regular feature in later conferences in the early years.

The Shade Tree Conference included field observations on types of cavity fillings (led by Bartlett) and canker spots and cavity fillings (led by James A. G. Davey, vice president of the Davey Tree Expert Company). Presentations were made on a variety of topics and were limited to five minutes each. The first speaker, A. F. Burgess of the Federal Bureau of Entomology, spoke on gypsy moth control. The final speaker, Dr. Haven Metcalf, forest pathologist for the USDA, discussed the care of trees, including tree surgery and the healing of wounds. Other presentation topics included municipal shade tree problems, tree surgery, wound healing, facts about insects, leaf fungi, practical pruning, wood-rotting fungi, training methods for tree experts, and the use of lead arsenate. Note the early emphasis on tree surgery and complete absence of the words *arborist* and *arboriculture*. Another noteworthy aspect of this first conference was Britton's use of the word *profession* ("tree surgery is a comparatively new profession,") suggesting that the care of trees required expertise derived from informed practice with high standards. Britton predicted that the value of trees and the profession of protecting them would become more appreciated and more important with time.

The first STC at Stamford was so successful that the participants voted to meet again in 1925. Haven Metcalf was elected chairman, and W. O. Filley, Connecticut State Forester, was elected secretary. In 1925 a third officer, vice chairman,

Fig. 10.1 Haven Metcalf, ISA president 1925–27. Courtesy of the ISA Archives.

was added, and W. A. McCubben, a plant pathologist in the Pennsylvania Department of Agriculture, was the first to fill that position. In addition, the conference voted for a committee of five to explore the use of case records in the care of trees, which was the first committee formed by the conference for a technical project.

The second conference held in Boston attracted more scientific participants than the first one, with no significant change in numbers of commercial tree men. For the first time, Britton mentioned the possibility of a permanent shade tree organization, but he actually advised against it, suggesting occasional conferences in different parts of the country.

At the third conference in Philadelphia in 1926, a committee of five was formed to consider a permanent organization. Dr. Ephraim P. Felt, entomologist at Cornell University, was elected chairman and Filley was reelected secretary. The third conference closed with a consensus that there was a need for a permanent organization of those concerned with shade tree welfare. Several resolutions were adopted, including resolutions emphasizing the need for research on adaptability of trees and shrubs to urban conditions, recommending state licensing of tree workers, and stressing the need for a suitable and easily identifiable name for the organization.

The fourth conference met 22–23 March 1928, in Washington, D.C. This provided members of the conference an opportunity to become known at a national level and to become acquainted with federal agencies and scientists interested in tree care. Four bureau chiefs of the USDA (entomology, chemistry and soils, plant industry, and the Forest Service) addressed the STC. The most significant event of this conference was its endorsement of the articles of organization

Fig. 10.2 E. P. Felt, ISA president 1928, editor 1929–33, 1935–36. Courtesy of the ISA Archives.

recommended by a committee appointed at the 1926 conference. This action created the National Shade Tree Conference (NSTC), marking the formal beginning of a new era in the history of arboriculture.

NATIONAL SHADE TREE CONFERENCE

As discussed in the articles of organization and adopted at the annual meeting in 1928, the goals of the National Shade Tree Conference were "to stimulate greater interest in the study of shade tree problems; and to exchange ideas for enhancing the beauty and usefulness of shade trees." The organization was designed to consist only of commercial arborists and scientific tree specialists such as plant pathologists, entomologists, foresters, horticulturists, and others. Other persons interested in trees were to be welcomed only by invitation of the executive committee. The officers of the NSTC were to consist of president, vice president, and secretary-treasurer, but no one engaged in commercial work (i.e., commercial arborist) was eligible to be an officer in any capacity. H. M. Van Wormer of Richmond, Virginia, one of the last surviving of the article signers, said the reason for this restriction was that commercial arborists were worried about giving advantage to a competitor.

The executive committee included the three designated officers plus two commercial members appointed by the president. In addition to presiding at meetings, the president was to approve meeting arrangements and appoint committees. The secretary-treasurer was to do the routine work, having much responsibility with little authority. In the statement on finances, the commercial tree companies and individuals who were ineligible to become officers were required to finance the NSTC and have exclusive voting power on all assessments. Noncommercial members (including the officers) had no vote power on financial matters.

The articles of organization were prepared by the Committee on Permanent Organization, four of whom were commercial arborists (Charles F. Irish, Francis A. Bartlett, Lewis H. Meader Jr., and W. O. Hollister). The single noncommercial member was A. F. Burgess, who was chairman. The articles were signed by each of the fourteen commercial arborists present. The National Shade Tree Conference became an institution in 1928.

Organization and Governance

The first elected officers for NSTC (in 1929) were H. H. York, president; A. F. Burgess, vice president; and Rush P. Marshall, secretary-treasurer. York was a plant pathologist from the University of Pennsylvania, Burgess was a USDA entomologist from Massachusetts, and Marshall was a USDA forest pathologist at Yale University. Two conferees appointed by the president and the officers constituted an executive committee of five. Although the articles did not specify, it was generally understood that the two conferees would be "active" members, that is, commercial tree workers. The first two conferees appointed were Charles F. Irish of Cleveland, Ohio, and Norman Armstrong of Poughkeepsie, New York.

The fifth STC in Brooklyn, New York, in 1929 was the first at which the organization met under its official name, the National Shade Tree Conference. It was notable because the nonscience members outnumbered the scientists for the first time. This was seen as a good omen for those actually responsible for tree care. The trend of nonscience members being well represented at the conferences has continued into the 1990s.

At the 1930 conference in Cleveland (the first held outside the Northeast), NSTC added the office of acting editor for publication of the proceedings. This office would grow in importance as the conference increased its publications. The first editor was Dr. Ephraim P. Felt.

The Arborist and Arboriculture

The 1930 conference endorsed a proposal for a new committee to draft a plan, including a constitution and bylaws for a professional organization for operating tree men for consideration at the 1932 conference. As a result of this action, an organization of commercial arborists, to be called the American Society of

Arborists (ASA), was formed within the NSTC. It elected Charles F. Irish as president, Orville W. Spicer of New York as vice president, and Norman Armstrong of New York as secretary-treasurer. Although this first organization would be short-lived, it was the forerunner of the National Arborist Association (NAA).

Of special significance was the recognition and adoption at this time of the term *arborist* in place of *tree surgeon*. This marked the end of an era in which most tree care work had been narrowly confined to cavity excavation and filling, pruning, and wound treatment. It recognized that *tree surgery* was too narrow a term to reflect the variety of tree treatments emerging in the 1920s and expanding significantly in the 1930s. In support of the term *arborist*, Charles Irish noted its earlier use in England for more than 300 years.

The word *arboriculture* was first used in the proceedings of the NSTC by Charles Irish in 1932, in his paper "Highlights in the Early History of Arboriculture." Thus the use of *arborist* and *arboriculture* in the 1930s represents the earliest general acceptance of these terms as distinctly different from forestry within the accepted meaning of these terms today.

The Constitution

The NSTC's 1935 meeting in Philadelphia had a much higher attendance. This was a direct tribute to the energetic public relations of NSTC secretary Richard P. White. A constitution and bylaws were approved. The constitution, which formally established the name of the organization as the National Shade Tree Conference, listed six purposes; defined categories of membership; designated officers, executive committee, and standing committees and their duties; provided for an annual meeting; adopted Robert's Rules of Order; and provided for amendments and bylaws.

The constitution proposed an addition in the section on "initiating and fostering research," to include "to publish, or sponsor the publication of, the results of such an investigation." This gave added emphasis to one of the original two purposes in the articles of organization, but went farther by making a specific commitment to see that results were published. This change gave the NSTC a practical significance that for the first time went beyond its original educational goals. The two principal defects in the articles were continued in the constitution—commercial members could not serve as officers and none but commercial members had full voting powers. In addition, the bylaws required the NSTC to arrange for commercial and educational exhibits for each annual meeting.

The NSTC voted to revise its constitution in 1941. After careful study by Dr. Lewis C. Chadwick, NSTC president E. N. Cory, and A. Robert Thompson, the revision was based on a broadened scope of arboriculture and growing membership of the NSTC. The major changes included elimination of classes of dues; officer eligibility for all members; and creation of regional districts to be represented by an elected member, who in turn sat on the board of governors for voting on controversial matters.

The revised constitution delineated six geographical regions from the United States: New England, Eastern, Southern, Central, Midwestern, and Western. These regions could have one or more chapters elect members (and alternates) to the board of governors. Individuals not affiliated with a chapter made provision for election of an at-large member to the board. Another important feature of the revised constitution was the provision for proposing and amending the bylaws at a single annual meeting. This made it possible to increase dues when an increase was needed to take effect the next fiscal year.

Regional Conferences

The Western Shade Tree Conference (WSTC) began in 1934 under the able and colorful leadership of Edward H. Scanlon of Santa Monica, California. Recently appointed city forester and with the support of his city administration and the Los Angeles Chamber of Commerce, Scanlon organized a one-day conference in Santa Monica. Scanlon's conference attracted more than 100 people—an unexpected amount. In his own words, the Western Conference brought to the region a "new era in tree culture." In 1937, on behalf of the WSTC and writing as its executive secretary, Scanlon sent a statement to the NSTC meeting in Philadelphia, expressing the hope that the WSTC would unite with the NSTC and create a central national headquarters and official organization publication. In 1942 the WSTC formally became a chapter of the NSTC.

The Florida Shade Tree Conference was founded on the campus of the University of Florida in Gainesville under the leadership of H. S. Hewins, head of the university's department of forestry. The first meeting, in 1934, was a two-day affair. At this meeting a decision was made to form a permanent organization to be known as the Southern Shade Tree Conference. Successive meetings were held in Florida in 1939, 1940, and 1941. At the 1942 meeting a constitution and bylaws were adopted as those of the "Southern Chapter of the NSTC." At this same time, NSTC members in Ohio petitioned the conference successfully to become a separate chapter.

Membership growth was stimulated through chapter development, with NSTC membership in 1948 exceeding 1,000 for the first time.

Events in Early NSTC History

Lewis Chadwick was elected NSTC editor in 1936, becoming active with the January 1937 issue of *Arborist's News*. This was the beginning of his long tenure as an officer in the organization. After serving as editor for two years, he became executive secretary in 1937, secretary-treasurer in 1939, executive director in 1963, and emeritus executive director in 1969 until his death in 1994. More than any other individual, Chadwick influenced the growth and direction of the conference in its transition from the NSTC to the ISTC and ultimately to the ISA.

In 1937 the NSTC approved funds to defray expenses of its officers to attend meetings. All of the officers at this time were scientific members and had no funding for travel from their educational or research institutions. Funding officer travel created a precedent of financial support for elected officers that would be continued as one of the many costs of holding annual conventions. Such a policy was extended in later years to attract and support outstanding speakers.

In 1946 the NSTC adopted a Code of Ethics for Arborists and created a fund for research. The Memorial Research Fund was seen as a new opportunity and an obligation for arborists to sponsor at least part of the new research, of which they were the principal beneficiaries.

The next year, the NSTC adopted an official emblem centered on a green deciduous tree with a full crown and trunk enclosed by a circle that included the organization name.

In 1948 the NSTC decided that a single representative on the board of governors could represent members of the conference living outside the United States. In the same year a commercial arborist, Charles R. Irish, was elected NSTC president for the first time. Prior to this only academics had served as leaders, so this was a significant step in the development of the NSTC.

In 1949 a committee was formed to prepare an annual budget for the organization, establishing a precedent for all future operations. Executive secretary Chadwick took this occasion (on the conference's twenty-fifth anniversary) to assess the state of the NSTC. In commenting on certain strengths and weaknesses, Chadwick saw great value in establishment of chapters, noting the increase in national membership with the proliferation of additional state and national meetings. On the negative side he saw weakness in the provisions regulating duties and responsibilities of the board of governors because of the natural lethargy engendered among individuals meeting only once a year to vote on measures without proper information or preparation. On both observations he was prophetic. The continuing creation of new chapters would accelerate new membership, and the lethargy of the board of governors would ultimately lead to its dissolution in favor

Fig. 10.3 The 1949 National Shade Tree Conference, Baltimore. Courtesy of the ISA Archives.

of a more responsive and responsible board of directors. He stated that the two principal publications of NSTC, the *Annual Proceedings* of the National Shade Tree Conference and the *Arborist's News* periodical, were the foremost sources of arborist literature in the world.

Incorporation

In 1955 the NSTC became incorporated as a nonprofit corporation of the state of Ohio. Listed in the articles of incorporation as trustees were L. C. Chadwick, Columbus, Ohio; T. W. Parke, Columbus, Ohio; C. Fenner, Lansing, Michigan; H. C. Wilson, Shelby, North Carolina; and Paul E. Tilford, Wooster, Ohio.

In 1957 NSTC secretary Chadwick suggested new policy directions for the organization, including additional cooperation in joint meetings with other organizations with mutual interests, greater emphasis on publications on research and education, and extension of executive committee membership terms to three years from two. These changes led to the first joint meetings with another organization in 1956 and in 1958 when NSTC met with the American Association of Botanical Gardens and Arboreta.

INTERNATIONAL SHADE TREE CONFERENCE

In 1960 Canadian members petitioned the NSTC to change the organization name from *national* to *international* because the conference included a substantial number of Canadians.

Fig. 10.4 Paul Tilford, ISA editor, 1938–67. Courtesy of the ISA Archives.

The organization became the International Shade Tree Conference (ISTC) in 1961. With its new name, conference leaders began to think of a greater role beyond the United States and Canada. This would lead in time to expansion to Europe. In 1963 the ISTC created a new office of president-elect, and made the immediate-past president a member of the executive committee. This change established a precedent for automatic succession that would be repeated in a later period when election as vice president virtually ensured succession first to president-elect and then to president.

In 1963, nineteen standing committees were listed, although the constitution provided for only two. One of the new standing committees established at this time was the awards committee. New awards were created for excellence of authorship (the Author Citation) and outstanding performance (Award of Merit).

By 1964 it had become apparent that new action had to be initiated for the future of the ISTC because of two problems. One concerned the increasing growth, complexity, and responsibility attached to the position of secretary-treasurer. The other concerned the inadequate resources provided this office to carry out its assigned responsibilities. Chadwick, secretary-treasurer from 1938 to 1964, had substantial support from his employer, Ohio State University, but had operated the office of secretary-treasurer out of his home. The heavy burden of work and responsibility for ISTC could no longer be continued on a part-time basis.

To provide additional resources to aid Chadwick, Mark Mowrey of Mark Mowrey Associates in Columbus was retained in 1965. In effect, he became a part-time acting secretary. This was a first step toward putting the routine workload of the conference on a full-time business basis. Thus, the management of the conference and its publications began a new era that would lead in time to major changes.

In recognition of his unique services, the conference changed "Chad's" official status in 1966 from secretary-treasurer to executive director. In that same year, the executive director was bonded and the annual meeting was formally called a convention rather than a conference. Each of these changes reflected the need for additional administrative resources.

Another important change concerned the frequency of executive committee meetings. Since its inception in 1935, the executive committee carried out pressing business of the conference between annual meetings, first by correspondence and later at intervening regional meetings. In 1964 the executive committee held its first interconvention official meeting. It met in January 1969 for a second interconvention meeting. This would lead in time to regularly scheduled business meetings in midwinter at the site of the pending annual convention. In the 1980s the executive committee began meeting four times per year, twice just prior to a board of directors meeting as well as between board meetings.

Dr. Paul E. Tilford retired as editor in 1967 after thirty years of service. Noel B. Wysong of River Forest, Illinois, served in that capacity for the next two years. Chadwick retired as executive director in 1969 to an emeritus status after thirty-three years of continuous service. In 1969 the executive committee appointed Ervin C. (Cal) Bundy as full-time executive secretary and Dr. Eugene B. Himelick as a nonpaid executive director. Both resided in Urbana, Illinois. A native of Illinois, Bundy was thirty-six years old and a graduate in ornamental horticulture from the University of Illinois at Urbana-Champaign. Following army service he had served as a professional floriculturist, arborist, superintendent of university grounds, and general manager of a commercial nursery. Bundy had his own horticultural and consulting service, experience as a high school instructor in horticulture, and had been a member of the ISTC for several years.

Himelick, a native of Indiana, was forty-three years old and had a B.S. from Ball State University, an M.S. from Purdue, and a Ph.D. in plant pathology from the University of Illinois. Well known since 1952 as an able tree disease and tree care specialist at the Illinois Natural History Survey, Urbana, he was the author of numerous research and educational publications and was an active member of the conference serving on many committees and the board of governors.

As executive secretary, Bundy was responsible for the overall management of the organization under the direction of an executive director. The executive secretary was appointed annually and was responsible for the development, organization, and implementation of programs and activities to further the objectives of

TABLE 10.1

APPOINTED AND EXECUTIVE OFFICERS OF ISA
(EXCLUDING EDITORS)

PERIOD	PERSON	TITLE
1924–28	W. O. Filley	Secretary/Treasurer
1928–29	G. P. Clinton	Secretary/Treasurer
1929–33	R. P. Marshall	Secretary/Treasurer
1933–37	R. P. White	Secretary/Treasurer
1937–63	L. C. Chadwick	Secretary/Treasurer
1963–69	L. C. Chadwick	Executive Director
1968–69	M. L. Mowry	Secretary/Treasurer
1969–79	E. C. Bundy	Executive Secretary
1969–79	E. B. Himelick	Executive Director
1979–86	E. C. Bundy	Executive Director
1979–	E. B. Himelick	Advisor
1986–	W. P. Kruidenier	Executive Director

the conference. He was authorized to employ appropriate staff necessary to carry out the administrative activities of the organization subject to the approval of the board of directors. He was also responsible for carrying out other duties or programs as directed by the executive committee and the board of governors.

As the new executive director, Himelick was selected to serve on a part-time basis. He continued as plant pathologist on the staff of the Illinois Natural History Survey and as professor at the University of Illinois. In his new role as executive director of the ISTC, he was to serve, initially, without salary as liaison between the ISTC executive committee and the executive secretary, with authority to delegate responsibilities to the secretary as needed to oversee and direct the functions of the conference. He also served as chairman of the program committee for the conference.

After the office of executive secretary became appointive, constitutional revision was essential to accommodate this change. The executive secretary was eliminated as an ex-officio member of the executive committee and was required to be present at all meetings but had no vote. This move recognized the change in the position from one of policy making to that of policy execution.

A final note on the changing of the guard in 1969 was the formal recognition of Lewis Chadwick's thirty-two years of consecutive service. Already showered with many professional and academic honors, his official award was Honorary

Fig. 10.5 Gene Himelick, executive director of the ISA 1969–79. Courtesy of the ISA Archives.

Fig. 10.6 E. C. "Cal" Bundy, first full-time executive director of the ISA. Courtesy of the ISA Archives.

Fig. 10.7 Dr. Richard J. Campana, (author) ISA president 1967. Courtesy of the ISA Archives.

Life Membership in the organization that he had built and sustained. Following the organizational changes in 1969, several significant developments occurred over the next six years that would further transform the organization.

The origin and development of special-interest groups, such as the utility and municipal arborists, began with special discussion sessions at conferences in the 1950s and 1960s. Beginning in 1969 these arborists sought and were granted special status as special-interest organizations within the conference. A new article of the constitution in 1969 provided for "associated special-interest groups" within the conference. The term "special interest" group was changed in 1993 to "professional affiliation."

In 1973 the conference undertook a major revision of its constitution and bylaws. Since the last revision in 1941, many changes had been made by amendment but there had been no complete review. Important changes in the bylaws were as follows:

- Chapters and their geographical limits were listed, along with a statement on members-at-large.
- A statement was included providing for affiliated member association in chapters within the parent association.
- The new, separate responsibilities of the executive secretary and executive director were spelled out for the first time.
- Whenever possible, policy and procedures were extracted and placed in a Manual on Operational Policies and Procedures that outlined detailed guidelines for officers, committees, the board of governors, and others.

Fig. 10.8 ISA past presidents receiving honorary life membership: (left to right) Spence Davis Jr., Noel Wysong, F. E. Martin, H. C. Wilson, George S. Langford, Ray Hirt, Karl Dressel, Albert W. Meserve, and Homer L. Jacobs. Courtesy of the ISA Archives.

The fiftieth anniversary of the conference in 1974 was marked by the creation of a new professional journal. Dr. Dan Neely, ISTC editor since 1970 and plant pathologist at the Illinois Natural History Survey in Urbana, was appointed editor of the *Journal of Arboriculture* in January 1975. Dr. Neely served with distinction as editor of the *Journal* through September 1996. During his tenure, the *Journal* became internationally recognized as the premier arboricultural research journal. As editor, Neely also served on the executive committee until his retirement at the end of 1996.

To commemorate the fiftieth anniversary in 1974, the ISTC microfilmed the entire forty years of *Arborist's News* for sale to its members and other interested parties such as libraries, and, in July, Neely prepared a Golden Anniversary Issue of *Arborist's News*, which included previously unpublished papers presented in the first four conferences (1924–28) of the STC.

INTERNATIONAL SOCIETY OF ARBORICULTURE

The organization that began as a conference in 1924 became a society in 1975. After earlier encouragement and discussion with the executive committee and Executive Director Himelick, Vice President Hyland R. Johns, from Willow Grove, Pennsylvania, recommended the organization change its name to International Society of Arboriculture (ISA). The executive committee accepted the proposed new title with enthusiasm. Thus on 1 January 1976, the ISA was born. This new name, along with the creation of the new *Journal of Arboriculture*, gave the society a new professional status. The society made another significant step with the

Fig. 10.9 Dr. Dan Neely, ISA editor 1971–96, president 1999. Courtesy of ISA Archives.

creation of the Memorial Research Trust Fund in 1976. A new constitution and bylaws for the newly created ISA were adopted in 1976.

In 1978 the ISA executive committee became the ISA board of directors, which was made up of six regional representatives, the immediate past president, and appointed officers of the ISA. Only the regional representatives and past president would have a vote.

By vote of its members, the ISA board of governors was terminated as the governing body of the society in 1985. By the same action its responsibilities as organizational and corporate authority of the ISA were transferred to the ISA board of directors, and the duty of the board of governors to elect board members was transferred to affiliated chapters of the ISA.

A full-time executive director position was created in 1979, and the position of the executive secretary was eliminated. Ervin Bundy, the current executive secretary, was appointed as the first full-time executive director. Himelick was appointed executive director emeritus and was asked to serve as advisor for one year. For the first time in its history the organization had a principal executive officer who was a working arborist and whose priorities were not academic.

After seventeen years as executive secretary and executive director, Bundy resigned as executive director. As the first full-time executive employee of the society, his management established many precedents that served the society well, and under his leadership, the ISA grew larger, stronger, and more diversified. The 1970s saw rapid growth of the society with membership topping 3,000 professionals by the end of the decade and more than 4,000 by 1987.

William P. Kruidenier of Urbana, Illinois, succeeded Bundy 1 July 1987. He had a background in landscape architecture (B.S. and M.S. degrees in this field from the University of Illinois, with special focus on design, construction, and administration). A certified arborist through the Illinois Chapter of the ISA, Kruidenier was city arborist of Urbana when he was appointed the executive director of the ISA.

In 1988 the ISA headquarters office was moved from downtown Urbana to a historic building in Leal Park, also in Urbana. The woodframe building, a Greek revival cottage built about 1856, is considered architecturally and historically significant for eastern Illinois and is on the National Register of Historic Places in Urbana. Located in a two-acre park, the new headquarters building was surrounded by 200-year-old trees. Due to continued rapid growth of the ISA in the 1990s, the headquarters moved from Urbana to a purchased facility in Savoy in 1992 and again in 1998 to a 15,000-square-foot facility in Champaign, Illinois.

A European office was opened near London in 1997 to service the European membership. The board of directors determined it was critical to establish an office in Europe in order to better meet and serve the needs of the growing European membership. Within eighteen months of opening the European office, membership had grown from around 600 to more than 1,000 members.

The ISA approved its first strategic plan in 1988 entitled "Blueprint for Action." This six-year plan, along with its succeeding six-year strategic plan entitled "ISA 2000," set the stage for rapid expansion of ISA into arborist certification, nonserial publication development, and public education efforts that would fuel the growth of the tree care profession, professional development, and public education. The society's growth can be seen in the membership statistics: 5,000 in 1989; 6,000 in 1992; 7,000 in 1994; 8,000 in 1995; 9,000 in 1996; 10,000 in 1997; and 11,000 in 1998. Much of this growth reflects the development and implementation of the ISA arborist certification program.

A milestone in ISA's history occurred in 1989 when the first Chapter Leadership Workshop was held at the headquarters. The *Blueprint for Action* recognized the need to train ISA members involved in leadership at the chapter level and called for hosting a leadership workshop. The purpose was to train the volunteer leaders in how to effectively administer their chapter and local programs as well as give the leaders an opportunity to learn more of the workings of the society. The workshop became an annual training event, hosted by ISA officers and staff. Chapter and professional affiliation leaders as well as chapter certification and research trust liaisons were invited to participate.

CHAPTERS

In 1941, with the sweeping revision of the constitution described earlier, the NSTC had described six geographical regions for the United States. A seventh area division was created for Canada when a Canadian Chapter was formed in 1950. Within these regions provision was made for the creation of regional chapters. The first chapter to be created was in Ohio in 1942.

It was joined in 1942 by the Western and Southern Chapters that had begun as independent conferences. The Canadian Chapter was created in 1950, the Midwestern Chapter in 1954, the Pennsylvania-Delaware (Penn-Del) Chapter in 1960, and the New England Chapter in 1964. The Canadian Chapter was notable because it represented a regional unit beyond the national United States, as well as the formal beginning of an international role for the organization. The formation of the Penn-Del Chapter was notable because it was originally centered on the Delaware River Valley and was intended to include only eastern Pennsylvania and Delaware, as the Delaware Valley Chapter. This caused a serious split among NSTC members in Pennsylvania because there were the eastern and western factions in the same state. By insisting that the states could not be split in creating new chapters, the conference resolved this issue, but only after much bitterness and discord.

The New England Chapter had a difficult time becoming established for the most unexpected reason. New England was already rich in arborist meetings because it was the regional birthplace of the NSTC, and state arborist associations preceded the conference and additional ones formed later by 1964. Thus, resident members of existing organizations were apprehensive about losing their identity and at first resisted creation of an ISTC chapter. The earliest chapter meetings, therefore, were jointly sponsored with earlier arborist organizations in Massachusetts and Connecticut.

Beginning in 1974, twelve new chapters were being created rapidly. State chapters were created in New Jersey, Indiana, and Kentucky in 1974, and a new regional chapter (Rocky Mountain) was established in 1975. In 1977 a new state chapter was formed in Michigan and a provincial one in Quebec, Canada. The Quebec Chapter (The Societe Internationale de Arboriculture-Quebec, Inc.) was the first one authorized to use a language other than English in its proceedings and publication. With the addition of the Quebec Chapter, both Canadian cultural language patterns were now represented.

In the following year (1978) two new state chapters (New York and Texas) and a regional chapter (Mid-Atlantic) were formed. At the same time, the state of West Virginia became a part of the new Mid-Atlantic Chapter. With these changes, every ISA member in the United States and Canada had chapter affiliation. In 1980 a new state chapter was formed in Wisconsin, as well as the society's first international chapter, Pacific Northwest (Alaska, British Columbia, Oregon, and Washington, with Idaho added in 1997).

New chapters formed in Illinois (1983) and Minnesota (1989). Scandinavians took the initiative to establish the first European chapter when, with 110 members from Denmark, Sweden, Norway, Finland, and Iceland, the Scandinavian Chapter was accepted officially by the ISA in 1987. In this same year western Canadians in the provinces of Alberta, Saskatchewan, and Manitoba formed the Prairie Chapter. The eastern Canadian provinces in the following year created a new Atlantic Chapter comprising the Maritime Provinces of Nova Scotia, New Brunswick, Newfoundland, and Prince Edward Island (which caused the Canadian Chapter to be renamed the Ontario Chapter).

The ISA experienced continued expansion in the 1990s with chapters forming in Europe (Germany/Austria and France [1991]; United Kingdom/Ireland [1992]; Italy [1994]; Norway [1995, thus changing the name of the Scandinavian Chapter to Denmark Chapter]; and Sweden, Spain, and the Czech Republic [1998]); one each in Brazil (1995), Mexico (1996), New Zealand (1997), and Australia (1997); and two in the United States (Florida [1996] and Utah [1999]).

Over the decade of the 1990s, many chapters experienced tremendous growth and greater demands from their memberships for educational seminars, newsletters, arborist certification workshops, and program development coordinated with the international headquarters in Champaign. Due to this increased demand for service, seventeen chapters had full- or part-time chapter administrators in 1998. In response to this increased service demand from chapter members through the chapter administrators, ISA offered its first Chapter Executive Workshop in 1998 in an effort to develop a closer working relationship with the chapters.

SPECIAL-INTEREST GROUPS (PROFESSIONAL AFFILIATIONS) WITHIN THE SOCIETY

Municipal Arborists

Beginning in 1947 municipal arborists and city foresters held extensive, informal evening meetings at annual conferences. They were concerned with such items as brush disposal, highway planting contracts, chain saws, stump removal, gas in soils, evaluation of city trees, cleaning roots from sewers, house moving, and Dutch elm disease. By 1957 they had their own Municipal Arborists and City Foresters Committee.

By the mid-1960s the municipal arborists were probably as numerous and strong as members of any other special-interest group in the NSTC, with the exception of the commercial arborists. In 1964 under the leadership of Edward H. Scanlon, Cleveland forestry commissioner, they created a new organization of municipal arborists independent of the NSTC, called the Society of Municipal Arborists (SMA).

The formation of the SMA represented a direct challenge to the leadership of the conference. It divided the NSTC and caused a net loss of membership over a five-year period. The utility arborists broke the ice in 1970 to become the first special-interest group within the society, and the municipal arborists were not far behind with the Municipal Arborist Association (MAA) in 1972.

To help avoid or resolve potential conflicts between the new urban forestry program of the U.S. Forest Service and the older horticultural views in arboriculture, the ISTC created an Urban Forestry Committee in 1974. In 1980 this committee merged with the 116 members of the Municipal Arborists Association to form a new special-interest group within the society known as the Municipal Arborist and Urban Forestry Society (MAUFS). By 1983 the MAUFS had a membership of 180, was publishing six newsletters per year, and had established a much-coveted Distinguished Forester Award for outstanding contributions in municipal arboriculture or urban forestry.

In 1993 discussions pertaining to a possible merger began between the SMA and the MAUFS. After a number of years and many heated debates, the two organizations officially merged in August of 1997 at the ISA Annual Conference in Salt Lake City. The merged organization was called the Society of Municipal Arborists and remained a professional affiliation within the ISA. By virtue of the merger, the combined organization grew from 200 members to more than 500 within one year. In 1998 the SMA met with the National Association of Tree Officers (an English association of municipal tree officers) during the ISA Annual Conference in Birmingham, England, and signed a letter of mutual interest and cooperation, thus signaling another step in the internationalization of arboriculture.

Utility Arborists

Perhaps the earliest evidence of utility arborist interest in the NSTC occurred in 1947 with the appointment of the Committee on Street Lighting and Tree Planting. Edward H. Scanlon urged a broader scope for the committee, and its title was later changed to Utilities and Trees Committee. The first meeting of a group of utility arborists—at Rutgers University in 1950—had fifty participants. By 1966 the utility arborists had their own standing committee in the NSTC. In that year they scheduled their first paper session at the annual conference and had a membership of ninety-one. By 1967 its roster had grown to 346.

With thirty-two chapter members, the Utility Arborist Association (UAA) became the first special-interest group in the ISTC in 1970. The charter president was Herbert J. Cran. Membership was limited to active or retired employees of a public utility who were members of ISTC. Its purpose was "to provide a stable organization capable of sustaining long range programs and communications to benefit the public utility industry." By 1973 the membership roster was 141; the organization had a functional staff of officers and directors from each region, and there were nine functioning committees.

The UAA is the only nationwide organization in both the United States and Canada devoted strictly to the profession of tree and vegetation management on utility properties. Richard E. Abbott served as the volunteer executive director/ editor of the UAA for the first eight years. Bill Hamilton served as the executive director from 1980 through 1983. Ric Ulrich, a driving force behind the significant growth of the UAA in the 1980s, served as its executive director and editor from 1983 through 1992. In 1992 the UAA hired its first paid, part-time executive director, Derek Vannice, who worked out of the ISA office thus increasing communication and joint program development. During the late 1980s and 1990s the UAA experienced increased visibility and recognition within the tree care profession and reached a membership of more than 1,200 by 1998.

The Arboriculture Research and Education Academy

The Arboriculture Research and Education Academy (AREA) was created as a special-interest group within the society in 1973. As scientists and educators, Dr. John A. Weidhaas (of Virginia Polytechnic Institute) and Dr. E. B. Himelick noticed that the numbers of scientists and educators in the society was small in relation to total membership, and sensed the need for more tree care scientists to attend ISA meetings and for better communication between scientists and practitioners. Thus, Weidhaas proposed the creation of a special-interest group, which became known as AREA, and he became its first president.

Membership in AREA is open to ISA members employed in or retired from the scientific and educational community. It sought those engaged in research, extension, teaching, management, or regulation in programs sponsored by educational institutions, governmental agencies, arboreta, botanical gardens, museums, or private industry in which the person's major responsibility was research or education. The purpose of AREA was not primarily to attract new members but to encourage interdisciplinary cooperation and coordination and attendance at ISA meetings.

In 1980 AREA initiated a paper session at the ISA annual conference, similar to those in scientific societies, and has followed the scientific societies in encouraging poster presentations. In 1987 AREA initiated a new project to compile a roster for an ISA speaker's bureau. Throughout the 1990s AREA became more involved in planning the annual conference program. A "Call for Papers" was utilized to encourage scientists to submit conference presentation topics for the following year's annual meeting. An AREA representative served on the program committee that selected submissions for the main conference program. Scientific sessions as part of the main program provided delegates with the latest research information and featured researchers whose work was most relevant to the practicing arborist.

A Student Society

In 1980 a group of students in the urban forestry program at the University of Wisconsin, Stevens Point, called an informational meeting to organize the student society of arboriculture. Dr. Robert Miller was their advisor and university representative. In 1982 the student organization petitioned the ISA for recognition as a special-interest group for all students in the ISA; it became the Student Society of Arboriculture (SSA).

The SSA began with a charter membership of fifteen and by 1985 it had thirty-five participating members. Despite these modest numbers, the SSA represents all student members in the ISA, which numbered more than 350 in 1998. Since its inception the SSA has raised money locally on the Stevens Point campus to develop a tree nursery; plant, dedicate, and maintain campus trees; and develop Arbor Day programs in the community. The purpose of SSA is to initiate an outreach program to all student members of ISA, to stimulate the development of other local campus student organizations, to survey other student organizations, and publish a quarterly newsletter of its own. The SSA also provides a job-referral service for its members.

ISA encouraged student involvement at its annual conference by providing reduced registration fees and free housing for a limited number of students. The students would assist with speaker needs and host an evening session of SSA. The SSA hosted its first annual student conference in 1997 in Stevens Point, Wisconsin. A result of this conference was to have the SSA present a plan for establishment of "student branches" throughout the society. In 1998 the society approved establishment of "student branches" within ISA chapters, and in that year had established student branches in four chapters.

The Society of Commercial Arboriculture

The interests of most commercial arborists in the United States and Canada were well represented by the National Arborist Association (NAA). For many years the NAA met jointly with the NSTC and the ISTC. When the NAA began to meet separately in the 1960s, a liaison committee of the ISTC was formed to maintain cooperation between the two organizations. From this committee, a new Commercial Arborist Committee was created within the ISTC in 1968. The new committee was charged with preparing a program of special interest to commercial arboriculture for annual meetings, depending to some degree on help from the NAA.

By 1980 a survey of ISA members indicated a clear need for the ISA to provide an opportunity for non-NAA commercial arborist members to have more input within ISA. The members expressed a need for the continuity between annual meetings that could be provided by a special-interest group. The petition for organization included 145 signatures, confirming the strength of its supporters. The petition was approved by the ISA and the Society of Commercial Arboriculture (SCA) was born in 1982. Yvon Fournier of Canada became its first elected president. Within a year of its founding, its membership had increased to 180 so that with the UAA and MAUFS arborist groups, it now constituted a third strong supporting group within the ISA. By 1984 it had begun publishing a newsletter and by 1986 had special projects to increase membership, increase newsletter production, and provide truck and letterhead logos available for sale to members. The SCA supported the ISA International Tree Climbing Championship (Jamboree) from its inception and served as a major cash prize donor over the years.

A major function of the SCA was to host a field tour during the ISA annual conference. This often included a tour of a local commercial arborist's operation providing delegates an excellent opportunity to gain insights into innovative company management strategies. By 1998 membership had grown to more than 850, and SCA contracted with ISA for its first part-time executive director, Sharon Lilly, who worked out of the ISA office.

ANNUAL CONFERENCE AND TREE CLIMBING CHAMPIONSHIP

Historically, ISA has held its annual conferences in August. The four-day events are highlighted with speakers from around the world who feature the latest research and information on subjects ranging from commercial to utility to municipal arboriculture. The conferences begin with a field day featuring an out-door equipment display, International Tree Climbing Championship (ITCC, known as the Jamboree until the ISA board approved major rules and a name change in 1996), and an opening ceremony and reception. The annual conferences are a family event, often bringing together more than 1,500 delegates during the 1990s. The society held its annual conference off the North American continent for the first time in 1998, and more than 1,200 delegates attended from more than thirty-six countries.

The ITCC or Jamboree, held annually at ISA annual meetings, had tradition-ally been a colorful project with origins dating from tree climbing contests in the early 1940s. In 1942, the year in which the Western Shade Tree Conference merged into the NSTC, the Western Conference was reported to have held the first tree climbing contest in the conference. Similar contests were reported in Massachusetts at a later date. The NSTC conducted a tree climbing contest for the first time at its annual meeting in 1951, held in Cincinnati. The event was so successful that a special committee was appointed to formulate rules and regula-tions for additional contests, and the report of its chairman, R. D. Lowden of Bos-ton, was accepted in 1952. Tree climbing contests at the national meeting were held either infrequently or not at all during the 1950s and 1960s.

ISA executive director Eugene Himelick initiated the first Jamboree contests of the newly organized ISA in 1976, and the first International Jamboree was held in St. Louis, Missouri. The goal of the event was to demonstrate skills; however, safety in tree work was an essential component of the competition. The first world champion tree climber (in 1976) was Tom Gosnell of Santa Barbara, California. In 1980 the Jamboree was discontinued because of lack of insurance liability cover-age, but was reinstated in 1981. The same problem occurred from 1987–89.

Despite the insurance problem, the ISA was committed to continuing the an-nual Jamboree. In May 1989 the executive committee approved a new insurance program that allowed the Jamboree to occur during the August conference in St. Charles, Illinois. This commitment to international and chapter jamborees proved very important to the society. Many climbers became involved in professional activities and development and new techniques were introduced to the profession during the Jamboree.

In the mid-1990s a committee was appointed by the board to review the Jamboree policies and rules. The result of the committee's activity was to recom-mend major changes in order to "internationalize" the Jamboree. The board ac-cepted the changes as well as a name change to International Tree Climbing Championship. The committee developed a formal rule book and training video to standardize the ITCC around the world. The efforts of hundreds of volunteers each year allowed this program to become one of the most visible and successful programs of ISA. By 1998, more than 900 contestants from 16 countries were participating in ITCC events. The International Tree Climbing Championship brought together the world's best climbers to display their skills along with the latest in climbing techniques and equipment. From its humble beginnings, the ITCC had grown to prominence in the 1990s and had a tremendous impact on improving tree care and climbing techniques for the practicing arborist.

As an example of the visibility the ITCC gave the profession, the ITCC was featured on *Sky-TV* in 1998 and shown in 123 countries.

Arborist Certification

Establishment

In the early 1980s the Western Chapter of ISA introduced an arborist certification program. Although certification and licensing programs existed in several states, this was the first ISA program. Several other chapters adopted programs of their own in the 1980s. Within the ISA *Blueprint for Action* strategic plan, it was noted that ISA was to investigate development of an arborist certification program that was international in scope. The ISA appointed a committee chaired by Sharon Lilly to consider establishment of an arborist certification program. Based on the committee's review and strong recommendation in 1991, the board approved moving forward with a certification program as proposed by the committee. The proposal recommended implementation of a certification program administered jointly by the society and its chapters. The ISA was to develop and administer the program and the chapters were to administer the tests and provide regional workshops and promotion.

In 1992, after three years of development, ISA launched an unprecedented program of arborist certification on an international scale. The goal was to raise the level of professionalism in arboriculture by educating the providers of tree care services. While it could not solve all of the problems of the tree care industry, the certification program did more to raise the level of education in the tree care profession than any other single program in the history of arboriculture.

The ISA certification program was a voluntary, nongovernmental program, administered by the ISA, and not associated with any governmental licensure. Although ISA arborist certification was designed primarily as an educational program, it was not associated with any college, degree, or educational title in the schooling system. It crossed all levels of education. The program tested and certified an individual's knowledge in the field of arboriculture, and attested to a generally accepted level of knowledge in tree biology, soil and water relations, tree installation and establishment, tree identification and selection, diagnosis, maintenance practices, and other disciplines of the tree care profession.

Objectives

In establishment of the certification program, specific objectives were considered essential. First, the program was developed to continually improve the level of technical competency of personnel in the tree care profession. Second, the program was developed to provide a measurable assessment of the knowledge and competence required to render high quality service. Third, it was determined that certification should give individuals incentives to improve their level of knowledge because of the correlation between certification and recognition, remuneration, and prestige. Since the ISA wanted to provide a means of recognition among peers, it was determined that the program should encourage those in the profession to be aware of the profession's performance standards.

In addition to meeting these objectives, the certification program has benefited arborists and the profession in other ways such as the establishment of a uniform standard by which professionals can be measured and providing an incentive, through the recertification requirements, for continuing education. Certification serves as a tool to help employers, both in training personnel and hiring new employees. Finally, the program provides new and expanded educational materials and programs for the professional arborist.

One of the keys to the program is that it is open to all eligible arborists. In order to qualify for the exam, an individual must have three years of practical experience or two years of experience plus a college degree. Membership in ISA is not required.

The ISA arborist certification program has been successful in many ways. Tree care providers have gained a better understanding of tree biology and the effects of various maintenance practices. As a result, there is a noticeable decrease in the incidences of poor pruning practices such as topping. Some individual arborists felt that the process of studying for and passing the certification exam changed the way they do business. Companies began requiring their employees to become certified and/or offered a bonus or raise in pay for becoming certified.

In 1992 there were 2,500 ISA Certified Arborists. By 1998 there were more than 10,000 with more than 250 exams offered annually through ISA chapters in Canada and the United States. In 1998 arborist certification was also offered through the United Kingdom/Ireland Chapter. In addition, more than twenty-five arborists representing other countries became ISA Certified Arborists.

The program has been successful for ISA. Membership in the United States and Canada increased dramatically from the program's inception in 1992. Demand for and sales of books, tapes, and other educational materials increased to the point where ISA was producing four major nonserial books per year. The recertification requirement to accumulate thirty Continuing Education Units (CEUs) in a three-year period has increased attendance at meetings, seminars, and workshops through the 1990s.

ISA Publications

Proceedings of Annual Meetings

The first appointed committee of the NSTC was for publications. The publication committee's first mission was to prepare a set of meeting proceedings. A periodical for abstracts and papers was also proposed. Accordingly, its first publication was the *Annual Proceedings of the 1929 Conference* in Brooklyn, New York.

In 1936 the Western Shade Tree Conference, based in California, had not yet merged with the NSTC but had begun to produce proceedings and papers comparable to those of the NSTC. To the mutual advantage of each organization, the NSTC arranged to print and distribute the WSTC publications along with its own proceedings and publications. This arrangement continued annually until the WSTC became a regional chapter of the NSTC in 1942.

In 1958 the business aspects of the organization became so voluminous that business transactions, including all reports from committees, were published separately from paper presentations, questions, and discussions. The practice of publishing business affairs and papers as two separate items continued into the early 1970s when paper presentations were printed in *Arborist's News*. The business proceedings continued to be published and distributed to members until the late 1970s, when again the volume became too expensive to handle. From that time until business proceedings ceased being published in 1986, they were sent only to leaders, executive committee members, board of governors and/or directors, and committee chairs. As a replacement for the business proceedings, ISA began publishing an annual report in 1988 that is distributed during the annual conference.

Arborist's News

The first monthly periodical was appropriately entitled *Arborist's News*. It began publication 1 November 1935. The issues were organized and produced by Dr. Richard White, secretary-treasurer, in New Brunswick, New Jersey. Dr. Ephraim P.

Felt of New York was the editor during the first two years of publication (1935–36). Dr. Lewis Chadwick was elected editor in 1936 and served until 1938 when Paul E. Tilford succeeded him. Felt was a distinguished entomologist from Cornell University, Chadwick a professor of horticulture, and Tilford a research plant pathologist, both at the Ohio State University.

The early issues of *Arborist's News* were composed primarily of abstracts of newly published papers on shade tree care, announcements from the leadership of the NSTC, and book reviews. Also included were abstracts of publications in the fields of entomology, fertilization, pathology, and planting. Beginning in 1935, *Arborist's News* included short articles by society members and case histories on tree care.

Tilford continued as editor until 1966. During his editorship, the publication continued to increase in size and scope. Noel B. Wysong, retired chief forester of the Cook County Forest Preserve District in River Forest, Illinois, succeeded him in 1967. Wysong served for three years and was succeeded by Dr. Dan Neely, a plant pathologist at the Illinois Natural History Survey and professor at the University of Illinois at Urbana.

Arborist's News ceased as an independent publication at the end of 1974 with volume 39. The last issue—the Golden Anniversary Issue—contained the historic papers, programs, and minutes of the first four meetings of the National Shade Tree Conference, never before published. It also included the articles of confederation and a reproduction of the signatures of the original thirteen signers of that document. In 1974 ISTC executive director Himelick and editor Neely arranged to microfiche all issues of *Arborist's News* for posterity.

Himelick and Neely presided over the termination of *Arborist's News* as a periodical in 1974 and the initiation of the *Journal of Arboriculture* as a new professional publication. *Arborist's News* lived on as addendum pages in the *Journal*, reduced to the function of monthly society news. During the forty years that it functioned on its own, however, *Arborist's News* was recognized as one of the foremost sources of arborist literature in the world.

In 1992 the *Journal* became bimonthly and *Arborist News* (note the change in spelling) was reborn as a greatly expanded and improved bimonthly magazine. The society removed the addendum pages from the *Journal*, thus enhancing its value as a refereed scientific publication.

Journal of Arboriculture

The first and most significant publication of the ISA began in 1975 with the *Journal of Arboriculture*. The *Journal* is a publication devoted to the dissemination of knowledge in the science and art of growing and maintaining amenity trees. Articles are scientific, educational, or technical in nature. An editorial board of twelve renowned scientists reviews and approves all manuscripts.

Nonserial Publications

The first nonserial publication of the NSTC was *Transplanting of Trees and Shrubs in the Northeastern and North Central United States,* published in 1943. A joint publication in cooperation with the National Arborist Association, it was published in bulletin form in response to a request from the Camouflage Division of the Armed Forces. It was rewritten in 1981 by Eugene Himelick and renamed *Transplanting of Trees and Shrubs Manual.* It was copyrighted by the ISA and revised in 1987 and 1991. The publication, whose authors are Dr. Gary Watson and Dr. Eugene Himelick, underwent a major revision in 1997 with the title changing to *Principles and Practices of Planting Trees and Shrubs.*

Immediately following the end of World War II in 1945, the NSTC created a second publication called *Model City Ordinance for Tree Management.* The 1953 revision had a voluminous title—*A Standard City Ordinance Regulating the Removal, Planting and Maintenance of Shade Trees in Public Areas, and Standard Arboricultural Specifications and Standards of Practice.* A third edition of fourteen pages was revised, updated, and reprinted by the ISA Publications Committee with the cooperation of ISA editor Neely and executive director Himelick in 1972. With its title reduced to *A Standard Municipal Tree Ordinance,* it provided relevant information for people and municipalities interested in creating, revising, and improving ordinances relative to planting, maintenance, and preservation of shade and ornamental trees.

Shade Tree Evaluation was published for the first time in 1957 under the direction of the late Norman Armstrong. For the first time the society was able to provide a sound basis for evaluating trees. In essence it had devised a formula based on (1) a unit value per square inch of the tree bole at breast height; (2) species of tree; (3) tree condition, and later to include; (4) tree location. It was practical and easy to use for an informed and conscientious arborist and was widely accepted by attorneys and courts as a valid basis for assessing individual tree values. It has been revised and updated seven times, the last revision (1992) being titled *Guide for Plant Appraisal.* The Council of Tree and Landscape Appraisers (CTLA) was responsible for later revisions. The *Guide for Plant Appraisal* is arguably one of ISA's flagship publications.

Arboriculture as a Career by the ISTC was issued as a leaflet in 1961. Revised and reprinted in 1963, it was revised again in 1974 as *Opportunities in Arboriculture.*

As a joint effort with the NAA in 1988, the publication was revised and renamed *Careers in Arboriculture* as a four-color brochure of sixteen pages, describing the field of arboriculture and various career opportunities in it.

In 1976 the publication of single sheets of arboricultural abstracts in specialized areas of plant pathology, entomology, physiology, selection and genetics, and horticulture began. They were initially funded by the Memorial Research Trust. About 80 papers were abstracted in 1979; by 1986 the number had risen to about 120. Publication of the abstracts continued until 1998 when the ISA board voted to terminate this program in favor of placing abstracts within the *Journal of Arboriculture*.

With the increased focus on publication development through the 1990s, the ISA established "families" of publications targeted to meet the needs of its professional affiliations. While many publications serve multiple disciplinary needs, the ISA arboricultural families included commercial, utility, municipal, and research/education. The society also produced a variety of youth education and public relations materials available in book, brochure, or press release formats. A number of the publications have CEU workbooks and tests available for the certified arborist.

By the mid-1990s, ISA became an outstanding resource for the latest arboricultural information. The society was constantly producing new educational material to keep members current with the latest professional practices. By 1998 the ISA had established itself as the publishing house for scientific and applied information on the care and management of urban trees with more than ninety selections of books, brochures, videos, audiocassettes, and public relations and public education materials. In 1998 sales of ISA books, videos, and public information materials exceeded $700,000, compared to sales of less than $50,000 in 1989.

The increased focus on publication development grew out of the society's strategic plans and was greatly enhanced by the certification program, which was causing a tremendous interest in professional development within the tree care industry. Not even the drafters of the ISA strategic plans could have envisioned the rapid growth of the publication house. ISA publications began in 1943 from a desire to improve professional practice.

Following are some of ISA's major publications as of 1999: *Arborists' Certification Study Guide* (by Sharon Lilly—the major publication of ISA in the 1990s); *Arboriculture and the Law* (authored by Victor Merullo and Michael Valentine); *Arborist Equipment* (by Donald Blair—this publication served as a one-stop source of technical information about tree care tools and equipment); *Tree Climbers' Guide* (by Sharon Lilly); *Plant Health Care for Woody Ornamentals* (John Lloyd, coordinating author) along with a companion *Guide to the Plant Health Care Management System* (multiple authors); *Trees and Development* and *The Evaluation of*

Hazard Trees in Urban Areas (both by Nelda Matheny and James Clark); *Guide to Report Writing* (authored by Dorothy Abeyta for the American Society of Consulting Arborists, published by ISA); and *Golf Course Tree Management* (by Sharon Lilly for ISA, published by Ann Arbor Press).

ISA also focuses on research-oriented publications such as *Landscape Below Ground* (1993 proceedings of an international workshop on tree root development in urban soils edited by Gary Watson and Dan Neely); *Trees and Building Sites* (proceedings of the 1995 Trees and Buildings Conference edited by Gary Watson and Dan Neely); and *Landscape Below Ground II* (1998 proceedings of an international workshop on tree root development in urban soils edited by Gary Watson and Dan Neely).

Many of the society's publications have been translated into French and Spanish. Recently, the ISA ventured outside the United States to publish its first truly non-U.S. publications entitled *Arboriculture and the Law in Canada* (by Julian Dunster and Susan Murray in 1997) and *Arborists' Certification Study Guide* (revised for the United Kingdom in 1999).

In addition to the more than twenty-five publications designed for youth, consumer information, and public relations, ISA also publishes thirty videos on topics pertinent to each of the professional affiliations. The videos range from topics of tree damage and hazard assessment to utility and municipal concerns and maintenance techniques.

In the late 1990s, with certification for tree workers under development, the ISA began to focus more on training of tree care personnel with publications such as *Arborist Equipment* and *The Tree Climbers' Guide*. In partnership with ArborMaster Training, the ISA produced a series of fourteen training videos on climbing techniques, equipment, and chain-saw use and safety. Each video came with an extensively illustrated study guide and CEU workbook.

ISA RESEARCH GRANTS

Humble Beginnings

At its 1936 annual meeting, the NSTC approved a project pertaining to lightning injury, a milestone in the history of the NSTC, because it was the first research project it sponsored. No other organization or institution was then in a position to gather such data over a period of years from such wide geographical sources. The project was under the direction of A. Robert Thompson of the U.S. Department of Interior Park Service and resulted in publication of a body of much-valued information.

It was clearly recognized by 1946 that NSTC scientists working outside of the conference had conducted most of the research on tree care. A research fund was needed so that arborists could sponsor research for which they were to be the principal beneficiaries. A committee to establish this fund was chaired by Dr. Curtis M. May, plant pathologist with the U.S. Department of Agriculture Division of Forest Pathology, and included Paul Tilford and Lewis Chadwick. The research fund was formally started on 12 December 1946, with the transfer of $2,000 from the general fund of NSTC to the Memorial Research Fund.

The first research project sponsored by the Memorial Research Fund was a fellowship awarded to the Ohio State University (for $1,950) for a study in 1948–49 to investigate prevention of fruiting of certain ornamental trees by application of spray materials. It produced some of the earliest data that would in time prevent unwanted flowering and fruit production of urban trees.

The second research project from the NSTC Memorial Research Fund was initiated in 1952. Called "Effectiveness in Shade Tree Disease Control by Addition of Chemicals to Nutrient Solutions Supplied to Roots," it was a cooperative study between the University of Maryland, College Park, and the Division of Forest Pathology of the USDA, under the direction of Dr. Curtis May, Beltsville, Maryland.

Two new projects were approved for support in 1955: "Study of the Nutrient Requirements of Ornamental Trees and Plants by Foliar Analysis" and "Stimulation of Tree Growth by Antibiotics." The first of these went to the Ohio State University, with Dr. Chadwick supervising. The second went to the Division of Forest Pathology, with Dr. May supervising.

In 1960 the NSTC initiated a major project on "Soil Aeration and Growth of Various Tree Species." Through a fellowship at Duke University, Dr. Paul Kramer, supervisor and graduate and postgraduate student, George Yelenosky, made a significant contribution to knowledge of soil aeration. This study noted outstanding differences in species tolerance to various levels of aeration.

A grant was given to Dr. Richard E. Harris of the University of California at Davis to study "Factors Influencing Trunk Development of Young Landscape Trees." Completed in 1970, this study yielded data of value in avoiding later stem problems by careful attention to planting details.

In 1968 the research committee first prepared an announcement for proposal applications for a research grant—$4,000 per year was to be granted for a period up to four years. This was the largest commitment in advance that the society had ever made and it drew twelve worthwhile proposals. The Research Assistantship Grant was awarded to Dr. Theodore T. Koslowski of the University of Wisconsin, Madison, for his proposal, "Effects of Transplanting on Physiological Responses and Growth of Shade Trees."

A new idea for fund-raising was proposed by ISTC president Olaf J. Andersen, an arborist from Houston, Texas. In 1972 he and his wife donated a Book of Remembrance to the society. The memorial gift accomplished two goals—honoring a departed loved one, and contributing research funds to the society.

The Research Trust

John Duling of Muncie, Indiana, always a strong advocate of research, proposed the establishment of a tax-exempt Memorial Research Trust Fund in 1972. Funding for the trust began in 1974. The first trustees were Hyland R. Johns (Pennsylvania), chairman; Jack R. Rogers (California); Ray Gustin (Maryland); Yvon Fournier (Quebec); Eugene B. Himelick (Illinois); John Duling (Indiana); and Olaf J. Andersen (Texas). The fund was to be administered by Cal Bundy, then executive secretary of the ISA. In 1977 the fund's board of trustees increased the number of its at-large members from two to seven, making a total of twelve board members

The first business meeting of the trust took place in 1976 at the annual meeting in St. Louis. Bundy was appointed administrator of the trust, which had donations and pledges of $42,419. By the end of 1977, more than $45,000 had been committed to the trust. The first two grants awarded went to Dr. A. L. Shigo of the U.S. Forest Service for studies on internal infection in trees and to Dr. Richard J. Campana of the University of Maine to study the systemic fungicide, benomyl.

The trust's legal operations began to grant funds in 1977. Of thirty proposals that were properly screened and recommended, six were funded for $500 each. These were awarded to the Universities of Illinois, Massachusetts, and Tennessee, the Morris Arboretum (University of Pennsylvania), and Colorado and Oregon State Universities. These first grants were for areas of special arboricultural interest in integrated pest control, tree evaluation, tree genetics, and breeding.

In 1981 the ISA Canadian Chapter moved to create a separate Canadian Trust within the ISA. This allowed funds raised in Canada to be used to support arboricultural research there as well as in the United States.

In reviewing the trust program after 12 years, Dr. Francis W. Holmes, Research Committee Chairman in 1986, noted the record of support for 116 projects on 294 subjects in 57 institutions for a total expenditure of $118,500.

In 1989 in a joint venture by NAA and ISA, a $60,000 grant was made to the Illinois Natural History Survey. It was entitled "Health Maintenance Option Approach to Implementing IPM Strategy." Integrated pest management (IPM) had been in great demand for several years, and this grant was designed to enhance insect and disease control of amenity trees with fewer chemicals and lower dosages. An extended project, it included five stages in the production of a publication to guide application of the IPM campaign. Based on a marketing analysis of tree care consumers, the IPM name was changed to Plant Health Care (PHC), and new publications and educational brochures were introduced to the tree care professional in 1992. This initial work in developing PHC allowed the profession to focus on long-term management practices that improve the survivability of plants in the urban environment. A number of publications emerged from PHC, most notably the *Plant Health Care Compendium, A Guide to the Plant Health Care Management System,* and *Plant Health Care for Woody Ornamentals.*

Between 1975 and 1998, the trust funded more than 250 grants totaling more than one million dollars in research on five continents. Throughout its history, the trust has funded groundbreaking research in areas of tree management and maintenance, planting, plant health, tree failure, soils, environmental benefits, and many other areas. The research has benefited commercial, municipal, and utility arboriculture. When it benefited the profession, the trust partnered with public and private organizations to further its research efforts.

The majority of funding to support research was generated through the chapters of ISA. Two annual functions have added revenues to the research trust funds each year. The first event of note is Tour des Trees, an eight-day bicycle tour that finishes at the annual conference field day. The second event is a golf outing, held on the day before the ISA field day. These two events, along with chapter fundraising activities, permitted the trust to fund more than $125,000 in research each year between 1995 and 1998. The trust also established an endowment fund in 1994 that grew to $125,000 in 1998. The endowment fund was established with the goal of funding research from interest earned off the principal.

OTHER ACTIVITIES

Film Production

In 1954 the conference undertook a major project requiring $25,000 to produce a film entitled *Trees and Their Care.* At this time, time-lapse color photography was a new technological advancement, and the observations of plants as they grow became very popular. In that year NSTC past president Noel Wysong began a seven-year campaign to raise $25,000 for the project. Assisting him in fundraising was NSTC past president Earl Martin of Toronto. Produced by prominent nature photographer John Ott of Chicago, the film was shown for the first time at the 1961 annual meeting of the ISTC in Minneapolis.

The film was a 16-mm sound movie in color, twenty-nine minutes long, and showed the detailed growth and development of tree buds, flowers, and leaves. Of special interest were the opening of flowers and leaves and the development of insects shown by time-lapse photography. Following a period of sales and rentals, the handling of the film was turned over to the International Film Bureau of Chicago. For its professional efforts in producing a film of such high quality and value to arboriculture, the ISTC received an Award of Merit from the American Horticultural Council.

The ISTC's other venture into filmmaking came in 1975, with a new film on pesticides. *Pesticides: Play It Safe* was a training film designed for professional pesticide applicators.

Tree Recognition

In 1975 and again in 1987 the ISA, in cooperation with the NAA, initiated a bicentennial tree recognition program to commemorate the U.S. Declaration of Independence in 1776 and the signing of the Constitution in 1787. The goal was to locate trees known to have been living witnesses to events in 1776 and 1787. Once located, each tree was to be marked with a bronze plaque designating it as a duly recognized bicentennial tree. Appropriately, the program was initiated in October of 1975 by the planting of an American elm on the White House grounds in Washington, D.C. The elm was a scion of the John Quincy Adams elm destroyed by Dutch elm disease.

American National Standards Institute

In 1968 the American National Standards Institute (ANSI) organized a committee designated as Z-133 to prepare national standards to make trimming trees safer. The National Arborist Association was acting secretariat of the committee for solicitation of comments for a proposed standard. The ISTC Ethics and Professional Status Committee supported the project and appointed Herbert J. Cran of Connecticut and Freeman L. Parr of New York to represent ISTC. The Z-133 standards recognized and addressed the hazards later referred to in the U.S. Occupational Safety and Health Act of 1970. Eventually, the ISA replaced the NAA as the secretariat of ANSI Z-133.

ISA Awards

In 1963 the conference created awards to recognize productive authors. The Author's Citation was given to authors of outstanding publications for sustained excellence in the publication of timely information pertaining to the field of

Fig. 10.10 The NAA/
ISA bicentennial tree
program, Bob McCon-
nell and Hyland Johns.
Courtesy of the ISA
Archives.

arboriculture. Not limited at first to members of the organization, it has been awarded to scholars in many areas of plant science, including botany, forestry, and horticulture. Early nonmember recipients were Fred R. Kilner, editor of *American Nurseryman*; Dr. Cynthia Wescott, author of *The Plant Doctor*; and Dr. Donald Wyman, horticulturist of the Arnold Arboretum of Harvard University.

The Award of Merit was designed to recognize outstanding meritorious service in advancing the principles, ideals, and practices of arboriculture and is the highest award given by the society. The first five recipients were past or present officers of the society: Norman Armstrong, Rush Marshall, Charles Irish, Lewis Chadwick, and Paul Tilford.

Special Awards of Merit were given to people outside of the society for the first time in 1967. Lady Bird Johnson, wife of U.S. President Johnson, was honored for her national crusade on natural beauty and strong support for urban tree planting throughout the country. Governor Harold E. Hughes of Iowa was honored for his strong support of research in arboriculture and Dutch elm disease. In 1970. President Richard M. Nixon was honored for his support of legislation for a National Arbor Day throughout the United States.

In 1978 ISA president Yvon Fournier of Quebec initiated a new series of annual awards to stimulate chapter competition in striving for excellence and achievement in fulfilling ISA goals. Known as the annual Banner Awards, each chapter received a large silken banner for display at its meetings that identified the chapter and year of origin. Citations were awarded to chapters in six categories: membership increase, special projects, quality of newsletter, attendance at annual meetings, presidency of the ISA, and hosting the ISA annual meeting within the chapter area. Each citation was to be affixed to the chapter's banner. The first banners were awarded at the ISA convention in Quebec in 1979.

ISA on the Internet

In 1995 the executive committee contracted with the University of Illinois to establish an ISA home page on the Internet. The site was established in 1995 with a focus on plant heath care information, a "chat page" for tree workers, as well as general information on ISA and its various programs. There were more than 1,000 "visitors" to the page in the early months, and the site grew to over 80,000 visits per month in 1998. The page is continually expanded to include information on the trust, annual conference, publications, International Tree Climbing Championship, and much more.

SUMMARY

The International Society of Arboriculture had its beginnings as a northeastern regional conference of about thirty-five tree scientists and commercial arborists in 1924. Membership grew to 11,000 in 1998 with members on five continents. From 1943 to the present, the ISA has produced numerous technical publications, videos, audiocassettes, slide presentations, and consumer information brochures.

CHAPTER ELEVEN

The Asplundh Tree Expert Company

"A better way" —Asplundh Company motto

A third national tree company emerged in 1928. The Asplundh Tree Expert Company is not only the largest of the three but a very different kind of organization than either the Davey or Bartlett Company. Whereas the earlier companies first emphasized individual tree care and gravitated to line clearing, Asplundh began exclusively with line clearing, and has since broadened its scope. Organized by a team of brothers, the Asplundh Company became a growing family dynasty.

A history of the Asplundh Company, prepared after its first seventy years, has provided the primary basis for this review. Despite Asplundh's extensive diversification beyond vegetation management, this text emphasizes only those company functions that have significance for line clearance or tree care.

BEGINNINGS

The Asplundh family had its origin in America before the end of the nineteenth century. In 1882 Carl Hjalmar Asplundh emigrated from Sweden to America and went to work for a pharmaceutical company in Philadelphia. At the same firm he met Emma Steiger, another new immigrant from Switzerland, whom he married. Settling in the small town of Bryn Athyn, a suburb of Philadelphia, they had nine children, with eight surviving. The last born, a son named Carl, arrived a few months after his father's death in 1903. Carl and two of his older brothers, Griffith

Fig. 11.1 The Asplundh brothers who founded the company, left to right: Lester, Carl, and Griffith Asplundh. Courtesy of Asplundh Tree Expert Company.

(Griff) and Lester, were the founders of the Asplundh Company in 1928. Another older brother, Oswald (Ozzie or O. E.), played a key role in arboriculture before that time. Ozzie worked at first as a gardener, then began his own business in landscaping and tree surgery.

The three Asplundh brothers collectively were far better prepared to launch a new tree company than either the Daveys or Bartlett. Griffith, the oldest of the three, graduated from the Forestry School of Pennsylvania State College (now University). Lester, next in age, had gone to Swarthmore to emerge with a degree in electrical engineering, and had worked for a major utility company. Carl was a business administration graduate from the Wharton School of Finance at the University of Pennsylvania. After Griffith finished forestry school (ca. 1926), he formed his own tree company (Interstate Treecraft) in western Pennsylvania, apparently planning to build a clientele in both Pennsylvania and Ohio. With this kind of background and talent, the company was launched in 1928, the year before the greatest economic disaster in North American history.

The Asplundh Company was founded on 28 August 1928, in Glenside, Pennsylvania. From its inception, the founders decided to provide service only to public utilities so that the company began by trimming trees around telephone and electrical wires. The decision to limit work to line clearing came about from a dispute with a property owner over the granting of permission to trim his trees. The Asplundh decision had historical significance because of the combined impact of the substantial expertise focused on the single tree care practice of line clearing.

Griffith became the company's first president, Lester was vice president, and Carl, secretary-treasurer. They began with $2,500 in borrowed money and a few climbers (two crews, two trucks, one secretary, and three bosses). With little to go

Fig. 11.2 O. E. "Ozzie" Asplundh, oldest of the Asplundh brothers who went into arboriculture and initiated his three brothers into tree work before they founded the company. Courtesy of the Asplundh Tree Expert Company.

on financially, the company was quickly a sales success. The Asplundh Company had 30 pioneer trimmers, and a fleet that consisted of two secondhand stake-body trucks. The primary tools in those days were axes, saws, ropes, and ladders. Other vehicles were owned by the employees or were rented. Before a year had passed, several more crews had been added to keep pace with expanding work.

Early in the company history Asplundh acquired a visible corporate image by its orange machines. The "Princeton" orange reminded Carl of his massive football opponents from Princeton University. Seen as impressive and imposing, the orange was adopted to give Asplundh a distinctive company image. The company attributes much of its early success to training and supervision of its tree workmen. There was a strong spirit of competition with other emerging companies.

Asplundh organized its first tree school in Huntington Valley, Pennsylvania, in 1929. Unlike either the Davey or Bartlett schools, the Asplundh school was limited to training for line clearance. It was committed to excellence and quality control. Because of the Depression, many small tree care firms had gone out of business. And some of their men came to Asplundh for work. These arborists were retrained to what Asplundh insisted was its "better way."

THE DEPRESSION AND WAR YEARS

With all three of the young executives pushing sales, the company began with tree trimming contracts with Philadelphia Electric, Pennsylvania Power and Light, Public Service Company of New Jersey, New Jersey Power and Light, Keystone Telephone Co., and American Telephone and Telegraph. In that first year they operated only in Pennsylvania and New Jersey. In 1930 the company had its first major line-clearing job in Maine for the New England Telephone and Telegraph

Company, clearing a fifty-mile right-of-way (ROW) from Clinton to Bangor, Maine. When clearing a path through heavily wooded growth, the method in those days (before the chain saw) was to clear-cut, using axes, two-man saws, and plenty of sweat.

In 1931 Asplundh established its first branch office in Columbus, Ohio. There was no record of geographic expansion in 1932–33, but things picked up again in 1934. The company expanded into Maryland with a contract with Baltimore Gas and Electric. In 1934, despite the difficult times, the company had enough work to require larger quarters, and the company made its move to Homestead Road in Jenkintown, Pennsylvania. In the next few years Asplundh moved south and north from its Philadelphia base with new operations in Virginia, the Carolinas, New York, and New England.

To survive the Depression the Asplundh Company had to be innovative. Without the backlog of experience of the Davey and Bartlett Companies, it had, in its own words, to develop "a better way." The primary aspect of its better way would be to develop new and superior equipment. Lester's engineering background came into play early. In 1929 he developed a hand-cranked aerial platform to get men into the treetops faster and safer. Although slow and cumbersome, it was a forerunner of the aerial device to appear twenty-five years later.

In that same year he developed a larger circular saw, ominously called the "mankiller," mounted on the front of a tractor. Horizontally oriented, the spinning blade was pushed into the tree trunk to sever the stem. Although neither the platform lift nor the saw proved practical, they were indicative of the innovative improvement of machinery that would later become a hallmark of Asplundh development.

Asplundh was the first of the tree companies to use the newly invented power saw. Although not generally available until after World War II, the power saw eventually revolutionized the entire tree care industry but probably affected line clearing earlier and more directly than other aspects of the industry.

Like the Davey and Bartlett Companies, Asplundh was also affected by the Depression, and 1932 was the worst year for sales. Wages were low, with climbers making only fifty-four cents and foremen from seventy-five to eighty-seven cents per hour. The three Asplundh brothers went without salaries in that year. Unlike the Bartlett and Davey Companies, however, Asplundh's clientele included utility companies. They kept clearing ROWs as the utility industry kept growing. Thus, the company was able to grow, and because of the availability of newly laid-off private or commercial arborists, was able to meet demands for new crews. In 1934 and 1935, with new contracts and a favorable geographic expansion, the company continued to grow and prosper. In 1936 O. E. Asplundh gave up his own tree business and joined his brothers. With his sales expertise he helped Asplundh push farther into the Midwest as the company established a new office near Chicago.

The disastrous Northeast hurricane in 1938 provided an opportunity for Asplundh to expand into Long Island and Boston. The dire need for fast cleanup after the hurricane provided Asplundh with an opportunity that it was to recognize and act on. It would lead in time to a nationwide storm emergency program.

By 1939 the company had again outgrown its office space. A new location was acquired in Jenkintown, Pennsylvania, with land for expansion, and a large garage for equipment storage and tool repair. As operations extended both south and west, a new office was established in the nation's capital and another in Texas. At this time working districts were divided into four geographic regions. The three founding Asplundh brothers directed the East Coast operation; Daric Acton became regional vice president for an area that included western Pennsylvania, West Virginia, Indiana, and Tennessee. West Jordan was regional vice president for Ohio and Michigan; and O. E. Asplundh, with headquarters in Chicago, was regional vice president for all points west.

POSTWAR INNOVATIONS AND MECHANIZATION

After the war the company moved quickly to retool, improve, and expand. Carl Asplundh listed six points that would be stressed: replacement of old trucks with new ones, with bodies designed especially for Asplundh work; new field equipment for line clearing to be the best available; improvement of work methods; reactivation of tree schools; a new emphasis on safety; and expansion of present territories and opening of new divisions. In line with such field improvements, the Asplundh offices were automated for the first time in 1948 with new IBM computers.

Because of the shortage of steel in the war period, truck bodies were still open with wooden stakes. When overloaded, these were not safe. Unsightly protruding branches often scratched cars, and became a public image problem. Overhanging loads sometimes brought damage claims. To meet this problem the company designed and had made solid steel side panels for the beds. The new design made it possible to contain the loads and increased the carrying capacity of the truck. The new trucks gave brush disposal an improved image.

Emphasis on safety was underlined when Harry Ertel was appointed to develop a new safety program in 1946. As the first safety director, Ertel initiated new first-aid and tree rescue techniques. When Ertel became a company manager in the Carolinas in 1951, Harold Masters joined the company as the safety director. With his assistant, Bob Herder, they accelerated the Asplundh safety program.

To supplement their program they used a film, *The Breath of Life*, co-produced by Asplundh and the Aetna Life and Casualty Insurance Company. It was dubbed as "The Masters and Herder Traveling Road Show." Traveling many miles, the show visited crews in the field and gave programs on safety practices. Company posters depicted a cartoon character called "Hap Hazard" (an accident-prone buffoon) who was said to be most effective in demonstrating what should *not* be done. When Masters transferred to New England in 1961, Herder became the new safety director.

In the wake of rapidly developing technology and new personnel, there arose a need to acquire expertise in such areas as care of new equipment (especially chain saws and power sprayers), new chemical sprays, and new office procedures. To meet these needs, a series of schools was initiated for general foremen who were brought to the home office from around the country. The principal of the first schools was Hyland Johns, then a young graduate forester.

By 1960 the training school had become known as the Asplundh Supervisory Training Program, with Johns as its leader. The one-week program included courses in chemical brush control with several class lectures, group discussions, equipment data, and field trips to rights-of-way operations for application of knowledge and training. Johns wrote the first *Spray Foremen's Training Manual* in 1951. From the late 1950s through the 1980s he served Asplundh as a liaison agent between field operations, the main office, and industry organizations such as the ISA, achieving the rank of vice president and board member. Throughout his career with the Asplundh Company and beyond, he became an outstanding leader in arboriculture.

As the company grew in the 1950s, more space was needed to service all the machines, tools, and equipment. Regional service centers, with adequate space and full-repair facilities, were established in New Jersey and North Carolina. These units were staffed with full-time mechanics and shop personnel.

By 1959 the Asplundh Company had expanded north, south, and west, with the formation of three regional affiliate companies: New England Tree Expert Company, Florida Forestry Corporation, and Pacific Tree Expert Company. The latter affiliate included operations in Washington, Oregon, and northern California, establishing the Asplundh Company as the first of the three national tree companies to become nationwide. This made it the largest of the national companies, although it began operations twenty years later than Davey and Bartlett.

Chemicals to kill brush, evolving from research during the war, became popular new tools for ROW maintenance. The company introduced a spray service to kill brush in 1946. In 1952 Asplundh began a long-range program of testing new chemicals in cooperation with the American Chemical and Paint Company and Pennsylvania State University. Following development of the new chemicals for brush control along ROWs, the company moved quickly to acquire and develop or convert new machinery to get the chemicals to the brush. The company acquired surplus jeeps, trucks, and tractors and converted them with the addition of tanks, pumps, and hoses. Four-wheel-drive vehicles were used for rough terrain, huge airplane bomber wheel tires were used to make a swamp buggy, and a Caterpillar tractor was adapted for spraying chemicals.

New inventions supplemented these adaptations. "Special shear dozers" were used for clearing ground. A new brush hog was developed to be towed behind a tractor. Asplundh claimed a "new phase" of chemical application, when trucks mounted on a railroad flat car were used to spray chemicals along the railroad ROW.

Griffith Asplundh died suddenly in 1948, active to the end as the first president of the company. He had led the company in its most trying years, guiding it successfully over the formidable obstacles of the Depression and war. His leadership had made it possible to exploit the new opportunities ahead in the decade of the 1950s. This period was characterized by the advent of new machines (the Asplundh chipper and lift in particular), new ROW developments, use of aircraft, and new vegetation control techniques and chemicals.

The new steel truck bodies had resolved the problem of confining tree waste and this, in turn, led to a better solution to waste compaction and disposal. Before the chipper was perfected, several other ideas for disposal had been tried without success. These included a truck-mounted furnace for burning at the job site, a wire-bundling device (similar to a hay baler), and even a series of circular saws to section the brush.

A chipper made by a Massachusetts engineering company (Fitchburg) had rotating blades and sliced branches like a meat cutter. Asplundh engineers studied this. Not satisfied with this concept they set out to develop their own machine in 1948. The Asplundh machine had a heavy cast-metal rotor with parallel blades that pulled the branches into it, rather than having an operator push them in. The chipper was a big success, leading to creation of a chipper assembly facility to produce machines for Asplundh. In time Asplundh made and sold chippers to other companies.

The efficiency of the Asplundh chipper was increased in 1953 by addition of a flywheel to give added torque, while maintaining chipping uniformity. This increased its production capacity, as did enlargement of the blade. When palm fronds jammed the exhaust chute, a blower was developed to push the materials through. Both torque and blower became standard chipper features. As demand for the Asplundh chipper increased, a new subsidiary called the Asplundh Chipper Company was founded to deal exclusively with manufacture and sales of chippers.

The success of the Asplundh chipper created the problem of how to confine, transport, and dump the chips. After several unsuccessful trials, these problems were solved by the invention of a new completely enclosed steel body on a split-dump truck. Prior to this, unloading of chipped material was done manually with pitchforks and bale hooks.

In the early 1950s Asplundh used telescoping cranes to lift men 100 feet up in a bosun's chair, and then lower large stem sections to the ground using steel cable. Possibly the first in the tree industry to use cranes, Asplundh saw this as the prelude to something better in the future, such as the aerial lifts to come.

When mechanically sound aerial bucket lifts were produced by other companies in the 1950s, they were a positive step toward the goal of putting a man to work in the treetop with efficiency and safety. When Asplundh first used these models in 1953 they did not have proper electrical insulation. Although production gradually improved, later models did not eliminate the hazard of electrocution. The Asplundh Company solved this problem by testing and demonstrating a new product called "spiralloy," reported to be as strong as steel. The product was made of spun glass fiber and epoxy resin. Asplundh made its first Trim-Lift booms with the new material in 1958. Production requirements to make new lifts and chippers again called for expansion. The Philmont, Pennsylvania, plant was expanded, new factory space was acquired at Chalfont, Pennsylvania, and Asplundh took over more of the work previously subcontracted. The recognition of the superior quality of the filament fiberglass developed by Lester Asplundh not only changed the way Asplundh would do business, but provided the industry with a safe aerial lift that had a structurally sound boom.

Carl Asplundh became president of the company in 1952 when Lester had to step down due to a severe respiratory ailment. About this time the second generation of the Asplundh family began moving into the company, starting out working on tree trimming crews in the field. Asplundh's policy is to promote from within if possible, and to have all company employees begin at the bottom so that even the top executives have experience at all levels in the company.

In the 1950s the company resumed its strong in-service training program for all levels of employees, including foreman training classes, middle-management meetings, and special subject seminars. Its *Foreman's Manual* included a wide variety of information from company policy to first aid and safety. In commemorating its first twenty-five years, the company created a scholarship program in 1954 for sons of its employees at the University of Massachusetts. Designed to provide opportunities at an early age for young men interested in line clearing, it involved a work-study sequence of six months of college, six months of company field work, a final nine months of college, and six more months at work to qualify as a foreman. The supporting coursework centered on a basic training in arboriculture. It included tree identification and planting, diagnosis and treatment of tree disease, identification and control of tree pest insects, fertilization, pruning, tree repair, and removal. Financial support included payment for work periods, college tuition, partial payment for college board and lodging, and additional support from a loan program. Only high school graduates were eligible, and selection was competitive for the six most promising applicants.

O. E. ("Ozzie") Asplundh died in 1955 at the age of 65. Like the passing of Griffith, the first company president, his departure severed another significant link with the past.

In 1959 the company created a formalized Storm Emergency Plan. The Northeastern hurricane of 1938 had provided an opportunity for the Asplundh Company to learn about and to meet the emergencies created by storms on an organized basis. Because of its line-clearing expertise the company was constantly in demand from utilities for emergency work during or following storms. Asplundh-trained tree trimmers were in special demand because of their experience in working around hot wires. Eventually the Asplundh Company compiled a nationwide *Storm Emergency Personnel Listing.* The Asplundh listing included the names and phone numbers of hundreds of responsible Asplundh supervisory personnel in cities and towns throughout the United States and Canada. This folder was designed to ensure good communications while assisting in prompt restoration of utility power service. Its *Storm Procedure Manual* ensured efficiency of crew operations, accurate accounting, and customer satisfaction. Every storm emergency within its geographic sphere of operations was charted and monitored at the Asplundh headquarters in Pennsylvania. It was the first service of its kind to be developed by any of the tree companies individually or as a consortium.

In 1957 even greater care was given to training of skilled line-clearance personnel. A department for personnel and training was created and headed by Hyland Johns. This led to the creation of the Asplundh Supervisory Training Program in 1960 under the joint direction of Johns and Edward Asplundh.

With the economy booming in 1960, electric and telephone lines kept expanding to meet the needs of an expanding population. New equipment was introduced, including a helicopter, a large-wheeled spray truck for rough terrain, two types of tracked vehicles, a four-wheel-drive truck, and a new portable backpack spray unit. The helicopter crews showed that aerial spray of chemicals for brush control held promise for future use. The large-wheeled truck ("Big Squirt") was more compact and maneuverable than the earlier "swamp buggy." One-tracked

Fig. 11.3 Hyland Johns, Asplundh vice president. Courtesy of the Asplundh Tree Expert Company.

vehicle, the "Muskeg Bombardier," could travel over the most difficult swampy ground with a full complement of chemicals and sprayers. The other, adapted from a World War II army tank, was used for large spray jobs.

A NEW GENERATION

The new generation of Asplundh executives appearing in key positions at this time consisted of seven sons of the founding brothers. Each had performed successfully as a junior executive and by the early 1960s was ready for larger responsibilities. Each of the Asplundh second generation was well educated, representing a variety of backgrounds in forestry, engineering, law, and business. Three of these seven would become president—Barr in 1968, Edward in 1982, and Chris in 1992.

The sudden deaths of two key executives brought a new team of executives to the fore of the company. President Carl Asplundh Sr. and Treasurer John A. Gaffney died in 1967. Gaffney, a college classmate of Carl's at the University of Pennsylvania, had been a loyal and important company employee since 1928. Lester Asplundh returned as president temporarily and board chairman on an acting basis. In 1968 Barr Asplundh, son of Griffith, was elected president, and Lester continued as board chairman. To emphasize loyalty, productivity, and localization of utility services, nine field managers (all nonfamily) were named as new vice presidents, and Vice President Hyland Johns became a member of the board. After fifty years of service and growth President Barr Asplundh noted that the company that had begun as a small tree care concern in 1928 had grown into "the largest utilities service company in the nation, if not the world." By then Asplundh had 9,000 employees.

Two innovations were made in 1970 to maintain and improve communications within the widespread corporate structure. The first was a decisive move to cope with a nationwide strike by postal workers. Operation "Roadrunner" consisted of a self-made courier service, involving Asplundh Aviation planes and commercial airlines. With an unusual display of cooperation, efficiency, and precision, thousands of invoices and checks were processed in time to prevent unnecessary slackening of operations. Another problem with communications in that period was solved by establishment of toll-free WATS lines. With such lines installed at Asplundh headquarters in Jenkintown, it became possible for the Asplundh administration to have direct, localized, and personal contact with its widely spread customers and employees.

As the company moved into its fifth decade its early slogan "Line Clearance Exclusively," was no longer true, as different kinds of services for utilities were added. A new growth retardant, Asplundh Sproutgard, to treat fresh pruning cuts, and a new soil sterilant, Clearway, were developed by the Chemical Department founded in 1946. Clearway, applied in dry granular form by rotary spreader, was designed to eliminate weeds and grasses. Reflecting the true Asplundh spirit, it was clearly visible with its bright orange dye.

GROWTH AND DEVELOPMENT

By 1973 the growth and development of the company meant that more space was needed in the home office. A new building on a new twelve-acre site was purchased and occupied in 1973–74.

A new dimension of chemical brush control was developed in 1975 with the organization of the Asplundh Railroad Division. Specifically designed spray trucks (Hy-Rail) with their own rail wheels traveled on rail lines distributing chemicals to maintain railroad ROWs.

By the 1970s the company's safety program was so effective that it anticipated many of the new federal safety regulations. The Occupational Safety and Health Act (OSHA) was passed by Congress in 1971. The OSHA laws designated line-clearance work around live electrical lines as hazardous. Strict safety policies and procedures had been in effect at Asplundh long before the OSHA regulations. Bob Herder's expertise was recognized by the federal government and he helped to write the tree trimming standards.

In another effort to provide "a better way," the company responded to complaints of "noise pollution" from its chippers by creating a new machine with less noise. The new "Whisper Chipper" was quieter but did not sacrifice chipping power. Trademarked in 1973, the new chipper was also purchased by customers

Fig. 11.4 Asplundh aerial lift truck and "Whisper Chipper." Courtesy of the Asplundh Tree Expert Company.

outside the company. Since noise is known to reduce human energy, this innovation was seen as conserving energy as well as reducing pollution.

In 1978—its fiftieth year—the company listed its thirteen principal services and divisions by percentage of sales. The five most significant company activities, representing 94.2 percent of sales, were line clearance, manufacturing, underground distribution construction, chemical operations, and brush control. Eighty-eight percent of the company's activities were related to arboriculture. Despite the diversification, more than seventy-two percent of sales came directly from line clearance.

The next decade of Asplundh history (the 1980s) was characterized by new brush control initiatives; a second president (and senior executives) from the second generation of Asplundhs; major physical plant alterations and development; a new Municipal Tree Division; continued geographic expansion; and the creation of an Asplundh Family Management Program, with the debut of a third generation of Asplundh family leaders. Unfortunately, it was also in this period that the last of the founding Asplundh brothers, Lester, passed away, separating the company from the final link with its beginnings. Succeeding Griffith in 1949, he had been the second company president and served until 1982 as either president, executive vice president, or board chairman; he passed away in 1984.

In 1981 the company's Chemical Department initiated a new program for controlling growth of trees. This specialized service involved injection of growth regulators. A logical extension of earlier brush control methods, it became an additional tool to control brush for utility clients. This led to a new division in 1985 to market vegetation management products to utilities and government agencies.

In 1982 Barr Asplundh became chairman of the board and was succeeded as president by Edward K. Asplundh, son of the late Carl Asplundh Sr. Following duty in the air force, Ed began the new phase of Asplundh operations in aerial transportation and then was elected to the board of directors in 1964. He became the second company president with a business background from the Wharton School of Finance.

The company began a period of major, physical plant development in 1982. New distribution centers for tools and supplies were established in Indiana and Virginia; and chipper manufacturing was moved from the Pennsylvania Philmont Plant to Chase City, Virginia. In the following year, a plant to manufacture fiberglass booms was purchased in New Castle, Delaware.

Company growth and expansion continued in the decade of the 1980s. Of special interest to arboriculture was acquisition of fourteen tree service companies in the United States and Canada. Five of these were in British Columbia, Alberta, and Ontario; the others were based in seven states from New England to Arkansas. In 1984 the Asplundh Company became truly international in scope with the acquisition of the Molsberry Division of Reichhold Limited in Edmonton, Alberta. It became known as the Fred McComb Division of Asplundh Utility Services, Ltd. By 1990 the company had expanded farther so that it was involved in every state, with new operations in Hawaii, the Virgin Islands, the eastern Canadian provinces, and France. It was thus the first American tree company to be involved in Europe.

Need for more space for administrative staff led to a new headquarters addition in Willow Grove in 1984, to be used primarily for the Equipment Department. Continued growth in Asplundh's operations warranted a second addition, which was completed in 1989.

In 1984, reflecting the increasing interest of the company in tree care beyond utility line clearance, a Municipal Tree Department was established. Although previously engaged in urban forestry contracts, the company had made no special effort to pursue this work. With the new division, field managers would be better prepared to perform such work and compete for contracts. The first division manager, Robert Tate, had professional experience as an urban forester, educator, and consultant. The growth and success of this division demonstrated the company's continually expanding focus.

After sixty years of company management by members of the Asplundh family, it was decided that a Family Management Development Program would be initiated for the third generation of Asplundh family employees. By 1988 there were eleven family members in the program in positions ranging from foreman to sponsor. The aim of the program was to ensure that family trainees had a solid foundation in the line-clearing industry so that they would be well equipped for future responsibilities.

The seven-year program begins only after each participant has earned a college degree. Beginning as a groundman/climber, each trainee moves to crew foreman, general foreman, supervisor, and division manager before eligibility for a sponsorship position at main headquarters. This formalization of training for top executive management follows the company tradition of having all employees begin at the cutting edge of action in the field.

In 1993, in the Asplundh Company's sixty-fifth year, it expanded its operations by acquisition of certain assets of the Southeastern Public Service Company. In the following year the company was heavily involved in clearing ice storm debris from roads and power lines in 14 states with more than 1,650 crews from 25 management regions.

In 1995 Robert Asplundh retired as board chairman, and Paul Asplundh, son of the late Griffith Asplundh, was elected as the new chairman. In this same year the company gained more specialized equipment in the Pacific Northwest with the acquisition of certain assets of D & M, makers of the Slashbuster mower, enabling it to increase productivity and serve new markets.

In an effort to boost utility-related arboricultural research, Asplundh contributed $50,000 to the ISA Research Trust in 1995. Although the Asplundh Company had supported the trust for many years, with Hyland Johns serving as its chair, this donation was the beginning of a renewed support for research and a commitment to help raise much-needed research funds.

At this time, as Pacific Gas & Electric accelerated its tree trimming program in northern California, Asplundh had 200 crews from all over the United States at work at one time in order to get the job done. Also in 1996 the Asplundh One-Call went international with new One-Call centers in Ontario and Sydney, Australia. It also closed operations in France and sold its Ford dealership that year. In addition, it branched out into new utility services by acquiring Underground Utility Locating, Inc.

In 1997 Paul Asplundh retired as board chairman and Carl Asplundh Jr., oldest son of the late Carl Asplundh, was elected chairman. The company also moved to increase its role in the underground utility business by the purchase of Central Locating Services Ltd. in Syracuse, New York.

In 1998, as it celebrated its seventieth anniversary, the Asplundh Company played a major role in helping utilities restore power after the disastrous January ice storm in the northeastern United States and adjoining provinces of Quebec and Ontario. More than 580 tree crews and 100 construction crews were mobilized. More than 300 crews were sent to Canada and 30 crews plus lift trucks were airlifted by the military from North Carolina to Maine. This operation was the first of its kind in the history of the company.

S U M M A R Y

From its founding in 1928 on the eve of the Great Depression, the Asplundh Company survived the stresses of deep economic depression and war to continue growth and geographic expansion, essentially through leadership in line clearing and service to expanding public utilities. Today the company is the largest line-clearing contractor in North America and possibly the largest tree care company in the world. With more than 13,000 employees and about 13,000 pieces of rolling equipment, it operates in all of the fifty states, three Canadian provinces, and the Virgin Islands.

CHAPTER TWELVE

The Depression and the Hurricane

"Every other one of the unemployed became a tree trimmer"
—Winston Parker

In many respects, 1933 was the cruelest year of the Depression. The new Roosevelt administration had just begun, and the economy reflected a full three years of business stress following the market collapse in 1929. In the first hundred days of his first administration, President Roosevelt launched his New Deal. Among the many programs initiated were some of interest to arboriculture; those to control the gypsy moth and Dutch elm disease are reviewed in other chapters. Legislation creating the Rural Electrification Administration (REA), the Works Progress Administration (WPA), and the Civilian Conservation Corps (CCC) will be discussed here.

In those first 100 days, four billion dollars were appropriated by Congress for emergency relief of unemployment. More than one billion went to the REA, 600 million to the CCC, and 500 million to the WPA. The REA gave an enormous boost to the electrification of rural America and the power companies designed to build utility lines across the countryside. The program provided work opportunities for thousands of arborists and became in time the economic mainstay of the arborist industry, whereby it would survive not only the Depression but also the upheaval of the war that followed.

One of the earliest, most popular, and successful programs advanced in the New Deal was the Civilian Conservation Corps, popularly known as the CCC. It was created by the emergency of the Depression, it was terminated by the emergency of war. It was a significant move for both forestry and arboriculture. The government philosophy behind initiation of the CCC was more pragmatic than

Fig. 12.1 Tree moving and planting was a major emphasis in arboriculture during the Depression. Courtesy of the Davey Tree Expert Company.

ideological. Its primary goal was to keep young men out of the private labor markets, off the street corners, and out of the cities. The logical solution was conservation in the woods, on the prairies, in the fields, and even in the parks.

At its inception the CCC aimed at a population of 250,000 young men. They came from the streets and slums of teeming cities, from small towns, suburbs, and from hardscrabble farms. Despite their numbers, they were but a small part of the fifteen million unemployed at the time. The authorizing legislation called for emergency conservation work for young men from impoverished families. A voluntary organization, its members received low wages (about 20¢ per hour), lived in barracks housing, had few benefits except for food and medicine, and were located at camps in rural or forested areas. Under the administrative responsibility of the army and General Douglas MacArthur, young men worked hard physically and played in healthy settings while restoring the environment through conservation initiatives.

Though preoccupied with tree planting above other considerations, the CCC also became involved with tree disease and insect control and provided valuable service to stem the spread of Dutch elm disease, gypsy moths, and white pine blister rust. Possibly its single most successful project was the planting of 200 million trees in the shelterbelt from Texas to Canada, designed to minimize the disastrous effects of wind, snow, dust, flood, and soil erosion. The shelterbelt was a figurative wall consisting of two rows of trees planted over the prairies to avoid another dustbowl disaster like that of 1936. In addition to massive tree planting, some of which went into the urban forest, another major contribution of the CCC to arboriculture was the emergency tree clearing following the 1938 hurricane in the Northeast.

Promoted actively by President Roosevelt himself, the CCC represented a significant milestone in conservation over a ten year period from 1933–42. During this period more than 2,500,000 young men from poor homes were fed, clothed and paid by the army in 2,652 camps throughout the United States. Their work was supervised by a large number of agricultural and forestry scientists and conservationists in a wide range of constructive projects. Of special interest to arboriculture was its planting of three billion trees and creation of 800 new state parks. The extent of its contribution in 1942 dollar value was estimated at two billion dollars. After the war many CCC men were attracted to arboriculture and forestry for their careers.

The National Recovery Act (NRA) of 1933, designed to restore the economy by raising standards and prices, was called by some "economic self government." In essence it was a plan to empower each industry to make its own rules governing prices of its products or services and wages of its employees. Sought by President Roosevelt, it was passed by Congress as the centerpiece of the New Deal. The legislation authorizing the NRA required all industries to formulate a code of regulations governing working conditions for its employees.

By relaxing some provisions of the antitrust laws, the NRA allowed a fully representative trade group to balance production against consumption and stabilize prices. Its primary goal, however, was to raise workers' income, which would mean increased prices. Although it was declared unconstitutional in 1935, it was taken seriously by every industry, including commercial arboriculture.

To meet the requirements of the new NRA, those in the arborist industry began to discuss how to reach agreement on a code or plan. The act applied only to commercial arborists. It was thus of special interest to a loose organization of commercial arborists that preceded the formal establishment of the National Arborist Association (NAA) in 1938.

In 1933 the Emergency Relief Act, better known as the Works Progress Administration, or WPA, appropriated $500 million to assist 18 million men on relief. Shade tree plantings were encouraged as relief projects. These projects were selected because they provided visible objectives, were of mutual benefit not only for employment but also to the nursery industry, and resulted in the beautification of urban sites. The men involved in the WPA also reinforced control of gypsy moths and Dutch elm disease, and in the hurricane emergency of 1938, removed downed trees.

TABLE 12.1
NEW DEAL PROGRAMS AND
THEIR EFFECTS ON ARBORICULTURE

PROGRAM	FUNDING (MILLIONS)	RESULTS OR EFFECTS
Civilian Conservation Corps (CCC)	600	Planted trees
		Built parks
		Controlled tree disease and insect pests
Works Progress Administration (WPA)	500	Trimmed trees
		Lowered arborist standards
Rural Electrification Administration (REA)	1,000	Financed electrification
		Supported utilities for line clearing
National Recovery Act (NRA)	None	Threatened management in arboriculture (later declared unconstitutional)
		Required self-regulation of arboriculture

Early in the program, one of its projects involved tree trimming in public parks. To attract skilled workers the government offered wages of $1.20 per hour, which was $.50 more than that paid by even the largest companies, such as Bartlett and Davey. As a result the tree companies began losing some of their best men to the government, and could not afford to train more men and risk losing them to the government as well. It was clear to both Martin Davey and F. A. Bartlett that the federal pricing policy threatened their livelihood, already under severe financial stress because of the Depression. That was when Bartlett and Davey went to Washington together to call on President Roosevelt. The government agreed to reduce its pay scale to eighty cents per hour, only ten cents above the arborist rates of seventy cents. The differential was enough for the government to attract some skilled workers on a temporary basis, because the work was only seasonal and not recurring, but it was not sufficient to draw away most skilled men from permanent jobs. Without these trained, skilled workers neither company believed it could have survived this most difficult period of financial stress, as many tree companies did not.

Using WPA labor, many cities in the United States made surveys of existing tree plantings as the first step in management of municipal trees. The city of Cleveland received a federal grant of $179,000 for a shade tree census. Of more

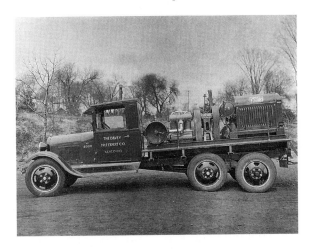

Fig. 12.2 The Davey Compressor mounted on truck, 1930. Courtesy of the ISA Archives.

than 118,000 trees surveyed, there were 105 different species, which included 5,000 elms, 20,000 maples, and 20,000 sycamores.

The newly organized WPA also began to prune trees in public parks. Unknowingly, the federal program created new problems for the tree care industry. Government bureaucracy, with its ever-changing regulations and shifting personnel, tended to lower standards through ignorance and/or neglect of tree care practices and standards. By giving untrained men an opportunity to learn tree trimming at a low level of competence, it created a large group of people who believed they were suddenly professional arborists. After the federal program was over, some of these lesser skilled men were involved in tree care work, to the detriment of the working reputation of those who were both well trained and competent.

In 1938 the NSTC created a special committee, in cooperation with the newly organized National Arborist Association, to prepare specifications and forms for establishing tree planting standards. The need arose because of the lack of training and care by many WPA workers involved in planting programs.

One of the casualties of the Depression was a reduction in federal appropriations for gypsy moth control in 1936. Fortunately, this was partly offset by aid from labor provided by the WPA and the CCC. The WPA was helpful in controlling Dutch elm disease. In 1937 the federal government created 3,000 WPA jobs for winter work in eradication of dead elms or those dying of Dutch elm disease. Out of $3,280,000 appropriated for the fiscal year, almost one-third was spent. In 1938 almost a million dollars from WPA funds was provided for winter eradication of elms deemed hazardous for spread of Dutch elm disease.

Each of the three national tree companies had its own particular problems. The Davey Company, then the largest, was especially vulnerable because its organization was the most spread out and had the most to lose. It suffered a drop in business volume from $3,000,000 to $700,000 in two years. This meant widespread layoffs, severe reduction in pay, and successive reduction of expenses at all levels. Overextended, with a serious cash flow problem, it barely survived.

With less to lose, but nevertheless with business declining, the Bartlett Company was also pressed financially. Growth was arrested; some field offices were closed; staff was cut; and employees at all levels, including the owners, took pay cuts. Programs and meetings were cut, and advertising was curtailed.

The impact of the Depression on the Asplundh Company was similar in some ways to that of the other two, but quite different on one critical point. The Asplundh Company began operations on the eve of the crash, thus was not large when the economy collapsed. It had fewer resources to help it survive, but its goal to serve public utilities exclusively gave it an advantage over the other two. Despite the Depression, electric power was growing and would grow more with new federal funding to extend power into rural areas throughout the country. Many of the smaller tree care companies did not rely on large estates for continuous work. They were able to exist by doing necessary work for less wealthy customers. Others began doing utility work.

Some unemployed men began doing the work in the early years of the Depression. Beyond the few who were good and honest, were many who just wanted enough money to survive and didn't care how they got it. Things were so bad that the public began to associate the "tree expert" with a bad arborist at best and a con man at worst.

THE GREAT NORTHEASTERN HURRICANE

Climatic disasters such as hurricanes, tornadoes, and ice storms and snowstorms have had and continue to have a significant impact on arboriculture. Space and time preclude a general review of storm damage to urban trees since arboriculture became established as a recognized practice about 1900. One of the most disastrous hurricanes in the Northeast, however, has a unique place in the history of arboriculture. It may not have been the greatest of the hurricanes, or have caused the most human suffering, but no other storm had a greater impact on urban tree populations than the great New England hurricane of 1938. It came near the end of the Depression, when organized arboriculture was still in a formative stage, and it hit one of the most heavily populated areas of North America, which probably had the most dense stands of urban trees on the continent at that time.

The Northeast hurricane of 21 September 1938, was devastating to humans, buildings, and trees. From its origin in the South Atlantic Ocean between Africa and South America, the storm took at least five days to swing west and north toward New England. In midocean on 16 September, it brushed east of the Bahama Islands on the nineteenth, passing Cape Hatteras by 7 A.M. on 21 September.

Roaring up the Atlantic coast, the winds hit Long Island broadside from the south at high tide in early afternoon. On the north coast entire houses were reported blown across Long Island Sound to pile up on the shores of the Connecticut coast. South of Boston, a steady wind was clocked at 121 miles per hour with gusts up to 186 miles per hour. Wind speeds at the top of the Empire State Building in New York City were recorded at 120 miles per hour and at the top of Mt. Washington in New Hampshire at 163 miles per hour.

Brushing eastern Pennsylvania, New Jersey, and New York, the hurricane headed north up the Connecticut River Valley, bisecting Connecticut and Massachusetts as its center moved between Vermont and New Hampshire. The Northeastern hurricane was the deadliest of any recorded up to that time. More than 600 people were killed, 30 miles of railroad beds were washed out, 5 billion board feet of timber were felled, and 10 million urban trees were downed. Preceded by four days of constant rain, the storm uprooted and destroyed trees by the hundreds in single plantings. In the Harvard University Forest in central Massachusetts, only 340 of 2,200 planted trees (15 percent) remained undamaged. At the Arnold Arboretum of Harvard University 1,500 trees were downed.

In New York City more than 21,000 park and street trees were destroyed, with an estimated cost of replacement and repair in 1939 dollars of almost $1,500,000. Probably hardest hit was Long Island, which was in the direct path of the hurricane center.

In New Jersey the storm created such a disturbance that the New Jersey Bell Telephone Company hired 500 extra operators. Following the storm, the company funded the maintenance of 5,000 newly planted trees to see that they were properly trimmed, staked, and straightened. The damage in Newark, New Jersey, required the work of 600 men to clear the streets and roads of downed trees. Despite such a massive effort, the city was still clearing away trees that were leaning on buildings five weeks after the storm.

Damage from trees falling on buildings was also a serious problem. A police/fire report in one New Jersey town listed thirty-five buildings so damaged. To remove the trees, the city had to increase its tree crews by 261 percent. A tally of the trees down in Irvington, New Jersey, showed the following: 560 were street trees, 182 trees fell on houses, 121 were in backyards, 52 in school yards, and 17 in parks.

Somewhere between ten and twenty percent of the shade tree population in New England was reported ruined or damaged by the storm. Including both woodland and urban areas, 150 million trees were said to be destroyed or injured in southern New England alone. In urban areas about one million large shade trees were believed to be affected.

It was widely believed that about fifty percent of the trees that were lost had their roots torn out of water-soaked soils. It was also noted that ninety percent of the badly damaged trees had internal decay. On a bright note, however, one survey noted that ninety percent of cavity-filled trees resisted stem breakage.

The damage to trees was most serious where the entire tree was dislodged or large sections were torn or broken. Whole trees (some extremely large) were uprooted and laid prone, their roots exposed. Others were partially uprooted and leaning, often on wires, poles, houses, and garages. Some trees were broken at the trunk or had large sections or branches sheared off. More often than not, these separations were associated with decay, old wounds (including both root and trunk rot), or high angle branching.

From surveys of the damage across the towns and cities of the region, a general consensus emerged. Trees of all kinds were damaged in the hurricane, but there were significant differences between species. The species that had the most damage on a per-tree basis were those with well-known structural defects, such as poplars, willows, soft maples, and Siberian elms. The single species with the greatest amount of loss was the elm. Hundreds of thousands of American elms, with sixty percent of many shade tree populations on streets and highways, were destroyed. This was attributed mostly to their vast numbers, advanced age, and large size. To these factors can be added their massive spread, high angled branching, shallow roots, and natural occurrence on low, wet sites.

Of the conifers, white pine was the most severely damaged, and spruce less so. It came as no surprise that the harder-wooded deciduous trees—such as oak, hickory, and beech—did well. Sugar maples in southern New England experienced little breakage, but were damaged by much uprooting. In northern Vermont, however, greatest damage was reported on tapped sugar maples. Twenty percent of those tapped for sugar were blown down, and of all downed maples an estimated seventy-five percent had been tapped. Downed maples also experienced masses of infestation by tent caterpillars. In general shade tree and ornamental tree losses from the hurricane were greater in built-up community centers than in open countryside.

The business of cutting wood with hand tools was a monstrous task in which thousands of men were involved. In New Haven it took three days to clear the streets and open lanes, without even disposing of the wood. It took another three months to complete the removal of all tree and wire hazards. At the end of that period there were still thousands of hazardous trees needing attention.

The available labor was quickly mobilized to remove the hurricane debris. Large crews of men were required, and they came not only from government sources such as the WPA and the CCC, but also from private arborist companies. Both Bartlett and Asplundh had large numbers of men involved.

TABLE 12.2

FACTS ABOUT THE GREAT NORTHEAST HURRICANE OF 1938

ITEM	NOTES
Origin	South Atlantic Ocean
General path	North, from east North Carolina to New England
Central path over land	Western New England and Connecticut River Valley
Wind speed	60 to 180 mph
Areas affected	Coastal North Carolina, Virginia, and Maryland; eastern New Jersey, Pennsylvania, and New York; all of New England Areas worst affected were Long Island, New York, and Providence, Rhode Island
Trees affected	More than 5 billion board feet of timber trees damaged; many more urban trees damaged (10 million in Massachusetts alone). More than 1 million trees destroyed. Total value of loss (in 1938 dollars) was greater than $100 million.
People affected	30 to 40 million (estimated) were affected in some way; 600 known fatalities
Total losses	Incalculable; probably in the billions (1938 dollars)

So much work was being done by inexperienced men that the Massachusetts Tree Wardens and Foresters Association held a special meeting to call the attention of state officials to damage being done by inexperienced workers without proper supervision. The association finally stabilized the situation by making it clear that much of the needed work was required by law to be done under the supervision of tree wardens.

The Bartlett Tree Company hired an entire CCC camp from mid-Maine (250 men including the company commander) because they had been trained in rope climbing. These men were distributed throughout New England and received regular wages and living expenses. The company had 1,500 men clearing hurricane debris from state highways. On the Hunnewell Estate in Wellesley, Massachusetts, fifty men were involved in clearing the massive destruction of trees in the private arboretum. This arboretum had one of the finest collections of conifers in North America.

In New York City, with 2,285 stumps to remove, the federal government assigned 500 men from the WPA to supplement the city tree crews. Even after the trees and stumps were removed, the city still needed another $100,000 to repair sidewalks uprooted by the trees that had been blown down. The WPA received $539,000 from Congress for cleanup of downed trees in the hurricane area, and also funded elm sanitation crews to remove dead trees and those dying of Dutch elm disease.

Crews of WPA and CCC workers were called to clear brush from roads and near buildings. Another 40,000 WPA men and 40 CCC camps in the area were assigned to fire hazard reduction, with the Forest Service coordinating activities.

THE EASTERN SHADE TREE CONFERENCE

Arborists felt it was important to restore the urban tree populations and reduce their vulnerability to future storms. There were clearly lessons to be learned for restoration and rehabilitation of what would be known later as the urban forest. To assess the damage and learn for the future, a special conference of tree-oriented individuals was organized. The organization committee consisted of Dr. B. O. Dodge, pathologist of the New York Botanical Garden; Dr. E. P. Felt, director of the Bartlett Tree Research Laboratories; and W. O. Filley, forester for the Connecticut Agriculture Experiment Station.

The conference met 8–9 December 1938, at the New York Botanical Garden. Filley was elected chairman and presided at all sessions. Dr. Rush Marshall of the USDA Division of Forest Pathology served as conference secretary. Marshall was a past president of NSTC. It was decided at the outset to publish the proceedings for the benefit of individuals and organizations that were interested in tree care work but could not be present. A ninety-nine page proceedings was published in March 1939 as *Eastern Shade Tree Conference* and is still available at the New York Botanical Garden.

Filley outlined the principal purpose of the conference as a broad discussion of hurricane damage to shade trees. He noted that the reason for the conference was the emergency caused by the hurricane, that the damage under consideration was confined to New England and neighboring states, and that this conference would be a single event with no permanent organization. Of the twenty-six presentations made, eleven were directly related to the hurricane, four concerned tree disease, three were on insect problems, and eight were on other aspects of shade tree care.

The conference was supported financially by eight contributing patrons, of whom little is known, except for F. A. Bartlett and Frederick Law Olmsted of Boston, descendant of the eminent Olmsted of landscape fame. There were 208 registered attendants, 14 of whom were women. Of the nine states and districts represented, only Ohio, Michigan, and Washington, D.C. were beyond the hurricane zone. Dr. Dressel of Michigan, NSTC president, and Executive Secretary L. C. Chadwick of Ohio were present. Also represented were university and college professors; botanical and tree scientists from private, state, and federal research institutions; and representatives from city, state, and federal parks.

Although the Eastern Shade Tree Conference was not an official function of the National Shade Tree Conference (NSTC), it was definitely initiated by those who were early leaders in the NSTC. For all practical purposes these same leaders were largely responsible for seeing that the impact of the hurricane on shade and ornamental trees was recorded. The New York Botanical Garden also played an important role by hosting the conference and publishing its proceedings.

H U R R I C A N E   L E S S O N S

This catastrophic storm in an area with great urban density of trees and utility wires made it clear that large towering trees constituted a serious liability for future storms. The lesson could not be clearer. Future plantings should deemphasize planting of large tree species on urban sites, or at least limit them to sites without overhead wires. New selections for future planting would include trees less liable to disease, decay, and breakage. The internal conditions of individual trees were noted for vulnerability to storm breakage. Both scientists and arborists were in agreement that basal stem or root decay could be a great menace in future wind damage.

From L. C. Chadwick's survey of hurricane effects on shade trees, it was learned that both oaks and beeches were quite wind resistant, that cabling saved many trees from serious damage, and that newly planted trees that were strongly and properly guyed survived, while others did not. As expected, full and thick tree crowns with great wind resistance were more damaged than those with lesser crowns.

The hurricane was the prime test for wind resistance, calling attention to the need for care in site planning and selection of trees for root depth at maturity. It focused on the need for greater care in pruning to avoid internal decay in stems. It reemphasized the logic of not planting trees directly under wires, and warned again of the liabilities in curbside plantings between sidewalk and road. In a later paper Colonel Dodge of Windham, Massachusetts, stressed four points that summarize some of the principal ways for arborists to prevent or minimize future storm damage: (1) a routine, scheduled pruning of all large trees near wires or residential property; (2) cabling of weakened crotches and unsupported large limbs; (3) reinforcement of split trunks with steel rods, such as wood screws; and (4) feeding to promote growth and maintain vigor.

As devastating as it was, there were some positive aspects to the hurricane. It swept away much that was diseased, decayed, dead, or weak. It also provided an unusual opportunity for enterprising arborists to assess how the damage occurred and to avoid mistakes in future plantings. It provided a good chance to study root systems and growth patterns, and relate these to soil conditions. This hurricane foreshadowed the demise of very large trees in urban plantings and motivated arborists to create storm emergency readiness plans.

SUMMARY

The Depression had a generally adverse impact on arboriculture, but also occurred when power-line installation was on the increase. Despite a depressed market for all other kinds of arboriculture, line clearing for utility companies became the mainstay of the arborist industry, supported by federal funding for rural electrification.

CHAPTER THIRTEEN

Dutch Elm Disease

"A mysterious dying of elms" —Dina Spirenburg,
early Dutch plant pathologist, 1918

Dutch elm disease (DED) is the most serious tree disease in the history of North American arboriculture. Unknown to science or arboriculture, this new disease was detected in Western Europe immediately after the end of World War I in 1918. Its origin and cause unknown, it progressed over most of Europe, including England, over the following two decades. It decimated both rural and urban elms in Europe and was found in North America for the first time in 1930.

NATURE OF THE DISEASE

The causal organism of Dutch elm disease (*Graphium ulmi* Schwarz) was first isolated in 1921 by Maria Beatrice Schwarz, a graduate student in plant pathology, but her results were neither universally accepted beyond the Netherlands nor acclaimed within. As a result, progress on disease control was delayed for almost a decade. The work of Schwarz was repeated and confirmed in 1929 by another graduate student, Christine Buisman. Two years later a graduate student in entomology, J. J. Franzen, proved that two species of European elm bark beetle were carriers of the causal fungus. Beginning in 1929 Buisman began to seek elms that might resist the disease. Her expanded program included all known elm species in the world and in time was most successful.

In addition to her work on selection for disease resistance, Buisman began a thorough and continuous study of the disease that continued to her death in 1935.

Fig. 13.1 Diseased American elm in New Jersey (1933). Courtesy of the department of plant pathology, Cornell University.

In addition to her confirming the cause of the disease in 1929, she discovered the perfect stage of the fungus, renaming it *Ceratostomella ulmi*, and cleared up confusion over other, similar elm diseases caused by fungi and bacteria. Recently the causal fungus has been renamed *Ophiostoma ulmi* (Schwarz) Nannfeldt. From 1928–35, in a series of publications she discussed the inoculation of young elms, susceptibility and resistance of various species of elms, the disease distribution in other countries in Europe as well as in the Unites States, and the advisability of developing resistant elm strains from Asiatic species.

At the time of her death in 1935, she was at the height of her productivity and was clearly the foremost authority on DED. Her work on resistant elms was taken over by another plant pathologist, Dr. Johanna Went, who began a new breeding program to find resistant hybrids. In later years, this program reached its highest productivity and effectiveness under an eminent forest geneticist, Hans M. Heybroek.

DED is characterized by pronounced foliar wilt resulting from the inability of water to move upward through vessels. The fungus pathogen is carried to healthy trees by elm bark beetle vectors that breed in diseased trees, where the fungus produces spores. Produced in a sticky matrix in the insect galleries, the fungus

Fig. 13.2 Gallery formed by the elm bark beetle vector of Dutch elm disease. Courtesy of the department of plant pathology, Cornell University.

spores stick to the adult insects as they emerge. The beetles then feed on healthy elms by chewing through the bark and into the wood of twig crotches and small stems. As the insects feed, the fungus spores sticking to the outsides of their bodies are rubbed off in the newly exposed wounded elm tissue, where they germinate and colonize the elm vessels. As the fungus develops in the elm tissues it produces enzymes and toxins that interact with biochemicals of the host tissue. The vessels become impaired as water conduits and the affected stems die when water is deficient. Weakened and newly dead stems are then colonized by elm bark beetles that invade the tissues in the bark and wood for breeding. The new brood of adults contact new fungus spores in the wood and bark and carry them to new healthy trees when they feed. Thus, the beetles pick up the fungus in breeding and deposit it in feeding.

INTRODUCTION TO THE UNITED STATES

American arborists and scientists had viewed the rise and spread of Dutch elm disease in Europe with grave concern, anticipating ultimate introduction to the

United States. Several warnings were given to the American public as early as 1928 by those who had seen the destruction of the European elms or had followed progress of the disease across Europe. Several Americans went to Europe to observe the disease, including F. A. Bartlett; Dr. J. S. Boyce of Yale University; and Dr. Haven Metcalf, chief forest pathologist in the USDA. Their independently issued reports left no doubt of the danger that this disease posed for the extensive urban stands of elm here.

As one of the leading arborists of the period, Bartlett was the first to sound the alarm for arboriculture. North American pathologists and entomologists were concerned not only for urban elms, but for those of the forest as well. By 1930, all of the above were closely involved with the new National Shade Tree Conference (NSTC). Thus, when the disease was first reported in North America in the summer of 1930 at Cleveland, Ohio, both arborists and scientists were keenly aware that the dreaded menace to the elms was now a reality; and the NSTC became the earliest platform for informing the arborists in North America of what was ahead.

The first known case of the disease in North America was found not by a scientist but by a perceptive and eminent arborist—Charles F. Irish of Cleveland. His company's illustrated poster, dated 3 July 1930, was the first published report of the disease in the United States. As general manager of the forthcoming National Shade Tree Conference to be held in Cleveland about a month hence, Irish had a dynamic message for the convening arborists.

Later, a short publication by the Ohio Experiment Station noted that Dr. Curtis May had examined diseased elms in both Cleveland and Cincinnati and had isolated the causal fungus. Dr. Buisman of the Netherlands, who was traveling in the United States at that time, confirmed identification of the pathogen isolated by May as the causal agent for Dutch elm disease. Appearing before the NSTC of that year, May noted that his organization, the Ohio Agriculture Experiment Station, had no funds available to look for other diseased trees, and appealed to the conference for help in detecting new cases of disease. During the following year (1931) four more infected elms were found in Cleveland, but none in Cincinnati. Subsequent scouting in 1932 revealed no more infected elms and the disease was believed to be eradicated in both places. In 1933, however, another diseased tree was found in Cleveland and two more were discovered in 1934.

When the disease first appeared in Ohio, the Office of Forest Pathology in the USDA cooperated with the Ohio Agricultural Experiment Station at Wooster to eradicate it. Infected trees were promptly cut and burned, and with federal help, extensive statewide scouting was undertaken to determine the distribution of the disease. More infected trees were found in Cleveland in 1935, but no additional ones were reported there by the fall of 1936.

At first it was not understood how the disease had come to America from Europe. Because of the U.S. quarantine, there had been no importation of nursery stock from Europe since 1912 except by special permit, and it was not considered likely that this could be the source of infection. But European elm burl logs, known as Carpathian elms, were highly prized by American furniture manufacturers for veneer stock, and large quantities had been imported on an annual basis in the 1920s. One report indicated that these log shipments arrived as partial payment for unresolved World War I loans to France, but this is not certain. What is certain, however, is that they were the means for the introduction of the DED fungus and the ensuing epidemic that would decimate the elm populations of both the United States and Canada.

Following the discovery of a new and heavy infection in Maplewood, New Jersey, a few miles west of New York City, in 1933, a new shipment of elm burl logs from France was intercepted at the port of New York. The Dutch elm pathogen, *O. ulmi*, was isolated from these logs; and two European bark beetles (*Scolytus scolytus* [Fab.]; *S. multistriatus* [Marsh]), notorious agents of elm disease transmission in Europe, were identified. The fungus was isolated from individuals of both beetle species.

In the same year (1933), additional shipments of elm logs bearing the DED fungus and beetle carriers were intercepted at Norfolk, Virginia; Baltimore; and New Orleans. With these interceptions the pattern of introduction became clear, especially because all of the infected trees were located near points of transportation such as wharves, railroads, and veneer mills. The final evidence confirming the fungus introduction on elm logs came in 1934 with the discovery of a diseased elm near the piers in Norfolk where elm logs from Europe had been unloaded from ships.

In cooperation with the Department of Agriculture, immediate steps were taken to eliminate the source of inoculum from abroad by the Bureau of Plant Quarantine. A quarantine directive (Quarantine N. 170) was issued, effective 21 October 1933, regulating importation of logs. This law forbade the entry of elm logs except by special permit, and then only when the bark had been removed prior to shipment. It also forbade importation of other parts of elm plants, but unfortunately did not exclude elm wood products.

After Cleveland and Cincinnati in 1930, the third independent infection area around New York City in 1933 quickly became known as the most serious of all. The first diseased tree found in that area that yielded the DED fungus died in late summer of 1932, if not earlier.

By the fall of 1933, 677 diseased trees had been found around New York City in three states (New York, New Jersey, and Connecticut). Of this number 628 were within 15 miles of the Hudson River and New York Harbor, and extended from Paterson, New Jersey to New Brunswick, New Jersey; Staten Island; western Long Island; and the southern half of Westchester County, New York. A single infected tree was found just across the border on the Cushman Estate at Glenville, Connecticut, in the late fall of 1933. For the next ten years disease spreading from the New York area would become the focal point of research and control efforts in the United States.

Additional independent infections were later discovered in 1933 and 1934 at Fort McHenry in Baltimore, Norfolk, and Indianapolis. By the fall of 1934, it was clear that importation of infected elm logs from Europe was responsible for introduction of what would become the most devastating urban tree disease in North America.

Early Spread in the United States

From the infections in Cleveland; Cincinnati; Baltimore; Cumberland, Maryland; and Norfolk, no additional diseased trees were found in either 1936 or 1937. New infections were discovered, however, in Athens, Ohio, and Wiley Ford, West Virginia, in 1937. The infection rate in Indianapolis had increased steadily from four in 1934 to 32 in 1937, indicating the potential for a serious new infection. This had become the principal source of new infections in the new region in the Midwest, from which the fungus would be spread west into Illinois and north into Michigan and Wisconsin.

By then it was clear that overland spread of the disease was not being checked, despite eradication efforts. The heaviest infection, centering around New York City, had spread considerably to include 7,500 square miles in the tri-state area. DED was firmly established in the whole northern half of New Jersey, the western half of Long Island, and in increasingly larger areas of New York state and Connecticut.

Twelve years after the disease had been discovered in the northeastern United States, 65,000 diseased trees had been discovered and removed in an area of 12,000 square miles. This was the equivalent of 5.4 diseased trees per square mile. During this period almost six million additional dead, weakened, and woodland elms that could have facilitated spread of the disease had been destroyed. This aspect of the sanitation program was largely responsible for the relatively small number of infected trees discovered in 1942. The progress made in isolated areas was an example of the value of eradication measures. A report was issued in 1943 that no diseased elms had been found in Cincinnati since 1930; at Brunswick, Maryland, and Portsmouth, Virginia, since 1935; and in Norfolk since 1936.

Fig. 13.3 North American spread and distribution of Dutch elm disease. Courtesy of the department of plant pathology, Cornell University.

Once DED was known to be well established in the Northeast in 1933, the federal government became active in a massive control project, unfortunately called "eradication," and established a federal DED laboratory in Morristown under the direction of Dr. Curtis May. This laboratory was unique in that it was established in an abandoned "speakeasy" (an illegal barroom during the era of Prohibition). According to May the DED fungus itself was isolated "at the bar," lined with laboratory petri plates of potato dextrose agar. Subsequently, entomologists from the USDA Bureau of Entomology and Plant Quarantine joined the pathology team under May. Relocated to more respectable lodgings at a later date, the DED laboratory was active in Morristown until the financial strains of World War II curtailed financing for DED control. Established to confirm new cases of disease by culture, the laboratory carried out a variety of experiments on the fungus too numerous to review here. One of its important discoveries was the ability of the DED fungus to produce easily discernible, asexual fruiting bodies (coremia) on elm bark and wood. Above all the DED laboratory became the headquarters of the ambitious federal program to eradicate the disease from North America.

With the advent of war, continued federal support on a regular basis was not possible. The expenditure of federal funds for removal of infected trees was absolutely prohibited sometime before 1945. A summary of the status of Dutch elm disease in 1943 indicated that up until 1940, when funds and labor were still available, definite progress in the eradication program was being made. But with curtailment of funds, reduction in efficiency of crews, and the shortage of labor, only a limited program was possible. Consequently eradication work in 1941 and 1942 was hopelessly inadequate for thorough coverage of infected areas.

DED in Canada

The disease was expected in Canada after introduction to the United States and measures were taken to prevent its entry. Despite preventive efforts, however, the disease was found for the first time by Dr. Rene Pomerleau of the Dominion Forest Service in 1944 in the St. Lawrence River Valley, first at Sorel and later near Lake Peter about fifty miles upstream of Montreal.

The infected area was approximately forty miles long. Twenty-eight infected trees were found and more were expected with more intensive scouting in 1945. An intensive scouting was undertaken in Nova Scotia, New Brunswick, and Ontario. These examinations revealed the disease to be widespread and well established over an area in Quebec 160 miles long and 90 miles wide, but was not yet found in other provinces.

Since the European elm bark beetle, so effective in the United States in spreading the disease fungus, was not known to be in Canada, Canadians were optimistic about possibly eradicating the disease. This hope would be short-lived, however, because the native American elm bark beetle was present and able to spread the fungus in a somewhat similar way.

Postwar Spread

Following the war, with no federal eradication program in force in the U.S. for more than five years, the disease was able to spread unchecked. By 1946 it had moved west through Pennsylvania and overlapped into the Ohio River Valley within the range of another lethal elm disease known as elm yellows (elm phloem necrosis). The combination of the two lethal diseases was conducive to even more massive and rapid destruction than seen before. Elm yellows, then thought to be caused by a virus (now known to be caused by a phytoplasma), killed elms in advance of Dutch elm disease, which provided an enormous substrate of elm tissue conducive to enhanced breeding of insect vectors. By 1946 it was clear that Dutch elm disease was moving northward in New York state toward Canada, as infection from Canada moved southward into northern New York and Vermont. By this time it had already spread south, probably from Ohio and Indiana to Kentucky and Tennessee.

In 1945 the major infected areas included larger areas of New York, Pennsylvania, New Jersey, Connecticut, and Massachusetts. Small isolated infections were active in Delaware, Maryland, West Virginia, and Indiana.

By 1946 the disease had spread to Ontario from Quebec, and secondary introductions of the disease developed by a gradual northward spread from the United States over a wide geographic front from 1947 to 1975. The earliest infections in Ontario from the United States were reported in 1950 at two separate points, one contiguous to Niagara in northern New York and the other in the extreme south of the province near Michigan (Detroit-Windsor). The earlier infections probably developed by spread from the New York City area, and the later ones from Midwestern sources in Ohio.

By 1957 a new area of disease had developed in the Maritime Provinces as the fungus spread northward through Maine into New Brunswick (Houlton-Woodstock area). The most recent point of disease spread from the United States occurred in 1975 in Manitoba, probably as a northern extension of the diseased area in Minnesota (Red River Valley). The occurrence of the disease in Canada from these different points representing individual introductions was complemented by spread of the fungus between infection areas, thereby shrinking the unaffected areas. In 1981, DED was found in Saskatchewan, and by 1983, it was known to be in six Canadian provinces.

By 1968 the disease had crossed the Great Plains of the central United States and spread into the mountain states of Colorado and Idaho beyond the range of native elms. The far western stage of the disease (1970–80) was marked by its occurrence in each of the northern Rocky Mountain states and its spread beyond the last mountain barriers to all of the Pacific Coast states, occurring in the coastal areas of San Francisco and Portland, and inland in Washington. Occurrence of the disease beyond the range of native elms into arid and semiarid areas was a significant development in its history.

DAMAGE AND IMPORTANCE IN NORTH AMERICA

When DED was first found in the United States, the native American elm was the most threatened of the various elm species here. The largest, finest, and most planted of our elms, its natural range extended from the Atlantic Ocean to the foothills of the Rocky Mountains, and from the watersheds of the St. Lawrence and Ottawa Rivers in Canada to the Gulf of Mexico. Within this range were five other species of native American elms, but none was as vulnerable as *Ulmus americana*, the urban elm. In the mid-1930s, it was without question the most heavily planted and most highly valued of shade trees in eastern North America, and was commercially important as a timber tree in the Midwest and upper South.

Its greatest value, however, was as a street and landscape tree in both large cities and small towns throughout the United States and Canada; it also made up thousands of monocultural stands in every region of eastern and midwestern North America, except the Deep South. In the Northeast, especially in New England where some specimens were literally older than the nation, millions of dollars of real estate value depended on its health and well being.

The decimation of the elm populations of cities, towns, and roads was accompanied by tremendous financial losses and many new expenditures. The cost of removing dead and dying trees was enormous; there was a negative impact on real estate values, and the dollar value of elms decreased significantly. Additional costs included disease control efforts, new plantings, and research and education.

When the serious nature of the disease threat first became apparent to the federal governments of both the United States and Canada, action occurred on several fronts, including quarantine legislation and funding for detection and containment. Left to themselves for the decade following World War II, individual states and provinces grappled with detection, education, regulation, research, and control. For the most part, however, the twin burdens of losses and control efforts fell on local cities and towns, at great public expense.

IMPACT ON ARBORICULTURE

On the positive side economically, the DED was an opportunity for unemployment relief during the Depression, when the federal government appropriated millions of dollars and hired thousands of men in its abortive eradication program. Of much greater significance, however, was the stimulus given to the green industry by the enormous need for arborist services, because nurseries, botanical gardens and arboreta needed chemicals, machines, and trees for replanting. Because the disease had spread far and wide in the Northeast and Midwest by the time the control effort got under way on a large scale, it became the centerpiece of significant expansion of arborist services to cities, towns, institutions, and homes. With more far-reaching consequences than the immediate loss of tree populations was the influence of DED in emphasizing the deplorable state of urban trees in most cities and towns. This led ultimately to the rise of the urban forestry movement following federal legislation to stimulate more large-scale tree planting. DED also stimulated education and research.

Disease Control

Efforts to control Dutch elm disease were essentially blind until the cause of the disease and the way it was spread were finally established ten years after its first appearance in Europe. Thus, during that first decade there were no control practices carried out with serious intent. During this period early removal of diseased trees and pruning of isolated infected branches probably had a small, temporary effect on slowing the spread of the disease or saving individual trees.

After 1929, however, with the cause established, sanitation of diseased trees became imperative, and the Dutch began a search for resistant trees. A few years later when the role of bark beetles in serving as vectors for the pathogen was proven, the role of sanitation was broadened to include elimination of diseased wood to eliminate the vectors as well as the pathogen. This was the situation until well into the 1930s, when the pathogen was introduced into North America. From this point on, except for resistance in host species, the initiative on disease control passed to North America.

The history of methods for disease control is reviewed here in the order in which different methods were pursued vigorously or were accepted. In some cases the early use of a control method was abandoned as hopeless until new information and more research gave it more promise. These methods include (1) sanitation to eliminate or reduce sources of fungus inoculum and potential insect vectors; (2) selecting and breeding elms for varieties resistant to the pathogen; (3) suppression of vectors to minimize probabilities for infection, including spraying of insecticides; (4) severance of grafted roots to prevent fungus transmission; (5) pruning to eliminate fungus infections; and (6) use of systemic fungicides to prevent infection or enhance recovery. Other methods proposed for control were either ineffective or were not tested sufficiently for recommendation. The use of toxic chemicals to kill elms to prevent vector breeding, use of pheromones to trap vectors, and use of biological control agents against pathogen or vectors all show promise for future use. No single method, however, or even a combination of methods has been completely effective in disease control, except for limited numbers of trees or for short periods of time.

Sanitation

Sanitation alone was later demonstrated in many studies to be significantly effective in reducing probability of infection, and in slowing the rate of disease increase. Of greater significance now is its role as a baseline control method that enhances the success of every other effective control method in reducing or limiting infection pressure, by keeping local populations of pathogen and vector at low levels. Beginning in the late 1940s, used in comparison against, or in tandem with insecticide spraying of DDT, it was used and abused amidst heated controversy over the next two decades of municipal control of DED.

Sanitation alone was successful in eliminating disease altogether (eradication) or in limiting spread of the disease when first detected in new elm populations. Even after both pathogen and vectors were well established in elm-rich areas, the disease incidence was often reduced by a significant degree through sanitation alone. It soon became clear, however, that in places where the elm is native as in eastern North America, complete sanitation was physically and economically impossible, so that inoculum pressure ultimately increased beyond control, and other methods were required for direct disease control to supplement sanitation. When such methods were used, in addition to sanitation, their effect was enhanced locally by good sanitation, and often failed in its absence. In practice, this has been true for every additional measure of direct control considered effective and acceptable.

Spraying

By 1946 the use of DDT (dichloro-diphenol-trichloroethane) to control elm bark beetle populations was only in the experimental stage, but seemed promising. By the early 1950s it was being used regularly, following recommendations by the USDA for spraying healthy elms—with one dormant application before leaves emerged, and a second foliage application after the first formed leaves had reached normal size.

When the disease was in the early stages in new areas, DDT was very effective in preventing infection, especially when used with careful, complete, and timely sanitation practices. Throughout the 1950s DDT was used by arborists in the Midwest, but its efficacy was questionable in eastern areas where beetle populations were increasing beyond the range of control.

Despite heavy and intensive spraying, the vector-fungus population pressure favoring DED was too much for large-scale protection of healthy elm populations, even with spraying and sanitation combined. It also became apparent that with the many uncertainties connected with spraying (i.e., weather, psychological factors), the requisite time and care were conducive to reasonable protection only for relatively small numbers of trees. In addition, the immense volume of spray chemical then used for an entire population of elms would soon be considered prohibitive for ecological reasons.

Fig. 13.4 Spraying of elms to prevent infection by elm bark beetles. Courtesy of Larry Schreiber, USDA-ARS.

TABLE 13.1

EARLY DUTCH-ELM-RESISTANT TREES DEVELOPED
IN THE NETHERLANDS (*Source: Holmes 1976*)

YEAR	RESISTANT ELM	ORIGIN
1937	Christine Buisman elm	Selection
1948	Bea Schwarz elm	Selection
1961	Commelin elm	Selection
1963	Groeneveld elm	Selection
1975	Lobel elm	Hybrid
1975	Plantijn elm	Hybrid
1975	Dodoens elm	Hybrid

DED-Resistant Elms

Buisman's research in Holland was the beginning of a long and productive program to determine the relative susceptibility of different elm species. Dr. Johanna Went, Buisman's successor, began hybridizing elms in 1937 in search of greater resistance. Following the war the Dutch program was headed by a young forest geneticist, Dr. Hans Heybroek, who would take the program to its greatest success with the production of several useful resistant elm species and hybrids.

Meanwhile, Dr. Donald Welch of Cornell University was trying to find resistant American elms. By the mid-1950s Welch had produced some resistant elms following successive inoculations over several years, but was unable to obtain any resistance in resulting progeny. In continuing Welch's work at Cornell, using long-tested resistant trees, Wayne Sinclair of Cornell established an ambitious program for further selection and propagation in the 1970s, but abandoned the project when his elms resistant to DED were found to be highly susceptible to the elm yellows phytoplasma.

By 1973 a resistant hybrid between Japanese and Siberian elm had been developed by Dr. Eugene Smalley and associates at the University of Wisconsin. Known as "Sapporo Autumn Gold Elm," its early form resembled that of the American elm more than other resistant trees produced to that time. In 1975 another resistant elm known as the "Urban Elm" was released by the USDA Shade Tree and Ornamentals Laboratory in Ohio. It was a cross between Siberian elm and a resistant Dutch selection.

TABLE 13.2

DUTCH-ELM-RESISTANT TREES DEVELOPED IN NORTH AMERICA

YEAR	RESISTANT ELM	PARENTAL GEOGRAPHIC ORIGIN	PARENTAL GENETIC ORIGIN
1973	Sapporo autumn gold	Asia	Hybrid (*Japonica pumila*)
1976	Urban elm	Europe and Asia	Hybrid (*Carpinifolia pumila*)
1985	Liberty elm	North America	Hybrid (*Americana*)

After many years of intensive research, supported by the Elm Research Foundation in Harrisville, New Hampshire, a new American elm highly resistant to DED and closely resembling the American elm was available by 1985. Known as the "Liberty Elm," it was produced in quantity and has been distributed extensively in North America. Later testing by Dr. Denny Townsend of the U.S. National Arboretum found several new disease-tolerant American elms; one of the best is the Valley Forge elm, which commemorates an American historical site.

Repellents

Various chemicals, repellent or toxic to the principal insect carrier (*Scolytus multistriatus*) of the DED pathogen, were reported to deter some activities of this vector. As early as 1941, reproduction of the European elm bark beetle in elm logs or standing trees was prevented by ax-frill application of copper sulphate and sodium arsenite solutions to newly infected trees. By 1974 several other chemicals were shown to prevent such reproduction when injected or pressure-injected into elms in early stages of disease. These included sodium arsenite; potassium iodide; cacodylic acid; and the systemic insecticide, MST. These chemicals were more effective in killing healthy trees on woodland sites—rendering them unavaiable for beetle infestation—than in diseased counterparts because of better chemical movement in healthy trees.

The Systemic Trial

About 1965 the Shell Oil Company developed a powerful chemical named bidrin for use as a systemic insecticide against the bark beetle vectors of the Dutch elm disease fungus. Having a high mammalian toxicity, its introduction into trees required extreme safety. Special precautions were taken to protect applicators and prevent escape of the chemical into the uncontrolled environment. Applicators were required to wear protective clothing and face shields and leave no containers unattended at the tree sites. To prevent the chemical from coming into contact with anything but the container, the injection device, and the tree, the Mauget Company devised a clever injection device. The chemical was sealed under pressure in small plastic containers. Sharpened steel tubes hammered radially into the outer woody tissue of trees around the main stem up to four feet above the ground were used as conduits for introducing the chemical into the water conducting tissue. Released under pressure when the seal was broken by attachment to the open end of the protruding tubes, the chemical moved quickly into the tree.

Good distribution of the chemical upward in the tree was favored by pressure from the container and normal upward flow of water in the wood. Because an excessive amount of chemical was toxic to the trees, great care had to be exercised in calculating an effective but safe dosage. Elaborate formulations and tables were made based on estimated volume of vessel-carrying capacity in stems. The chemical was effective in preventing beetle feeding to the extent that it became distributed in small twigs, but it had little or no influence in deterring the fungus. Once introduced into the tree there was always the question of whether the beetle, while deterred and ultimately killed, might not have transmitted the fungus before dying, In the end, bidrin was considered too "hot" to handle with excessive risk to humans, the trees, and the surrounding environment, and it was abandoned.

TABLE 13.3

CHRONOLOGY OF MEASURES TO CONTROL DUTCH ELM
DISEASE, BY ORIGIN AND PRACTICE

PRACTICE	FIRST RECOGNIZED	FIRST PRACTICED	WIDESPREAD USE IN NORTH AMERICA
Sanitation	1919, Europe	1919, Europe	1938
Spraying	1946, North America	1946, North America	1954
Resistance	1929, Europe	1936, Europe	1960s
Root graft severance	1960,* North America	1960, North America	1965
Surgical pruning	1920, Europe	1946, North America	1972
Chemical injection	1942, North America	1972, North America	1976

*Transmission of disease by root graft was discovered.

Root Graft Severance

With the discovery in 1960 that the causal fungus of DED could be transmitted from diseased to healthy trees by grafted roots, hopes for disease control became more complicated. Unfortunately, nothing was then known about how often root grafting occurred either in natural stands of elm or in those lining streets and walkways. This may explain why little or nothing was done to prevent this kind of disease spread for at least twenty years.

Elm yellows disease in the Midwest was killing street elms progressively in rows of trees that were between twenty and thirty feet apart. Intensive research was also being done at that time on oak wilt, a vascular disease very similar to Dutch elm disease. The research showed that root graft was its primary means of spread, and that spread could be minimized or halted by mechanical severance of roots. This led to the discovery that many elms within forty feet of one another were often linked by grafted roots, and that mechanical severance could also be used to prevent disease spread in elms.

By the mid-1960s a soil fumigating chemical called Vapam (sodium methyldithiocacbamate) was shown to kill grafted roots and prevent passage of the fungus. Unfortunately, the chemical could also kill the healthy tree to be protected if the applied dosage was too high, or applied too near the healthy tree. When applied carefully, it reduced root graft infections by fifty percent, and was widely used for some time, especially in the Midwest, where soils and sites were most congenial to its application. Where sidewalks and utility lines are not present, mechanical severance of grafted roots by trenching with a spade or by machine has been effective and less dangerous to healthy trees.

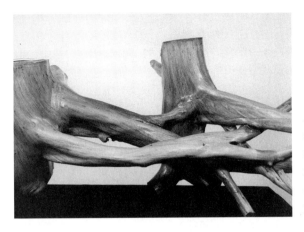

Fig. 13.5 In 1965 it was discovered that the disease could be transmitted through natural root grafts. Courtesy of the department of plant pathology, Cornell University.

Eradicative Pruning

The possibility of controlling the disease by eliminating a single infected branch from an elm was demonstrated relatively early in both Europe and North America. It was seldom used, however, because it failed in most cases. The basis for general failure seemed to be confirmed by spore movement studies in the 1930s, leading to the impression that fungus was extensively distributed within the tree by the time the earliest visible symptoms appeared. Despite this, there was some successful pruning in the 1950s. Following new data in the 1960s from measuring the rate of downward spread of the fungus from twig inoculation sites, interest in pruning as a control measure was revived.

By 1976, with the advent of new and effective systemic fungicides and new injection technology, it was clear that eradicative pruning supplemented by chemical injection could be a most effective tool in eliminating disease tissues from elms with visible symptoms. It was also shown that chemical injection before pruning was significantly more effective than pruning first, and injecting later. The size of tree and extent of infection were found to be the significant factors. Large trees with limited infections could be pruned successfully, whereas small trees with deep infections were likely failures.

Chemical and Biocontrol

The process of introducing chemicals into elms to control the disease has been investigated successively since the mid-1930s, first in the United States and later in Europe. By the mid-1940s, the new synthetic-organic chemicals stimulated new interest for effective chemotherapeutants, especially against Dutch elm

Fig. 13.6 Injection of an American elm by Dr. L. Schreiber. Courtesy of Larry Schreiber, USDA-ARS.

disease. Many new chemicals were tried and evaluated beginning in the early 1940s, especially by G. Zentmeyer of the Connecticut Agriculture Experiment Station.

In 1960 a major development in fungicidal chemistry yielded a new systemic fungicide involving 2-aminobendizole. Considered a basic discovery, it led to testing of a new, highly active systemic fungicide called benomyl (trade name Benlate) that was highly toxic to many plant pathogens, including the causal fungus of DED. Benlate was first produced commercially by the Dupont Chemical Company; it was first available as a powder but was insoluble in water.

To obtain a soluble product to inject into elm trees, the U.S. Forest Service achieved solubility in hydrochloric acid, obtaining methyl benzimidazole carbamate in hydrochloric acid (MBC-HCL). In 1972 the EPA granted registration of MBC for use by trained arborists as an "aid" in the control of DED.

Meanwhile, Canadian pathologists found that the phosphorous form of solubilized MBC was also highly effective against *C. ulmi* within elms, and could be used with no apparent toxicity to elms if special care was taken to observe dosage rate and amount injected into trees. In the United States and England, however, pathologists found the hydrochloride form to be highly effective at higher levels of MBC with no greater toxicity to elm tissue than the phosphorous MBC. Despite this, almost all of the data on the phosphorous MBC, now known as Lignasan BLP (benomyl lignasan phosphate), was derived by the Canadians until 1975, and much of this was obtained by direct underground injection into severed roots.

By 1976 a phosphate derivative of MBC, developed by Canadian Dupont, was registered by the EPA but unfortunately was marketed with dosage levels too low to be as effective. Known as Lignasan, the dosage specifications were later adjusted to achieve maximum effect, and it became one of the first commercially successful systemic fungicides for use in trees.

Meanwhile, another benomyl derivative was in the making. In the late 1960s a new chemical, 2-(thiazol-4-yl) benzimidazole, had been developed for use against earthworms. Produced by Merck and found to be toxic to the DED fungus, it was registered by the EPA in 1977 as a hypophosphate salt, called Arbotech, for injection into elms. As successful as Lignasan, it had a greater residual capacity and was modified to enhance effective control against DED for periods of up to three years after injection.

SUMMARY

Dutch elm disease was a strong catalyst in promoting professionalism in modern arboriculture and urban forestry on a worldwide basis. DED brought together professionals in regional groups, many of which would later form chapters of the International Society of Arboriculture. DED also stimulated federal, state, and local legislators to work with arboricultural professionals to plan management programs and define budgets for long- and short-range tree care programs. This type of cooperation and coordination with financing had not been seen before Dutch elm disease swept across the country.

CHAPTER FOURTEEN

The National Arborist Association

"Trade association is the salvation of small business" —Anonymous

The National Arborist Association (NAA) dates its origin to 1938 when it first used that name. Its roots go back to 1931, however, when a move to create an associate membership in the National Shade Tree Conference (NSTC) exclusively for tree workers was defeated. After working with scientists and municipal foresters to establish the conference from 1924 to 1928, a small group of enterprising commercial arborists decided in the early 1930s that they needed a trade organization confined to private, commercial arborists. The NSTC endorsed a proposal for a new committee of three to draft a plan, including a constitution and bylaws for a professional organization for operating tree men for consideration at the 1932 conference. In the following year, with the NSTC meeting in Rochester, New York, on the recommendation of a committee report, the American Society of Arborists (ASA) was formed within the conference, consisting only of commercial arborists. Elected as officers were Charles F. Irish of Cleveland as president, Orville W. Spicer of Connecticut as vice president, and Norman Armstrong of New York as secretary-treasurer. The articles of organization of the NSTC had provided that two commercial members would be on the NSTC conference executive board. With the creation of the ASA, the conference voted to have the president and secretary of the ASA as its two executive board conferees. When final action was taken, however, the president and secretary were not listed as the ASA as intended, but as the "National Association of Arborists."

Of much significance was the first recognition and adoption of the term *arborist* in place of *tree surgeon*. This marked the end of an era in which most tree care work had been narrowly confined to cavity excavation and filling, pruning, and wound treatment, beginning in the 1920s and expanding significantly in the 1930s. In support of the term *arborist,* Charles F. Irish noted the earlier use of the word *arboriculture* in England for more than 300 years.

This newly formed ASA-NAA did not survive. Near the end of the 1935 NSTC meeting, W. G. Aborn, NAA president, announced that the National Association of Arborists had voted unanimously to disband, noting that the NSTC had broadened the membership and had a commercial committee that would function along the lines for which the National Association of Arborists had been formed. Funds of $39.39 remaining in the NAA treasury were voted as a contribution to NSTC.

Before its demise the NAA was faced with a most unusual challenge created by passage of the National Recovery Act (NRA) in 1933. This act required every commercial trade interest to organize so that it could set its own industrywide wages and prices. Considered both necessary and desirable, it would transcend the scope and activity of the small and weak association of arborists hastily formed in 1932, and would also involve the NSTC. Not really organized for a job of this scope, the commercial arborists, still within the NSTC (as the ASA), passed the responsibility on to the NSTC. The NSTC, however, was not a commercial organization, and was in no position to represent the arborists as seen under the NRA. Two years following its enactment, the U.S. Supreme Court declared the NRA unconstitutional.

THE NAA IS BORN

The National Arborist Association had its genesis in a small group of commercial arborists that were active in the National Shade Tree Conference from its inception. Not wanting to destroy or replace the NSTC, which they had supported from the beginning, they sought to find an accommodation in cooperation with the NSTC. After the aborted trial of the ASA-cum-NAA within the conference, which ended in 1935, they remained inactive until 1937.

At the 1937 NSTC meeting the commercial arborists decided to create an independent organization of commercial tree workers without withdrawing support from the conference. They selected a committee of six, charged with planning a new organization of commercial arborists to meet at the 1938 NSTC meeting. The chairman of this group was Charles F. Irish, and the others were Sam A. Parmenter of Kent, Ohio; Orville W. Spicer of Stamford, Connecticut; J. Gonzenback of Louisville, Kentucky; I. B. Dewson of Ridgewood, New Jersey; and W. O. Hollister

Fig. 14.1 Charles F. Irish, NAA president, 1937, and organizational chairman. Courtesy of the National Arborist Association.

of Kent, Ohio. This would become the National Arborist Association, separate from, but in support of, the NSTC throughout its development to the present time.

Charles F. Irish was one of the most prominent and knowledgeable arborists of the period. He had developed the first air gun for aerating compacted soil, discovered the first case of Dutch elm disease in North America, and was a strong advocate of research. He was probably the most influential working arborist of his day, and became the first commercial member to be elected president of ISTC (1947).

The list of charter members of the NAA included forty-two names. Missing from this group were representatives from both the Bartlett and Asplundh Tree Companies, but individuals from the Davey Tree Company were charter members. From the outset the Davey firm was to contribute up to fifty percent of the NAA revenues, which was based on volume of work. The Bartlett and Asplundh Companies would in time become active members.

From its inception the NAA stated clearly that it would be a trade association whose members would be "commercial arborists" or "tree experts." The stated objectives of the NAA were to disseminate information and to promote research. The NAA also resolved to support and cooperate with the NSTC and, for decades, required all NAA members to be members of the NSTC.

The first elected members of the NAA were H. M. Van Wormer of Virginia, predsident, J. Cook White of Boston, first vice president, C. L. Wachtel of Wauwatosa, Wisconsin, second vice president, and W. O. Hollister of Kent, Ohio, secretary-treasurer. A president and vice president were elected annually, whereas the secretary-treasurer was continued as an anchor to guide and direct the organization.

Fig. 14.2 Dr. Paul Tilford, NAA executive secretary, 1946–65. Courtesy of the National Arborist Association.

W. O. Hollister of the Davey Tree Company served for three years until 1941. In that year the NAA hired Dr. Paul E. Tilford of Wooster, Ohio, on a part-time basis as its first paid executive secretary. At that time Tilford was a research plant pathologist at the Ohio Agriculture Experiment Station in Wooster. Later he became full-time and served also as editor of the NSTC.

GOVERNANCE

The arborists who assembled in 1938 adopted a constitution that created a board of directors. Described as a nonprofit organization of business competitors, the NAA was made up of individuals, partnerships, and corporations. Its two broad purposes were to promote greater appreciation of shade trees and to assist its members in the practice of tree preservation. Its first broad purpose was essentially public education for recognition of trees as assets, and its second was to aid its members in the practice of tree work designed to save trees.

Its constitution empowered the board to employ an executive secretary by contract and charge him with publication of information of service to members. The NAA member dues would be determined by a schedule based on the volume of business, with quarterly payments. Following adoption of the constitution, and after consideration of nine different names, the assembled members agreed on the National Arborist Association.

Three years after the NAA was established, the United States was at war. The NAA was involved in several cooperative actions with the NSTC during this time, including a joint camouflage project, preparation of a tree planting manual, and development of a national postwar tree planting policy for the federal government. All private tree work had a low priority during the war and most, if not all,

NAA companies and their managers were involved in various war effort community activities.

Dr. Paul E. Tilford resigned his position at the Ohio State University in 1945 to become the first full-time executive secretary of the NAA. He was elected editor of the NSTC in 1946. His dual role as NAA secretary and NSTC editor led to a close symbiotic relationship between the two organizations, with each benefiting from the other over a twenty-five-year period. With plans to enlarge and initiate new activity, the NAA established its national office at Tilford's residence in Wooster. The office remained there until Tilford retired in 1965, when it was moved to Washington, D.C. Tilford's wife, Esther, became an alternative secretary in assisting her husband. In 1966 the NAA emblem was registered in the U.S. Patent Office as its official trademark.

During its first thirty years the NAA held its regular annual meeting during the NSTC conference. This was a dinner meeting of short duration, because in those early years there was limited communication between members and limited growth in numbers. In 1952 the NAA initiated a two-day winter meeting—the first was held in Philadelphia. The winter meeting would in time become the annual meeting of NAA. To celebrate its first twenty-five years, the NAA met in St. Louis, Missouri, in 1963, and planted a black gum tree in the Missouri Botanical Garden near an oak planted by the NAA at the NSTC meeting in 1938.

At the NAA annual winter meeting in 1966, President Edwin Irish presented the retiring Tilford with a letter from President Lyndon B. Johnson honoring the NAA for the excellence of its contributions. The letter was seen by the NAA as a personal tribute to Tilford for his fine work with the organization for twenty-five years. Highly competent, able, and effective, he gave the association a stability and respected professional image. An able writer, he edited everything published by the NAA until 1966 and was the author of scores of papers on arboriculture. After retiring, Tilford was elected mayor of Wooster, Ohio, and served in this capacity for several years before his death in 1986.

Following Tilford, the NAA hired Clarke W. Davis of Tampa, Florida, as the new executive secretary. He had a background in business administration and public relations at the Universities of Maryland, South Florida, and Tampa, and two years' experience with the Florida Nurserymen and Growers Association. The NAA headquarters was moved from Wooster to Washington, D.C., at 15th and H Streets. Emphasis on publicity and public relations would be a new priority for the NAA and the tree care industry.

With no background in either tree care or publishing, Davis was not chosen by the NAA to carry the editorial work handled by Tilford. The NAA engaged Noel B. Wysong of River Forest, Illinois, past president of NSTC, to prepare press

Fig. 14.3 Robert Felix, NAA executive vice president, 1974–96. Courtesy of the National Arborist Association.

releases for public relations. Each month these notes on shade tree care subjects were mailed to a large list of newspapers and magazines, as well as to NAA members.

With Clarke Davis as the new secretary, the NAA began a period of change that would be short-lived, terminating in 1969. Some significant changes in governance were made during this interlude. There was an increase in the number of board of directors, and two new membership categories were created. The new association members were not commercial arborists, but those in businesses related to supplying and servicing arborists, typified by the commercial exhibitors at meetings. Associate members would have no vote and could hold no office. Privileged membership was available to retired professional arborists, who also would not vote or hold office.

During the spring and summer of 1969, there arose a question of misuse of funds by Secretary-Treasurer Davis. Following a careful review of the situation by a select committee, his resignation was requested and submitted on 10 September, and his resignation was effective on 30 September. A multiple management group was retained to manage NAA over a period of three years.

The next management period of NAA began with the appointment of Robert Felix in 1974. A native of Lynnbrook, New York, and a business graduate of Adelphi College in 1956, Felix had served as chairman of the NAA finance committee in 1967, treasurer in 1969, and president in 1972. Mrs. Felix was hired to handle the clerical work. The NAA moved its national headquarters several times in these years, going from Washington, D.C.; to Wantaugh, Long Island; to Bedford, New Hampshire; and then Amherst, New Hampshire. Felix began his new position determined to "initiate an aggressive program for the NAA" that would include education, safety programs, and a broad public relations program. More successful with each passing year, Felix continued to manage the NAA with distinction until his death in 1996.

Lacking Felix's strong leadership, the NAA entered a challenging period. The association weathered a tough transition with the vision of a strong board of directors, the capable management of a team of senior staff, and the dedication of its entire paid staff as well as a cadre of volunteers.

MEMBERSHIP AND GROWTH

Despite the thirty commercial arborists who voted to accept the original constitution in 1938, the NAA actually began with only nineteen individuals and company members officially represented. The dues were fifteen dollars, to be progressive with business volume. The only original requirements were to represent a commercial tree company and to be a member of the NSTC. In 1946 the NAA established a new requirement for membership: in addition to three years of experience in the business of arboriculture and membership in the NSTC, an applicant had to have a suitable recommendation by one or more members. By 1947 membership had increased to include 102 members in 22 states, but was still limited to those in the eastern half of the country. In the postwar period, membership steadily rose to 162 by 1950; by 1963, its twenty-fifth-anniversary year, there were 203 members from 33 states and provinces.

Following a dynamic period of activity in education, beginning with the Home Study Program (HSP) of 1970, membership climbed steadily. By 1975 twenty-one of the original forty-two charter members were still alive. By 1979 the membership represented 50 percent of the commercial tree care industry in the United States, with more than 270 member companies.

In 1986 the association again revised its application requirements for membership. Until this time, it had been possible to remain selective to be sure that its members were of high professional quality. Now it was necessary to represent the entire shade tree industry, so the membership could no longer remain exclusive. Requirements for new members were simple—a completed application form and certificates of insurance.

In 1987 the NAA began a new campaign to increase membership, designed to offer commercial arborists new opportunities for professionalism. Membership more than doubled and by 1988 it had exceeded 800.

In 1955 membership dues, based on a sliding scale, were a minimum of $50 for an annual business volume not exceeding $25,000. For large companies the dues were $4,960 plus $0.21 per thousand for a business volume exceeding

$10 million. After thirty years, minimum dues had risen to $325 for member companies with an annual business volume of less than $100,000, and for companies with an annual volume over $200 million, dues were reduced to $2,000.

By 1979 Robert Felix of the NAA estimated that there were 7,000 arborist firms in the United States with gross annual sales of more than one billion dollars. This represented a significant industry made up of thousands of well-trained, well-educated men and women, well equipped with tools and machines. With barely more than ten percent of the companies as NAA members, the association had plenty of room for additional growth and development.

On 19 October 1990, the NAA reached a membership milestone when it added its 1,000th active member firm. That represented a healthy start on the 15,000 tree care companies the NAA sought to serve.

Contracting arborists in the United Kingdom voiced a strong interest in bringing the resources available through the NAA overseas, and in 1995 a UK chapter of the NAA was formed. Eventually the UK formed a permanent committee, hired a part-time administrator, and began hosting meetings for the growing number of NAA-UK members.

In July 1995 amendments to the NAA constitution and bylaws created the NAA affiliate member. This nonvoting category of membership addressed a growing international interest in NAA membership. Since a large number of member services, including training programs and management guidelines to legislative and regulatory representation, were of no direct benefit to members from other countries, dues for affiliate membership were based on the administrative costs of providing membership.

In 1997 the NAA experienced an unprecedented growth in membership of more than thirty percent, indicating a great demand for the business management assistance it offers its members. Strong growth carried over into the next year.

In 1998 the two sister organizations, the ISA and the NAA, held a pivotal joint meeting of their executive committees. Their goal was to find ways of preserving the unique identity and mission of each organization while at the same time enabling them to pool their talents and resources to a greater degree for the good of the industry. The facilitated meeting was highly successful, resulting in a number of initiatives as well as a closer working relationship between the respective boards and staffs.

ACTIVITIES AND ACHIEVEMENTS

In 1939 the NAA began to press for legislation for its interests. When a law was proposed in Pennsylvania for licensing of arborists to protect trees, the NAA urged its members to support it. In that same year it urged the federal government to develop a research program on a newly discovered lethal disease of plane trees known as canker stain.

During the war the NAA was instrumental in bringing about a decision by the War Manpower Commission to recognize line clearing as essential, making it possible for draft deferment and use of critical materials such as steel for tools and trucks. After the war, in cooperation with the NSTC, the NAA financed a representative in Washington who urged the army to assume responsibility for tree planting around VA hospitals. This was followed by a letter to the Veterans Administration explaining the work of arborists and urging the use of professionals for the maintenance of those trees.

Following the war the NAA turned to supporting education and research in arboriculture. In 1945 the association made its first award for research. The recipient was a dedicated and distinguished plant pathologist of the Natural History Survey and the University of Illinois at Urbana-Champaign. Dr. James Cedric Carter received a cash award of $500 and a recognition plaque for his landmark research on bacterial wetwood of elm. This was the first award of any tree care organization for outstanding research on a major shade tree problem.

By 1949 the wage and hour laws created during the war, plus the rise of unions, were of much concern to NAA members. In that year committees on unions and safety practices were established for the first time. In response, the NAA provided $500 in expenses for members to appear before the National Labor Relations Board (NLRB) regarding the status of arborist company employees. The NLRB ruled that such employees were agricultural and the NAA ascertained that employees of most of its members were exempt from most provisions of the law with respect to unionization. In 1950, however, it approved support of legal expenses of up to fifty percent for one of its members, Frost and Higgens in Boston, to negotiate a union contract.

At its annual meeting in Boston in 1952 the NAA endorsed a policy of charging a uniform fee of $100 for each day, or a portion thereof, plus expenses for expert witness services. In 1954 it required that its members charge for all tree inspections, although free estimates for work and charges were allowed. By 1963 it had endorsed a policy for charging fees for any kind of consulting, including making calls, inspections, and advising.

By 1952 the NAA was again involved with legislation on both federal and state issues. With the United States at war in Korea, the draft of eligible young men became an issue. In a petition to the Labor Department it sought to include line-clearing supervisors and foremen on a list of essential war activity personnel, as in World War II. Another request from the NAA was directed at the Office of

Price Stabilization; it requested that tree care service work be exempted from a general price freeze. These issues were complicated by the federal legal position that wartime rulings (including exemptions) were not in force because the United States was not legally at war.

The NAA continued to support research and education in the 1950s. In 1952 it funded Professor L. C. Chadwick, executive director of the NSTC, to attend the International Horticultural Congress, and helped to establish a Shade Tree Research Fellowship at Rutgers University in New Jersey. In 1955 it contributed toward the establishment of the new Arbor Day Foundation, and also urged the Secretary of Agriculture and the Department of the Budget to include sufficient research funding to allow the National Arboretum to be completed and to operate with adequate scientific staff and research facilities. With a view toward establishing a program in apprentice training, an NAA committee met with a Labor Department representative to consider establishing standards and policy so the Labor Department could approve such a training program in tree care.

In 1992 the NAA teamed up with ISA and Allegheny Power to undertake an in-depth debris disposal research project. The intent of the $100,000 program was to find economically viable means for disposing of wood waste, which accumulates in small quantities from utility and residential/commercial tree care operations.

PUBLICATIONS

Two years after its founding in 1938, the NAA began publishing a four-page quarterly newsletter known as *The Commercial Arborist*. It became a monthly in 1942 and then was discontinued until after the war. The NAA's first bulletin in arboriculture was published in cooperation with the NSTC; *Transplanting of Trees and Shrubs* was produced in 1943 for the War Department in order to emphasize camouflage using trees.

After the war the NAA published a small leaflet—*Shade Tree Work for Vets*—in which it sought to attract young, new blood to the profession; 3,000 copies were distributed. In 1946 the monthly newsletter was resumed initially as a four-page issue under the name *Arbor Action*. From 1948 to 1950 three new informative publications were produced—one on fertilization and two on DED. *Fertilize and Spray—Then Your Trees Can Feed Themselves* not only reinforced good arboricultural practice, but was a subtle reminder to arborists that *fertilization* of trees is not *feeding* trees. *Elm Diseases—What It Takes to Be an Arborist,* prepared by Dr. Paul E. Tilford, was published in *Consumers Research Bulletin* in 1949. The NAA itself published *Facts about Dutch Elm Disease—The Goat with Green Glasses,* of which 19,000 copies were distributed.

Three additional publications were produced from 1955 to 1960, including *National Tree News* in 1955, *Pruning Standards for Shade Trees* in 1958 (of which 5,000 copies were produced), and *A Guide for Fertilization* in 1960. In 1965 the NAA published *Safety Practices for Arborists,* an update of a 1953 report by Karl Kuemmerling of Ohio. The NAA supported the ISA with $1,500 for the work of the ISA Evaluating Committee to revise, update, and enlarge the *Tree Evaluation Book,* first initiated by the ISA and the NAA in 1957.

In 1968 the NAA published a four-page pamphlet on career opportunities in arboriculture. Designed to aid its members in recruiting, it included duties, physical requirements, and educational training, as well as descriptions of tools and equipment used. A new colorful update of this pamphlet was produced in cooperation with the ISA in 1987.

In 1984 the NAA created a new publication, *The Tree Worker,* which was produced as a monthly at nominal cost. Designed literally for the men working in and under the trees, it contained up-to-date information on technical materials and methods, safety, customer relations, and pertinent news items.

In June of 1990 NAA published the first issue of *Tree Care Industry* (*TCI*), the only trade journal written by arborists for arborists. It is mailed to almost 14,000 commercial, utility, and institutional arborists. Monthly issues offer a combination of special features and articles from recognized leaders in the industry plus departments such as "Washington in Review," "Labor and Law Update," and an industrywide calendar of events.

PUBLIC RELATIONS

From its earliest years the NAA was conscious of its perception by the public. With a constant eye on public relations, it sought to provide public service where possible and to cooperate with other organizations for its own good as well as the public good.

Beginning in 1950 it provided the office space for editing and publishing of *Arborist's News* for about fifteen years. This came about because of the dual role of its secretary, Paul Tilford, as the elected NSTC editor. In 1951 it supported, in vain, an Ohio arborist licensing law, and in the following year made its first direct contribution to research in helping to establish a Shade Tree Fellowship at Rutgers University. In 1955 it passed a resolution to urge Congress to provide manpower and facilities for the National Arboretum. When certain areas were rocked by a series of devastating storms in 1956, it organized a strategic shifting of tree crews of its member companies to ease the many emergencies arising from trees destroying homes and power lines and blocking highways and communication.

Feeling the need for professional advice to increase publicity and advertising, the NAA employed Ralph Head and Associates in 1963, a public relations firm. The NAA set the following goals for the PR firm: (1) assemble available data; (2) analyze and interpret data; (3) define the problems and opportunities; and (4) develop a working plan for the NAA.

In 1978 the NAA joined with the International Society of Arboriculture (ISA), the American Society of Consulting Arborists (ASCA), the American Association of Nurserymen (AAN), and Associated Landscape Contractors of America (ALCA) to form the Council of Tree and Landscape Appraisers. Representatives from these organizations revised the *Shade Tree Evaluation Guide.* The NAA also initiated a speaker's bureau of its members who had special expertise and talent to educate other members, other arborists, and the public on arboricultural subjects of common interest.

As the newly organized ISA began moving toward an endowed Research Trust Fund to support research in arboriculture in 1976, the NAA gave its early support with $1,000. In addition, the NAA proposed that it cooperate in raising funds for the ISA Research Trust Fund by initiating a program with two procedures: (1) each member company of NAA could be asked to contribute a quarter of one percent of annual billings; and (2) members could match contributing funds from clients who wished to contribute.

In the fall of 1985 the NAA received an invitation from the Statue of Liberty— Ellis Island Foundation to contribute its services for tree pruning on these two islands in preparation for bicentennial ceremonies in 1987. Following thirty years of neglect, the trees were badly in need of pruning. In November 1985 more than 100 arborists, including 88 top climbers, converged on the islands. Commercial arborists from twenty-three NAA member firms from Connecticut, New York, and New Jersey were joined by twenty students of arboriculture from the University of Massachusetts, Amherst. The beautification of the two islands by these arborist volunteers was reported to be worth $30,000.

From 1987 through 1991 the NAA continued the bicentennial tree theme for a public relations campaign. The focus was to recognize 200-year-old living witnesses to the signing and ratification of the U.S. Constitution. The bicentennial tree program was responsible for erecting bronze plaques next to historic trees throughout the country.

In July 1993 NAA staff attended the first National Youth Environmental Summit in Cincinnati to impress on these decision makers of tomorrow that

arborists are pro-environment and that the trees we plant today will require continual professional care if they are to become part of tomorrow's urban forest.

Standards

In the 1970s NAA director Robert Felix had a close working relationship with
both the Environmental Protection Agency (EPA) and the Occupational Safety
and Health Administration (OSHA), and was consulted often. The NAA was especially active on safety codes of special interest to OSHA, and represented the
arboricultural industry to the American National Standards Institute (ANSI) for
many years after its founding of the Committee on Arboricultural Standards.

The NAA Standard Practices Committee was established in 1944. By 1949,
with W. S. Speed as chairman, the committee recommended that the NAA adopt,
as standard practices, the cabling and bracing methods described by A. Robert
Thompson of the National Park Service and the Department of Interior in the *Tree
Preservation Bulletin* No. 3. The earliest standards to be used by the NAA, they
foreshadowed a far more detailed and extensive list of published papers on recognized methods of tree care.

In 1958 the NAA published *Pruning Standards for Shade Trees.* This first
publication on standards was prepared under the committee chairmanship of
Freeman Parr. Included were divisions on pruning at four levels: Class I, fine
pruning; Class II, medium pruning; Class III, safety pruning; and Class IV, drop
crotch pruning.

By 1958 it was clear that standards on fertilization were needed. By 1962
Parr's committee had produced a second set of standards, *A Guide for Fertilizing
Shade and Ornamental Trees.* In that same year the NAA standards committee
approved publication of the final draft of standards for lightning protection of
trees. These were updated and revised in 1980 in cooperation with the National
Fire Protection Association in Boston; the new standards were published as *Protecting Trees from Lightning Damage.*

By 1978 the NAA had updated and revised its standards on pruning and
installation of lightning protection systems, and prepared new standards on hydraulic sprayer calibration. The audience for these publications, in addition to
arborists, consisted of various federal, state, and city officials; park officials; nurserymen; utility companies; and road officials.

The NAA was instrumental in organizing the ANSI A300 Committee, which
held its first meeting on 19 March 1991. It produced a document entitled "Standard Practice for Shade Tree Maintenance." Fifteen professional organizations,
companies, and government agencies were invited to participate. The purpose of

the A300 committee is to develop consensus standards for the care and maintenance of shade trees. Nine priorities for tree care categories were set at the initial meeting, with the first priority being pruning practices.

SAFETY PRACTICES

Safety has always been important to working arborists, given the nature of their work. After the war there was even more emphasis on safety because of new tools and fast-moving machinery. Soon there were organized efforts on behalf of accident prevention, including voluntary adoption of standards, and more recently, legally imposed compliance with accepted standards. By 1949 the association had a safe-practices committee, and by 1953 it expressed the need for a safety manual and wide publication of basic safety rules. The first safety rules adopted by the NAA were based on those of A. Robert Thompson, published in 1940 as *Tree Preservation Bulletin* No. 8, and entitled *Safety for Tree Workers*.

In 1953 Karl Kuemmerling, chairman of the NAA safety committee, made the first of his many reports on safety. With twelve other committee members, he was responsible for the first NAA publication on the subject—*Safety Practices for Arborists*. His initial report stressed the need for teaching and promoting safety as a routine practice. When it was updated by the NAA in 1965, many types of new equipment had been introduced, which created new safety problems. Accordingly, the update included new sections on aerial lifts, tree cranes, and brush chippers.

The NAA first gave safety awards in 1958, but it was preceded in this area by several of its member companies. One of the earliest companies interested in worker safety was Farrens Tree Surgeons in Jacksonville, Florida. Major emphasis on accident prevention decreased accident frequency; this saved the company large sums of money and caused insurance premiums to decrease proportionately.

When OSHA regulations became functional in 1970, the NAA and its member companies were already prepared for legally imposed safety standards. The year before, a new committee on standards had been created by the American National Standards Institute. The Z-133 committee concerned itself with safety requirements for pruning, trimming, repairing, maintaining, and removing trees. Meeting regularly this committee continues to revise and update tree care safety standards. Prior to the establishment of this committee, safety requirements for arborists had been based on the general duty clause of OSHA, which was primarily for utility line clearance, not for arborists.

By 1986 OSHA made it mandatory to report all accidental exposure to occupational damaging noise exposure, such as that from prolonged use of chain saws. As a result, it also required audio testing of all operators of noise-making machines. While cooperating with the OSHA rules and regulations, the NAA has not hesitated to raise questions about unnecessary or unfair restriction. Original OSHA regulations required that all tree workers working around live electrical wires maintain a distance of ten feet from wires. Through its work in the ANSI Z-133 committee, the NAA showed that trained, qualified workers could work around electrical wires at a two-foot distance, while all others must maintain the ten-foot rule.

Almost since its inception, the NAA has been engaged in governmental activities at the federal level. In March 1994, after nine years of input by the NAA, OSHA promulgated 29 CFR, part 1910.269. The regulation is commonly known as the Line Clearance Tree Trimming Vertical Standard. Thanks to the NAA's consultation, the burdensome and unworkable portions of the standard were toned down. The result of the effort was an explicit OSHA standard that applied to all tree care personnel working near electrical conductors. The phrase, "OSHA has accepted the NAA approach," appears constantly throughout the standard's preamble. With the able assistance of key members, the NAA was able to save the industry from being crippled by misguided government regulations, while at the same time championing safe work practices.

Awards

In 1958 the association established its first annual award for internal recognition of its members. This first annual safety award was upgraded in 1963 to the Safety Award of Merit. By this time most of the large tree companies had come to recognize good safety records as more than routine, and the NAA move in this direction lent additional force and attention to the importance of safety in arboriculture.

In the following year the NAA established a second internal award. A Leadership Award of Merit was presented to Dr. Paul Tilford, NAA executive secretary, for his dedication, initiative, and achievements over the previous nineteen years in helping to give the association a recognized professional status.

The Paul Tilford National Arboriculture Foundation, created in 1982, provided for fifty charter fellows, each of whom would make a $1,000 contribution to support research in arboriculture. Another award, the Freeman L. Parr Award for outstanding communication achievements in the field of arboriculture, was designed to recognize NAA member firms that advanced the field by communicating with newsletters and brochures.

In 1995 the NAA instituted a recognition program called the Excellence in Arboriculture Awards. The purpose of the Excellence Awards is to recognize

Fig. 14.4 Ray Gustin Jr. (right), NAA president, 1958, presents the NAA Award of Merit to Ross Farrens, NAA president, 1946. Courtesy of the National Arborist Association.

professionalism manifested in tree care projects undertaken by NAA member firms, as well as to recognize those firms' clients for their dedication to tree preservation.

The projects are evaluated against pre-established criteria by a panel of judges. Originally, the panel of five Excellence judges represented the ANSI A300 Committee, the International Society of Arboriculture, the National Arborist Association Standards Review Committee, and the American Society of Consulting Arborists, with the final judge chosen "at large" by the Excellence in Arboriculture Committee.

The entry categories for awards are as follows: tree health management for residential projects under $5,000, residential projects over $5,000, commercial projects under $5,000, and commercial projects over $5,000; heritage—pro bono tree care for historic trees; Arbor Day—pro bono tree care in connection with Arbor Day activities; tree relocation; construction site tree preservation; and the Judges' Award. Awards are presented at a gala event at the association's Winter Management Conference.

PROJECTS

Since its inception in 1938 the NAA has been involved in a variety of programs of interest to arboriculture. Many of these have been sponsored in cooperation with the ISA and discussed in previous chapters. Early projects in NAA history have been covered in other sections. The following selections are reviewed here to reflect the significant role of the NAA projects in arboriculture since 1960.

As discussed previously, the NAA sponsored a tree recognition program to mark the bicentennial event. Then in 1987, thirteen companies in greater Philadelphia volunteered equipment and crews to prune and fertilize all the trees at the

Fig. 14.5 H. M. Van Wormer (center), NAA president, 1938, presents Dr. Paul Tilford the NAA Award of Merit. Gerald Farrens, NAA president, 1977, looks on from the right, as do Kenneth B. Kirk (far left), 1978 president, and his wife Vi. Courtesy of the National Arborist Association.

historic Independence Hall and Liberty Bell Pavilion. With fifty workers, seven trucks and chippers, plus three fertilization trucks, more than 100 trees were treated.

National Arborist Day at Arlington National Cemetery on 16 October 1993, was touted as NAA's gift to the American people and the environment. More than 400 tree care workers from NAA member firms in seventeen states took time to care for the trees that shade and adorn the national memorial. Many of these trees are the only living witnesses from the Civil War era, when Arlington was created. In 1998 the NAA returned to Arlington. The association's second Arborist Day at Arlington was an overwhelming success, this time with almost 600 members volunteering their time to provide much-needed care for trees throughout the 600-acre cemetery.

In January 1995 the National Arborist Foundation (NAF) received a grant of $85,000 to develop computer models and related promotional materials on the economic and environmental benefits that result from maintaining large trees. The grant was made by the National Urban and Community Forestry Advisory Council. The NAF matched the grant amount with the help of other tree care trade associations, ISA chapters, and related groups.

NAA EDUCATION

In 1969 the NAA initiated its first nationwide training program for arborists. Its first course was prepared for foremen and/or crew members of NAA-affiliated shade tree companies. This was the first educational program for commercial arborists not sponsored by a commercial company for its own employees or offered by an educational institution. Designed to increase knowledge of arborists' work and safety practices, it was tailored to meet specific needs of participants and increase their effectiveness. The program was seen as an aid to recruiting and training tree workers, as well as an opportunity to raise standards of workmanship.

In the following year (1970) the NAA launched a Home Study Program (HSP), available at first only to its members. In 1971 it decided to market the HSP publicly so that it would be available to nonmembers as well. The initial program was designed to provide professional arborists with increased technical and practical proficiency. The program included eight individual study sessions including introduction to commercial arboriculture, tree anatomy and physiology, soils, pruning, tree identification and selection, fertilizing, and watering. Endorsed by the ISA, the original HSP was so successful by 1978 that it had been taken by 1,200 arborists.

Series I was soon followed by Series II, a 400-page second course that contained eight assignments on diagnosis of ornamental tree problems, nonparasitic injuries, tree insect problems, tree disease, pollution damage to trees, pest management for ornamental trees, fertilization and watering of trees, and maintenance and repair practices. A third HSP course was prepared for crew foremen and a fourth as an electrical hazards awareness program. The program on electrical hazards awareness reflected the concern of both arborists and OSHA over the dangers of working around live wires.

In June 1990 the NAA and ISA submitted a formal grant request for $50,000 to the EPA for its Integrated Pest Management (IPM) project, a research and education project that could reduce reliance on conventional pesticides. Studies show that pesticide use can be reduced by more than seventy-five percent with sound IPM practice. Although denied the EPA grant, the organizations pressed on, ultimately receiving a grant from the U.S. Forest Service. The charitable foundations of the NAA and ISA awarded an $83,000 contract to the Illinois Natural History Survey to study public perception of IPM and develop marketing and operational strategies.

In 1992 the NAA and ISA began selling each other's programs at member prices. Shortly thereafter, the NAA's Home Study Program for Arborists and Crew

Leader Home Study courses became the first self-study programs accredited through the ISA arborist certification program.

In 1994 the NAA's popular Electrical Hazards Awareness Program (EHAP) was revised to help employers comply with OSHA training requirements that took effect in January 1995. In 1994 every active member received a copy of the new EHAP, which consists of a field handbook, two hazard tree decals, and a one-page "tailgate" (on the job) lesson.

At about this time, the NAA released the first draft of the Professional Tree Care Specialist program. This two-tiered, members-only program recognized employees who reached measured levels on knowledge and training and helped employers develop a realistic training curriculum.

Beginning in 1975 the NAA initiated programs in technical seminars, slide cassettes, and symposia. The first technical seminar, held in 1986, focused on fertilization of urban trees, considered by some as the most controversial tree care practice. A second seminar in 1977 focused on pesticide application and calibration of equipment to remedy improper practices leading to hazardous pesticide use in the environment, excessive application of chemicals and use of fuel, and wasted time. Beginning in 1981 the NAA initiated a series of seminars in different regions of the United States for training in sound financial management principles.

In 1976 the NAA began a series of slide/cassette training programs with the first one on cabling and bracing. Consisting of eighty color slides with cassette narration as well as a script, it became available to nonmembers for fifty dollars. Designed as a training aid, it could be used to supplement field experience of other training programs. By 1977 the NAA had produced five more slide/cassette training programs on basic instructions for a tree care trainee, climbing techniques for the professional arborist, tools and techniques of pruning, the reasons for pruning, and spraying techniques. In 1978 there were two programs available on tree fertilization, focusing on the rationale for feeding and the process of applying nutrients to trees and shrubs. By 1982 a program on targeted spray applications for shade and ornamental trees became available. It was designed as a guide to limit distribution of spray materials to specific trees. In that same year, in order to enhance safety training, the NAA produced a slide/cassette program on the critical area of aerial rescue.

In 1978 the NAA began the first of its symposia. With breakthroughs on new systemic chemicals and new tree injection systems to control Dutch elm disease, the NAA recognized a need for clarification of issues surrounding effective and responsible use of these new tools. Its first educational symposium, opened to the public at large, was available to limited numbers of attendees. A full two days were spent at the National Arboretum in Washington, D.C., for a series of paper

Fig. 14.6 Tree climbing and rigging demonstrations at the Tree Care Industry (TCI) Expo, 1998. Courtesy of the National Arborist Association.

presentations and discussions. Papers were presented on all aspects of Dutch elm disease research and disease control practices. Essentially educational in nature, this seminar represented a needed and worthwhile public service.

In 1979 the NAA began a new safety tailgate program designed to provide safety training for all practicing arborists. The course was designed to be taught in the field and used ANSI Z-133.1 standards as a basis for understanding the program, entitled "Safety Requirements for Pruning, Trimming, Repairing, Maintaining and Removing Trees and for Cutting Brush."

In 1987 the NAA began to use videotapes for communication. The ANSI Z-133 standards were produced in a four-part series called *Professional Tree Care Safety*, and included general requirements, personal protection, equipment procedures, and operational practices. New tapes became available for those who had finished the first four parts.

In 1986 the tape entitled "Proper Pesticide Applications Techniques for Urban Trees" was sponsored by the Specialty Group of Union Carbide Agricultural Products, Inc. The first of its kind for the arborist industry, it was prepared in response to increasing reluctance by insurance companies to insure arborists who apply pesticides, and it was designed to demonstrate that arborists are properly trained to apply pesticides. At this same time, the NAA completed three instructional videotapes on hydraulic sprayer calibration and pesticide application to trees. These were a part of the NAA-sponsored "On Target" program. In 1987 a revised version of the four-part safety series was produced to update newly revised ANSI safety standards. This was followed by a video in 1989, *Chipper Use and Safety*. Designed to prevent chipper accidents because of malfunction, the tape stressed continuous, proper maintenance and repair. In cooperation with the ISA, NAA and *TCI Magazine* sponsored TCI EXPO '90, first annual trade show and seminar program in October 1990 at the Richmond Convention Center in Richmond, Virginia. TCI EXPO '90 highlighted key suppliers of equipment, materials, and services to the tree care industry. In 1992 the NAA broke new ground when it introduced a thirty-foot-tall demonstration tree at TCI EXPO in Baltimore. In 1994 *Ropes, Knots and Climbing* introduced recent advances in climbing techniques and equipment that were revolutionizing tree climbing. The video focused on tools and techniques for beginning and intermediate climbers.

In 1998 the two-part video program entitled *Rigging for Removal* was introduced. Featuring Donald Blair, Ken Johnson, and Robert Phillips, three of the foremost rigging experts in the United States, it quickly became a best-seller. Continuing an approach it had used successfully in the past, the NAA hosted a series of rigging workshops around the country.

SUMMARY

The NAA is the only national organization that represents the entire commercial shade tree industry, devoting itself exclusively to the furtherance of commercial arboriculture. Following a false start in 1931, it was established in 1938 with forty-two charter members. It is designed to serve commercial arborists who meet and exchange information and promote cooperation. It also serves to gather and disseminate information; foster and promote research; encourage sound legislation; maintain good ethics; cooperate with allied organizations; conduct public relations; and promote membership interests.

CHAPTER FIFTEEN

Insecticides and Fungicides in Arboriculture

"Where there is much there are many to consume it" —F. Bacon

Although it was known long ago that chemicals could be used to control pests, experimental work to test such chemicals did not begin until about the mid-1600s, and they have only been used to any significant degree in arboriculture the past fifty years. Before 1850, and even well beyond it, proposed insect control measures were cultural, mechanical, crude, labor intensive, of a nontechnical nature and, at best, only partially effective.

As with insecticidal materials, fungicidal chemicals can be traced to ancient times for use in preventing or alleviating plant disease. The fungi that caused disease, however, were less known than the insects, and, in most cases, neither seen nor recognized. Nonetheless, in 1,000 B.C., Homer noted the use of sulfur as a curative agent for ailing plants. In 470 B.C. Democritus is said to have recommended sprinkling pure amurca (olive tissue that remains after pressing to remove the juice) on plants to control blight. Despite these interesting observations, there is no documentation of successful use of chemicals to control plant disease of any kind before the end of the Renaissance in the 1600s, and major developments in the use of fungicides for control of tree diseases have occurred only in the past hundred years.

INSECTICIDES

The known use of insecticidal materials goes back to the Sumerians in about 2500 B.C. In China, about 1200 B.C., chalk and wood ash were reported to control insects; so-called "botanicals" (of plant derivation) were used to treat stored grain. Each of these materials was presumed to have insecticidal properties. About the same time in Greece, Homer referred to "pest averting sulfer," apparently burned in dwellings to fumigate against insects. Arsenical materials of unknown composition were also used to kill insects in that period. Several centuries later (ca. 350 B.C.) Aristotle noted fumigation as a long-established practice. Two hundred years later, the Roman Cato recorded the use of oil sprays, oil with bitumen (of coal origin) in sticky bands, oil and ashes, and sulfur and bitumen ointments. Cato also noted the fumigation of grapevines against insects with a mixture of olive oil, sulfur, and pitch. By 200 B.C. arsenic was known in China. In 100 B.C. the Romans used a specific botanical against rats, mice, and insects. Hellebore, derived from a plant of the same name, had insecticidal properties. Thus, by the end of the ancient period, three sources of insecticide were known: minerals, oils, and plants.

No new development of insecticides was reported from the Roman era until the end of the Renaissance. Beginning in the 1600s, botanicals of insecticidal value, such as nicotine and derris, had been discovered. One of the earliest natural products used as an insecticide was a water extract of tobacco. Such extracts were sprayed on plants in Europe in the 1600s and were in use in the American colonies by the mid-1700s.

In the late seventeenth century (approximately 1670) arsenic was used successfully in the colonies against ants. Known earlier to the ancients in Greece and China, this was the first record of its use in the Americas. In the late eighteenth century, the newly independent Americans had begun to use soap, turpentine emulsion, and tar to control insects. The first United States vice president, John Adams, painted apple trees with tar to discourage caterpillars. By 1800 whale oil was used against scale insects; kerosene emulsion was used as a contact poison; and soap, mercuric chloride, and arsenical sulfates were combined in a hellish witches' brew described as most effective against many troublesome insects.

By 1800 three plant-derived insecticides were recommended for insect control. The dried roots of hellebore, a perennial weed in both Europe and North America, had insecticidal properties. From 1800 to 1850 quassia (from the quassia tree from tropical American forests) was mixed in a phosphate paste and used as an insecticide. Pyrethrum powder was introduced into western Europe and North America in the 1800s from eastern Asia. It was made from flowers of *Chrysanthemum cinerariifolium* and was also known as Persian louse powder.

Tobacco liquid, dust, and fumigation were all used during the 1800s to kill insects, and by mid-century, tobacco was combined with soap for the same purpose. (The principal toxic ingredient, nicotine, was a stomach poison to insects. By the early 1900s, nicotine combined with sulfur—nicotine sulfate—was sold commercially. By 1917 it was commercially available in a dry carrier for dusting.)

Toward the end of the 1800s a chemical called rotenone, also known as derris dust, was used as an insecticide in the United States. It was derived from *Derris* plants and related genera of the pea family (Leguminosae). Derived as a dust by grinding roots of *Derris* plants, it became quite popular by 1933 and has since been synthesized, making its production less difficult.

By 1940 a sesame oil was used as a synergist for pyrethrum insecticides, greatly enhancing its insecticidal value. First synthesized as a pyrenoid called allethrin in 1949, it was developed as a photo-stable synthetic pyrethrum (permethrin) in 1973. Long lasting when stored in darkness, it breaks down quickly in light so that it is not hazardous in the environment.

Petroleum oils have been used as insecticides for more than 100 years. Some arborists consider them the best available control for scales, mites, plant bugs, psyllids, and some moths. Long used as dormant sprays, improved technology and formulations make petroleum oils competitive with the new synthetic organic compounds. Because the oils are phytotoxic to some plant species, arborists must pay careful attention to plant species sensitivity.

Inorganic Insecticides

The period from 1800 to 1900 was characterized by empirical trials of numerous materials to control insect pests. Most, if not all, of these chemical materials had their origin from plants, petroleum sources, or minerals, but the most effective were inorganic, including sulfur compounds, arsenicals, and copper sulfate.

The usefulness of soaps for insect control was known as early as 1842. Especially effective against soft-bodied sucking insects, such as aphids, leafhoppers, and certain scales, insecticidal soaps were also said to be effective against almost all arthropods. Because their efficacy was short-lived, soaps had to be applied repeatedly for effect. Discontinued with the advent of organic pesticides in the 1940s, soaps have recently been resurrected.

One of the first insecticides that could be targeted against a specific plant pest was Paris green. Of European origin, it first appeared between 1860 and 1870 in the United States for use as a spray against the Colorado potato beetle. Paris green was first synthesized as copper-aceto-arsenite in 1865. In 1867 it was mixed with kerosene for use as an emulsion spray against potato and fruit insects. It was the first successful insect stomach poison.

The first chemicals that were effective for control of tree insects came into use or were devised to control serious insect pests introduced to North America from

TABLE 15.1

CHRONOLOGICAL LISTING OF SELECTED ORGANIC
AND INORGANIC INSECTICIDES

Organic pesticides

PERIOD	MATERIAL	SOURCE
200 B.C.	Bitumen	Coal oil
100 B.C.	Hellebore	Botanical
1600s A.D	Tobacco	Botanical
1800	Oil	Whales
1858	Pyrethrum	Botanical
1867	Kerosene	Petroleum
1877	Benzene hexachloride	Synthetic
1890	Derris	Botanical

Inorganic pesticides

PERIOD	MATERIAL	SOURCE
1200 B.C.	Wood ash	Natural
1000 B.C.	Sulfur	Natural
800 B.C.	Arsenic	Natural
1822 A.D.	Mercuric chloride	Synthetic
1859	Phosphorus paste	Synthetic
1860	Paris green	Synthetic
1875	Lime sulfur	Synthetic
1891	Lead arsenate	Synthetic

abroad. The San Jose scale was introduced into North America on ornamental plants from China and caused serious annual losses in orchards by 1880. It had no natural enemies in the new ecosystem. All of the then-known insecticide types (lead arsenate, nicotine sulfate, various oils) were ineffective against the scale. The only chemical with promise was lime sulfur. In the early 1900s lime sulfur combined with oil emulsions provided satisfactory control; by 1917 lime sulfur with oil had become established as a standard dormant treatment.

While ineffective against the San Jose scale, Paris green was the first chemical used effectively against the gypsy moth. It had been used in Ontario against cankerworm in 1884 and other tree insects, and may have been the first synthetic insecticide used for the control of shade tree pests. Paris green was followed by London purple, another arsenical, developed in England. An arsenite of lime, this new chemical was effective against many leaf-eating insects, including leaf beetles, cottonwood slugs, and elm cankerworm. Mixed with tar, it was applied to the trunk; used alone, it was applied to leaves. Often mixed with flour in a paste or with ashes, London purple was first used as a spray on trees in Illinois. By 1872 it had been used successfully against apple cankerworms and by 1887 against apple codling moths. Until that time, Paris green and London purple were the most valuable agents against chewing insects.

Both of these chemicals were soon superseded by lead arsenate. The unexpected emergence of the gypsy moth by 1880 led to the development of lead arsenate for gypsy moth control in 1892. First created in 1891 for use specifically against that insect, by 1910 it was recommended for control of a wide variety of leaf-eating insects and was used early against plum curculio. Combined in an emulsion, it was used with kerosene and hot water against various scale insects. When first used in 1892 in Massachusetts, lead arsenate was formulated as a dinitrophenol compound (salt of 4–6 dinitro-o-cresol). By 1903 it was available commercially. For the next fifty years it was perhaps the most effective and widely used insecticide for shade tree insects and was not replaced until after World War II by DDT and other new chlorinated hydrocarbons.

Organic Insecticides

Early in the 1900s, the heavy use of lime sulfur against San Jose scale in apple orchards led to insect resistance to this chemical. By the 1920s the effectiveness of lead arsenate against apple codling moth began to wane, and successful fumigation with hydrocyanic acid from 1915 to 1940 also lost its insecticidal punch as citrus insects became resistant. As early as 1914, A. L. Melander, an entomologist at Washington State College, posed a question with far-reaching complications: Can insects become resistant to chemical sprays? This early concern with developing resistance was given little concern until the age of DDT, several decades later.

It was also clear that the value of some effective insecticides was limited because of toxicity to plant tissues treated for protection against insects. In 1908 arborists in Massachusetts noted that various spray mixtures and banding recommendations were not always dependable, and much injury occurred from their use. Accordingly, in some of its publications, that state emphasized the need to watch out for "bogus tree doctors with quick sure-cure nostrums." This early warning was symbolic of a problem that has plagued modern arboriculture since its origin at the turn of the twentieth century.

Although production of synthetic organic chemicals for pest control did not materialize on a large scale until the 1930s, by 1877 benzene hexachloride (BHC) was used, probably for the first time, against museum insects. A few years later (1892) naphthalene cakes were effectively used against other insects. The British filed a patent in 1896 to use inorganic fluoride as an insecticide. Carbolineum arrived in 1892, and the Germans introduced potassium dinitro-o-cresylate as a new insecticide late in that century.

By the early 1930s miscible petroleum oils were used for scale control, pyrethrum and nicotine were used against aphids and thrips, and lead arsenate against a variety of leaf eaters. By 1937 new organic compounds were sought as effective substitutes for lead arsenate against which some targeted insects had shown increased resistance. Attention was directed toward phenolics, phosphoniums, chromatic salts, thiazines, thiocarbamates, and thiuram sulfides, of which the latter two showed most promise. One of the new synthetic organic compounds, paradichlorobenzene, was used effectively against both clothing moths and peach borers.

The organic synthetics that first appeared in the early 1930s were believed to have enormous biological potential. By 1940, however, only two dozen insecticides were available for plant protection, each effective against only a few pests and for short periods at high dosages.

One of the earliest special groups of the organic insecticides developed in the mid-1930s was the chlorinated naphthalenes. These became the basis of three of the most poisonous chlorinated hydrocarbon insecticides (aldrin, dieldrin, and endrin) developed in the age of DDT (see next section). Of these, endrin was considered to be the most poisonous of all.

Following early production of DDT, other chlorinated hydrocarbons (CHCs) were produced. Before the end of World War II, benzene hexachloride (BHC) became more widely available. It was soon followed by rhothane (DDD), toxaphene, chlordane, methoxychlor, lindane, heptachlor, endrin, dieldrien, and isodrin— almost all of which were in use by 1950. Most of these proved effective against a wide variety of shade tree and shrub pests without evidence of plant injury.

TABLE 15.2

EARLY USE OF INSECTICIDES IN ARBORICULTURE

YEAR	INSECT	MATERIAL
1891	Gypsy moth	Lead arsenate
1917	Borer	Carbon disulfide
1930	Scale	Petroleum oils
	Aphids, thrips	Pyrethrum, nicotine
	Gypsy moth, Japanese beetle	Lead arsenate

The Era of DDT

The period from 1940 to 1970 has been called the Era of DDT. These thirty years were marked by a historic peak of chemical pesticide use in all aspects of the environment, including arboriculture. This period was characterized by the development of chlorinated hydrocarbons, new organic phosphates, new miticides, increased insect resistance, systemics, a biological insecticide, and pheromones. The period began with the dramatic advent of DDT and ended with its banishment.

The first of the postwar organic insecticides, including DDT, were the chlorinated hydrocarbons, known for their high toxicity and longevity. The insecticide dichloro-diphenol-trichloroethane (DDT) was first formulated by Austrian graduate student Othman Zeidler in 1873, but its insecticidal properties were not well known until the chemical was resurrected in 1938 by Paul Mueller, a Swiss chemist with the J. R. Geigy Company in Basel, Switzerland. In that year, this new insecticide was credited with saving the Swiss potato crop from the ravages of the Colorado potato beetle. Discovery of its insecticidal capacity at that time made it possible to use DDT in World War II, and Mueller received the Nobel Prize for his work in 1948.

With World War II in progress, the Geigy Company sent a sample of DDT to a New York subsidiary with data on the insecticidal potency of its compositions. Included in that data was information on the effectiveness of DDT against the typhus-carrying body louse, a common scourge among military units living under primitive conditions of sanitation. By the fall of 1942 DDT was available to protect U.S. troops from the louse-borne typhus virus in the North African campaign. It was also used extensively in controlling mosquito-borne malaria in tropical areas of the South Pacific battle zones.

Although poisonous to the central nervous systems of insects and less toxic to birds and mammals, it was considered harmless to humans. It had no effect on protozoa, bacteria, fungi, or internal mammal parasites such as nematodes or flatworms. In 1945 no cases of toxicity to humans were known. Many soldiers were dusted with it from head to foot with no apparent health effects.

By 1948 it was known that DDT could control tent caterpillar, Saratoga spittle bug, pine tip moth, lace bug, almost all leaf-eating caterpillars, thrips, plant bugs, aphids, beetles, leafhoppers, catalpa sphinx, certain ants, and wasps. It had little or no effect on red spider mites and allied species, some aphids, scales, beetles, mealy bugs, plant lice, grasshoppers, boll weevil, cinch bug, and Mexican bean beetle.

The influence of DDT was worldwide and dramatic, surpassing in the minds of some the impact of gunpowder and penicillin. Of special interest to arboriculture,

DDT exceeded any previous expectation for insect control. Control against difficult insects such as gypsy moth and spruce budworm was successful for the first time. Its most important use, however, was in control of insect-borne, human disease. As mentioned previously, the Allied armies in Europe, Africa, and the South Pacific were able to function without serious problems from malaria and typhus. By 1955 worldwide eradication of malaria seemed at hand, and the virtual extinction of many common insect pests, such as the common housefly, was predicted.

On the downside, the heavy and continued use of DDT began to show some undesirable results in the 1950s and 1960s. Some of the insect targets were found to have developed resistance to it. Some natural predators of tree pests not killed by DDT were themselves destroyed, leaving the unaffected pests to flourish and become more damaging as a result. Damage to both target and nontarget tree species was also recognized: not only were dormant sprays toxic to many smooth barked trees and shrubs such as maples and lilacs, but foliar applications were known to burn the leaves of Siberian elm (*Ulmus pumila*). Finally, evidence began to surface that DDT might be hazardous to the health of animals and humans. Perhaps the most important characteristic of DDT that made it so successful in the beginning was its longevity in the environment. By the late 1950s this same characteristic loomed as a detriment when it became clear that DDT had been distributed on a worldwide basis and was accumulating at high levels, through food chains, in fish; birds; and mammals, including humans. These factors led ultimately to the complete ban of DDT in 1972 for dissemination into the environment.

The loss of DDT for control of insect pests of shade trees and ornamental plants was a special blow to arboriculture. Perhaps most seriously affected were extensive and intensive control programs of Dutch elm disease and gypsy moth. Despite assurances from pest control authorities, none of the alternatives proposed could match the effectiveness of DDT against a wide variety of insect problems. This had a demoralizing impact on arborists, commercial and municipal, that led in time to the virtual abandonment of control programs for Dutch elm disease and other insect pests. Of even greater significance, the ban on DDT became the symbol for igniting the pesticide controversy as a dominant public issue that continues today.

The Carbamates and Phosphates

Just as DDT was being resurrected in Switzerland, another class of chemical was formulated for insect control. Known as carbamates, the first major success (carbaryl, sold as Sevin) became available for use in the late 1950s. As a chemical group, the carbamates have had more significance and greater use as fungicides than as insecticides.

In 1944 in Germany, Gerhard Schrader introduced the chemical bladen, which would lead to the later development of the organophosphorus (OPPs) insecticides after World War II. These were known as the "soft insecticides" for their reduced persistence in the environment, and included some of the most highly toxic chemicals known, such as parathion. Also included were malathion; schradan; TEPP (tetraethyl pyrophosphate); demeton; and others, including some with a narrow, specialized spectrum.

Discovered in Germany, parathion was the earliest of the broad-spectrum OPPs but, because of its high toxicity to humans, it had limited use. Extremely effective against a wide variety of agricultural and ornamental pests, it had an unpleasant odor, and as with TEPP, was especially effective against aphids, spider mites, and scale insects. In contrast to other organophosphates with mild toxicity to mammals, parathion was extremely toxic to humans and over time was responsible for some fatal poisonings (involving careless use and deliberate suicide). Because of its high toxicity, parathion was and continues to be used only under special conditions and often only by permission of regulators.

The next organophosphate of value for ornamental and shade tree use was malathion, developed in the United States and used in the early 1950s. Considered a milestone in the emergence of selectively toxic OPPs, malathion probably controls as many insects as does parathion with a longer effect. Available at first with a distinctly distasteful odor, it was soon purified and deodorized.

Systemic Insecticides

Another of the many new developments following World War II was the advent of systemic chemicals for insect control. Such chemicals were absorbed by plant tissues and translocated throughout the plant. These chemicals are not generally toxic to plants but are toxic to insects that consume treated plant tissue. By 1949 absorption and translocation of systemic chemicals had been established. Some materials could be absorbed directly by application to leaves and stems; others were absorbed freely by roots, either by direct application or from the soil.

The history of systemics in agriculture can be traced to World War I, with attempts to find chemicals that could be absorbed by plants to make them toxic to insects and fungi. The chemicals involved included pyridine, magnesium sulfate, barium chloride, and potassium cyanide. Success was tempered by the risk that edible tissue might be too toxic for human consumption, especially when arsenate or cyanide was involved. While effective, these and other successful chemicals considered too toxic for safety were eventually abandoned.

The systemic insecticides developed in the United States in the postwar period came largely from the work of Gerhard Schrader in Germany, who in 1940 discovered that the organic phosphorus and fluoride compounds were readily absorbed by plants. Most future systemic insecticides would be organic phosphates, such as bidrin, Meta-Systox, and Di-Syston.

By 1957 there were no systemic insecticides used to control shade tree insects, but in the following decade, a number of new compounds were tested. Some had significantly less mammalian toxicity than the organophosphates from which systemics were derived. Uptake of the chemicals through soil was in most cases prohibitive because of toxicity, expense, and problems with achieving proper distribution. This led in 1965 to the creation of a trunk mini-injection system (known as the Mauget method) for getting bidrin into trees. Only partially successful, Bidrin was abandoned for various reasons, including toxicity and lack of safety and effectiveness. Despite this, the use of systemics for control of tree insects improved with new chemicals and new injection systems, so that use of systemic insecticides in arboriculture is now an established practice.

Biological Insecticides

The accidental introduction of the Japanese beetle (*Popillia japonica*) was the occasion for the development of a new kind of insecticide, *Bacillus thuringiensis*, popularly known as *Bt*. Apparently the Japanese beetle was introduced on nursery stock from Holland in 1911, only a year before passage of the first U.S. plant quarantine law in 1912. Probably surviving in soil around the spruce trees on which they were carried, the pest was first detected in 1916 at Riverton, New Jersey. Sodium cyanide was used to kill the grubs. While ordinary lead arsenate was ineffective, a specially coated type prepared by the USDA provided effective local control.

Despite this, by 1919 the Japanese beetle had spread from 2.5 square miles to an area encompassing 48 square miles, and eradication was abandoned in 1920 with 103 square miles infested. Omnivorous in its diet, the beetle fed on 300 species of woody and herbaceous plants including maple, sycamore, linden, oak, cherry, honeysuckle, and azalea. By 1938 it had spread from New England to Virginia and points west of the Atlantic states.

In 1933 a disease of the Japanese beetle was discovered in New Jersey. It was caused by a bacterium called *Bacillus popilliae,* thus its common designation as *Bp*. The bacterium had been discovered in 1901 in Japan causing a disease of silkworm insects, but the Germans named it and first used it for beetle control. In

1935, ninety percent of the Japanese beetle population in the United States was found to be infected with *Bp*, known as "the milky disease." The first successful attempt in the United States to use a microorganism to control an insect came in 1939. From 1939 to 1952 *Bacillus thuringiensis* spores in a chalklike dust were applied to plants fed on by Japanese beetles in fourteen eastern states, resulting in both a significant decline of the Japanese beetle population and its damage in all of the states where *Bt* was used. By 1945 the Japanese beetle was considered of minor importance until there was a resurgence and extensive spread in western states.

In 1965 USDA scientists induced *Bt* to produce spores in a liquid fermentation medium, opening the path to low-cost industrial production of spores and the first synthetic microbial insecticide. By the mid-1970s several variations of the *Bt*-based bacterium were available under such trade names as Thuricide HPC, dipel, and biotrol. These were essentially formulations of spores and diamond-shaped crystals, both produced by the bacterium. Both spores and crystals must be eaten by the insect for effect. The crystals paralyze the wall of the caterpillar's gut, and insect feeding ceases. The bacteria then invade the insect tissues and multiply in the insect blood until it dies. Under the trade name, Thuricide HPC, *Bt* was approved for aerial application in 1973 by the EPA.

Pheromones

As early as 1896 it was known that females of certain insects, such as gypsy moths, had an odor that attracted males. In 1953 the chemical produced by the gypsy moth female was isolated, and by the 1970s it was identified and produced commercially, first as gypure, later as disparlure. This gypsy moth sex attractant, known as a pheromone, was the first to be produced and used in arboriculture to bait moths for population studies. In the late 1960s and early 1970s scientists from the U.S. Forest Service and the State University of New York discovered a new pheromone. Produced by the female of the European elm bark beetle (*Scolytus multistriatus*), it was a powerful attractant to male beetles. By 1975 these pheromone chemicals were isolated and identified.

New pheromones and pheromone-baited traps were used for borer control in 1973, eastern and western spruce budworm control between 1974 and 1976, tussock moth and oriental fruit moth control in 1986, and probably others. By 1982 at least 350 pheromones were said to be effective against 350 species of Hepidoptera alone. By then such chemicals, said to be used for "biorational control," were required to be registered with the EPA, as were all other pesticides.

Integrated Pest Management

In *Silent Spring* (1962) Rachel Carson noted examples of successful biological control of certain pests without recourse to pesticides and urged more research in this area. Integrated Pest Management (IPM) recognizes the practical reality of learning to live with insects and disease at acceptable levels of tolerance. The evolution of IPM was a natural consequence of excessive use of chemicals for pest control after World War II and the unfavorable results that developed, including release of materials hazardous to nontarget organisms, development of resistance and resurgence of pest populations, and the unintended rise of new pests of little or no previous consequence. Entomologists and plant pathologists began to reemphasize nonchemical or biological methods for insect or disease control in the 1960s. By 1971 more than ninety percent of research for insect control by government and universities was directed toward nonchemical methods.

TABLE 15.3

SELECTED U.S. FEDERAL PESTICIDE LAWS

YEAR	LAW	NOTES
1910	Pesticide Purity Act	Prescribed standards for product purity
1938	Pesticides in Food	Kept illegal pesticides out of food
1947	Federal Insecticide, Fungicide, and Rodenticide Act (FIFRA)	Required registration for interstate shipment of pesticides; prohibited label tampering, required proof of efficacy and safety
1954	Miller Pesticide Residue Amendment to Food, Drug and Cosmetic Act	Required full data on toxicity and health hazards
1958	Food Additive Act (Delaney Amendment)	Prohibited carcinogens in food additives
1964	FIFRA, amended	To include nematicides, plant growth regulators, defoliants, and desiccants
1970	Environmental Protection Act	Created Environmental Protection Agency with broad powers
1972	Federal Pesticides Control Act	Governed legal registration and use of pesticides

Given the development of IPM programs around annual cash crops, it is not surprising that arborists did not adopt IPM until 1982. One of the first such programs was initiated by John Holmes and John Davidson in cooperation with an arboriculture company and the entomology department at the University of Maryland. Involving 11,000 plants on twenty-six client properties, the program began with a biweekly monitoring program. Aside from plant diseases, twenty-five different pests were identified for treatment. The most significant change in the new IPM approach, compared to previous treatment, was a ninety-four percent reduction in the volume of chemicals sprayed.

By 1985 standards for commercial arboricultural IPM programs were proposed by entomologists at the University of Maryland. These included recognition that pesticides may not be the best solution for every pest problem, retention of a trained IPM manager, maintenance of IPM-related records, and a communications effort to sell the program.

In 1990 the Illinois Natural History Survey and the University of Illinois completed a joint project of the ISA and NAA on development of a national campaign to implement a PHC (Plant Health Care) strategy for trees. Designed to develop an effective strategy to market and implement PHC programs in arboriculture, the project began with on-site reviews of seventeen arboriculture companies with IPM programs. Some of the early findings indicated that profits came from increased sales of basic tree practices other than spraying; that enhanced education and training were essential; that careful monitoring enhanced quality of tree care; that health care programs for trees may not be for every arborist; and that some programs, of necessity, could not include IPM beyond a limited number of specific problems.

FUNGICIDES

The development of fungicides progressed slowly in both Europe and North America until the Irish Potato Famine (1840s) that shook the botanical and chemical worlds to "hurry for humanity." The first application of sulfur spray or dust to foliage occurred in England in 1824 to control powdery mildew of peach. Ten years later in England, a mixture of sulfur and lime (calcium oxide) was used to control peach leaf curl. The first fungicidal application in the United States occurred in 1833, with boiled lime and sulfur used together to control powdery mildew of grape. Of special interest to arboriculture is the fact that these early fungicides were applied to woody plants.

Some of the earliest inorganic fungicides in North America were the copper compounds, copper sulfate in particular. As early as 1840 copper sulfate was reported as an effective spray in Nova Scotia against fruit diseases, but it was Olivier in France who in the late 1800s first clearly demonstrated its value to control a specific tree disease (pear scab). No work had been done with copper fungicides in the United States before 1880; however, by 1890 testing with copper sulfate had produced good results against apple scab and by 1896 against peach brown rot, plum pocket, sycamore anthracnose, canker, and other diseases of woody plants.

Before 1850 only six chemicals were known with fungicidal properties. Four of these (sulfur, arsenic, mercury, and glycerides) were first known as insecticides. The other two were copper sulfate and zinc chloride (known for wood preservative properties). Later, in France, another copper fungicide was found to be effective. Known as *eau celeste* (heavenly water), it was an ammoniated copper.

By 1881 ordinary washing soap was used in the United States for wetting sulfur in water to control powdery mildew of peach. Beginning in 1883 sulfur and its compounds were used successfully in the United States against many fungal plant pathogens. The first liquid fungicide was hyposulfite of soda, which was used against the pear and apple scab fungus in 1883 and 1884. In 1886 sulfur combined with lime was used against powdery mildew. In 1905 lime sulfur and calcium polysulfide were found to be too caustic on some tree species, such as peach, but by 1907 a new formulation of lime sulfur prepared by self-boiling had been developed. In 1910 the New York Agriculture Experiment Station at Geneva published one of the earliest papers on this fungicide, concerning the manufacture and use of lime sulfur.

Overshadowed by bordeaux mixture (see next section) and lime sulfur for about thirty years, sulfur dust was resurrected after World War I following successful development and uses of new dusts introduced about 1900. By 1902 two new fungicide dusts had appeared, bordeaux mixture dust from the United States and copper carbonate dust from Germany. Neither had wide use or acceptance until an Australian plant pathologist resurrected copper carbonate dust for use against wheat bunt during World War I. In 1918 a copper-lime dust of fine micronation was introduced as a substitute for bordeaux mixture. This development stimulated the resurrection of sulfur dust by careful attention to micronation, giving it a new use as a fungicide. From that time, both copper and sulfur dusts were widely used as alternatives to liquid sprays for foliage disease control. Despite this, the volume of dusts used was considerably less than that of liquid sprays.

Bordeaux Mixture

The fifty years from 1890 to 1940 is called "the period of bordeaux mixture" because use of this first universally successful fungicide was predominant during this time. But the period was also characterized by the rise of sulfur fungicides, the revival of dusts, the beginning development of organic compounds, and the elucidation of insoluble coppers.

TABLE 15.4

FUNGICIDE USE BEFORE 1900

The Pre-Scientific Period

YEAR	DISEASE	PLANT	CHEMICAL
1000 B.C.	General	General	Sulfur
470 B.C.	Blight	Olive	Amurca
1705 A.D.	Decay	Wood	Tar
1767	Decay	Wood	Copper sulfate

The Pre-Synthetic Period

YEAR	DISEASE	PLANT	CHEMICAL
1807	Bunt	Wheat	Copper sulfate
1815	Decay	Wood	Zinc chloride
1824	Mildew	Peach	Sulfur and lime
1832	Decay	Wood	Creosote
1834	Leaf curl	Peach	Sulfur and lime
1840	Leaf disease	Fruit	Copper sulfate
1845	Blight	Potato	Copper sulfate
1845	Mildew	Grape	Lime and sulfur
1861	Mildew	Rose	Copper sulfate
1873	Bunt	Wheat	Copper, lime sulfur, and soap
1881	Scab	Apple	Copper sulfate
1881	Mildew	Peach	Lime sulfur and soap
1885	Mildew	Grape	Bordeaux mixture

In 1885, after extensive testing, Alexis Millardet published his discovery of bordeaux mixture, by then reduced to a mixture of copper sulfate and lime. It was the first fungicide made in the United States and was effective in controlling many fungal diseases of plants: brown rot of peach and cherry; leaf spots of peach, maple, and plum; leaf curl of peach; rust of cottonwood; shot hole; rust and black knot of plum; powdery mildew of many woody plants; and many other plant diseases. By 1886 bordeaux mixture had wide commercial use against black scab of apple and pear and black knot of plum.

Bordeaux mixture became widely accepted as the standard fungicide against most fungal diseases of woody plants, even though it had some limitations, such as phytotoxicity. By 1907 its toxicity to plant tissues had become widely recognized. Despite this, bordeaux mixture remained a standby for disease control for another fifty years until supplanted by the new synthetic organic compounds produced after World War II. Given its known phytotoxicity, its continuous use over such a long period made possible the extensive observations of its value as an herbicide and stimulated early interest in the possibility of using chemicals to kill unwanted plants.

Organic Fungicides

The early period of organic fungicides in North America included the continued use of the older inorganics while new research on the organics was under way. Except for formaldehyde, all materials used to control fungal diseases of plants had been inorganic until 1913. In that year, the Germans used chlorophenol of mercury to control bunt of wheat. This was the first use of mercury to control a plant disease, although mercury had been used successfully against wood decay fungi. This first synthetic organic fungicide was also the first metallic organic compound to be used as a fungicide. Especially effective against many plant pathogens, it soon replaced copper for many uses as a protectant.

Following the rise of the insoluble copper compounds in about 1930, was the discovery of dithiocarbamates in 1934. This was the real beginning of organic fungicides. With the approach of war at the end of the 1930s, shortages of copper and mercury provided the impetus to search for and develop new organic fungicides. The earliest of these had their origin in the early 1930s when the DuPont Chemical Company began research in 1931 on dithiocarbamic acid. One of the early compounds from this group of value to arborists was ferric dimethyldithiocarbamate, better known as ferbam.

TABLE 15.5
LATER (AFTER BORDEAUX MIXTURE)
FUNGICIDE DEVELOPMENT

YEAR (APPROX.)	DEVELOPMENT	NOTES
1902	New copper dusts (use delayed until 1917)	Bordeaux mixture, copper carbonate
1908	Revival of lime sulfur	Apple scab
1913	First organic since formaldehyde	With mercury
1918	Revival of sulfur dust	Finely micronized
1918	New copper-lime dust	Fine micronation
1920s	Fixed coppers	Low solubility
1934	Dithiocarbamates	Real beginning of organics

The advent of organic fungicides and their significance has been described by James Horsfall of the Connecticut Agriculture Experiment Station. Until 1956 the organic sulfur compounds were the most rewarding of the new organics. The most important of these were the derivatives and analogues of dithiocarbamic acid, then considered the core of the carbamates. In 1934 Tisdale and Williams made fungicide history with a patent on tetramethylthiuram disulfide (TMTD or thiram), disclosing its fungicide properties as well as those for sodium, cadmium, and ferric salts of dithiocarbamic acid. This work was considered significant for directing research into a new fungicide area. Within twenty years the dithiocarbamates were being used to control diseases not controlled satisfactorily before, such as apple rust and bitter rot of apples. These new chemicals largely replaced both elemental sulfur and lime sulfur and had driven bordeaux mixture from its last major stronghold in plant pathology (potato blight). Despite this, copper fungicides still persisted for some diseases of stone fruit trees and other plants.

Having a broad spectrum for toxicity, thiram was first field tested on foliage against apple scab in England in 1935. Despite this, only the discovery in 1938 of another chemical type (chloranil, discussed below) prompted the marketing of dithiocarbamates in the United States. Thus, the earliest data on field trials in the United States was on ferbam to control downy mildew (1942) and on the metallic dithiocarbamates (1943).

Meanwhile a different type of dithiocarbamate with strong fungicidal properties was formulated in disodium ethylenebisdiothiocarbamate (nabam). The addition of a zinc sulfate lime mixture to help it adhere to foliage improved its performance. The new mixture was patented as zineb in 1948. When further study resulted in a new compound, zinc dimethyldithiocarbamate, ziram was born. Nabam, zineb, and ziram were the genesis of the ensuing family of highly successful carbamates that would dominate the market for many years.

Chloro-p-benzoquinone (chloranil) was the first of many quinones to be useful as fungicides. An analogue used earlier as a seed protectant, p-benzoquinone dioxime was used successfully against cherry leaf spot. Chloranil was patented in 1944 and opened a new era in plant pathology. Although not used in arboriculture, chloranil stimulated wide commercial use of all fungicides and was probably the last significant development until after World War II.

Following the end of the war in 1945, the most significant innovation in fungicide development was the advent of many new organic compounds. These included organic sulfates such as fermate, dithane, and methesan, and organic mercuries such as phenyl mercury. Until 1945 sulfur and its compounds were some of the oldest fungicides still in use for control of tree diseases. Widely available and inexpensive, they were nonhazardous to plants and animals. Despite this, they had limited effectiveness until about 1948 when they were changed by particle micronation, which increased adherence to plants.

The effectiveness of many fungicides was increased about this time by additives that could temper the toxic quality or improve the ability to stick to or spread over a plant surface. The additives were classified in three groups: diluents, wetting or dispersing agents, and sticking agents. Such additives could have a positive or negative impact on fungicide effectiveness by improving compatibility with other chemicals, by retaining effectiveness and compatibility with insecticides or other fungicides, or by being toxic to plant tissue designed to be protected.

While some of the older inorganic fungicides (such as the sulfurs, coppers, bordeaux mixture, and lime sulfur) were still in use after 1948, there was even more interest in the newer possibilities following the spectacular success of the chlorinated hydrocarbon insecticides. The early organic fungicides used in 1950 for shade tree diseases tended to be specific for only a few diseases and not as effective for a broad spectrum of uses. At that time the most promising fungicides for shade trees were considered to be organic mercury, the dithiocarbamates, and the dinitro compounds. The organic mercury (phyenyl mercury triethanol lactate) marketed as Puratized Agricultural Spray (PAS) was effective as a foliage spray to control various leaf diseases of deciduous trees, such as leaf spot and leaf anthracnose. By the mid-1950s PAS had become a standard control for sycamore anthracnose.

As we have seen, among the new fungicides with promise were the carbamates in general, and the dithiocarbamates in particular. One of the earliest and most useful for shade tree diseases was ferbam, available by 1953 to control root rot, rusts, and leaf spots. Especially useful in protecting leaves of ornamental trees and shrubs from infection by rust fungus spores, it was sprayed successfully on apple, crab apple, hawthorn, and other broad-leafed trees. The dinitro compound (elgetol) was also applied as a water spray on fruiting fungus galls on cedar trees to prevent sporulation and subsequent infection of Rosaceous host species.

Another new fungicide of this group showed great promise. Known as captan, it offered greater prospects for control of more diseases than any other fungicide. Among diseases controlled through soil application were apple scab, leaf spot, brown rot of citrus and peaches, black spot of roses, and damping-off. Another group, known as quinones, had value as foliage and fruit sprays, with effective control of elm leaf spot and promise for reducing sycamore anthracnose.

Recent Developments and Innovations

The period following World War II included many innovations, including the development of organic chemicals used as protectants for external application or systemic materials that could move into and move through healthy or diseased plants. Among these were the antibiotics, the chemotherapeutants, and the systemics.

Following the dramatic discovery of the medicinal efficacy of the antibiotic penicillin, plant pathologists began to test and seek antibiotics for use in plant disease control. A chemical known as expansin, identical to medicinal penicillin, was used to control Pythium root rot in plants in 1939. In the following year another antibiotic isolated from a *Penicillium* fungus species known as griseofulvin was used as a systemic fungicide against the powdery mildew pathogen.

The medicinal antibiotic streptomycin, discovered in 1944, was used successfully to control fire blight, a bacterial plant disease. In 1952 streptomycin was shown to be absorbed by plant stems from external application, and by 1953 it was used regularly to control fire blight of apple and pear. By 1956 it was mixed with clay particles for application as a dust. From 1948 to 1956—three new materials—Aureomycin, Agrimycin, and Terramycin—were introduced, each of which was successful against bacterial plant disease.

TABLE 15.6

ANTIBIOTICS USED FOR CONTROL OF PLANT DISEASE

YEAR	MATERIAL	USE
1938	Expansin	Pythium root rot
1939	Griseofulvin	Powdery mildew
1949	Actidione	Coniferous rust
1953	Streptomycin	Fire blight (bacterial tree disease)
1956	Agrimycin	Crown gall (bacterial tree disease)

In 1946 another antibiotic, cyclohexamide, was shown to be active against fungi. Because of early evidence of phytotoxicity, its use was believed to be limited. But, when introduced commercially as actidione, it was useful in controlling rust disease in trees without serious phytotoxicity. First used successfully to control cherry leaf spot and rose mildew, actidione achieved most distinction in the control of the rust diseases of apple and cedar trees. This chemical was applied as a water spray to cedar foliage with established galls, which prevented emerging fungal structures from producing spores to infect apple trees.

The concept of curing infectious disease in a plant by chemical treatment (chemotherapy) following expression of symptoms is an old one but had no practical application until 1940. In that year Frank Howard of the University of Rhode Island revived interest in chemotherapy with success in treating bleeding canker of maple caused by the *Phytophthora* fungus. He did this by chemically inactivating (antidoting) a fungal toxin rather than by killing the pathogen or inducing resistance of the plant. A few years later (1946–47) plant pathologists at the Connecticut Agriculture Experiment Station used chemotherapy to reduce the severity of Dutch elm disease and cure peach of a viral disease. Also germane to chemotherapy was the new information on movement of antibiotics in plants.

By 1958 plant pathologists had tested several fungicides (including 8-quinolinoline benzoate) showing promise as chemotherapeutants against Dutch elm disease and oak wilt, but none was satisfactory for one reason or another. Meanwhile the Bartlett Tree Company had formulated a new material, called carolate, that also showed early promise as a chemotherapeutant against Dutch elm disease. Unfortunately for arboriculture, none of these materials proved satisfactory.

Following almost two decades of intensive research and testing for a chemotherapeutant fungicide for wilt disease of shade trees, two breakthroughs occurred. One involved the development of a truly systemic fungicide—benomyl; the other involved the development of a new injection system to achieve satisfactory distribution of the chemical in the woody stem structure.

The limitations of surface-applied fungicides for disease control led to a search for chemicals that could penetrate plant tissues and move within the plant beyond sites of introduction. During the 1940s and 1950s, work in England and the United States indicated relative ease of root uptake and distribution of some chemicals, including chloramphenicol, cycloheximide, and sulfonamides. But it was discovered that movement of chemicals from leaves into stems and roots was more difficult. Up until the mid-1960s there were no systemic fungicides that gave adequate field control of plant disease. In most cases, those available were too toxic to plants for practical use.

By 1966 the development of three systemic chemical types of high toxicity to fungi but not to plants represented a significant new development for plant disease control. The first of these (in 1966) were the oxathin derivatives, especially fungitoxic to rust fungi of pine and juniper, including white pine blister rust and cedar-apple rust. Of special interest to arborists were the benzimidazoles, including benomyl and thiabendazole (TBZ), both highly effective against wilt and a wide range of other plant diseases such as powdery mildew, apple scab, and Verticillium wilt. In addition, benomyl also acted as a mite ovicide and repelled some nematode larvae. The development of the two benzimidazoles were of special interest to arboriculturists because of their potential for internal chemical control of Dutch elm disease.

Benomyl was first introduced by the DuPont Chemical Company about 1970 as a dry powder called Benlate (methyl 1-(butylcarbamoyl)-2 benzimidazole carbamate). Insoluble in water, it was first applied as a water suspension to leaves or soil for uptake by elm tissues. Applied to soils under elm trees, it was effective against the Dutch elm disease fungus only in prohibitively large quantities. Sprayed on leaves and absorbed into elm tissues, its movement into woody stems was too limited for safety. Injected as a water suspension into elm stems, its effectiveness was also restricted by limited movement. By the early 1970s the need to solubilize benomyl for effective movement and distribution in elm stems stimulated research toward this end.

Research by the U.S. Forest Service produced a solubilized benomyl product in hydrochloric acid. Known chemically as methyl benzimidazole carbamate hydrochloride (MBC-HCL), it was more popularly called the "golden juice" because of its light brown color. With an extremely low pH, the juice was soluble, injected well, moved well in elm tissue, and was highly effective. This solution prevented infection and induced recovery after symptom development. Later commercial improvement by DuPont resulted in a solubilized benomyl phosphate (Lignasan) that was even more effective. Even later, the Merck Chemical Company developed a solubilized thiabendazole (Mertect) that was equal to Lignasan in effect. Other systemic chemicals designed for tree disease control continue to be introduced.

Fungicides in Jeopardy

Coincident with the development, testing, and success of the systemic chemotherapeutant fungicides were the critical evaluating and testing of all fungicides similar to that described earlier for insecticides. By 1980 some of the new organic fungicides developed in the postwar period were marked for cancellation. Following the demise of DDT in 1972, the first fungicides to be canceled were the organic mercuries, highly valued in arboriculture for control of leaf and twig diseases. As with DDT for insecticides, the ban on mercuric fungicides was a precursor of things to come.

After reviewing the ethylenebisdiothiocarbamate (EBDC) registered fungicides (maneb, mancozeb, metiram, nabam, and zineb), the EPA concluded that the risks from continued use of these products outweighed the benefits and proposed cancellation of many of the uses previously allowed. A sixth EBDC (amobam) had been voluntarily canceled several years before. The EPA review included use of EBDCs on food and ornamental plants and addressed industrial and homeowner uses as well. The risks cited resulted from exposure to ethylenethiorurea (ETU), a common contaminant, as well as metabolite and degradation products of these pesticides. The EBDCs were also found to pose carcinogenic risks to consumers from dietary exposure, and presented risks of carcinogenic developmental and thyroid effects to those who mixed, loaded, and applied these pesticides.

Concerned with the public view of pesticides as related to environmental quality and food safety, the American Phytopathological Society issued a position statement in 1990 on the significance of fungicides. Noting that plant diseases limit food production and that fungicides are key components in disease control programs (protecting seeds, foliage, roots, flowers, and fruits from infection) it called attention to the following facts:

- When used prudently, fungicides are beneficial in providing plant health for the public at large.
- Regulation of such chemicals must have a scientific basis and cannot be entirely risk free.
- Regulation and evaluation must be based on recognized scientific procedures, rather than on public perception, emotion, or speculation.
- Improved plant health management systems must combine several disease control methods to minimize fungicide use and lessen future need for such chemicals.

The American Phytopathological Society endorsed the need for new fungicides, indicating the continued need for their use in the foreseeable future, and the group stressed the need for timely and accurate information as critical to safe and reasonable pesticide use.

Summary

Pre-science use of insecticides from the ancients to colonial America, without knowledge of chemistry, included fumigation by sulfur and the use of oils, ashes, plant derivatives, crude ores, arsenic, smoke, and soap. The nineteenth century is known as the inorganic period for insecticides, while the twentieth century is known as the organic period. The most recent period in pesticide history is characterized by the seeds of dissent, regulations, Integrated Pest Management, the rise of pro-pesticide action, and a continuation of the debate on use and safety.

Efforts to control plant diseases in ancient times by use of materials that we now know to have fungicidal value were essentially blind. Unlike insects, fungal pathogens could not be seen nor was their existence known before the microscope was developed in the 1600s. Thus, unlike insecticides, fungicides as materials designed to control fungal disease of plants or prevent wood rot became known only about 300 years ago. Chemicals with known fungicidal properties were first used on cereal plants, then fruit trees, followed by forest trees and finally ornamental trees. They were first used to prevent seed infection, then foliage disease, and then diseases of stems, and finally roots.

CHAPTER SIXTEEN

Herbicides and Tree Growth Regulators

"Chemicals that kill plants or inhibit growth" —National Academy of Science

Materials used to kill unwanted plants can be traced to at least 1200 B.C., when armies in biblical times used salt and ashes to destroy crops of conquered lands. Such examples of scorched earth in warfare may be the first reports on the use of nonselective herbicides. Selective herbicides were not synthesized, and large-scale application did not begin until the early 1940s with the advent of 2,4-D. Although both growth regulators and herbicides had their origin in growth hormones following the advent of 2,4-D in 1942, the development of herbicides for use in arboriculture preceded that of growth regulators by two decades.

HERBICIDES

The interest in selective weed control by chemicals did not begin until the end of the nineteenth century. By 1896 it was seen that certain weeds among the grapes sprayed with the fungicide bordeaux mixture were killed. Other fungicides containing copper salts applied to broad-leafed weeds were also found effective in selective weed control. By 1900 other chemicals used for control of insects and fungus diseases were also found to have herbicidal properties. Such chemicals as potassium and ammonium salts, iron sulfate, sulfuric acid, and copper nitrate were then used as selective herbicides. Copper sulphate, in particular, was used to selectively kill weeds in grain fields.

After 1900 other chemicals were tried. Sodium arsenite had wide acceptance for weed control along railroad rights-of-way (ROWs) in the 1930s and was used for this purpose up to 1960. Before this time petroleum oils had also come into use as contact weed killers.

Advances in organic chemistry, beginning about 1932, led to the development of the synthetic dinitrophenol cresolate (DNOC), which was first used for weed control. It was first used in France and was patented in the United States in 1935. Although it had some selective capacity, DNOC was used more effectively for total weed control.

Following this development, many new chemicals were tried as herbicides. Inorganics and materials such as ammonium thiocyanate, ammonium nitrate, and ferric sulfate were used in foliar applications, where they probably caused plasmolysis and ultimate desiccation of leaf cells. In this same period pentachlorophenol was introduced as a wood preservative against decay fungi. Later it would be found to have herbicidal value.

By 1939 interest in new chemicals was high, stimulated in part by new discoveries in growth hormones. Of particular interest to arborists and foresters at that time were several chemicals used to kill trees. Calcium chlorate, potassium chromate, and various arsenicals were applied to woody stem tissue, exposed by girdling or by drilled holes. Arsenic oxide placed in ax cuts was used successfully to kill eucalyptus trees in California.

One of the earliest inorganic weed killers used in arboriculture for brush control was ammonium sulfamate (AMS). Patented in 1942 by Dupont with the trade name Ammate, it had many desirable qualities, including low mammalian toxicity, nonvolatility, no odor, water solubility, and ability to translocate in plants. It was used either directly on or in wounded tissue, or formulated with water or an oil-water emulsion for spray. Despite its high cost and dermal irritation to users, by the late 1940s it was widely used along with the two principal phenoxies for destroying worthless trees. Ammate was the most successful and most widely used of the inorganic herbicides for at least two decades.

The Organic Herbicides

Prior to 1942 most chemicals used in the production or management of plants were largely fertilizers, insecticides, or fungicides. Two new types of chemicals then emerged that had great promise to manage plant growth. One type (the phenoxy herbicides) was selectively phytotoxic, so that unwanted plants could be destroyed without threatening the more desirable ones. The other type (the growth regulators) was found to influence rates of growth, so that various plants could be

TABLE 16.1

INORGANIC MATERIALS AND CHEMICALS

USED AS HERBICIDES BEFORE 1945

YEAR	MATERIAL
1200 B.C.	Ashes; salt
1896 A.D.	Bordeaux mixture; copper sulfate
1900	Sodium arsenite
1940	Inorganic salts (thyocyanate, sulfate, nitrate, borate, chlorate)
1942	Sulfuric acid; ammonium sulfamate

manipulated for one purpose or another. The surge of organic chemistry associated with the end of World War II set the stage for the rise of organic herbicides. By that time there were already more than 100 chemicals available for weed control, but most of them were inorganic.

The first of the phenoxy herbicides, 2,4-D, evolved from early basic knowledge on plant hormones. The phenoxy herbicides have been called "hormone poisons" because they resemble naturally occurring auxins in being able to move through plant tissue and alter growth. Certain synthetic compounds, not occurring in plants, were shown to produce similar effects. Referred to as synthetic auxins, the best of these was 2,4-dichlorophenoxy acetic acid (2,4-D). Unique in its time, it was able to kill broad-leafed plants without affecting grasses. It was seen immediately as a selective weed killer for lawns, and later as an herbicide for unwanted woody plants.

Four characteristics made 2,4-D effective and valuable: a minute amount was highly effective; it was highly selective in affecting the dicotyledon plants, while not affecting the monocotyledons; it was systemic in plants, it translocated readily, and was effective at points distant from the site of introduction; and it was inexpensive, ensuring that it could be used readily and widely.

For many years 2,4-D was considered the most generally useful of all known herbicides. It was rapidly destroyed by soil bacteria, and it did not persist in soil. Its popularity and success stimulated the search for new and better chemicals for killing unwanted woody plants. By 1952 one side effect was evident: many shade trees were damaged by 2,4-D drift from lawn spraying operations.

The Other Phenoxies

The phenomenal success of 2,4-D led to intensive studies to find organic herbicides for even greater effectiveness in weed killing. By the mid-1940s it was discovered that by adding another chlorine atom to the phenoxy ring of 2,4-D, its activity as an herbicide was enhanced. The resulting chemical, 2,4,5-trichlorophenoxy acetic acid (2,4,5-T), was even more effective as a weed killer of woody plants. Of enormous significance to arborists and foresters, it would become the most significant herbicide in vegetation management on a broad scale for thirty years.

The first formulations of 2,4-D and 2,4,5-T (sodium and potassium salts) were not easily absorbed by foliage. Formulations as esters had faster and greater leaf absorption. The first ester formulations, however, were too volatile, and often caused unintended damage by drift to nontarget vegetation. By the mid-1950s, this too had been corrected by decreasing volatility with high molecular weight alcohols. Later the phenoxies were formulated as amines for rapid movement into plants and with invert emulsions to reduce drift from aerial application.

Other chemical modifications of the phenoxies were of interest to arborists. 2,4-dichloro-phenoxypropionic acid (2,4-D-P) was used for woody brush control when 2,4,5-T was in short supply during the Vietnam War. Silvex (2-[2,4,5-trichloro-phenoxy] propionic acid), 2,4,5-T-P, resembled 2,4,5-T. Silvex affected species of maple and oak that were resistant to both 2,4-D and 2,4,5-T. A final modification of interest for woody plant control was the creation of 2-methyl-4-chlorophenoxyacetic acid (MCPA). Closely related to 2,4-D, it could sometimes be converted to 2,4-D by certain plants and not others, allowing at times a unique specificity. Considered as a single group of woody plant herbicides, the phenoxies represented the core of organic compounds around which most formulations were constructed for at least three decades.

By 1971 the herbicides used for control of unwanted woody plants included AMS and the two phenoxy compounds 2,4-D and 2,4,5-T. Of these, 2,4,5-T was the most toxic to woody plants, but 2,4-D was about as toxic or even more toxic for some species. Amitrol (aminotriazole) was considered especially effective on a few important species, such as poison ivy and poison oak, especially when combined with ammonium thiocyanate.

Bromacil became available in 1952 under the trade name Hyvar. A water-soluble, wettable powder, it was clear, nonvolatile, and odorless. Treated foliage dropped quickly so it was especially useful in killing overhanging branches along rights-of-way.

Another new herbicide of the 1960s was dicamba, sold under the trade name of Banvel. Available in both liquid and granular formulations, it was one of many derivatives of the substituted benzoic acids. A systemic, it was very effective in control of woody brush when used in combination with the two principal phenoxies. It was especially valued for being able to control so-called hard-to-kill tree species, such as ash, mesquite, maple, pine, gum, sagebrush, and sourwood.

Fig. 16.1 Spraying for line clearance brush control. Courtesy of the ISA Archives.

Also introduced in the 1960s, picloram was used for effective control of woody species not easily controlled by other herbicides. It was soon used to replace 2,4,5-T by many vegetation managers. Often used in combination with other herbicides such as 2,4-D in Tordon formulations, it was used to control oak, maple, sourwood, mesquite, red cedar, and pine. Most often used in combination with phenoxies, it delayed the killing action, permitted greater translocation, and was more effective than either chemical type used alone.

Dioxin is a contaminant produced in the process of manufacturing 2,4,5-T. Known chemically as 2,3,7,8-tetrachlorodibenzo-p-dioxin, it is referred to as TCDD. It is believed that some of the teratological effects attributed to 2,4,5-T are caused by TCDD. Dioxin is a cancer-producing agent and its presence in phenoxy formulations led to the removal of 2,4,5-T from the market. It was later determined, however, that the level of dioxin in 2,4,5-T was far less than that considered sufficient to cause cancer.

By 1970 the Edison Electric Institute (EEI), made up of ninety-eight investor-owned utilities stretching from Maine to California, was sensitive to public criticism from the Vietnam experience with 2,4,5-T, and gave serious thought to discontinuing the use of pesticides in line-clearing activities. In that year it initiated a long-term research program on the effects of herbicides in the environment in nine areas from New England to the Pacific and Gulf Coasts.

By 1972 it had completed two phases of its study. The first effort involved an intensive survey of the literature on herbicides. Phase two, involving studies on thirty-six permanent field plots, had yielded the first year of data. From more than 1,000 publications, 150 were selected for reference in preparing a booklet in

TABLE 16.2

CLASSIFICATION OF PRINCIPAL ORGANIC HERBICIDES
USED IN ARBORICULTURE

Before 1950	Substituted aliphatic acids
Petroleum oils (DNOC), 1932	• TCA
• 3,5-dinitro-o-cresol	• Salapon
Arsenicals, before 1940	Arylaliphatic acids
• Cacodylic acid	• Dicamba
• Phenoxyaliphatic acids	• TCBA
2,4-D, 1942	• TCPA
2,4,5-T and others, 1942	Phenol derivatives
	• Pentachlorophenol
After 1950	• Nitrophenol
Nitrogen heterocycles	Bipyridiums
• Aminotrole	• Paraquat
• Picloram	Saturated aliphatics
• Bromacil	• Methyl bromide

1973 on herbicide use on electric utility ROWs. Focusing first on the broad environmental effects of herbicides, it noted the changes in ROW ecological communities and nondeleterious effects on wildlife before turning to a review of the principal herbicides used.

In 1972, when DDT was banned by the Environmental Protection Agency, it became clear that 2,4,5-T would be under special consideration as another potential hazard. Following new state requirements regulating its use, in 1974 the ISTC represented the Pesticide Users Conference and the Green Industry Council in a dispute with the EPA over use of 2,4,5-T. Early in 1979 the EPA announced its immediate suspension, with the intent to cancel all use on forest trees and ROWs vegetation. In the following year this suspension and that of silvex was challenged unsuccessfully in the courts. Silvex and 2,4,5-T were finally banned completely when suspension on use of both chemicals became final in January of 1985.

Unfortunately, some herbicides can be absorbed from the soil solution; 2,4-D and MCPP are not absorbed. Herbicides found distinctly injurious to woody ornamentals and shade trees included dicamba (Banvel), picloram (Tordon), tebuthiuron (Spike), and bromacil (Hyvar). Despite this, herbicides have now become standard tools in line clearing of ROWs and for other purposes in arboriculture.

GROWTH REGULATORS

Plant regulators are organic compounds that promote, inhibit, or otherwise modify plant growth in small amounts. They are based in naturally produced plant hormones. The term *hormones,* coined by animal physiologists in 1904, refers to naturally occurring compounds. Most plant regulators in use today are synthetic. By definition, hormones cannot be synthetic. There are four or five classes of plant hormones recognized, depending on one's viewpoint. Auxins, gibberellins, and cytokinins are three clearly delineated hormones. A fourth group includes plant inhibitors, while ethylene is also recognized as a plant hormone not identified with any of the others.

Like most effective herbicides, growth-regulating chemicals have been known only since the 1930s. The first of these were naturally occurring plant hormones. Those most useful included several weak acids, such as indole acetic acid (IAA), indole butyric acid (IBA), naphthalene acetic acid (NAA), phenylacetic acid (PAA), and naphthalene acetamide (NTA). By 1939 NAA was used to prevent preharvest fruit drop. At that time various natural-based, but synthetic, growth regulators were used to enhance rooting for survival of transplanted trees; to reduce number and size of fruit seeds and improve quality; to develop seedless fruits; to stiffen stems of grasses; to prevent sprouting of stored tubers; and to stimulate rooting of cuttings for propagation of ornamental woody plants and shrubs.

The first growth hormone, indole acetic acid (IAA) was discovered in the early 1930s and revolutionized propagation of cuttings. Although propagation from cuttings had been practiced before this discovery, the new growth hormones initiated a train of innovations in plant propagation. Mist propagation was developed in the late 1940s, and mechanized controllers of mist systems were developed in 1960. After a commercial growth hormone was developed in 1955, it played a key role in commercialization of tissue culture, and by 1965 tissue culture technology had replaced budding for propagation.

Some of the early growth-regulating chemicals such as indole acetic, indole butyric, and naphthalene acetic acids were relatively insoluble in water, but solutions were easy to make with the use of alcohols. Mixing the chemical with fat made a paste. Not known to occur widely in green plants, by 1942 these chemicals were made synthetically and sold commercially for treating plants. More than fifty such compounds were reported to have growth-regulating properties. Some were effective when vaporized by heat and affected plants in the form of a gas. In addition to the acids named, the following chemicals were known to be useful: indole propionic, phenylacetic, and naphthalene acetamide (NA).

Available at chemical supply houses, these materials were used for rooting of cuttings in propagation of woody plants, by soaking, dusting, spraying, and ringing. They were also used to control preharvest fruit drop and to stimulate rooting in transplanting. Future uses were expected in other plant-growing practices, such as setting fruit in the absence of pollination, stiffening weakly formed stems, preventing tuber or bulb sprouting in storage, and seed treatment for increased yields. Beginning in 1935, the research on the use of growth regulators expanded rapidly so that by 1942 there were more than eighty-five published papers in this area.

Tree Growth Regulators

The tree growth regulators of today have their origins in chemicals naturally produced in plants, known as auxins. Auxins have been known only since 1926, when the active chemical substance in an oat shoot was quantified, isolated, and identified. By 1934 the principal active material isolated was named as indole acetic acid (IAA). By 1955 it was shown to occur in human urine, yeast and fungi, and corn endosperm.

By 1963 it was recognized that there is no aspect of plant growth and development in which auxin does not play an important role. A few examples are noted: apical dominance in woody plants, rooting of cuttings, cambial growth, callus formation, and regulation of leaf abscission. Following identification of IAA as an auxin, it was soon synthesized and available for testing.

After 1945 new information on hormones included the discovery of gibberellins and cytokinins; the significance of inhibitors, such as abscisic acid (ABA), also became apparent at this time. Later the inhibitors would be recognized as a new, fourth class of hormones. Finally, in a later period, ethylene would be accepted as a hormone. In contrast to the auxins discovered by studies in physiology, the gibberellins were found in 1926 by Japanese plant pathologists working on the "bakanie" disease of rice. Exudations from the fungus (*Gibberella* sp.) causing the disease stimulated growth of diseased seedlings. By 1935 the active substance was isolated and named gibberellin. Through a combination of poor publicity and the war, the gibberellin work was not widely known until 1950. By 1955 research in the United States had shown that gibberellin markedly increased stem growth implants. First field tested on grapes in 1957, by 1962 commercial application was used to produce larger and longer berries.

Evidence suggesting the influence of cytokinins on plant growth goes back to 1913 with stimulation of cell division by a substance other than an auxin. Actual discovery of the first cytokinin (kinetin), however, did not occur until the 1950s. From an extract of yeast DNA, a purine was identified and named kinetin. In addition to increasing cell division, increasing leaf size, overcoming apical dominance, and breaking dormancy in seeds, it mobilized nutrients, and prolonged the shelf life of vegetables; and in contrast to auxins and gibberellins, the first naturally occurring cytokinin in a higher plant was not isolated until well after synthetic ones were in use to regulate plant growth.

Evidence of ethylene's toxicity to plants was apparent more than 100 years ago as a by-product of kerosene combustion, but was not discovered as a ripening agent in fruit on trees until the 1960s. Accepted by plant physiologists only in the past two decades as a plant hormone, it is now considered to be more significant in plant development than first believed. By 1969 an ethylene-yielding chemical known as ethephon first became available commercially for field application. First applied on woody plants in the early 1970s in ISA-supported research, it was shown to be effective in increasing growth in Monterey pine.

Development of Inhibitors

The view that natural plant inhibitors function as growth chemicals like other plant hormones was not accepted until the 1960s. Despite this, plant inhibitors were discovered as early as 1928 because of the knowledge that juglone from walnut trees, excreted by roots, inhibited the growth of plants, such as lilac, which were nearby. From the literature, it is clear that plant inhibitors are common in a wide range of plants.

Probably the earliest and possibly the most important and widespread of these plant inhibitors is ABA, or abscisic acid. Inhibitors had been discovered in seeds by 1934; in ash trees by 1949; and in fruits, leaves, and stems by 1957.

By 1949 new synthetic organic chemicals were produced that would retard stem elongation, increase green color in leaves, and affect flowering without malformation of the plants treated. As synthetics, retardants are clearly distinct from hormones that are naturally occurring, and from herbicides, which are growth stoppers or malformers. Growth retardants may also differ from other inhibitors that completely suppress cell division of the shoot meristem.

These retardants were eventually used to control plant size. By slowing cell division and elongation in stems, they could control height growth without malformations of plant tissues or complete suppression of growth or organ development.

By 1950 the first known retardants, nicotiniums and quaternary ammonium carbamates (QACs), were discovered to reduce stem elongation in beans. Amo-1618, discovered by 1955, was the most effective of the QACs. Two of the most significant of the early growth regulators of woody plants were maleic hydrazide (MH) and chlorflorenol (CF). MH was probably the first growth regulator used in arboriculture. It was applied in 1952 in Brooklyn, New York, to de-fruit ginkgo trees. Another early use of MH in arboriculture occurred in the early 1960s, in the form of maleic hydrazide (MH30T). Long known to prevent sprouting of onions and potatoes in storage, MH30T was sprayed successfully for the first time to reduce growth of elms and sycamores in California. Later tests with other trees, such as poplars and eucalyptus, resulted in leaf burning and premature leaf fall. Further research showed that, with care and skill, chemical sprays could be used to limit growth and save on pruning costs. This was the beginning of chemical control of tree growth in commercial arboriculture.

TABLE 16.3

SELECTED TREE GROWTH RETARDANTS EVALUATED
IN THE 1970S (*Source: Dormir 1978*)

YEAR DEVELOPED (APPROX.)	NAME (COMMON OR TRADE)	SOME TREES AFFECTED
1955	MH	Broad-spectrum hardwoods and conifers
1957	Maintain	Elm, oak, pine, and others
1962	CCC	Catalpa, maple, oak, sycamore
1962	Phosphon	Cypress, oak, pine
1965	NAA	Elm, maple, oak, pine
1968	EHPP	Elm, oak, and others
1968	Alar	Elm, maple, pine, and others
1975	A-Rest	Elm, pine, dogwood, birch, and others
1975	Atrinal	Elm, ash, eucalyptus, and others

A compound known as CCC was discovered from another group of QACs in 1960 and was found to be more effective in retarding growth than any other compound. By 1962 maleamic and succinamic acids were found to be effective on both vegetables and ornamental plants. From these chemicals, CO 11 and SADH were found to retard growth in many plants, including woody ones. Two new groups of retardants, the phosphoniums and hydrazines, were reported by 1955. From the former came Phosfone-D, affecting more tree species than Amo-1618.

The EEI-Battelle Project

In 1958 the Edison Electric Institute began a research project at the Battelle Institute in Ohio to seek and evaluate potential tree growth retardants that might reduce maintenance costs under utility power lines. The objective was to see if the trimming cycle time to maintain pole clearance could be increased by chemical treatment. Battelle plant physiologists were joined in the project by an EEI steering committee, an advisory group of foresters and arborists, and several cooperating utility companies. The steering committee included representatives from nine companies in the eastern United States, and had the cooperation of fifteen utilities. Laboratory and field testing was completed by 1967. In early research more than 150 selected chemicals were tested for the ability to inhibit stem elongation without adverse effect on the tree. Despite some promising results, by 1962 none of the materials tested was considered fully satisfactory.

In 1963 the research focused on the narrower problem of inhibiting sprouting and regrowth after trimming. Promising results on greenhouse trees led to extensive field testing of napthalene acetic acid (NAA) on large trees. Data from teak trees treated in Puerto Rico showed that sprouting was negligible where pruning cuts were treated with the ethylester of alpha-naphthalene acetic acid (ETNAA). In 1964 five utility cooperators initiated local field tests to determine formulations, application time, and species response. By 1965 the numbers of utility cooperators had increased to fifteen, with all data funneled to Battelle for analysis and evaluation; the project was completed by the end of the 1967 season.

Numerous tree dressing formulations had been evaluated, with each cooperating company doing specific tests, including some on mixed species as present on regular line-clearing operations. Specialized tests were made on variation in formulation, treatment time, and dosage. More than 20 inhibitor-fortified dressings applied to 14 species of trees were evaluated, involving 17,000 cuts on 1,180 trees. Data had been collected from maple, sycamore, elm, oak, ash, willow, and poplar; silver maple was the species most widely investigated. Consistent with early observations ETNAA was the most effective in preventing sprout emergence, but was only partially effective in retarding stem elongation. Despite the large number of chemicals tested, no "miracle chemical" was discovered. The data on ETNAA, however, showed it had sufficient capacity for growth inhibition to warrant manufacture, and it was marketed in an asphalt base under the trade name Tree Hold. The Asplundh Tree Expert Company also marketed a liquid dressing of the same material for aerosol application, known as Sprout Guard.

In summarizing the project, the cooperators had different thoughts based on their individual experiences. About 50 percent (8/15) of the companies involved continued to use ETNAA in wound dressings on cuts after the project ended. An additional 25 percent (4/15) continued its use with specific applications. All cooperator companies recognized the inhibition of sprouting, but results varied from little to complete. Overall, the research was considered successful, and represented a breakthrough for tree growth control by chemicals.

This first advance in growth control in arboriculture stimulated more research and led to a reevaluation of trimming methods promoting natural inhibition of sprouts. The latter complemented the chemically induced inhibition of sprouts. By the early 1970s the use of chemicals to retard growth was seen as "pruning with chemicals," which was somewhat misleading, since prevention of growth was not removal of established branches. The EEI-Battelle study was significant in showing that growth control could become an arboricultural practice of economic significance in the practical extension of trimming cycles.

Following the Battelle project, a new group of synthetic growth regulators emerged in the 1970s. Known as the morphactins, they were seen as different from earlier compounds in being effective over a wide range of concentrations without significant phytotoxicity. Comprising two types based on presence or absence of chlorine, they were known as chloroflurenols or flurenol. Based on early work in Ohio in 1969 in testing the ability of morphactins to alter growth, the results indicated that these new chemicals could be significant in limiting vegetative growth beneath power lines. Despite this, however, there was some phytotoxicity.

During the 1970s Maintain CF 125 (a chloroflurenol) was used extensively as a basal treatment for growth control. In 1978 bark banding with morphactin was used to inhibit growth of several woody species. Species of both pine and acacia were successfully treated, but other unnamed species failed to respond. In the following year (1979), trunk bark banding with chloroflurenol was used to limit growth. A basally applied solution around the trunk reduced shoot growth in the tree tops. Later it was mixed with both an oil surfactant and water; it was injected into trees with good results. Effective in inhibiting tree growth beneath power lines, the morphactins were regarded as an important tool in reducing pruning cycles, and were used extensively over the next two decades.

As research continued on new growth regulators, other advances were made beginning in the early 1970s. In 1971 P. L. Neel, ISTC Research Fellow at the University of California, Davis, demonstrated that growth regulators could be used to manipulate trunk growth in large trees in a different way. In this case, using ethephon (an ethylene), he was able to stimulate growth. In 1983 indole butyric acid (IBA) was used successfully to increase root regeneration of small trees. Aside from scientific curiosity, however, the arborists' interests were centered on growth retardance rather than stimulation.

The Antigibberellins

With interest in growth regulators for arboriculture remaining strongest for retarding growth in line-clearing operations, the next significant development was a new generation of tree growth regulators that inhibit the growth hormone gibberellin. Beginning in the late 1970s and extending into the 1980s, three new compounds emerged as gibberellin inhibitors, which were able to reduce cell elongation without inhibiting cell division.

The first was paclobutrazol (Clipper), developed in England by the Imperial Chemical Institute (ICI) in 1977. Originally used for dwarfing fruit trees to reduce pruning costs in orchards, it and other gibberellin inhibitors would become very effective in reducing growth in right-of-way trees. First used experimentally in the United States in 1981, it was able to shorten internodes of stem growth, decrease leaf size, and darken foliage color. It was also noted that treated trees fared better under drought stress than comparable nontreated trees. The treated trees had greener, smaller leaves that appeared better able to retain water longer. Good results were reported on the treatment of many tree species, such as maple, oak, ash, and sycamore. Despite the good results, there was a question that paclobutrazol shortened the life span of trees treated, but it is far too soon to know whether this is true. The longest used of the antigibberellins and with the widest range of use by utility arborists, paclobutrazol was seen to have great potential for increasing tree-trimming cycles from two to four years. It was labeled for commercial use in 1986. Following paclobutrazol, floraprimadol (Cutlass) was introduced in 1983 with an experimental use permit. It is very effective like paclobutrazol, and was registered for commercial use in 1989.

Despite the effectiveness of growth regulators, there have been reservations about their use because of inconsistent results as well as damage to trees by injection. The most common method of introduction, trunk injection, can result in bark damage, necrotic tissue around drilled holes, and bleeding. In cases where trimming cycles are long, economic advantages are marginal, results are inconsistent, and there is public concern over widespread use of pesticides, some companies opt not to use tree growth regulators. Despite this, for many arborists, by the 1990s tree growth regulators had entered the main stream as effective chemicals for use in arboriculture.

SUMMARY

Materials used to kill unwanted plants had little use until it was discovered that the fungicide bordeaux mixture was toxic to certain plants as well as to fungi. This stimulated the search for additional, selective inorganic chemicals. Bordeaux mixture was soon superseded by a variety of materials, including the arsenicals and sulfurs. Recent information on herbicide use in arboriculture has made clear that they can be valuable as well as potentially dangerous.

Growth regulators had their origin in the discovery of plant hormones early in this century. By the mid-1980s chemical treatments of urban trees to retard growth had become widely practiced and accepted as a new tool in arboriculture. Despite this, negative data on efficacy and costs, combined with side effects that are damaging to trees, has begun to raise questions on the value of continuing the practice of what has become known erroneously as "chemical pruning."

CHAPTER SEVENTEEN

Pruning and Line Clearing

*"I know not how your trees should be faulty, if you reform all
your vices timely and orderly"* —W. Lawson, 1676

Arboricultural practices were prevalent in many ancient civilizations. In addition to planting and transplanting, the ancients undertook pruning and experimented with fertilizers. Even the art of grafting was known to the Romans, although probably not understood well. They were also known to propagate by cuttings, by layering, and by suckers from roots and stems. Not confined to trees and shrubs, these practices were used on plants of every type. There was little recorded on such practices, however, until the period following the Renaissance in Europe.

In this post-Renaissance period, one of the first to recognize and acknowledge the debt that society owed to the tree men who did the actual work was John Evelyn of England, in his *Sylva* of 1662. The following statement may have been the earliest acknowledgment of the care, dedication, and skill of the working arborist:

> Those walks and ranks of trees are sure to prosper whilst under the care and culture of the most industrious and knowing Mr. Wise (to whom, and to his partner, Mr. London) I now only acknowledged myself particularly obliged; but the whole nation for what they have contributed to the sweetest, useful and most innocent diversions of life, gardens and plantation.

When it became clear during the late nineteenth and the early twentieth centuries that trees on urban sites were subject to different stresses than forest trees, most plantsmen assumed and accepted that civilization was dangerous for trees. There were two obvious causes for stress. Under urban conditions fallen leaves removed from the site could result in a depletion of essential nutrients. Under the same conditions adequate water was often unavailable because of paving, soil compaction, construction, and physical obstacles to root growth and water flow. Trees weakened under these conditions could be more susceptible to insect infestation and fungus infection.

The bulk of work in arboriculture in North America at the beginning of the 1900s was in tree surgery that included cavity filling, trimming, and cabling/bracing. Interest in tree care services increased tremendously in the Roaring Twenties. New wealth and prosperity brought estates that were larger than those of the nineteenth century, and there were more of them. Moving large trees was in vogue. Most arboricultural work in this period was done on large estates, with one or more crews on a single property for one or more weeks. The cost of such jobs commonly ran into thousands of dollars, which was substantial at the time.

Although the arborists of the early 1900s were preoccupied with such tree surgery as cavity filling, they were also engaged in pruning. It soon became apparent that pruning was far more important than cavity work for general tree maintenance, especially when it became apparent that most cavities develop from improper pruning, or no pruning at all. It also became clear that pruning was essential throughout the life of the tree, and that the importance of early and constant pruning was often overlooked. In their preoccupation with cavity treatment, the early arborists failed to give pruning the priority that need and practicality would demand.

After the stock market crash in 1929, the amount of cavity work decreased sharply, never to regain its dominant position. Many arborists learned for the first time that their own survival depended on consideration of the client's pocketbook, because the big spenders were gone. As a result, the less expensive services of pruning, fertilizing, and insect control came to the fore. In addition, the growth of electric power in the 1920s created an entire industry of line clearance that continues to the present time.

Despite these changes, by 1935 most commercial arborists considered the field of tree care to involve only five major practices: pruning, fertilizing, spraying, cabling and bracing, and cavity treatment. Of these, the first four were accepted universally as of major importance; only cavity treatment was then in doubt. It was felt that its close association with tree surgery meant that it did not deserve as much emphasis as it had been given earlier, but it still had a place. Despite the claims of many arborists, it was becoming clear to many that cavity work would not cure internal decay, would not prevent its spread, and would not improve the health of the tree or lengthen its life.

Fig. 17.1 Early tree climbing saddle. Courtesy of the ISA Archives.

In this postwar period, serious thought was given to the quality of tree care practice by both teachers and practitioners, in light of the many new developments in tools and chemicals. In 1955 L. C. Chadwick believed that quality of workmanship in shade tree practices had slipped back twenty-five years. At least one practicing arborist agreed. After thirty-five years in the business and as the successful owner of a tree company, he was unhappy that the high ideals of his youth concerning proper practices had become dissipated in his own practice. After a lifetime of successful work in tree care, the late J. Cooke White of Boston expressed both concern and optimism in 1962, when he posed the following question: "What will happen to the care of trees—the most cheerful, colorful, romantic occupation on our planet?"

PRUNING

Next to planting, pruning may be the oldest tree care practice known. At present it is the most heavily practiced and the most important economically when including utility line maintenance. Over the past fifty years it has been the subject of more books than any other shade tree practice. Evolving through garden, orchard, forest, and bonsai practices, its role in modern arboriculture as a recognized practice dates only from the institutionalization of commercial arboriculture about 1900.

From ancient times pruning has been described as removal of limbs from a tree, whether they were alive or dead. Theophrastus in Greece saw no harm and much good in pruning away dead branches. Among the ancients to comment on pruning was Varro in the Roman era. He was critical of previous writings that failed to recommend regular pruning of olive trees. He was especially critical of tree "beating" because, while it removed the fruit, it reduced the future productivity of that tree.

In the 1600s William Lawson recognized many advantages of pruning fruit trees which could also apply to ornamentals: (1) appearance of the bole is improved ("cleane skinde"); (2) safety from winds (a low profile); and (3) increased strength of bole. According to Lawson's book *Ordering All Manner of Fruits*, "there is nothing so important" in tree care as pruning. Lawson wrote of the need to prune back the top of a tree to balance the loss of roots in transplanting, and he was clear in noting the advantage of small cuts over large ones to advance rapid healing. This latter perception, without the aid of modern research, remains sound today after more than 300 years, although more is known about wound closure and compartmentalization. On pruning per se, Lawson noted, "this is an art of dexterity and skill, acquired through practice, which is so important and yet so little regarded."

John Evelyn made some of the most perceptive observations of his time on the subject of pruning. In his massive treatise on silvics and silviculture in 1664, noting how valued it was to the ancients, he cited their belief that a Greek goddess presided over it. He also noted that the Roman name for one who pruned trees was *arborator,* from which the terms *arborist* and *arboriculture* were derived.

Noting that it should be done early to control form, Evelyn also cautioned against the unskilled who "deface, mangle and leave ugly stubs." He may have been the first in 1664 to recommend an upward cut first to avoid bark stripping, and noted that pollarding was "good for mast [fodder for animals], but not for timber." In this statement was recognition that bark stripping would ruin a tree for form and permanence, ending in early decay and death: "The elm so treated will perish to the root and certainly become hollow if it lives."

Pruning was defined by Evelyn as "all purgation of trees from what is superfluous." He was probably one of the first to note the abuse of trees by bunglers and frauds, calling attention to "Manglind [mangled by unskilled and mischievous bordurers]—armed with handbills" that made trees "full of knots, boils, cankers and deformed bunches [branches] to utter destruction." His words were clear evidence of the damage done by poor pruning, and the importance of pruning to the further development of the tree. Urging pruners not to leave "ugly stubs," he noted how they became "hollow and rotten," serving as "conduits to receive rain and weather," conveying "wet to heart and deforming the tree with ugly blotches, shorting life and marring timber." Above all, he noted that the cut should be "clean, smooth, and close."

Through his research and compilation of all the literature on tree care that was available to him, John Evelyn may have known more about pruning in his time than any other man. Except for cutting close, little that he said then has since been refuted, and most of his words ring true to this day.

Pruning was probably examined more closely in the 1800s by German foresters in silviculture than by any other group, including orchardists. Despite its value in growing high-quality wood in tree trunks, however, pruning was said to decrease other tree values, lead to decay, and leave disfiguring scars as sure signs of internal decay. With rising demand for more high-quality timber in the 1860s, pruning as a practice had to be readdressed, and German foresters sought a better approach to pruning. They were especially stimulated by the writing of their own Brunswick forester, Alers, as well as M. de Courval of France. The interest of Alers resulted from the need to prune dead branches (dry pruning) of spruce in close plantings to prevent engulfment by the bole of dead branch stubs.

Between 1860 and 1890 knowledge and efficiency in all aspects of pruning increased, and equipment improved as well. With enhanced pruning procedures came new pruning regulations put forth by governments, such as those from Prussia in 1865, as well as individual foresters, such as Hesse in 1899.

One of the most important aspects of improved pruning technique was the effort to avoid damage from improper pruning: this lesson was learned through practical experience and new research in plant physiology and mycology (pathology not having been yet recognized in name). The crude stumping of branches that led to internal stem rot was to be avoided by the new procedure of "close to stem cutting" followed by a thick layer of tar on the exposed wound, as recommended by De Courval. Results of limited internal decay fifty years after following such a procedure were hailed as significantly superior to the crude hacking leaving residual stumps.

During this period many unanswered questions were raised, debate was lively among foresters, and scientific research was pursued by Robert Hartig of Germany (the father of forest pathology) and others. Questions involving growth rates following pruning, wound healing, and internal decay began to provide a foundation for further research, but failed to solve the riddle of all the factors governing the onset of internal decay. Fungi as the cause of wood decay had yet to be demonstrated, and were only then discovered and proven by Hartig in this period. For the first time in the 1870s, a basic understanding of wood decay was firmly established from these and other studies.

The role of Hartig in pruning and decay is often cited, but sometimes misunderstood. Hartig's major contribution to an understanding of decay was in reversing the cause and effect concept to show that fungi caused decay, and not the opposite. He was also the first to underline this point by showing the relationship of macroscopic fungus fruiting structures (mushrooms and conks) to microscopic filaments (hyphae) of the same organism. Although he probably knew of the role of the branch collar in providing early wound closure, he believed erroneously, with just about everyone else of that era, that wound dressings would stop decay.

Significant contributions on pruning in Europe were made by M. De Courval of France in 1861, in his demonstration of the value of using coal tar residues from the newly established gas works to prevent decay by applying it to pruning wounds. The principles of pruning recorded in 1861 by De Courval were based on the successes he enjoyed from 1821–61 on his forest estate of Pinon in Aisne. Later in 1864 Baron Des Cars published a treatise on pruning that was based on De Courval. After the seventh edition in French, Charles S. Sargent, director of the Arnold Arboretum and professor of arboriculture at Harvard University, in 1883 translated the treatise into English (*Tree Pruning: A Treatise on Pruning and Ornamental Trees*) and wrote an introduction. This was considered to be the most comprehensive work on pruning ever published in English. The English edition of the treatise was made possible by a grant from the Massachusetts Society for the Promotion of Agriculture.

Des Cars advocated cutting close to and perfectly even with the trunk. One of his contemporaries, however, had a different view. M. De Breuil believed that amputations must be performed in such a way that the diameter of the wound shall not exceed that of the end of the branch. De Breuil's view may have been the first to sense that flush cuts could be damaging in creating unnecessarily large wounds. Disagreeing with De Breuil, Des Cars believed this would be disastrous, "For whenever a branch of large size is amputated in this way, it is evident that a cavity of the trunk will sooner or later appear." Adding further, "The secret of obtaining a complete cure in all operations requiring the removal of a branch either living or dead consists in cutting close to, and perfectly even with, the trunk."

A controversial aspect of pruning has been the question of tree topping. Topping is an old pruning practice, corrupted from a technique well established in Europe known as pollarding. In pollarding, all of the top branches are pruned, leaving only single stems from which many new branches would arise. Growing fast in whiplike form, such branches were deliberately produced for a variety of worthwhile uses, such as basket making or even animal fodder.

By 1976 topping of shade and ornamental trees was considered by most arborists to be an unprofessional practice. Some tree workers, however, did not agree, and used the following reasons to justify topping: a need for radical surgery after storm damage; client desire to preserve an abbreviated tree by reducing wind resistance; less costly practice than installing lightning rods or extensive cabling and bracing; need to correct major flaws in crown branching; need for compact tree crowns in small yards; client desire to lower branch growth for screening; client desire for removing tops that are dead from disease or freezing; and the desire to avoid overhead structural obstacles. Even in the late 1990s, topping is fairly common despite many publications that detail the problems associated with this practice.

The Branch Collar

Following the publications of Des Cars in the 1800s and H. Meyer-Wegelin's *Astung* in 1936, there was no change in pruning theory or practice until the latter part of the twentieth century. The dictum of flush cutting, initiated by Lawson and others more than 300 years ago, had survived all of its critics and doubters to become enshrined in new standards as conventional wisdom.

As early as 1756, Büchting said, "The branch collar should not be injured or removed." His view, even then, was not unique since many tree workers have uttered the same words for centuries. Büchting insisted that the pruning cut should be "just above the curled ring." On larger branches the vital significance of the branch collar was either not widely known or not accepted, and therefore ignored to favor the flush cut. Added to this was the regulation that pruning should be close to the stem, but not too close. In practice, this fine distinction was routinely disregarded so that flush cuts prevailed despite Büchting's recommendation.

All of this was changed by the research of a bright forest pathologist, Alex L. Shigo. Beginning his studies in forest pathology in 1954, over the following three decades Shigo issued a continual stream of research publications on disease and decay. Many of these publications helped to revolutionize the way arborists looked at trees. Among the new perspectives was what became known as the "collar cut."

Looking back in 1990, Dr. Dennis Ryan of the University of Massachusetts noted a change in pruning following the use of lightweight chain saws: "Our flush cuts became much flusher," with greater subsequent damage to the trees. Following Shigo, the role of the branch collar was defined and the "branch bark ridge" was described by Ryan in *TCI Magazine* "as the flare of wrinkled bark at the junction of a branch." Regardless of how the branch collar may now be described, its significance in pruning is clear.

Pruning Equipment

Up until the twentieth century, and even well into it, most pruning was done manually, without power or machinery of any kind. Even today, with many power tools including power pruners, manual pruning is still widely practiced. In the 1600s, tree workers used hatchets, hooks, handsaws, pruning knives, broad chisels, and mallets. Noting that only the best steel should be used and it should be sharp, Evelyn wrote in *Sylva,* "heavy and rude instruments mangle and bruise." Preferring a sharp knife for "twigs and spray" (probably branches), he used the chisels for "larger armes [branches] and such for amputation." Although we cannot be certain, it is generally assumed that saws were little used then, if at all, since they are not mentioned.

Apparently pruning saws did not come into general use until the latter half of the 1800s. Even De Courval did not generally recommend saws. Instead he noted that a straight blade, meaning a cleaving knife, was best. He considered a pruning hook unsuitable, and cautioned tree workers not to use spurs when climbing—both recommendations presumably designed to avoid unnecessary injury.

In Germany, following an investigation by an official commission in Baden, axes were forbidden for pruning and pruning saws were required. This occurred sometime between 1860 and 1890 when both the Baden and the Ditmar saws were in great demand. Other new pruning equipment at this time, in addition to saws, included paring irons, ladders, and climbing frames.

The next development occurred in England in 1883 with the introduction of the Waters Pole Pruner. With much of American knowledge on tree care taken from the English, this top pruner for clipping or cutting small branches up to one inch in diameter high in the tree was readily adopted in the United States. Available before 1900, it had a movable chisel and stationary hook combination. The improved Waters model in 1901 had the hook as well as a movable blade attached to a vertical wire. The wire served to activate the blade for cutting closure on the hook. This became known as the standard pruner. The chisel pruner, also from England, combined the chisel for vertical up cuts with a sharp hook for vertical down cuts.

Perhaps the first American model was made in 1912 by the Bartlett Manufacturing Company, an arborist supply firm in Detroit. With its own improved head with a compound lever, Bartlett produced top pole pruners for arboriculture for seventy years, changing its poles from wood to aluminum to fiberglass. Wooden poles were the established type until the 1950s, when lightweight aluminum became popular. After tree towers became standard by the 1960s, electrical hazards dictated a change to fiberglass. The Bartlett Company later produced mechanical

Fig. 17.2 Pruning an elm using ropes, saddles, and a tall ladder. Courtesy of the Forest History Society.

limb loppers for more than forty-five years, and hydraulic pruners for more than twenty-five years.

Up until the early 1900s most pruning in North America was done with straight-edged saws. A ladder was used for branches beyond reach from the ground. To prune from the ground, A. A. Fanno of California developed a pole saw in 1921 with a curved blade with its own special saw teeth. Said to be the first pole saw of its type, developed primarily for use on fruit and nut trees in California, it was an immediate success. The saws are made of high-quality steel and have been used continually from that time to the present by arborists, orchardists, nurserymen, foresters, and others.

The first of the Fanno saws was eagerly accepted by tree care workers, as were many other models, and led to the foundation of the Fanno Saw Works. When Fanno developed a twenty-two-inch brush-cut pruning saw for Davey tree workers in utility work, it was probably the first saw developed specifically for arboriculture. It was reported to have raker-style gullets for quick removal of large limbs.

Fanno continued to develop a wide variety of manual saw models used extensively in arboriculture, and ultimately expanded its market for international cooperation with Japan. One of its most recent models popular with arborists has what is called a Felco blade, thin at its top and thicker on the bottom with the teeth.

Fig. 17.3 Pruning a large limb with a hand-saw. Courtesy of the Davey Tree Expert Company.

Before World War II there were few power saws available in North America for pruning in arboriculture, although some powered pole saws, or servo-assisted pole saws, as well as hydraulic-powered pruners supplied by the Bartlett Company, were said to be in use. By 1940 farmers in California had developed the first pneumatic pruning tools, and the University of California and the USDA Extension Service had developed an air-powered pneumatic pruner that featured new design and engineering.

By 1945 the Miller-Robinson Company began selling Limb-Lopper pneumatic pruning tools. These early pruners were cumbersome, slow, and lacked power. Soon, however, farm tractors with built-in hydraulic systems were adapted to provide a power source for this pruning apparatus.

Early use of the chain saw for pruning the tops of trees was hotly debated. The early, two-man saws were never in question, because they were cumbersome and heavy. But, when new lightweight models for use by a single individual became available in the 1950s, they were wisely seen as a new hazard for pruning in the tops of trees.

Fortunately, the development of the aerial lift in the 1950s helped to allay some of this concern, but it was some time before such equipment became universally available and even today much pruning by chain saw is still done by arborists ascending into trees by use of rope and saddle climbing. Thus, the chain-saw hazard has been and continues to be an area of concern. When ropes are used, an accidental cut can be disastrous. When aerial lifts are used around high-voltage wires, electrocution is always a possibility. The increased use of aerial lifts and the new, rigorous standards for working around hot wires have at least minimized the hazard.

New tools have since been developed that are powered by electricity or gas. The new electric models with pressures only up to 150 pounds per square inch have a flexible hose about a quarter inch in diameter and shears that can complete a cut cycle as fast as one can operate the trigger. Small chain saws and hedge trimmers can be easily attached to extension poles up to sixteen feet in length.

Following the development of portable, gas-powered chain saws, lightweight pruning models, with a capacity for cutting branches up to five inches in diameter, were mounted on aluminum shafts with an extension to twelve feet. Because of the metal pole, however, these early saws were considered unsafe.

By the 1990s there were a substantial number of saw manufacturers and a variety of power tools for pruning, including gas-powered chain saws, hydraulically operated chain and circular saws, as well as pneumatic lopping shears and boom-mounted saws on aerial lifts, which were especially suitable for cutting and holding limbs.

LINE CLEARING

Line clearing as a practice came on the heels of the development of the telegraph, telephone, and electricity industries. Some of the first poles were established in between and around established trees. Others were set after trees had been cleared in forested areas. In any event, the management and maintenance of trees amid the newly established lines of poles was well under way by the early 1900s and growing rapidly as the electrification of America continued.

John Davey made it clear in his 1901 work, *The Tree Doctor,* that the utilities had a reputation for little or no skilled work in their early years. Davey himself had only contempt for those who mutilated trees, and in his view the worst offenders were the early line clearers for the telephone and telegraph companies. He sided with an irate public that deplored utility tree practices at that time. This situation was soon to change, however, according to Dr. L. C. Chadwick, who noted that utilities had begun to contract with commercial arborists for line-clearing work by 1919.

At first reluctant, Davey became the first of the national tree companies to clear lines for the utility industry in 1922. Risking embarrassment because of its reputation for skilled tree care, the company agreed to clear a power line in its hometown of Kent, Ohio, for the Northern Ohio Power and Light Company. The project was a success for both parties and a new industry was born. The experience showed that utilities wanted professional work, and that utility work could provide new opportunities for enhancing the growth of the industry. The Bartlett Company also began to do line clearing in 1922, and established a precedent by working under a written contract. In 1928 the newly formed Asplundh Tree Company began with service restricted to utilities.

During the 1960s utility arborists began to expand their role with the utility industry. Long considered a stepchild of the industry (a necessary evil), as professionals they were concerned about the instability of funds provided to support their work. After various studies, in cooperation with municipalities serviced by their work, they began to develop long-range master plans for maintenance of tree populations. Such plans required the cooperation of arborists representing both private and public interests, and were a good omen for the future of the industry.

Somewhat later (1968–72), utility arborists began to initiate "incentive contracts" for line-clearing work with commercial firms. One of the earliest private companies to become cooperatively involved was the Bartlett Company. In work under this program, the performance of crews improved, cost per tree trimmed declined, and the pay to the workers increased. Another coordinated utility program followed, with utility foresters developing master shade tree plans at no charge to the community. In such a program, the community was required to obtain easements from property owners in new developments with underground power lines.

The Asplundh Dominance

When it organized in 1928, the Asplundh Tree Expert Company chose to confine its work to the utility industry. Therefore, it is not surprising that this company would come to dominate the line-clearing industry. There is little in the development or progress of line clearing since 1929 that is not reflected in the history of the Asplundh Tree Expert Company.

At a time when all line-clearing work was carried out by manual labor only, the Asplundh Company acquired one of the earliest chain saws available to arboriculture. The only company at that time to use one, this was symbolic of the technological revolution that Asplundh would spearhead after the war. In time, the importance of line clearing following weather catastrophes would lead to the Asplundh Emergency Storm Service, organized along regional lines.

Line clearing was declared a necessity for national defense, so there was a continuous demand for it even during the war. This had two significant results. First, it allowed more tree care companies to survive the war years. In addition, it created a disproportionately large dependence on line clearing over all other kinds of tree work, reflecting a new turn in arboriculture. By the end of World War II the line clearers had moved from the "worst offenders in tree mutilation in 1901" to dominate tree care volume with standardized professional practices.

Southeastern Public Service Company

A fourth national tree care company, Southeastern Public Service Company (SEPSCO), operating largely in the southern United States, was created by a series of mergers of several tree care companies. The arborist most closely associated with its history was the late Ross Farrens. Farrens had a remarkable career in arboriculture, achieving success in the face of many difficult challenges.

Born in Nebraska in 1905, Farrens grew up in the Midwest. A high school graduate in 1924 from Herrick, South Dakota, Farrens completed the Davey Institute of Tree Surgery (DITS) course in 1926 and went on the road for Davey. He resigned from Davey with his entire crew and returned to Iowa to found the first Farrens Company.

Expanding for two years into Illinois and Wisconsin, he was unable to continue following the stock market crash of 1929. With his employees, he went to Florida to find new tree work. For the next few years he worked winters doing residential work in Florida and summers in the upper Midwest until, desperate for funds, he succumbed to "step down" to tree trimming for utilities. Farrens Tree Surgeons, headquartered in Jacksonville, Florida, was created in 1938. From his quality training and experience, Farrens was known in Florida as a man who could improve line-clearing service and reduce costs. His name, his reputation, and the company all grew. After time-out for military service he returned to Florida, expanded quickly into nine southeastern states, and incorporated as Farrens Tree Surgeons, Inc. in 1947.

In 1954 Farrens began a series of acquisitions and sales that expanded his managerial holdings in widely scattered tree companies, many of which became a part of a consortium known as SEPSCO. By 1965 his own company had 825 employees, 300 cars, 25 trucks, and an airplane, reflecting a tenfold growth in twenty years. In addition, there were two wholly owned subsidiaries in San Jose and Eureka, California.

With 825 employees in 1965, Farrens' company was said to be only one of fifteen divisions and one of four tree companies in SEPSCO. Together these companies represented one of the largest tree services for utilities in the United States. SEPSCO was purchased by the Asplundh Company in the mid-1990s.

Chemical Pruning

Until 1966 pruning of plants generally, and trees in particular, meant the mechanical removal of branches. In that year one of the first reports on tree growth regulation was described as "chemical pruning." Somewhat misleading, the

Fig. 17.4 Spraying chemicals by helicopter for line clearance (1960s). Courtesy of the F. A. Bartlett Tree Expert Company.

phenomenon described involved only the death of apical meristems of plants, without damage to leaves or axilliary buds. The net effect was reduction in linear growth for the next growing season, but not actual removal of branches already grown.

Some of the early chemicals involved were fatty acids and alcohols, such as methyl nonanoate and methyl decanoate. Earlier growth regulators such as maleic hydrazide and naphthylene acetic acid also inhibited growth, but caused other undesirable effects. The new chemicals were more highly selective and caused no undesirable effects on many trees tested, including maple, birch, pear, apple, azalea, elm, euonymus, and juniper.

By 1973 similar-acting chemicals, such as Slo-Gro produced by Uni-Royal Chemical, and Tre-hold produced by Amvac Chemical Corp., had become available. The former was absorbed by leaves and moved to rapid-growing terminals, inhibiting growth by preventing cell division. The latter, applied to newly cut wood surfaces, reduced initiation of sprouts. Reduction of growth by tree growth regulators is reviewed in chapter 16. It is mentioned here only to shed some light on the term "chemical pruning," which is somewhat misleading.

SUMMARY

Pruning is the most significant of all tree care practices. Affecting future growth and structure of the tree on urban sites, pruning is essential for the life of every tree. Pruning also prospered with the advent of line clearing, which is now recognized by the public as a way to lessen or prevent power outages.

CHAPTER EIGHTEEN

Transplanting

"Not every soil can bear all things" —Virgil

The Egyptians in 2000 B.C. were the first known to transplant trees by retaining the roots in a ball with soil. They also were the first to shape the hole and create a saucerlike depression to ensure adequate water for roots. Except for progress made in large tree moving, this was the state of the art in North America in 1900. The first trees planted were around permanent homes for the purpose of food, specifically for nuts and other fruits. This was followed by plantings for fibers and dyes. The value of shade or ornament from such trees was seen then only as an unexpected benefit.

PLANTING METHODS

We saw earlier that Lawson in England in the 1600s had much to say on methods of tree planting, including the following: a warning of excessive strain by guys on newly transplanted trees (obstruction of sap flow); incorporation of organic matter (oats) in planting holes, tree moving in the autumn only after leaf fall; successful moving of trees in winter; and warning against planting too deep because the majority of tree roots were near the surface. From this we can see how sound the basic knowledge of tree planting was more than 300 years ago.

By 1834 in England the success of transplanting small trees was said to be enhanced by puddling the roots in cow dung and loam. We can see now how the combination of wetness and loam could enhance survival of feeding roots, and how the cow dung could serve as a ready supply of nitrogen for nutrition. Even then it was claimed that transplanting could be done successfully at any time of the year. It was shown at that time that trimming roots before transplanting could enhance survival of transplanted trees. Although, such active horticulturists as George Washington in the 1700s did not hesitate to move some trees in winter with a frozen ball, it was the usual practice in 1830 to move trees only in the spring and fall.

Until 1900, the principal tool used for planting trees was the "sharp, shiny spade." By 1911 it was common to plant orchard trees in holes prepared by dynamite blasting. The Dupont Chemical Company produced special dynamite cartridges for this purpose, claiming that blasted soils contained more air, were more porous for water flow and fertilizer distribution, and broke compacted subsoil hard pans. The technique was widely practiced on rural sites, and was still used for excavating frozen ground as late as 1949. A few sticks of forty-percent dynamite could break a frost crust ten to twelve inches thick. It is not known whether explosions were used extensively by arborists.

TABLE 18.1

TREE MOVING: EARLY INTEREST AND PRACTICES

PERIOD	PLACE	NOTES
1500 B.C.	Egypt	Ferried by boat
300 B.C.	Greece	Noted by Theophrastus
1200 A.D.	China	Noted by Marco Polo
1600	Continental Europe	Well established
1636	Brazil	By land and water
1670	France	Massive transplanting of forest to Versailles
1750	England	Capability Brown's transplanting machine
1790	United States	Early frozen ball
1800s	England	Stewart's planting machine
1870	United States	Hicks's tree mover

There were many innovations in the early part of this century in various aspects of tree planting practice, including digging, lifting, pulling, carrying, moving, and finally establishing the tree on a permanent site. By 1920 tractors and other farm machinery began to be popular for growing and handling nursery trees. Prior to that period, mules, men, and the U-blade were used in harvesting nursery stock. First developed in the 1920s, the pneumatic spade had great practical value in breaking the soil hard pan around and under large root balls. Another pneumatic power tool useful in planting operations was the power auger for digging holes.

The practice of deliberately aerating soils to improve tree growth was new in 1920, because the need for oxygen for root respiration was a relatively recent discovery. It is clear from John Davey's book, *The Tree Doctor*, that he knew this, even if he didn't know why. Much of his remarkable success in nurturing sick trees back to health involved his sound horticultural training in improving soil quality, drainage, and thus aeration.

One of the earliest arborists to recognize the value of soil oxygen to tree growth and health was Charles Irish of Cleveland. Citing evidence of Greek horticulturists in 370 B.C. that growth of trees improved in well-drained soil, in the late 1920s he developed and patented an air-pressure gun to loosen compacted soils by aeration. He was the first to publicize the significant relationship between tree roots and soil oxygen. Irish magnanimously earmarked the funds proceeding from the patent to aid the National Shade Tree Conference.

As ball sizes of trees increased to several hundred pounds, special lifting equipment had to be used for both safety and efficiency. By the early 1950s a lifting boom attached to the hydraulic system of a tractor was used for loading. Later, this would be supplanted by newer, more powerful lifting machines for both loading and carrying. By 1949 a variety of power tools was in use to supplement the long-honored and still useful sharp, shiny spade. One of the most useful power tools for tree planting was the pneumatic spade. In the late 1940s the clam shell bucket digger became useful for digging large numbers of large holes for big trees, foreshadowing the advent of the backhoe machine digger in the 1950s and the tree spade in the 1970s. Another innovation of the 1970s was a gasoline-powered hole digger, capable of drilling planting holes.

On another note, antidesiccants or antitranspirants have been used since the 1930s to prevent water loss during or after transplanting trees and for evergreens during the winter. One of the earliest and most successful materials was Wilt-Pruf, first introduced sometime in the early 1950s.

By 1979 the long-accepted practice of root pruning to increase survival of transplanted trees was seen in a new light. New information showed that it had value only if a proper amount of time transpired between the pruning and digging. Its intended value would be nullified if the time interval was insufficient to allow new roots to develop. This was usually considered to be at least one or more years. Although this was a significant point, it was not new information; it was recalling information that had been learned when root pruning became an accepted practice several decades before.

By 1980 the use of organic matter as a soil amendment in transplanting was in question. It was clearly unnecessary for rich, loose loamy soils, but was still considered an asset for sandy soils that were too loose or clay soils that were too tight.

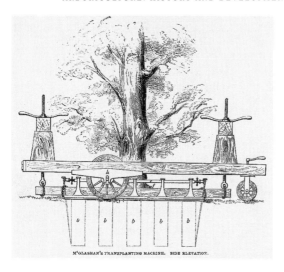

M'GLASHAN'S TRANSPLANTING MACHINE. SIDE ELEVATION.

Fig. 18.1 M'Glasman's transplanting machine. Courtesy of the ISA Archives.

MOVING LARGE TREES

Moving large trees for transplantation at another site is one of the oldest tree practices. By the sixteenth century the methodology of tree moving is said to have been well advanced. The machines used were essentially of two types, one for moving the tree vertically, the other for moving it horizontally. Since then the horizontal method has been preferred for large trees when and where it is practical.

Tree moving with a frozen ball was practiced early in North America. One of the earliest large trees moved in North America had been planted in the province of Spanish California in 1786. A giant palm—80 feet tall, weighing 60,000 pounds—was moved in 1924 by two derricks at a cost of $1,500. Planted near the site of what would become Los Angeles, it was purchased for the private grounds of E. Clement Wilson.

Back in England Sir Henry Stewart, who wrote *The Planter's Guide* in 1829, is said to have described a special machine that he developed to transplant trees. In his publication he also showed two photographs of earlier transplanting machines. One had been invented by the famous and colorful English landscape architect Capability Brown in the previous century. The other, also published about the same time in *Monteath's Forester's Guide,* was a three-wheeled vehicle with a tree vertically positioned "ready to be lowered by means of pulleys from a portable winch or crane." Stewart himself was said to be unusually successful in moving large trees, losing only one out of forty-five.

The practice of moving trees with machinery developed slowly in North America. The first tree moving equipment for the nursery industry was the Beeman-

Fig. 18.2 Vertical tree moving using winch truck by Murray Swanson (1931). Courtesy of the ISA Archives.

1-horse walk-behind tractor in 1919, which progressed to the Stark Improved Tree Digger in 1924. In 1937 large trees were moved by a single-operator crane produced by Garwood Industries, Inc. About ten years later, in the postwar era, an automotive tree mover was developed by Williams and Harvey Nurseries in Kansas City, Missouri. By 1950 this nursery had introduced its Rocker Mover for moving big trees.

The Davey Tree Company first began moving large, fully grown trees in 1926. Its early, crude equipment included a truck with tires made of solid rubber, a mounted power winch, and a two-wheeled cart. It could move a nine-inch diameter tree with this equipment. Later, Paul Davey developed a trailer with two wheels up front and six in the rear to support a heavy tree ball. With the trailer backed up to it, the tree was winched onto the trailer. Later, the trees were loaded by hydraulic-powered booms. Tree moving could and often did become a feat of careful engineering. In one difficult case reported in the Davey history, it moved a copper beech with a thirty-six-inch diameter. A large power shovel was used to trench around the tree, and a crew of coal miners was employed to undermine the root ball. Wedged out by huge timbers, the tree ball was winched to its new location on tracks laid in a specially dug trench (by power shovel). This tree was said to weigh 107 tons.

Before 1930 large trees (ten inches in diameter or more) were moved with a tree wagon or on a platform pulled by a truck. Eight ten-inch-diameter elms were moved from Cleveland to Baltimore by train in 1930. They were skidded from a swampy site onto a truck, then to a railroad flat car. The trees were successfully planted in Baltimore seventy-two hours later.

Fig. 18.3 Moving a tree to the top of Radio City in the 1930s. Photo by Henry Vaughn-Eames, courtesy of the ISA Archives.

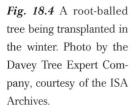

Fig. 18.4 A root-balled tree being transplanted in the winter. Photo by the Davey Tree Expert Company, courtesy of the ISA Archives.

In 1939 a record in tree moving was claimed by the Peck and Wadsworth Tree Company in Los Angeles. A live oak believed to be the largest tree ever transplanted at that time was moved successfully to the Calabasas ranch of the Warner Brothers film producers. With an estimated weight of 90 to 105 tons, 65 feet in height, and more than 13 feet in circumference, the tree had been side-boxed for 3 months in 14 feet square of soil at a depth of 7 feet. The box itself weighed more than two tons, and the specially built trailer on which it was moved

Fig. 18.5 Transplanting a large tree, moved in a vertical position. Photo by Charles F. Irish, courtesy of the ISA Archives.

had a capacity for 130 tons. It is too bad that moving such a tree on an epic scale was not recorded on film.

As with stump removal, pulling a large tree out of the ground was fraught with danger, with overstressed chains and broken cables. By 1949 a strong power winch with at least a 20,000-pound capacity mounted on a heavy-duty truck was considered suitable for most operations. Beginning about 1950, the practice of moving very large trees began to decline so that by 1970 most tree moving involved only moderate-sized trees. This trend away from the very large trees was attributed to increased construction of one-story homes in the new suburbs built after World War II.

Moving not-so-large trees was also being done by helicopter. In one case, a six-inch-diameter honey locust tree in Greenwich, Connecticut, was moved a mile in twenty-six minutes; this time included preparation, loading, unloading, and even planting. For lifting or lowering trees, most preferred small tree movers of the rocker type. Tree balls from two to seven feet in size could be moved by this method. Also used were winches with tripods, roller dollies, booms, plank and rollers, and platforms on skids or rollers.

In a 1951 review of moving trees with two-to-four-foot root balls, T. F. Mathieu of the Ohio State University found that moving by ball and burlap or by a platform was more common than belted slings or boxing with removable sides. Other methods used at that time included dollies with rollers; two-wheeled carts with a scoop; planks with rollers; two- or three-wheeled handcarts; clam shell shovel; tractor with shovel lift; front end tractor lift; and several other ingenious devices.

Despite this long history of moving large trees, as recent as 1968 the transplanting of a 60-ton oak tree, estimated to be more than 300 years old, was considered a new achievement in successful tree moving. Such an operation took place in Westlake Village, California, when a twelve-foot-by-twelve-foot box was constructed around the root system. Before top pruning, the tree was fifty feet tall, with a fifty-foot wide crown and a trunk diameter of more than four feet. The tree was moved with a 115-ton Owl crane and a special truck and trailer. Although there is still a great deal of large tree moving occurring today, there is little new in the engineering strategy of boxing, watering, hauling on flatbed trucks, and so on, with the exception of the tree spade.

THE TREE SPADE

Until the 1970s, most large tree moving had been done through a series of separate operations, including digging out the tree; burlapping or boxing to contain and support the roots; lifting by mechanical means; transporting by wagon, rail, or truck; and finally replanting in a previously dug hole. This process was changed dramatically by the development of the tree spade that could protect the root balls in a sheath of steel and do everything, except prepare the new site, in a single operation. The hydraulic tree spade is reported to have been invented by Albert H. Kornenek of Houston, Texas. Although the first commercial prototype was not produced until 1965, more than twenty years of experimentation had been invested in its development. The first model could dig a thirty-six-inch root ball.

In 1973 the Vermeer Company of Pella, Iowa, developed a self-propelled, truck-mounted model TM 700T tree mover. Hydraulically operated, its cutting blades could scoop out a soil tree ball in a matter of minutes, lift the balled tree out of the hole, move it on the truck-mounted machine, and set it into a hole previously dug to receive it. This machine could handle trees up to eight inches in diameter.

By 1984 the Vermeer Company developed a compact and highly mobile tree spade (TS-505) for transplanting trees of five-inch diameter. With a digging capacity of fifty inches in diameter and forty inches in depth, the TS-505 was designed to give the tree maximum room on the inside.

By 1991 the capacity of the spade had been expanded for use on a wider variety of soil sites, and especially for difficult situations. After more than twenty

Fig. 18.6 Large tree-moving project (1995). Courtesy of the National Arborist Association.

years of spade production, the Stocker Company of Jordan, Minnesota, was producing no less than eight types for hard clay, rocky, frozen, and sandy soils, claiming ease on the root balls and high tree survival rates. Despite its success, the spade was still limited in the size of trees that could be transplanted, and there was still a demand for moving large trees by the older, more laborious methods.

CONTAINER TREES

Although the use of containers to grow and transplant trees can be traced to 1500 B.C. in Egypt, the practice by nurserymen, arborists, foresters, and landscape architects did not become well established in America until after World War II. The first modern concept of growing trees in containers arose with a few adventurous nurserymen and growers in southern California. These first containers were reported to be dipped in and covered with asphalt. This led to the use of metal containers by 1946, when container tree growth had become established on a large scale. The Monrovia Nursery Company in California in 1926 was probably the first established container nursery, but container growing of trees did not become truly accepted on a large scale in nurseries for another thirty years.

By the early 1960s tree containers were not only used extensively for transplanting, but took on a new importance in stimulating urban plantings, both indoors and outdoors. Beginning in that decade, as indoor plantings became more popular, the size and use of containers for trees grew extensively. At the same time hotels, restaurants, and public buildings increased their use of indoor tree plantings for decor. Finally, with urban renewal as well as development of new communities, large containers and larger trees became common in outdoor plantings as well.

Container-grown trees, in the short term or long term, have had problems involving root limitations, climatic injury, and physical and chemical aberrations of soil or soilless media. Despite the problems, however, the number, size, and popularity of such containers have continued to increase over the past forty years, not only on outdoor sites, but increasingly inside large buildings, such as hotels, restaurants, and malls. In the history of planting trees, aside from such a practice in botanical gardens, indoor tree planting represents a new dimension in tree care.

Summary

Tree planting in urban areas increased significantly over the past 150 years as thousands of new communities arose and grew from coast to coast. Planting methods grew from the primitive stick and spade, digging by hand and moving trees by horse and wagon, to elaborate machinery for lifting, digging, moving, and setting on a massive scale. With postwar technology, tree planting was revolutionized by container trees, big tree moving, and unique planting methods for urban conditions.

CHAPTER NINETEEN

Fertilization

"Never blows so red, the rose where some buried Caesar bled"
—Omar Khayyàm

The history of fertilizer use began in early agriculture with the use of farm animals. Manuring is said to have been a well-established fertilization technique by 900 B.C. By the time of the Greek and Roman periods (ca. 500 B.C.–500 A.D.), the dung of horses, cows, sheep, goats, humans, and birds, and the remains of leaf compost were also being used for fertilization. Pliny the Elder of Rome successfully used green manure and wood ashes as fertilizer.

Long before the chemistry of fertilization was understood, many things were used to fertilize plants including animal manure, lime, leaf composts, ground bones, wood ashes, dried blood, saltpeter (potassium nitrate), guano, fish, seaweed, and probably other things not recorded. As early as 300 B.C., the Greeks were alkalizing soils with lime, and saltpeter, ashes, and human waste were used to enrich their groves of trees. This may be the earliest record of the fertilization of trees. A hundred years later the Romans knew the value of crop rotation (green manure), and leguminous crops (nitrification) in addition to liming and animal manure. The use of chemical fertilizer in Italy, however, was rare before the Roman Empire (ca. 14 A.D.).

Before 1860 Justus Von Liebig (1803–73) of Germany is credited with the development of the first sound chemical basis for the fertilization of plants. Probably the outstanding chemist of his age, Von Liebig was among the first to recognize that loss of soil fertility occurred because plants consumed the mineral content of soil. He was the first to experiment with fertilization by adding chemicals to soil. It was largely through his work that by the end of the nineteenth century, complete fertilizers were known to require the chemical elements for synthesis of protein and other vital building materials for plant tissues.

The American experience with fertilizer did not become significant for tree culture until arboriculture became an institution about 1900. It was only then that liming and the new concept of acidity based on hydrogen potential (pH) in the soil became the basis of soil fertilizer studies from 1900–50. During that period when the pH concept of soil chemistry was introduced and accepted, the role of lime in altering pH became critical. Of special interest to arborists was the discovery that adequate soil iron could be denied access to plants if soil acidity was significantly decreased by the addition of lime.

Orchardists in the early 1900s were probably the earliest to use synthetic commercial fertilizer for trees. One of the first methods devised involved suspension of a bag of manure in a barrel of water for days to obtain a nutrient solution.

By 1900 it was common knowledge that trees had many absorbing roots at various distances from the tree bole, but the precise location of these roots was and still is controversial, probably because there is so much variation among trees. In 1901, however, John Davey was definitive in asserting that the root system of the tree was proportionately comparable to its branch distribution. From this he believed that the critical absorbing roots were within the outer drip line of the foliage, and directed the application of fertilizer to those areas of soil. Most tree workers believed this to be true until at least the 1940s, when it was contested.

In the early 1940s Spencer Davis of Rutgers University called attention to the fact that most absorbing rootlets of most trees were not far from the trunk of the tree. More recently it has been shown that many such rootlets extended at least twice as far from the trunk as the radius to the drip line. Despite this, many arborists, foresters, and landscape specialists continue to follow the drip line method.

FERTILIZATION METHODS

Methods of applying fertilizer have changed greatly during the past century. Methods range from simple, soil surface deposition by hand of dry powder or granules, to dry or liquid soil emplacement, to power pressure to direct stem or root injection of dry or liquid slow-release materials. Until the 1940s application was simple and mostly manual. The earliest materials were dry and insoluble, surface spread, placed in holes or trenches, or mixed in planting soil. Holes were first made by punch bar, later by posthole diggers, and then by manual augers. The holes were

TABLE 19.1

PLANT FERTILIZATION: DEVELOPMENT
OF KNOWLEDGE AND TECHNIQUES

YEAR	OBSERVATION OR EVENT	PERSON (IF APPLICABLE)
300 B.C.	Plant food is pre-formed in soil	Aristotle
1583 A.D.	Elementary materials are taken from soil	Cesalpino
1648	Measured water uptake by tree	Von Helmont
1727	Something in the air is needed by trees	Hales
1779	Trees purify the air	Ingen-Housz
1791	Oxygen is produced by plants	Priestley
1804	Photosynthesis of plant food	De Saussure
1842	Performed first work with artificial fertilizers	Lawes
1850	Plants consume soil minerals	Von Liebig
1854	Plant growth is proportional to amount of materials available	Von Liebig
1855	Plants need both phosphorus and potassium; nitrogen from the air is not sufficient; fertility is possible with chemical added to the soil	Lawes and Gilbert
1878	Nitrification results from bacterial action	Schloessing and Muntz
1886	Nitrogen believed to be fixed from air by bacteria	Hellriegel and Wilfath
1910	Ten essential elements known; iron is only known trace element	
1920	Early synthetic nitrogen	
1930	Earliest liquid fertilizer	
1950s	Earliest slow-release fertilizer	
1955	Synthetic iron chelates	
1972	Spikes (Jobes) for extended slow-release fertilizer	
1990	Biostimulants developed	

made first in rows, then single circles at the drip line, and later in concentric circles. Applications were also made through a complex tile system, designed especially for aerating, watering, and drainage. Once the system was installed as a series of soil-embedded, radial tile lines, it was a useful conduit for the distribution of fertilizer, introduced in the watering.

From 1920 to 1940 there was a significant increase in the amount of fertilizer, mostly dry, used for shade trees. In the 1920s and 1930s a new method for application of shade tree fertilizer was pioneered by Charles Irish of Ohio and

TABLE 19.2

SELECTED EARLY MATERIALS USED AS FERTILIZER

YEAR(S)	MATERIALS	LOCATION(S)
500 B.C.–500 A.D.	Manure; leaf compost; wood ash	Greece and Rome
300 B.C.	Lime	Greece
200 B.C.	Legumes	Rome
1600 A.D.	Nitre (N); phosphorus (P); potash (K)	England
1650	Animal nitre; fish; cotton and bean seeds	Colonial New England
1700	Sewage	England
1800	First chemicals	France
1833	Coal ash	England
1841	Superphosphate	England
1870	Guano	Europe and the U.S.*

*Raw source from South America

E. W. Higgins of Massachusetts. Both were outstanding pioneers and leaders in arboriculture, building strong and productive tree care companies. The following account was drawn from an article in *TCI Magazine* by Bill Rae, president of the Frost and Higgins Company in Massachusetts.

Until 1940 fertilizer had been applied as a dry powder, either by spreading over the soil surface, beneath a tree, or by using punch bars and hand augers to make holes for granular fertilizers. Irish had the augers and soil injectors made by local foundries and sold them to other companies, with the stipulation that one-half percent of all sales of tree fertilization would be given to the Research Fund of the newly founded National Shade Tree Conference.

The complete apparatus involved a commercial air compressor, pneumatic earth auger and pneumatic soil injector, plus a granular fertilizer. Drilled holes were hand filled with fertilizer, and the fertilizer was blown by air through the injector into the soil where it was widely distributed. According to Rae, his company employees devised a special apparatus for the rocky soils of New England, using well points, plumbing pipe, and assorted valves and other fixtures. Irish saw that the aero-fertil method of fertilization allowed for better distribution of chemical, increased oxygen for root respiration, and increased roots for water absorption.

Beginning in the 1940s new applications involved liquid formulations for soil injection by needle and foliar application by spray. Established by 1950 the soil injection needle was fed under pressure from a hydraulic tank. During this same

Fig. 19.1 Drilling holes for fertilization, M. L. Davey, Sr. looks on. Courtesy of the Davey Tree Expert Company.

Fig. 19.2 Air gun used to aerate when fertilizing. Photo by the National Park Service, courtesy of the ISA Archives.

period, feeding holes were first made by power augers. After a lapse of about twenty years, new developments in the 1970s included direct stem and root injection of either dry or liquid material, soil implantation of spikes containing slow-release fertilizers, stem and root implantation of slow-release capsules, and soil implantation of slow-release fertilizer packets.

IMPLANTATION AND INJECTION

Until 1975 fertilizer for trees had been applied as dry chemicals in soil holes, as liquid solutions in water injected into soils under pressure, or applied as aqueous sprays to the foliage. During the 1970s new methods of application were devised, such as direct trunk injection by gravity or pressure and implantation of chemical tablets in holes drilled into wood.

By 1980 systemic introduction of chemicals for nutrition looked promising. Powder injections of ferric citrate and ferrous ammonium citrate gave good results for improving the nutrition in various oaks and sweetgums. Both implantation of encapsulated chemicals (Medicaps) and stem injection (Mauget) were introduced to fertilize trees. Each method was seen to have advantages and drawbacks.

SHADE TREE FERTILIZATION ADVANCES

Until the 1920s fertilizers used for shade and ornamental trees had largely been borrowed from work done on orchard or forest trees. There was literally no research on materials for shade trees at that time. In the following decade, however, both the Davey and Bartlett Tree Companies began to explore new formulations designed specifically for landscape trees.

Because of his background in gardening, John Davey was familiar with fertilization for at least twenty years before he founded his company, but little was known then of tree fertilization. He devised tiling methods for watering trees and used the same system for applying fertilizer. This method had special value where the roots of urban trees extended under pavement, walks, or roads. The first commonly used method, however, in the early 1900s, involved the punching of shallow vertical holes in rings around the tree out to the foliage drip line, into which dry fertilizer was placed and covered by soil, or watered in first.

According to the respective histories of the tree companies, Bartlett, in 1918, was the first to begin to seek a fertilizer especially suited for shade trees. George M. Codding, who joined the Bartlett Company in that year, did some of the earliest work on fertilization of shade trees in the United States, and Codding and Bartlett are said to have devised the first fertilizer designed specifically for trees.

Research scientists devised their formula only after years of experimentation. It was reported that Bartlett, as a trained horticulturist, had been seeking such a formula as early as 1905, even before he created his commercial tree company. By 1928 Bartlett and Codding had developed a formula that they considered the best fertilizer produced for trees. It provided the necessary elements for tree growth at the proper time and improved the mechanical condition of the soil as well. Claimed to be the first scientific shade tree fertilizer, and called "Bartlett Green Tree Food," it was also seen as the result of the first study of "malnutrition of shade trees." Not really a "food" in a true botanical or biological sense, its formula was patented and never divulged, and the research on which it was based was never described.

At a later date, the Davey Tree Company had also begun to experiment with fertilizing trees. It began exploring for a better fertilizer about 1922, when Red Jacobs arrived to begin his long and productive career at Davey. Beginning fertilization experiments in 1926, described earlier in chapter seven, he demonstrated that the shade trees he tested responded significantly to his fertilizer formulations. He showed that fall fertilization could be just as successful as that done in the spring.

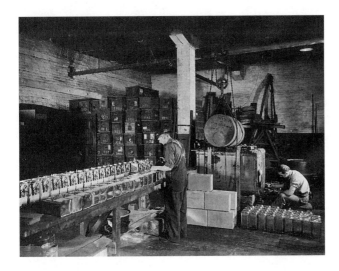

Fig. 19.3 Filling cans with Daveyite fertilizer (1938). Courtesy of the ISA Archives.

Jacobs's work was significant in that it created new opportunities for extending the fall work schedule, not only for Davey but for all arborists, and increased the amount of fertilizer used in shade tree care. From this research came a new formula for "Davey Tree Food" which became a rich source of revenue for the company. Like the Bartlett material, its formula was patented and not divulged. Unlike Bartlett's formula, however, the experiments were described and the data on tree response was available. Noting the great variation in response that he had seen, Jacobs concluded: "Possible combinations of tree species, soil types and fertility become almost endless." There were many unknowns, including fertilizer requirements of different species and the amount required under specific circumstances.

A few years later in 1934, A. P. Beilmann of the Missouri Botanical Garden experimented with various fertilizer formulations over several years. Concluding that the best fertilizer for shade trees was a 10-8-6 formulation, he also maintained that shade trees not only require large amounts of fertilizer, but that they cannot be overfed.

Dr. Carl Deuber, plant physiologist at Yale University, showed by a series of experiments that shade trees could indeed be overfed. From his work it was clear that excessive fertilization could bring about a physiological drought when excessive soluble salts caused water loss to plants by exosmosis. In effect, overfeeding could reverse the path of normal water absorption, so that water could be lost from the trees affected.

After A. P. Beilmann, Donald Wyman of the Arnold Arboretum in 1936 tested the response of small pin oaks to 15-30-0 or 11-46-0 ammonium phosphate and ammonium sulfate. After three years he found that both fertilizers increased growth significantly, with the phosphate salts being most effective.

From 1933–40, L. C. Chadwick of the Ohio State University fertilized elms in a massive test involving 500 nursery-sized American elms. Using 12-6-4 and 6-6-4 ammonium sulfate, a mixture of that and superphosphate, the chemicals were applied in spring, summer, and fall. His results showed that fall application was as good or better than other application times, and that complete fertilizers were better than nitrogen alone.

In 1950 Chadwick reported from more studies in the 1940s, using small Norway maples in his tests. Fertilized once in 1941 and again in 1947, stem growth was measured annually through 1948. Best growth occurred from surface application of a complete fertilizer applied to a mulch of stable manure. The complete fertilizer alone gave better results from surface application than holes made by punch bar or drill. No significant differences were seen between different application methods, comparing air or water, air and water, or holes made by bar or drill. In chemical deficiency studies nitrogen was most significant, but when phosphorus and nitrogen were combined, the stimulation was greater than with nitrogen alone.

Liquid Fertilization

Nothing has been found in the literature on liquid feeding of shade trees in North America until the 1930s. By 1934 information on liquid feeding for shade trees was considered fragmentary and contradictory. At that time it was believed that Beilmann had made more trials with different fertilizer formulations than any other tree specialist. The earliest tool for liquid feeding in soil may have been a "contraption" devised by Carl Fenner of Lansing, Michigan, in 1930. The liquid fertilizer was forced by pressure through hosing attached to a steel needle inserted into the soil. It worked well in light soils but not so well in heavy ones. To add to the confusion, liquid feeding of trees by jet method (soil needle injection) was carried out by an unnamed worker in Detroit about 1932, according to S. W. Parmenter, then of the Davey Tree Company. Its application by pressure was seen as an extension of the use of sprayers in that the same source of pressure was used.

In 1934 the Bartlett Tree Company claimed to perfect the first system of forced feeding with liquid fertilizer under pressure, known as the invigorate process. It was also known as jet feeding. Instead of dry form application, the fertilizer was wetted and forced by water to be distributed, as with air compression. One advantage cited was the lessened danger of rupturing a service line by an electric

Fig. 19.4 Fertilization experiment using the aero-fertil method. Courtesy of the ISA Archives.

or air-driven punch bar or auger. The story is told of just such an event caused by Davey men working near a client's driveway, where they punched through his water line, flooded his underground electric line, shutting off his electric service. Much to their dismay, the client was none other than Martin Davey, then president of the company.

Despite these reports, it was not until the 1950s that the needle method of injecting soils with liquid fertilizers with pressure from hydraulic sprayers became widely used. Noted for both speed and efficiency, liquid feeding under pressure by needle was felt to have some disadvantages, including loss of efficacy because of easy and fast leaching out of the injected soil, low efficacy in heavy soils without sufficient aeration, and perceived damage to soil structure. Such perceived damage was later discounted when the fragmentation of soil structure was seen to be offset by increased aeration.

Liquid feeding continued to be controversial at least through the 1950s, and there is nothing in the literature to indicate that the debate over wet versus dry feeding has ever been resolved. Soluble fertilizers first became available in 1954. One of these was a fish emulsion, injected by a soil needle under pressure from a sprayer. In 1956 water-soluble nitrogen also became available, and in the following years, two new devices were introduced for liquid feeding. The automatic Fert-O-Ject was available as a liquid fertilizer injector by 1958, and the Ross Root Feeder for the same purpose in 1959. The latter involved insertion of a fertilizer cartridge in a chamber of the apparatus attached to a garden hose.

Liquid feeding in the 1950s was viewed as a quick-acting fertilization response to ailing trees that needed quick treatment. With formulations of 10-8-6 or 10-6-4 considered most satisfactory, fertilizer was applied at a quarter pound per inch diameter from June to August for most satisfactory results. Application in light soils could be made at any time the ground was not frozen, but not in heavy soils. Despite the expected efficacy of liquid feeding, it was considered only as a supplement to, not a substitute for, dry feeding.

By 1968 twenty-two percent of all fertilizer was being applied as liquids—a forty-three-percent increase since 1965. Since that time liquid feeding has probably become the most popular method of fertilizer application for trees due to the introduction of slowly soluble, suspension fertilizer. In 1977 the Davey Company patented and began marketing Arbor Green after five years of research. This product offered all of the benefits of organic fertilizer—slow release, nonburning, nonleaching—in a powder form that could be injected as a water suspension into the root zone using traditional spray equipment. By 1981 liquid fertilization had become so widely used by arborists that the Doggett Corporation of Lebanon, New Jersey, claiming to service most of the tree care industry, advertised itself as the Tree Fertilization Company. A pioneer in the use of water-soluble fertilizers and foliage feeding before 1941, it was especially interested in deep root fertilization by hydraulic soil injection and controlled nitrogen release. In 1960, Doggett introduced the first soluble injection formulation. This was applied to the soil under hydraulic pressure.

FOLIAGE FERTILIZATION AND FOLIAR ANALYSIS

Following the advent of liquid feeding, two additional innovations occurred in the 1950s—foliage fertilization and foliar analysis. The first experiments in direct fertilization of trees by foliar spray were made in the 1930s, and one of the first to experiment with them was L. C. Chadwick of the Ohio State University. Noting that frequent sprays were essential, he did not believe that such sprays were likely to be used in commercial arboriculture due to the costs involved.

The first tree fertilizers applied successfully as foliar sprays were applied to apple trees in 1944. Ammonium nitrate (NH_4NO_3) and sulfate (($NH_4)_2SO_4$), as well as a commercial urea product (Uramon), were the first such chemicals to be used. By the 1950s the uptake of nutrients applied to foliage and small twigs had been clearly demonstrated in fruit trees, but was not seen to be significant by many arborists. Foliar applications were viewed as effective for a short period of time only, and for this reason could not be considered as a substitute for soil application. They were later accepted as a good way to supply deficient minerals, such as iron, on a temporary basis. Combined with soil applications they could be most effective. According to Pirone's *Tree Maintenance* in 1978, the entire concept of fertilization of trees had been changed "by the widespread interest in foliage feeding" in the 1970s.

After many years of dependence on soil tests for analysis, leaf tissue analysis was introduced to determine fertilizer requirements. In 1949 at the Ohio State University, leaf tissue analysis was considered the most reliable method for detecting deficiency of a necessary element such as iron.

One of the earliest fertilization studies in this area for shade trees was supported by the National Shade Tree Conference in 1955 under the direction of L. C. Chadwick. Seeking a foliar analysis index for fertilizer requirements of shade trees, he and his associates concluded that foliar analysis could detect incipient deficiencies before damage. Such analyses, however, failed to indicate specific causes of deficiencies, or amounts of fertilizer needed to correct them. It was also determined that such analysis could not completely replace soil tests. Chemicals shown to be deficient in leaves may not necessarily be deficient in soils. Iron (Fe) may be adequate in soils but inaccessible to trees if the soil is highly alkaline. Despite these shortcomings, tissue analysis became another useful tool for detecting deficiencies.

RECENT ADVANCES

In 1965, noting that most studies on tree fertilization originated from work in pomology and forestry and sought data on fruit or plantation yield, Neely and Himelick (Illinois Natural History Survey) began a series of fertilization studies on established trees. Their classic report in 1970 showed that nitrogen was the only macronutrient that increased tree growth, that addition of other nutrients was not beneficial, that all nitrogen sources were of equal value, that nitrogen applied on the surface was just as beneficial as nitrogen applied by solution injection or by placement in holes drilled or punched into soil, that foliarly applied nitrogen is only marginally better than no treatment, and that six pounds of actual nitrogen per 1,000 square feet of soil is an optimal rate of treatment. In their studies, application in the spring was more effective than fall application. They noted that application of fertilizers at transplanting time elicited no response until the trees became established, often the third year after transplanting. Most studies on tree fertilization after 1970 have been based on soil surface area treated rather than tree trunk size. Studies by van de Werken in Tennessee support or confirm the Illinois results.

CHELATION IN FERTILIZATION

Following the use of foliar sprays to fertilize trees, chemicals containing iron were introduced in the 1950s to control iron chlorosis. The common occurrence of iron in soils probably accounts for its discovery in 1910 as the first minor element essential for the health of all plants. By 1931 it was known that lime-induced chlorosis could be alleviated by adding iron salts to soil. This led to the discovery that iron could be present in adequate amounts in the soil, but be unavailable for absorption in alkaline soils. In such a situation, foliar application of iron was called for.

Before foliage feeding was developed, the information on treatment for iron chlorosis was coming from soil application and direct stem implantation. Chadwick successfully used iron sulphate in soil in 1936 and iron implants in stems in 1937. In 1937 even magnesium sulphate was curative for chlorosis in some ornamental plants, such as crape myrtle, both by soil application and foliar spray. In this case, the chlorosis reflected a magnesium deficiency, rather than an iron deficiency. By the 1940s iron implants in bald cypress were successful against chlorosis in Illinois, and injection of iron phosphate was successful against chlorosis of cottonwoods in Wyoming.

Chelates for plant nutrition, first available in the 1950s, were pioneered by I. Stewart and C. Leonard of the University of Florida for treatment of chlorotic citrus trees. Mobile and relatively stable at various levels of acidity and alkalinity, chelates were especially suitable for application by foliar spray or stem implant, and represented a new dimension for shade tree fertilization. Efficient as iron carriers, they were especially useful in the correction of iron deficiencies such as in pin oak. By 1959 chelates had become well established as effective chemicals for applying copper, manganese, and zinc, in addition to iron.

SLOW-RELEASE FERTILIZERS

During the 1960s and 1970s new developments in tree fertilization included slow- (or long-time) release fertilizers. Urea formaldehyde, used as early as 1950 as a nitrogen source, was one of the first of the slow-release chemicals, but was not widely used in tree fertilization until development of commercial slow-release products in the 1970s. Probably the first of the long-lasting chemicals to be so used was magnesium ammonium sulfate, popularly known as Mag-Amp, marketed in 1962. Produced by the Davison Chemical Division of W. R. Grace and Co., Baltimore, Maryland, it was inorganic and insoluble, said to be nonburning, and a long-lasting source of nitrogen and phosphorus. Its formula (8-40-0) included twenty-four percent magnesium oxide in addition to nitrogen and phosphorus.

T A B L E   1 9 . 3

D E V E L O P M E N T   O F   F E R T I L I Z E R   F O R   S H A D E   T R E E S

YEAR	MATERIAL	NOTES
1900	Dry inorganics	Used for orchard and forest trees
1920	Synthetic nitrogen	Dry; surface application
1920s	Ammonium sulfate	20-0-0; no standard recommendation
	Potassium nitrate	Surface bed in narrow trenches
1943	Vigoro	Rapid action
1945	Synthetic nitrogen	Postwar use; lack of standards
1950	Organic materials, urea, formaldehyde	Slow release
1951	Rapid-Gro	Rapid action
1955	Chelated iron	Treatment/prevention of chlorosis
1962	Mag-Amp	Slow release
1969	Jobes spikes	Slow release
1978	Esmigran	Granular micronutrients

The new slow-release fertilizers had one distinct advantage—they were safe to incorporate into soils when planting. Before slow-release fertilizers were developed, nitrogen sources were not recommended for use in planting holes because of the danger that quick-acting fertilizers could bring about physiological drought through increased concentrations of rapidly solubilized compounds. Such damage does not occur with slow-release compounds because of the delayed release of nitrogen.

S U M M A R Y

Shade tree fertilization in North America began with agricultural trial and error, and evolved into a science. Fertilization innovations through the years have allowed arborists to improve trees, to make their work more precise, to save trees from chlorosis, to extend the soil residual of fertilizers, to speed up or delay the tree reaction, and to stimulate better root growth. Despite these advances, there is still confusion about how fertilizers affect individual tree species and how their root systems develop.

CHAPTER TWENTY

Wound Treatment

*"Moisture is said to stimulate the growth of the callus, and the old
practice of covering the wound with a mixture of cow manure, clay
and lime had this in mind"* —George Stone, 1915

Evelyn, in 1662, urged pruning early in the life of a tree to avoid large wounds, and recommended plastering large wounds to keep them dry and hasten covering by bark. From this it was clear that his wound treatment was designed both to prevent ingress of water and to induce early healing. Evelyn saw clearly that pruning of large branches endangers rotting injuries of weather beyond protection with tar. Thus the use of tar for wound protection was recommended at this early date.

In 1800 Forsythe no longer referred to his famous composition for treating trees as a plaster but essentially as a tree wound paint. This is the earliest reference found on the use and application of painting. By 1834 the application of mud with bandages was said to be a better cure for wounds than the Forsythe composition.

T. Bridgeman, who wrote *The Young Gardener's Assistant* in 1840, was one of the first to call attention to wounds made by cankers. Recommending that tissue affected by cankers "be cut clean out," he also advised wound dressing to prevent water from collecting in the wound. Surprisingly, his dressing mixture included soot mixed with water and train oil, and was plastered over all wounded tissue. The goal was to seal the opening against "decay-producing air and moisture."

The first contribution to wound treatment by an American came in an 1867 publication entitled *American Pomology*. It was written by a medical doctor cum horticulturist named Dr. John A. Warder, then president of the Ohio Pomological Society. Warder would later become famous as a conservationist in the founding of the American Forestry Association in 1875. With special reference to wounds, he noted how large wounds of stone fruit trees were naturally protected by an effusion of gummy matter. He recommended that the exposed surface be covered with something to exclude atmospheric moisture whether this be paint, varnish, shellac, or common grafting. Of special interest to arborists, Warder was the first to use the term *tree surgery,* which was widely used long before the terms *arborist* and *arboriculture* were coined and adopted in North America.

Des Cars's book on pruning had been universally acclaimed both in Europe and North America, and his reputation was solid by the 1880s. Noted for his attention to the damage that even small wounds could cause, he said explicitly that "climbing spurs should never be used by good workmen." The contribution for which he became best known, however, was the heavy and lavish use of coal tar and/or its derivatives on pruning cuts to deter decay and promote rapid wound healing. His fame derived in large part from his outstanding record of preserving trees in the park system of Paris. He recommended a rather unusual mixture for treating tree wounds called fiacre, which was a mixture of loam and cow dung. Other preparations he recommended for wound treatment were also used in grafting, and these used resin, wax, or grease as a basis. Since these preparations were expensive and needed to be applied hot, they were largely impractical except on a small scale.

In 1898 L. H. Bailey, America's most famous horticulturist, published *The Pruning Book,* in which he wrote: "Wound dressings are preventive, not curative. They are akin to the antiseptic dressings of the surgeon, which prevent contamination of the wound and thereby allow Nature to heal it." Bailey sought a dressing that would be durable; both paint and tar were suitable, while wax and shellac were not.

Tree Wound Dressings

By 1890 the conventional wisdom in the new commercial world of arboriculture in America was to paint all new wounds. This had become the pattern before Davey endorsed it and the practice had been supported in all of the early literature on trees in that period. Until 1900, paint applications had included: varnish, shellac, tar, coal tar and bordeaux mixture, and lead paint. These were designed primarily to facilitate healing and prevent infection from decay-causing organisms.

Perhaps the first noncommercial American to comment on proper wound treatment in the new arboriculture was George Stone, professor of botany at Massachusetts State College in 1915. Noting how the early methods of Lawson, Evelyn, and Forsythe were used to cover new wounds in various ways, he saw in this the

TABLE 20.1

MATERIALS USED FOR WOUND TREATMENT

YEAR	MATERIAL	LOCATION
2000 B.C.	Mud, clay	Assyria
300 B.C.	Mud	Greece
1631 A.D.	Plaster plug	England
1640	Mortar	England
1664	Loam, hay, tar	England
1791	Lime, ashes, dung, sand	England
1805	Putty and paint, sand and wooden plug	England
1834	Clay and loam, paint and putty, small stones, tar and tallow	England
1840	Soot and oil	England
1864	Coal tar, wooden plug with coal tar	France
1867	Paint, varnish, shellac, grafting wax	United States
1898	Lead paint, tar and bordeaux mixture	United States
1900	Coal tar	United States
1916	Tar, creosote, paint	England

(Source: F. A. Bartlett, 1935 National Shade Tree Conference Proceedings)

need to keep the newly exposed cambium from drying out, making rapid healing possible. In his own words: "Moisture is said to stimulate the growth of the callus, and the old practice of covering the wound with a mixture of cow manure, clay and lime had this object in view."

This may have been the basis for the many dubious claims for "stimulating healing" that would appear in the coming decades. Stone was also a firm believer in the other reason for covering newly exposed wounds—to "prevent entrance of destructive organisms." He was not alone. Writing from England a year later, A. D. Webster, a horticulturist, was recommending "an application of tar, creosote, or paint, to prevent the entrance of wood destroyers and to aid in healing the wound." His recommendations were not new, but supported the prevailing view that dressings and fillings were designed to keep decay out. This view would prevail for another six decades, until it was finally accepted, about 1935, that such practices were probably in vain. Stone himself had recommended a painting of thick shellac in denatured alcohol or a thick coat of paint and warned that coal tar could be injurious. He noted also how bleeding from new cuts made painting unsatisfactory.

By 1920 J. F. Collins, USDA forest pathologist, was recommending immediate application of shellac as a suitable tree wound dressing to prevent drying and dying of newly exposed cambium. Several antiseptic or sterilizing preparations were in use at the time. Collins recommended commercial creosote in combination with shellac, and final waterproofing with thick coal tar or hot asphalt, but warned of possible injury with all tar-based materials. He also suggested sterilization with copper sulphate or bichloride of mercury, and noted the sterilizing value of the alcohol in shellac.

"Save the surface and you save all"—a slogan of unknown origin used by professional house painters in the 1920s—stimulated an investigation in 1926 by Dr. Rush Marshall, USDA forest pathologist, of materials used as wound dressings, seeking to determine the most satisfactory method of treatment. More than 100 materials were tested, including proprietary compounds and commercial paints and other products made for tree work, roofing, and wood preservation. Most materials designed for tree care contained asphalt, tar, or creosote. Paints included aluminum based, copper based, metallic roof paint, white lead, and zinc oxide. Shellac, varnish, and liquid rubber were also involved. Most materials were eliminated in early trials as too toxic or impermanent. The rest were tested for prevention or arrest of decay. Most oils, tars, and creosotes were found injurious to cambium. Heavy asphalt paste favored both callus growth and decay. Light asphalt paste favored less growth, but helped to prevent decay. Zinc oxide, a heavy mix with linseed oil, gave good healing and moderate decay arrest. None was better than a bordeaux paint mixture from Oregon State University. As the first critical evaluation of tree wound dressings, the study by Marshall was significant in failing to find any material that was completely satisfactory, but gave support to light asphalt, zinc oxide, and bordeaux mixture.

In 1929 Collins revised his 1920 USDA recommendations for wound treatment, but did not include rubber as a recommendation. Still recommending shellac to prevent drying and creosote to retard decay, he then advocated a third coat of thick coal tar for waterproofing. At this later date, he noted again and with greater emphasis that permanent waterproofing is possible only through constant reexamination and retreatment, again an omen of persistent dissatisfaction with any single method of tree wound dressing.

By 1936 a lanolin-based paint was seen by some as a significant improvement over previous paints and dressings because it prevented drying, enhanced callus growth, and prevented cracking of the wood. One material was a blend of lanolin and natural wound gum. Another, combining lanolin and asphalt, was especially promising with a fungicide added. Despite the promise that some mixtures showed, by 1937 it was clear that there was still no completely satisfactory tree wound

Fig. 20.1 A number of tree wound dressings were tried over the years. This composition was called magnesite. Photo by the F. A. Bartlett Tree Expert Company, courtesy of the ISA Archives.

dressing. In 1944 the U.S. Forest Service devised a new lanolin-based tree wound dressing that was combined with rosin. Blended with asphaltum, it showed promise over earlier lanolin formulation products. One of the best formulations included four parts of plastic asphaltum, two parts lanolin, and one part rosin. No latex-based paint was mentioned, however, by P. P. Pirone in *Tree Maintenance* when he enumerated asphalt, shellac, grafting wax, bordeaux paint, and even creosote as suitable dressings. Pirone also stressed the absence of any completely satisfactory dressing.

THE RISE OF ASPHALT

By the early 1890s the coal tar so strongly recommended by Des Cars in the previous decade was known to be injurious to cambial tissue, and other materials were sought for wound dressings. One of these was asphaltum, a coal tar derivative. Used first about 1912 following the pruning of orchard trees, it was mixed in varnolene or linseed oil, and it had to be applied hot. Its use produced mixed results because Marshall claimed it stimulated decay in 1932, but by 1937 it was considered better than a bordeaux-mixed dressing. In the late 1930s the Davey Company developed its own tree wound dressing called Daveyite. Considered both unique and sophisticated, with an asphalt base, it was manufactured from a special source available only from Egypt, Trinidad, and Utah. In 1938 the company used more than 1,600 gallons of the dressing in tree work. Despite further research by the company, it found nothing better over the next four decades. The Davey mixture, when applied in a thick coat, was said to stimulate decay; by 1959 it was able to spread a canker fungus when used as a nonantiseptic paint.

By 1940, following extensive testing, asphaltum in its varying formulations was found to be the most satisfactory material tested. Dissolved in a volatile, hydrocarbon solvent (gasoline, xylol, or benzene), asphaltum, by preventing cracking and checking, was superior as an impediment to decay. Water-asphaltum emulsion was found to give less protection over time than any other asphaltum mixture. Dissolved in creosote, asphaltum was injurious to elm, hickory, and maple, and was considered unsuitable. Dissolved in turpentine or mineral oil, it could injure the cambium.

As with creosote and coal tar, asphaltum was not always germicidal. It was not antiseptic to the spores of some fungi. Despite these detractions, asphalt seemed to be associated with less decay than any other material.

TREE WOUND CLOSURE

Before 1900 little was known of wound repair in trees to indicate that healing might be enhanced by treatment. The practice before this period was to preserve the capacity of wounds to be healed without stimulation. At least as early as 1901, however, in addition to prevention of decay, the use of wound dressings to promote healing had become a second major objective, along with the practice of wound treatment. While Davey observed the rapid healing of small wounds (three to four inches in diameter) without paint, he also advised painting all large wounds twice per year. In 1915 G. E. Stone noted how Forsythe and others 150 years before had sought to stimulate callus growth by retaining moisture on a fresh cut. Shellac and asphaltum were among the earliest materials claimed to stimulate healing, and by 1934 stimulation of callus growth was seen as occurring early in the growing period, usually between mid-February and mid-May. Despite the many early reports of growth stimulation from a wide variety of materials, additional reports failed to substantiate any of them.

Following the discovery and development of plant growth regulators in the 1930s, efforts were made to use them to stimulate wound healing by incorporating them into tree wound paint. A study was conducted by the U.S. Forest Service in the late 1940s involving more than 13,000 wounds, 600 trees, and 10 species. Growth-regulating chemicals were applied in lanolin, asphaltum, shellac, and bordeaux paste. Despite some evidence of callus stimulation, there was no significant increase in the rate of healing; there was a correlation between the healing rate and the rate of growth and discoloration of the wood, indicating that early onset of

Fig. 20.2 These construction injuries were "traced" and treated seven years earlier. Wounds have closed. Work by Norman Armstrong. Photo by A. R. Thompson, courtesy of the ISA Archives.

decay was always present. This may have been the first time that the healing rate was positively correlated with the growth rate of the tree. This could explain why earlier reports of callus stimulation failed to be sustained with increased application of promising materials. But this was not appreciated at that time, and new reports of callus stimulation would persist.

The 1970 study, "Healing of Wounds on Trees," by plant pathologist Dan Neely of the Illinois Natural History Survey and the University of Illinois found no increase of callus growth from wound dressing treatment. In 1979, in the "Tree Wounds and Wound Closure" study, he found that wound closure occurred at the same time of the year as cambium growth, that the amount of wound closure correlated directly with the amount of vascular cambium growth at the wound height, and that tree species per se had little influence on wound closure.

Germicidal Protection

Tree wound dressings were thought to need germicides to avoid spread of disease. In 1940 the newly discovered plane tree disease fungus was transmitted by sawdust from infected trees, having been transferred through dressings on pruning cuts on healthy trees. Within a few years, this same fungus was known to be easily spread to healthy trees in common asphalt tree paint. This called for the

TABLE 20.2

EARLY INFORMATION ON WOUND CARE

YEAR*	TITLE, AUTHOR / TOPIC(S)
302 B.C.	*Enquiry into Plants,* Theophrastus / Wounds, decay
1534 A.D.	*The Boke (Book) of Husbandry,* Fitzherbert / Wounds
1629	——, Parkinson / Cankers
1631	*The Countryman's New Art of Planting,* Mascall / Wound dressing and plugs
1640	*A New Orchard and Garden,* Lawson / Wounds, fillings
1664	*Sylva,* Evelyn / Cavities
1724	*New Improvements of Planting and Gardening,* Bradley / Cavity filling
1791	*The Culture and Management of Fruit Trees,* Forsyth / Wounds, cavities
1805	*The Forest Pruner,* Pontey / Wounds, cavities
1832	*Sylva Americana,* Browne / Filling
1834	*Encyclopedia of Gardening,* Loudon / Pruning, wounds, cavities
1840	*The Young Gardener's Assistant,* Bridgeman / Wounds, cavities
1864	*Tree Pruning,* Des Cars / Pruning, cavities, dressing
1867	*American Pomology,* Warder** / Wounds, cavities, surgery
1894	*Textbook of the Diseases of Trees,* Hartig / Wounds, decay, fungi
1895	*Principles of Pruning and Care of Wounds in Woody Plants,* Woods / Wounds
1898	*The Pruning Book,* Bailey / Wounds, decay, fungi
1900	*Gypsy Moth Report to the Massachusetts Board of Agriculture,* Forbush / Wounds, healing
1902	*The Tree Doctor,* Davey / Wounds, cavities
1912	*Tree Surgery,* Collins / Wounds, cavities
1916	*Tree Wounds and Diseases,* Webster / Cavities, decay, dressing
1918	*The Case of Tree Surgery,* Rankin / Wounds, cavities
1926	*Practical Tree Repair,* Peets / Wounds, cavities

*Information for listings through 1867 was taken from F. A. Bartlett, 1935 National Shade Tree Conference Proceedings.

**First to use the term tree surgery in the sense employed in 1935.

incorporation of a germicide in dressings to prevent such inadvertent disease spread. To prevent new infections, a tree wound dressing composed of a mixture of phenylmercury nitrate in gilsonite varnish was proposed. Orange shellac was also considered then to have high value as a germicidal dressing because of its alcoholic content. It was highly regarded for protection as well as stimulation of the cambium. A solution of copper sulfate was also recommended for germicidal treatment, but it was recognized that both copper and mercury compounds could be toxic to the tree's tissues. This was probably the first time that copper and mercury compounds were used against disease per se. At about the same time, insecticides were successfully incorporated into tree paint to deter insects, but this did not become a standard practice until much later.

By 1941 the germicidal dressings considered suitable included orange shellac and solutions of either copper sulfate or mercuric bichloride. Considered one of the best then in use, shellac was also a preservative able to penetrate wood. Although shellac was well known for protection of the cambium, it had the disadvantage of not being permanent. Solutions of both copper and mercury compounds had long been known for their germicidal value.

WOUND DRESSINGS IN TROUBLE

In the 1960s Donald Welch of Cornell University noted that experienced arborists, after using tree paints for many years, were not in agreement as to the practicality of such an operation, and that painting wounds was seen as an operation with far greater benefit as a mark of good workmanship than as a deterrent to the establishment of an infection through the cut surface. Calling attention to the lack of durability of practically all tree wound paints, he made it clear that a second or third application before total wound closure would be impractical. In the following decade, other voices were heard in posing the same question, but nothing significant happened until 1971 when arborists were presented with an unusual challenge from a research forest pathologist.

By the 1970s the need for tree wound dressings was well established in modern arboriculture. Widely accepted by both practitioner and client, a black-dressed wound was seen as a symbol of good tree practice and a trade badge of respectability. Into this tranquil acceptance of tree care expertise came an ominous challenge: Is tree paint really necessary? Based on extensive research of decay in living trees, the need for tree paint was challenged by USDA forest pathologist A. L. Shigo. Discoloration was seen to be universal in all cases one year after wound treatment, regardless of the material used. Within the following decade, the evidence against decay prevention was overwhelming. Shigo and others reported that the wound dressings they tested did not inhibit decay. By then, the evidence by Shigo and others in the United States indicated that there were no available wound dressings that inhibited decay.

SUMMARY

Although early arborists considered the use of some kind of tree wound dressings essential, by the 1930s there was much emphasis on seeking and testing new materials. At least by 1934 scientists generally acknowledged that no dressing to that time was completely satisfactory. By the 1970s, when tree wounds and their care were seen by some arborists as the number one problem in arboriculture, it finally became clear that no material could be guaranteed either to stimulate callus growth or prevent decay. Permanent sterilization of wounds was not possible; and beyond cosmetics or insect repellence, no wound treatment proved more effective than leaving the wood exposed and applying nothing.

CHAPTER TWENTY-ONE

Tree Surgery and Cavities

"Cavity filling for the rich was the beginning of arboriculture" —A. L. Shigo

The concepts of wound dressing and cavity filling are more than 2,000 years old, and predate that of surgery per se. By 1900, however, when modern arboriculture first became an institution, *tree surgery* was the term used to first characterize tree care practice.

In his 1901 book, *The Tree Doctor*, John Davey used the term *tree surgery* to describe what most tree care practices were at that time. Previously, the term had been used in 1867 by Dr. John Warder—medical doctor, pomologist, tree preservationist, and principal founder of the American Forestry Association. While Davey may not have coined the term *tree surgery*, he was the first in North America to develop it through his special care of old trees. F. A. Bartlett noted in 1935 that tree surgery was not standardized. Until 1904 he considered it to be in the same stage of development as human surgery was in the 1600s, when every barber was a surgeon. In his view there were substantial advances in tree surgery from 1904–34. During that time both Martin Davey and F. A. Bartlett considered their respective companies to be preoccupied with tree surgery.

The scope of the term *tree surgery* has been controversial. Some arborists applied it only where pruning or cavity work was involved, but others used the term to describe a wide range of varied tree care practices, including fertilization and spraying. In *The Tree Doctor*, seventy percent of the text covered tree surgery, most of which involved wounds, injuries, pruning, cavities, and soils and planting. Very little was said about filling cavities, while there was a great deal on pruning and wound dressings. In *Shade Trees in Towns and Cities*, Solotaroff wrote in 1911 that tree surgery was tree repair. By 1924 when the first National Shade Tree Conference was organized, tree surgery was still considered by both commercial tree care workers and botanical scientists to be a comparatively new profession.

A 1926 USDA publication, *Tree Surgery,* used the term interchangeably with *tree repair,* and limited its coverage to removing branches (pruning), sterilizing and waterproofing wounds (tree wound dressing), and cavity work. Two years later in 1928, the newly formed National Shade Tree Conference was asked by its members to find a better term to describe tree work. As *arborist* was used more and more in the 1930s, *tree surgeon* began to fade, although it included not only pruning, fertilization, bracing, and cavity filling, but the relatively new practice of spraying. By 1950 *tree surgery* had almost disappeared from the U.S. literature. Despite this, a book titled *Tree Surgery* was published in England in 1976 by Bridgeman, and the term was indexed and discussed in *Wyman's Gardening Encyclopedia.*

In the early 1900s Professor George Stone was considered the most learned scientist in tree surgery. A botanist at Massachusetts Agricultural College (now the University of Massachusetts), he gave lectures on shade tree management in 1885 entitled "Physiology and Pathology of Shade Trees." An inspiring teacher and a brilliant investigator, he stimulated such people as Harold Frost, A. W. Dodge, and F. A. Bartlett. According to his obituary, he attained recognition as "the best friend that trees ever had."

In addition to tree surgery Stone was active in many different areas, including shade tree management (urban forestry); spraying and spray equipment (he invented the Massachusetts Agricultural College high-pressure nozzle for tall trees); tree protection from wounds and treatment for cavities; materials and methods for crotch bracing, chaining, and bolting; tree guards and devices for protection against live wires; moving of large trees; and investigations on white pine needle blight (some of the earliest observations on what is now known to be caused by ozone and sulfur dioxide, among other things). Under his leadership the first organization of arborists in North America, the Massachusetts Tree Wardens and Foresters Association, was formed in 1913. Not surprisingly the Bartlett Tree Company did not accept John Davey as the father of tree surgery, but instead accorded the honor to George Stone, the professor mentor of Francis Bartlett in 1895.

In a 1965 paper, C. L. Wachtel discusses how tree surgery fits into modern arboriculture. Noting that the word *arborist* was practically unknown in 1925, he pointed to *tree surgeon* as the most common term for a tree worker. In those early years of modern arboriculture, probably most tree work was surgical—cutting out diseased wood, forming cavities, and either filling them or leaving them open. Good tree surgery was considered spectacular by an admiring public, and even artistic to some. It had some similarities with dentistry and was widely hailed by its practitioners as a new level of professionalism. By contrast, Wachtel noted how it was almost a lost practice by 1965, with "very little cavity or surgery work being performed today."

CAVITY FILLING

As A. L. Shigo said in *Modern Aboriculture* in 1991, "Cavity filling for the rich was the beginning of arboriculture." This statement was true for the start of institutionalized tree care about 1900 in North America, as cavity treatment became the core of tree care practices for the first three decades of the twentieth century. Of all practices in arboriculture, cavity filling has probably been the most spectacular, with the greatest public appeal. Probably more than any other practice, it literally sold the public on commercial tree care. The earliest attempt to cover cavities was recorded by Theophrastus of Greece in his *Enquiry into Plants* about 300 B.C. His efforts involved filling with stones and plastering the wounds with mud to prevent decay. This may have been the first purposive practice, linking wound treatment and cavities with decay. The history of cavity work, beginning with the ancients, was reviewed by F. A. Bartlett in 1935.

Over the past 200 years many materials have been used to fill cavities (with varying success and failure), including wood, brick, clay, mortar, cement, and lime. Only cement has survived into the present time. The practice of filling cavities was pursued so intensively and became so sophisticated that it was perfected in all aspects but one—it failed to arrest decay. It has now been practically abandoned and may in time become a lost art.

In the 1600s Lawson recommended to "Fill the hole with well-tempered mortar," the mortar being described by one author as manure, and by another as cement. If cement was the mortar, this may be the first reference to cement as a tree filling. Although cement was known for construction at least as early as the Romans, Lawson also closed his wounds with "a cerecloth doubled and nailed on, that no air or rain approach his wound." Here we see the first references to filling a cavity first and then sealing the surface. This was perhaps the earliest reference that excluded air and water.

In 1662 Evelyn was more specific in linking decay of wood with water. "Hollowness is contracted when by reason of the ignorant or careless lopping of a tree the wet is suffered to fall perpendicularly upon a part." He advised, "Cap the hollow part with a tarpaulin, or fill it with good stiff loam and fine hay mingled." This may be the first reference to leaving an open cavity, even though it was sealed.

William Forsythe became famous for his composition for filling cavities, which involved a strange mixture of "fresh cow dung, old lime, wood ashes and sand." He was awarded a grant of four thousand pounds sterling by King George III and Parliament for "his energy and zeal in devising his composition." Forsythe's composition was widely accepted and used for many years, but not without challenge from some of his contemporaries.

Pontey, in 1810, was especially critical of Forsythe's "composition." He noted Forsythe's own words, "As a most efficacious remedy to prevent the evils that I have described with all their destructive consequences and to restore sound timber, where the symptoms of decay are already apparent, I confidently recommend the use of my Composition." Pontey considered that to be a bold assertion unsupported by even a shadow of proof, and charged that Forsythe held wrongly that "No wound can be healed effectively, except it be dressed with his composition."

In the third edition of his book, *A Treatise on the Cultivation and Management of Trees,* Forsythe informed his readers that, "soapsuds were *useless,* the sand *unserviceable,* the lime rubbish a *nuisance,* and both sorts of ashes merely *capita mortua,* and, therefore, all of these articles are quietly dismissed and sent to their proper settlement, the *dunghill.*" From this it would seem that Forsythe had demolished his own formula, while continuing to claim credit for its merit. While his fame as botanist to King George III earned him many honors for his horticultural achievements, his method for filling cavities was largely refuted before he died.

Pontey had more of substance to offer. From his book, *The Forest Pruner* in 1810, he called attention to holes made by the falling of rotten branches, "calculated to receive and retain moisture, which, acting upon the core or pith as well as on the end of the wood, carries on the business of putrefaction with a rapidity scarcely to be questioned." He saw that the rate of decay was hastened by failure to remove branches "while they are only partially rotten."

He maintained that only large wounds require "plastering," and where necessary they should be "somewhat lasting." He noted also that neither "paint, tar, nor any such body be of material service if applied to a recent wound because the end of the stump shrinks and cracks afterwards so as to admit both air and moisture, and besides such means obstruct the first efforts of healing." In this he may have recognized how difficult it would be both to get a permanent seal, and how important it would be not to damage the healing process.

Finally, Pontey had a specific recommendation for treating the open wound or cavity: ". . . fill the fissures with good putty after which two coats of thick paint, applied to the end of the stump, would effectually prevent decay for many years." He recommended removal or drainage of all free water, filling with sand and plugging with wood. "The plug should be driven so as to be level with the inner bark as by that means. Nature's efforts would not be obstructed in growing over it. The plug should be caulked with oakum to exclude the air and moisture and afterwards painted over." *Webster's Dictionary* defines *oakum* as untwisted old rope, picked apart and used to caulk seams.

According to Bartlett in 1935, "The unfortunate reputation of commercial shade tree experts during the entire nineteenth century and the first years of the present decade came about wholly because of the widely publicized bickering and disagreement amongst Forsythe, Pontey, and other British tree experts." This controversy, which was bitter at times, was not only aired in the British Isles but was well known in Australia and in the United States. The spectacle of these commercial tree experts differing so violently among themselves to the point where each accused the other of dishonest motives had a dismal effect on the profession in general. Thus, Bartlett commented, "May we commercial tree experts of 1935 not derive a fruitful and valuable lesson from the affair of Forsythe and Pontey?" Not only was there much distrust and cynicism among early U.S. commercial tree workers, but the first two national tree companies (Davey and Bartlett) themselves collided and went to court over patents related to cavity filling.

THE PROBLEM OF DECAY

J. C. Loudon in 1865 in his *Encyclopedia of Gardening* made further observations on wounds and cavities stating that, "coating over wounds to *exclude air* is a useful process" and should never be neglected with large wounds. He recommended that clay and loam be painted on the surface of small wounds. "On large wounds, paint, or putty and paint, may be used; and in the case of deep, hollow wounds, the part may be filled up with putty, or putty and small stones, for the sake of saving the former, and then made smooth and well-painted. A composition of tar and tallow is also recommended as being very efficacious."

In 1883 Count Des Cars of France, in his book *Tree Pruning,* stressed the importance of cleaning out wounds, but also recommended painting them with tar. This appeared to protect exposed wound tissue and prevent decay. Like Pontey, he recommended closing the cavity mouth with, "a piece of well seasoned oak, securely driven in place." The end of the plug was then to be "pared smooth and covered with coal tar." This is one of the earliest treatments recommended for what would later be termed as nonfilled, but sealed cavities. This was the first record of the use of coal tar, or its related products, creosote and asphaltum, which would have far-reaching significance in tree care for the next 100 years. *Tree Pruning,* written in French, was published in more than seven editions over a period of nearly twenty years following the appearance of the original volume.

About this time, before the real cause of decay was known, the uncertainty of cavity treatment results gave rise to suspicions of fraud. According to one tree care professional, many so-called tree surgeons were in the same company as medical quacks.

The nature of wood decay was still in dispute until the eminent Robert Hartig of Germany in the 1880s showed clearly the relationship among wood, wood decay fungi, and the conditions under which such fungi cause decay. Professor Hartig, then at the University of Munich, wrote *Textbook of the Disease of Trees* in 1894. This work was a milestone in the scientific understanding of tree disease in general, and wood decay in particular. Hartig was the first to demonstrate clearly the cause of wood decay by macroscopic fungi and fruiting bodies, such as mushrooms and tree conks. The fungi have microscopic threads (hyphae) that invade the wood to cause decay. On wounds per se he wrote: "When water and air find easy access to a wound as in the case of root wounds and branch-wounds that have not been tarred, decomposition spreads fairly rapidly." He wrote further, "when air and water are excluded, wound-rot advances so slowly as only to reach a depth of half an inch in a century." Following Des Cars's earlier recommendation of tar, Hartig's knowledge and reputation went a long way in keeping alive the concept that tar could prevent decay.

Before the end of the 1800s, with the germ theory of disease and decay then accepted as conventional wisdom, the concept of sterilization or antisepsis used in medicine for humans was brought to bear on decay in general, and to cavity treatment in particular. Liberty Hyde Bailey of Cornell University, America's foremost horticulturist, with special emphasis on cavities, advised antiseptic treatment following removal of "rotten and discolored tissue." The advice was to "drive a plug of wood tight into the hole, paint the surface, trim the edges of the wood to live tissue and let Nature take her course." This is the first evidence of an attempt to prevent decay in trees by sterilization. Fostering the belief that the onset of decay in trees could be stopped by sterilization of exposed tissues provided a false sense of security in the coming decades.

In 1900 E. H. Forbush was interested in wounds. Following Des Cars he recommended coal tar as a wound dressing, but of greater interest, he conducted experiments on the rate and direction of callus growth over wounds and cavities. After studying 206 wounds over a three-year period, he found that 50 percent grew callus only from their sides, about 20 percent healed all around, another 20 percent healed only on tops and sides, and the remainder showed no consistent pattern. Although nothing was said of wound shapes, the fact that 186 of 203 (92 percent) healed from one or both sides appeared to be significant. This may have been the earliest American data on wound healing.

Fig. 21.1 Compressor and tools used to "clean out" a tree cavity. Courtesy of the ISA Archives.

THE GOLDEN AGE OF CAVITY WORK

The period from 1910–40 was characterized by the following: preoccupation of the two national tree care companies with cavity work, the emphasis by Davey on use of cement filling, the challenge by Bartlett to both Davey and cement, and a resolution of the problem of decay by forest pathologists. When tree surgery was stressed by John Davey in his book, the principal emphasis was on saving old trees with large wounds associated with internal decay of the tree trunk.

By 1900 cavities were seen correctly as the result of decay following wounding where circumstances favored growth of decay fungi. The tree cavity was considered analogous to the tooth cavity where further decay could be stopped, first by removing all evidence of decay and decay fungi, and refilling with a structural substance that would not only lend mechanical support, but would prevent further decay. For centuries tree cavities had been filled with wood, brick, stone, and other materials, and even cow dung, as we have seen. Of all the old remedies inherited from Europe, only cement was being used by 1900, and it would soon be challenged.

Davey pointed out in 1901 that there were several aspects to filling cavities in order to prolong the life of a tree. All decayed tissue had to be removed, and all tissue exposed to decay had to be treated antiseptically. The opening of the cavity had to be sealed or filled so that callus tissue would grow over the opening. Finally, it was important to strengthen the tree to prevent early stem breakage caused by the cavity. In fairness to the arborists of the day, they may have prolonged the

Fig. 21.2 A cavity filled with treated wood strips. The work was done by Frost and Higgins. Photo by A. R. Thompson, courtesy of the ISA Archives.

life of the tree when they slowed down the decay, and some mechanical stability may have been added to the stem. Despite this, these views would eventually be challenged and be successfully refuted.

In many cases, the cavity did close by callus formation, but there was no evidence then or since that decay could be completely arrested, or that wound treatments stimulated callus formation. The care and extent to which Davey and others practiced surgery convinced many that they had indeed discovered tree surgery for the first time. The only thing that differed from earlier tree surgery was the emphasis on closing the cavity and sealing the wound with attractive wound dressings. The work was neat, professional, and even artistic.

It became apparent that much had changed in the perception of treatment by the "surgeons" and the public, to give each more confidence in the work of tree men. The care and skill in removing rot from cavities, in cutting back into healthy tissue, filling the cavity, and coating with wound dressing contributed to the appearance of professionalism. Tree surgery provided the bulk of early work for Davey, Bartlett, and others. Though founded on tree surgery, the new tree care profession would have foundered if new and more challenging problems had not called it elsewhere.

The new surgery led to innovations. The Davey Company began bracing its cement fillings with iron crossbars extending horizontally across the cavities. Unfortunately, the swaying of trees in the wind cracked the cement and allowed water to enter the wound.

Fig. 21.3 Rubber was another material tried for cavity filling. Photo by
Van Yares Tree Service, courtesy of
the ISA Archives.

Until 1905 filled cavities had been sealed with a variety of materials, including wooden plugs, but never with metal. In that year a zinc sheet was first used to
provide a surface on which the cambium could roll. H. L. Frost, an arborist and
early partner of Francis Bartlett, used tin to close wounds. Wind swaying loos-
ened, dislodged, or crumpled the tin, displacing it, ultimately leading to stem de-
formity. In 1921 the Bartlett Company developed a rotary power drill for cleaning
decayed wood out of cavities. This led to additional confidence that tree men
were moving in the right direction.

After 1905 much attention was given to materials for filling large cavities in
trees. Various patents on methods and materials were sought and granted by the
U.S. Patent Office, including wood blocks and strips, and compounds involving tar,
asphalt, cork, magnesite, cement, and other materials.

Davey's primary contribution to cavity filling went beyond Forsythe's cleaning
the cavity of decay. He took special care to avoid unnecessary injury to living
tissue, and to shape the wound to avoid interruption of vertical translocation of
water and nutrients. His special contribution was in tracing the visibly affected
tissue back to healthy living tissue, and in removing some of this tissue to make
clean cuts to stimulate wound closure. Unfortunately, this meant enlarging the
area that had to be protected by new callus tissue. Cavities in that early period
were treated in one of three ways: (1) they were filled with solid material up to the
edge of the inner bark; (2) they were not filled, but closed over by a metal sheet or

Fig. 21.4 Filling a cavity with concrete. Work by Norman Armstrong. Photo by A. R. Thompson, courtesy of the ISA Archives.

something else at the level of the inner bark; or (3) they were left unfilled and open. Treatment by filling was the most common practice and the most expensive. The major reasons for filling cavities were to prevent ingress of insects and/or decay fungi, and to strengthen the stem.

Cavity work by the Davey Company did not change fundamentally from 1910–35. It was based on the assumption that decay could be stopped within a given area by removing the cause and preventing its reentry. By 1935, however, it was known that hyphae of the decay fungus could and did penetrate well beyond the limit of visibly diseased wood. Despite this, it was believed by arborists that it was "possible to keep a known sterile cavity of some size free from evidence of decay for some years . . . by a film of paint impervious to the passage of spores of wood-destroying fungi." The cavity filling was thought to prevent reinfection of the cavity.

At some point, Wellington Davey refined the use of concrete in cavity filling by application in sections and incorporation of rods and bars. After two decades cement was still viewed by the Davey Company as superior to anything else. Despite some disadvantages, such as high cost, it was the material used most often into the 1920s. Competing arborists were not so impressed, however, and the value of concrete came into question.

Fig. 21.5 A cavity filled with concrete and painted. Photo by the National Park Service, courtesy of the ISA Archives.

The Challenge to Cement

The challenge to cement was led by F. A. Bartlett, head of the only other national tree company in North America at the time. He believed that cement went unchallenged for so many years only because there was no other substitute available. He considered it unsatisfactory because it was heavy, rigid, and easily susceptible to breaking by wind action.

In 1919 Albert Vick, an arborist in Philadelphia, obtained a material used for decks of ships that was sufficiently flexible so that it could withstand continuous twisting and swaying without cracking. With some modification in formula, he created a new substance that would not shrink or crack under physical stress. Naming it Nuwood, he proposed it as a new and more effective cavity fill than concrete. Shortly after his development, Vick sold his company and rights to the Bartlett Tree Company.

The product developed by Vick was patented for exclusive use by the Bartlett Company. As described by Bartlett, it was unlike cement in that it was light and flexible enough to respond to tree swaying without cracking. It was said to be the only material meeting all requirements for a successful tree filler.

The Davey Company responded, and in 1921 initiated an independent investigation of the merits and demerits of materials for cavity filling. The wood product used by Bartlett was found to crack and disintegrate, releasing a toxic salt that damaged the tree, sometimes in one year. The Davey work using cement (patented) had held up over several years and was hailed as promoting the healing process. Despite the Davey faith in cement, the case against it continued to build.

In 1923, after many trials and disappointments, Harold Frost concluded that the use of cement was not satisfactory for filling cavities, and in the same year, the Massachusetts Forestry Association condemned cement for tree repair. In the following year the Massachusetts Forestry Association in *Bulletin No. 138* opposed the use of cement in the repair of trees with the following statement: "We are convinced that the use of cement in filling cavities in trees is a waste of money, and that it is not beneficial to the trees. So many examples have been found where decay had continued back of the cement, resulting in the loss of the tree, that many eminent arborists and foresters are emphatically opposed to its use."

The Davey Tree Company continued to promote the use of cement, noting in 1926 advertisements that Davey tree surgeons build their cement fillings in sections to prevent cracking and breaking, with the claim that sectional filling, patented and used exclusively by them, was the only thing that made successful tree surgery possible.

In 1926 Professor Peets of Harvard University noted in his book, *Practical Tree Repair,* that "the cavity is always at least a threat against the tree's life," and that "there is undoubtedly in the field of tree work a drift away from concrete." The final blow to the Davey position came in a published review of cavity filling in 1926 by Dr. J. F. Collins, USDA forest pathologist, showing cement to be the least suitable of a variety of recommended cavity fillings.

TABLE 21.1

MATERIALS USED TO FILL, SURFACE, OR SEAL TREE CAVITIES

FIRST RECORDED USE	MATERIAL	NOTE
1691	"Well-tempered mortar" (cement)	Fill
1883	Coal tar	Surface, seal
1900	Cement (use rediscovered)	Fill, seal
1905	Zinc, tin	Seal
1922	Wood strip, rubber	Fill
1923	Nuwood (trade name)	Fill, seal
1924	Flexifil (trade name)	Seal
1962	Urethane	Fill, seal

THE HEAL COLLAR

Another significant innovation by Bartlett was a wound treatment for capping filled cavities. Devised by Lem Strout and F. A. Bartlett, and known as the heal collar, it was designed to enhance wound closure. Publicly shown for the first time at the first National Shade Tree Conference in 1924, it was described as the application of human surgery to trees. The heal collar was a method of shaping a cut or wound to enhance the closing over a wound by active growth of the cambium.

The heal collar involved the use of surgical plaster on new cuts around the cavity walls to protect exposed cambium following the shaping of a cavity before filling. This was designed to prevent the newly exposed tissue from drying out and to stimulate new tissue growth. Waterproofing with asphalt inside the cavity edge, combined with a ring of roofing paper in an elastic cement, made a second collar. Setting of the double collar was followed by cauterizing the cavity interior to prevent internal decay. The material applied not only protected the cambial tissue from drying out, but did not injure it in any way to prevent growth. With this new technique, and the use of Nuwood as a filling, it was claimed that wound healing could occur in a few weeks instead of two years. The heal collar was patented, and eventually led to a lifetime guarantee for the success of all treatments by heal collar techniques.

OPEN CAVITIES

Although it was generally believed by most arborists until the 1920s that all tree cavities should be filled and sealed, some arborists covered or sealed cavities without filling. When cavity fillings were removed, it was often observed that decay had continued, and it was easier to re-treat to stop the decay if there was no filling to be removed. In the late 1930s, the subject "open versus filled cavities" became controversial.

Filling of cavities was a large and lucrative part of tree care work in the first three decades of the 1900s, and commercial arborists were not easily convinced that it did not represent perfection in tree care. As the oldest and largest organization, the Davey Company had probably filled more trees with cement than its competitor, and took its stand on cement defiantly into the 1930s. Likewise, with a new flexible filling material (Nuwood) and a unique surface finish (heal collar), the Bartlett Company fought for its position to continue cavity filling against increased evidence of failure to arrest decay by this method. By the end of the 1930s, open cavity treatment was seen as a less expensive and more sound approach to cavity treatment.

Fig. 21.6 Open cavity treatment. Courtesy of the ISA Archives.

THE CHALLENGE TO CAVITY WORK

By 1924 Haven Metcalf, chief forest pathologist of the USDA, believed that the primary objective of cavity filling was for appearance. He could see no evidence that cavity treatment prevented or even slowed the rate of internal wood decay. The arborists, however, were reluctant to accept this view.

By 1935 cavity work in arboriculture was becoming sufficiently controversial to require a state-of-the-art review by the National Shade Tree Conference. By then it was realized that the development of an effective tree wound dressing was more important than cavity research. It was believed that a successful dressing alone would prevent decay in new wounds, and in time, preclude cavity formation. According to Norman Armstrong, from 1910–20 cavity work—almost all fillings—was the major emphasis in commercial arboriculture. In the United States the terms *cavity work* and *tree care* were considered synonymous.

In 1935 the review of cavity work was presented at the NSTC conference by four commercial arborists and a research forest pathologist from the USDA. This review was highlighted by a carefully prepared history of cavity work by F. A. Bartlett; a spirited defense of cavity work and concrete by Jacobs of the Davey Company; and a stimulating evaluation of the place of cavity work in arboriculture by Norman Armstrong, whose insight and judgment carried the day. His primary conclusion: "Cavity work, aimed at eradication and control of heartwood decay, has no place in arboriculture." From this he hoped the future would bring, "no longer the cry of faker—no longer the brusque turn down. In their place, a growing regard and confidence."

Despite these developments, cavity treatment, including cavity filling with concrete, continued, although at an ever-decreasing rate, influenced largely by the economic depression. As late as 1933, based on its innovations with Nuwood and the heal collar, the Bartlett Company initiated its program to guarantee all of its cavity work. The decline of cavity work was well under way by this time, influenced not only by continued failure to arrest decay, but by increasing evidence that its claims could not be justified.

By the end of the 1930s, Dr. Donald Welch, forest pathology professor at Cornell University, refuted claims made that filling of tree cavities improved the appearance of trees, that mechanical strength provided by solid fillings was better than greater and larger callus growth formed at wound edges, and that removal of visible decay necessarily prolonged the life of trees. He called attention to the lack of evidence to support such claims and to evidence suggesting the contrary. In addition, he noted that most cavity treatments collected and were drained of water. Such alternate wetting and drying, providing both water and air, were ideal for decay fungi; they were more of an aid to decay than continuous saturation. Thus, he considered special provision for drainage to be worse than no drainage at all.

The Decline and Demise of Cavity Filling

The advent of war in the 1940s hastened the demise of cavity work, but other factors contributed. Since the 1920s, arboricultural practices had been diversifying because of new information and new demands, such as insect and disease epidemics. At least some of the decline could be attributed to more and better tree care, which precluded development of large cavities. Another major factor was the spread of Dutch elm disease in North America. It soon became the most compelling problem for commercial arborists in the eastern United States and Canada. Accordingly, little was heard of cavity work for almost three decades.

Following reports from Europe of a new substance for filling cavities, G. C. King, C. Beatly, and M. McKenzie recommended in 1970 the use of polyurethane for filling tree cavities, noting that earlier methods and materials were cumbersome, time-consuming, and expensive. The Vulta Foam 15F-1802 used by them was made by General Latex and Chemical Corporation in Cambridge, Massachusetts. This material was considered as effective as others and was both economical and time saving.

COMPARTMENTALIZATION OF DECAY

By the 1970s new work on decay in wood yielded information that would revolutionize old established concepts. Through a long series of research reports, Dr. Alex Shigo, research forest pathologist of the U.S. Forest Service, showed that trees could and did respond to wounds and subsequent infection by microorganisms in ways that would limit damage and further spread of decay. In effect, the tree could wall off damaged areas and seal them from new healthy tissues. Dr. Shigo described this mechanism as compartmentalization of decay in trees or, CODIT, as a model of the process.

Dr. George Hepting of the U.S. Forest Service was the first to describe compartmentalization of decay in trees in 1935. The significance of compartmentalization was not established, however, until after Dr. Shigo's intensive research from 1960–80. Beginning his studies in the 1950s, Shigo was the first scientist to dissect trees longitudinally by chain saw, the first to describe the succession of microorganisms leading to decay, and the first to emphasize the significance of the decay process in the light of modern botanical knowledge.

The concept of compartmentalization and its walls helped to explain why infection and decay were more extensive vertically in a woody stem; how and why it could spread less easily inward radially; how it could move even less circumferentially; and how easily it could be sealed from new wood by impregnable barrier tissue. With respect to cavity treatment, the barrier tissue concept is most significant because if the barrier were broken in cleaning the cavity, the new healthy tissue formed after the barrier was formed would then become infected and decay. This knowledge alone helped to clarify why open cavities, or those capped without filling, were better for the future health of the tree than the filled cavity.

In 1977, Shigo and W. C. Shortle, another forest pathologist with the U.S. Forest Service, called attention to the danger, in cavity excavation, of breaking the barrier wall that sealed off newly formed wood from wood that was discolored or decayed from earlier wounds. This could easily occur in a well-intentioned attempt to remove all decaying wood.

New trials on cavity filling technique introduced by Europeans in 1981 were thought to show promise, but the new material, polyurethane foam filler, when used by itself in post oak, was ineffective in stopping decay. Combined with a fungicide it had enough effect to encourage more study. Polyurethane foam filler had two positive qualities: it allowed cambial growth on its edges and was easily cut and shaped. By itself, however, it failed to prevent discoloration and decay.

SUMMARY

One of the three earliest practices in the newly institutionalized tree care profession of 1900, cavity work quickly accounted for ninety-five percent of tree care work. By the 1940s cavity work had dropped to five percent of arborist activity because of several factors, including general dissatisfaction with cavity treatment. By 1950 it was definitely a minor practice and would remain so.

CHAPTER TWENTY-TWO

Cabling, Bracing, and Lightning Protection

"Tree bracing—the simplest form of tree insurance" —O. Warner

CABLING AND BRACING

Mechanical, or structural, support for weakened trees may have been a concept many years before publication of the *Tree Doctor* in 1901, but there is little or no record of it. Davey noted that chains and rods had been successful in promoting tree survival for a hundred years, which would date the practice back to the early 1800s.

When Davey focused on the arts and skills required to preserve old trees, the need to prevent side branches from sagging, splitting, and breaking was apparent. Chains had been used to hold branches together, but because of their weight and capacity to injure bark tissue, they were unsatisfactory. They were first supplanted by metal pipes and iron bands and later by steel cables. Only then did the practice become known as cabling and bracing, or bracing and cabling.

The first cabling and bracing materials, including rods, screws, and hooks, were custom fashioned by blacksmiths, and at least one arborist (Blair in California) found it prudent to take a course in blacksmithy to make his own tools.

Davey and others developed methods of cabling trees before 1920. According to the Davey record, Wellington Davey, son of John Davey, did the initial developmental work. He used thimbles, eyebolts, and screw rods to form triangle and box cable systems. Except for minor improvements and extra high strength cable, there were no changes to this system until the mid-1970s. Cables not only weighed less and were thus less cumbersome, but were also less injurious when properly installed.

TABLE 22.1
DEVELOPMENT OF TREE CARE PRACTICES
(SHADE AND ORNAMENTAL TREES)

PERIOD/YEAR	PRACTICE	PLACE
5000 B.C.	Planting	Sumeria (Iraq)
1500 B.C.	Tree moving	Egypt
100 A.D.	Pruning	Roman Empire (Italy)
1600	Fertilization	Western Europe
1650	Surgery	England
1890	Pest control	United States
1900	Cabling and bracing	United States
1916	Lightning protection	United States

According to the Bartlett Tree Company history, Lem Strout in 1910 was the first to use steel cables to support weak crotches with eyebolt anchors in place of chains. This innovation was so successful that it remains the accepted practice today. In the early days of the Bartlett Tree Company, F. A. Bartlett's experimental farm was used for testing bolts and cables. According to Lem Strout, "the large, old pear and apple trees there probably had more bolts and cables in some of those trees than there were in any place in the country." Noting that some of the Bartlett cabling jobs had held up through hurricanes and ice storms for more than thirty years, Strout mused on how difficult and cumbersome it was for arborists before the advent of cables: "Imagine dragging around a hundred feet of heavy chain and working it high in the tree."

As cavity work got under way in the early 1900s, it soon became apparent that bracing in cavities was essential. The use of rods to brace cavities became so common that by 1928 the Davey Company alone used 87,000 feet of rod for this purpose. Bracing was also used to prevent damage that might require cavity work.

By 1937 various manufactured materials were available for cabling and bracing, including lag hooks, hook bolts, eyebolts, screw rods, eye nuts, the more durable copper-covered cable, and the proper combinations and strengths of cable and anchoring devices. The need for protecting cable loops with thimbles was recognized by this time, as was locking loops in place. Rods and bolts were used later in lieu of cabling to hold branches together. Perhaps the earliest standards for their use were developed about 1959. The National Arborist Association developed new cabling and bracing standards in 1987.

Fig. 22.1 Power installation of bracing rod. Photo by the F. A. Bartlett Tree Expert Company, courtesy of the ISA Archives.

Fig. 22.2 Bracing rods installed to support cavity treatment and weak crotch. Courtesy of the ISA Archives.

While rods were used to stabilize cavities, holes made to install them are wounds themselves that can begin the processes leading to decay. A 1977 study by Felix and Shigo, "Rots and Rods," showed how rot can develop from such wounds without proper installation. They showed how careful attention to size and number of holes; probing for sound wood; use of sharp tools; and proper sizes of rods, lags, eyebolts, and cable could minimize or prevent decay. They did not recommend wound dressings.

Fig. 22.3 The introduction of flexible cable was a significant improvement over chains and pipes. Photo taken by the National Park Service, courtesy of the ISA Archives.

From this study, new recommendations were made in 1980 for the installation of bolts and screws. Noting that the installation of each enhanced the spread of decay, lag screws were not recommended in decayed wood. In addition, Shigo recommended in 1980 that bracing and cabling work be done in the spring during growth to enhance good sealing by the new growth, or in the autumn during leaf fall to avoid early onset of decay before growth the following spring. In either case, the use of sharp tools was considered essential for rapid wound closure. A few years later, following a study on the wound effects of hardware used for cable installation, Shigo stressed care in the choice and use of washers at bolt endings, stressing avoidance of those with sharp edges, as well as use of a washer at both bolt ends.

TABLE 22.2

DEVELOPMENT OF CABLING AND BRACING

YEAR	EVENT	NOTES
1900	First equipment	Homemade, or by blacksmiths
	Steel chains dominant	Universal use
1910	First use of steel cables	Pioneered by Bartlett
1912	First use of power tools for installation	By Bartlett
1920	Early use of rods in cavities	By Davey
1923	First use of threaded rods	By Strout of Bartlett Company
1930s	First publication on cabling and bracing	By U.S. Park Service

Fig. 22.4 The installation of a lightning protection system. The conductor was nailed to the tree with copper nails. Photo by the F. A. Bartlett Tree Expert Company, courtesy of the ISA Archives.

In 1977 preformed tree grips were introduced to enhance the ease of seating fittings for cables. Considered a valuable innovation, they must be used with care, using only one-by-seven left-hand lay galvanized extra high strength (EHS) cable. Grips should never be shortened to fit a tight space and the cable must always be seated the full length of the grip. For safety reasons, only galvanized EHS cable has been used with the preformed grips; possible substitutes for EHS cable are nico-press fittings and stainless aircraft cable.

LIGHTNING PROTECTION FOR TREES

Almost every student of American history has heard of Benjamin Franklin's experiments with lightning and kites. It is not generally known, however, that he is said to have developed the first lightning protection systems for buildings as early as 1749. Lightning damage has been a serious problem in maintaining old, tall specimen trees of great value, often standing alone or in small groves, isolated from buildings or other trees. With their unusual height and splendid isolation, they were often struck by lightning.

According to H. Stevenson Clopper, a Baltimore arborist, it was Dr. J. B. Whitehead, dean of electrical engineering at Johns Hopkins University, who first recommended successful practices for tree protection. Although the types of materials and methods of installation varied from those used to protect buildings, the

Fig. 22.5 Digging a trench to run the conductor to the ground rod. Photo by the F. A. Bartlett Tree Expert Company, courtesy of the ISA Archives.

principles first established by Franklin were generally the same. Following the recommendations of Dean Whitehead, Clopper is credited in 1916 with the earliest protection of trees against lightning strike.

Following this earliest installation of a lightning rod in a tree, it was much criticized by forest technicians, insurance adjusters, and the public at large. The claim was made that a tree so protected would attract the lightning and be damaging to the tree. Experience showed, however, that it is not possible to prevent any tree from being struck by lightning, but with proper grounding of metallic conductors, the lightning charge is led harmlessly into the ground. By 1924 the Bartlett Tree Company had adapted Franklin's lightning protection system to protect shade and ornamental trees, claiming it was the first practical lightning protection system for trees. Given the earlier work credited to Clopper in 1916, the present writer has no explanation for this discrepancy of priority.

The Bartlett system, and probably others, is used by many arborists today. In effect, the accepted practice represents the installation of lightning rods to protect trees and is based on the same principles used to protect buildings. In 1925 the USDA Weather Bureau published an article, "Trees and Lightning Strikes," which unreservedly recommended the rodding of sound and valuable trees. In 1938 the U.S. Department of Interior, National Park Service published *Lightning Protection for Trees*, a bulletin reflecting, in part, information compiled by the first NSTC effort in this area. While much has been learned since then about the susceptibility of trees to lightning and the damage that it causes, many thousands of trees are now protected regularly by proper installation of effective lightning rods.

SUMMARY

Well established before 1900, chaining and bracing became cabling and bracing after introduction of cables. Both national tree companies were instrumental in establishing and expanding this practice. Lightning protection for trees, based on that for barns and homes, was begun before 1920 and became established practice before 1930.

CHAPTER TWENTY-THREE

Equipment

"From light, manual tools to heavy, powered machines" —Richard J. Campana

Although this chapter is concerned primarily with large equipment that dominates the practices it serves, something must be said of the manual saw, which preceded all of the most important tools and equipment now used in arboriculture.

The manual period began with the ancients using crude axes and saws fashioned of bone or rock, but later was characterized by metal-cutting instruments for manual use with the advent of the age of iron about 1000 B.C.

When arboriculture first became institutionalized in America following publication of *The Tree Doctor*, the basic materials used by a practicing "tree surgeon" were relatively simple. It has been said that full equipment for most arborists in the early 1900s consisted of nothing more than half-inch rope, a hand saw, and a can of paint.

The early machine age for tree care practice began with crude pumps for spraying chemicals, and was characterized by the development of a wide variety of simple, light devices powered by combustion engines or electricity. The modern machine period began after World War II and is characterized by sophisticated, powered, expensive machines, such as chain saws, tree towers, and wood chippers. It is significant that the materials needed in the practice of arboriculture were known mostly as "tools" until World War II, when the advent of more power machinery changed the reference from "tools" to "equipment." However, important manual tools remain in arboriculture; they are now seen as accessories to power-driven equipment.

The Automobile in Arboriculture

Before the automobile, the arborist had to use public transportation (horse car, trolley, or train) or a horse and wagon of his own to haul his tools around. In many cases crews would travel by train with all their equipment, and have to hire horses and wagons when they reached their destination. In other cases, again with tools and supplies, they would go by streetcar, holding long metal rods by hand outside the car windows. Thus it is clear that the advent of the automobile and all kinds of automotive devices were a boost to arboriculture, hardly appreciated today when automotive power is taken for granted.

The automobile gave arborists access to more clients and enabled them to be serviced in less time; it probably had more influence on tree care practice than any other single invention.

The automobile led first to the truck, then the sprayer, the tractor, the crane, the chipper, the digger, the aerial lift, the stump grinder, and the tree-moving spade, to mention a few. From trucks would come fixed or revolving ladders, towed chippers, aerial buckets, towering cranes, towed sprayers, backhoe diggers, stump grinders, and tree spades. Pressed into service by both the Davey and Bartlett Companies in the first decade of the 1900s, the auto was used first for mobility of the manager and his sales agents, then for movement of hand tools and supplies, and later for massive mobilization of men, tools, heavy equipment, and supplies.

Some arborists made innovations of their own to meet specific needs. Karl Kuemmerling of Ohio designed and built a self-dumping (gravity) trailer in the 1930s to be pulled behind large touring cars of that period. Later he made it into a hydraulic model and sold it to other tree companies.

The first trucks used in arboriculture were open with stake-paneled sides. The Asplundh Company took the lead, in 1949, in developing a steel-body truck for both safety and appearance. The resulting steel-body carrier not only lent more dignity to tree care work, but also freed the industry from potential lawsuits for damage caused by protruding tree limbs from the old stake-body models.

The wood chipper mandated a closed truck body for the chipped material. Accordingly, the Asplundh Company devised new truck and trailer equipment to resolve this problem. The company went even farther with its truck demands in 1968 when it created a truck dealership in cooperation with General Motors to ensure a steady supply of trucks. The need for a constant supply of suitable truck bodies for hauling wood debris from tree care and forestry operations has been met by manufacturers specializing in what are known as "forestry bodies." Many have said that the chain saw is the greatest innovation in the history of arboriculture,

Fig. 23.1 The pole pruner was one of the early tools developed for tree care. Photo by the F. A. Bartlett Tree Expert Company, courtesy of the ISA Archives.

but when one considers the mobility of tools and labor, even mobility of the chain saw, this claim may be challenged.

POWER TOOLS

In 1921 F. A. Bartlett and his associates developed an electric drill for cleaning the walls of tree cavities of decayed and infected wood. Bartlett saw this innovation as a new step toward professionalism in arboriculture. Based on this innovation, the Bartlett Associates claimed to be the first to perfect and use power machinery in tree care.

One of John Davey's sons, Paul, had an interest in and a talent for experimentation and invention. Between 1926 and 1929 he developed the first air-cooled power compressor, which led to development of the Davey Compressor Company. Davey's compressor was significantly smaller and lighter than the giant models currently available, but it could provide equal power output. In addition, his machine needed less maintenance, started more easily in cold weather, and consumed less fuel than the earlier models.

At a later date the Davey Company also devised a machine for cleaning cavities that was powered by compressed air. Although it was later abandoned for its lack of portability, the Davey experience with compression was significant in a much larger way. Paul's new power compressor had great potential as a new basic source of energy for a variety of machines. Another of Paul's innovations was the

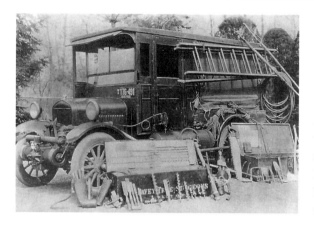

Fig. 23.2 Davey truck with the various tools used in "tree surgery" (1928). Photo by the Davey Tree Expert Company, courtesy of the ISA Archives.

Davey Power Take-Off, which made it possible to use the truck engine to power other equipment. The Davey Compressor Company became successful for power tools that were not related to tree care needs.

Following World War II several new machines were used for arborist or arborist-related operations. The brush hog, introduced in 1953, was a giant rotary mower hauled by tractor. Especially useful along rights-of-way and fence lines, it left in its wake a pulverized layer of ground wood, which was good for mulch. The introduction of hydraulic tree diggers revolutionized the digging of plants in nurseries in 1956. A new type of air-operated gun, similar to a jackhammer, was developed for planting young tree seedlings in 1968. This unique tool was created by John Walters of the University of British Columbia Forestry Department. The gun was loaded with plastic bullets (containers), each enclosing a young seedling. On firing, released air pressure forced the pellet with enclosed seedling into the ground.

THE SAW

As the most important of all arborists' tools, the saw and its development is of special interest. Saws made of volcanic glass and flint have been found or recorded in Babylonian ruins, in central Europe from the Neanderthal Age, as well as in biblical countries. From these early crude saws the two-man crosscut saw probably represented a gigantic step forward. The crosscut saw was developed in Germany and imported into the United States about 1870.

The earliest saws were the reciprocating type (back and forth). There is evidence that the circular saw was developed in England in 1777, but the Dutch claim that such a saw had been in use in the Netherlands well before that time.

Although the band saw was patented first in England in 1808, it was little used until the French perfected the joint. The first band saw in the United States was imported from France in 1868; this saw had improved on the first English model. Until the advent of the chain saw, the band saw was the most widely used of the power saws.

For the woodsman in the field, after the crosscut saw, the next step was a circular saw mounted on a platform parallel to the ground that could be moved into the trunk. Such a device was not only limited to small trees but also was vulnerable to damage from binding and awkward maneuverability. For the arborist in the early 1900s, however, the manual saws were the most important. For cutting trees, handsaws operated by one or two men were standard in both forestry and arboriculture until the advent of the chain saw about 1940. According to Milton Blair in California, in his work during the 1920s, he used tapered carpenter saws with reshaped teeth. Later he had the Stockton, California, Iron Works make hand-and-pole saws to his own design. Blair gave one of his Stockton-designed saws to the Fanno Saw Company in 1922. He credited this company with making the finest saws for tree work, citing its #14 handsome blade. Blair also described an unusual saw used by S. P. McClanahan of Palo Alto in the 1920s for sawing large trees. It was clamped to the log, and was powered by a gasoline engine, which rotated an arm that dragged a long blade back and forth.

THE CHAIN SAW

The chain saw was developed concurrently in Europe and North America, based on differing concepts of combining its two principal parts, the cutting saw chain and the power source. The cutting saw chain preceded the power source by about 300 years. The saw chain is said to have been invented in the 1600s in England. First used with hand-cranked machines in Welsh coal mines, it was still considered primitive when used in the mid-1800s in the United States. Over the next fifty years, from 1858 to 1905, at least twenty-five patents were issued in the United States for endless or sectional chains for sawing. The most significant figure in the early development of American cutting chains was Charles Wolf, who developed scratcher chains as early as 1910, and crosscut chains used on Reed-Prentice chain saws from 1925 to 1935.

Meanwhile, in Europe the German companies of Stihl and Dolmar were manufacturing a saw chain that served the European market. By 1939, at the onset of the war, world production of chain for saws had reached about 45,000 feet annually.

In the United States, the Disston Company initiated chain production in 1940. At the same time the Hassler Company improved the chain saw tooth. Hassler's improvement involving "bent-over teeth" made new chains adaptable to both electric and pneumatic chain saws. During the war years total saw chain production reached 1,500 feet per day including crosscut, scratcher, and Hassler improvements. Following the war, production was increased to 5,000 feet per day with further improvements in the Hassler patent. Following this, several American companies made improvements, such as a chain stabilizer and easy to file "half-circle tooth." Through these innovations and with increased sales, chain production had climbed to 2 million feet by 1950–51.

The first chain saws were stationary devices designed for indoor use in sawing logs. The first patent issued in the United States was to Harvey Brown of New York in 1858. Additional patents were issued in the following decades with no significant developments leading toward the chain saw as we know it today. From 1890 to 1920 new electric engines were developed. From 1920 to 1942 smaller gas engines were made. These were the only significant developments toward the evolution of chain saw efficiency before the 1940s.

A deck chain saw, made by the Potlatch Lumber Company in Idaho and in use by 1906, was an inspiration to the inventor Charles Wolf. After improving deck chain saws for the Union Iron Works of Spokane, Washington, Wolf designed and adapted the first semiportable chain saw in 1920. His models were produced by Peninsula Iron Works in Portland, Oregon, and later licensed to Reed-Prentice Corp. in Worcester, Massachusetts. The Wolf saw was portable but required a truck-mounted generator for electric power.

According to one report the first chain saw was patented in 1918 by James Shand of Dauphin, Manitoba. He reportedly came up with the idea while using a team of horses pulling barbed wire to saw off a fence post; he then arranged cutting teeth on a bicycle powered by a gasoline engine. Unable to sell his creation, he allowed his patent rights to lapse.

Before 1919 chain saws were specialty tools for use in extreme weather or for special applications. At that time there were few small combustion engines. But this situation changed in the 1920s when electric-powered saws became popular. Before the 1930s, large chain saws were used primarily as drag saws for bucking.

The Stihl Chain Saw

Despite this background in North America, the development of what would lead to modern chain saws was in Europe. Andreas Stihl developed an electric-powered bucking saw in Germany in 1926 and sold some in the United States in 1927 and 1928. This was the first portable chain saw. It was gas powered, it required

Fig. 23.3 An early two-man chain saw. Courtesy of the ISA Archives.

two men for operation, and it weighed 140 pounds. In 1932 he received an order for 3,000 of the new saws from the Soviet Union. By 1933, about 40,000 of these saws had been made and sold. In 1940 Stihl developed a gas-powered saw that weighed about 80 pounds. By 1936 he had an agent in British Columbia, Canada, who predicted sales of 5,000 if the machines were available. Working with Canadian and U.S. designers D. Smith and R. Shade, respectively, he reduced the weight of his saw and developed a seven-foot bar.

Industrial Engineering Ltd. in Vancouver, British Columbia, became the first chain saw manufacturer in North America to make portable two-man saws. The first model was the "K," a 150-pound, two-man saw. Known as the Beaver, it was designed for cutting eastern Canadian pulpwood. The company later became Pioneer Chain Saw.

Working with Stihl as a dealer, beginning in 1937, the Mill and Mine Supply Company in Seattle handled Stihl saws for the U.S. market. When the war precluded importation of Stihl saws from Germany, the company developed its own Titan chain saw.

The D. J. Smith Equipment Company, also in Vancouver, made the Stihl-inspired model A chain saw in 1939–40, before it was purchased by Reed-Prentice in Worcester, Massachusetts, in 1940. Reed-Prentice had tried unsuccessfully to develop a chain saw in 1929. In 1946 it used the newly developed 2-cycle McCulloch engine, reportedly the first engine weighing less than 100 pounds.

The McCulloch Story

After making engines for the Reed-Prentice chain saw for three years, McCulloch Motors of Havasu, Arizona, made its first chain saw in 1949. Weighing only forty-nine pounds at a cost of $400, it became popular quickly and took sixty-seven percent of the market in two years. The first chain saw producer to market by radio, it stressed the lightweight feature of its models. In 1953 it produced the super 33 model weighing in at twenty-two pounds. By 1961 it claimed to have a direct-drive chain saw, the lowest priced quality chain saw, as well as the lightest, most popular gear-drive saw.

In 1962 McCulloch became the first manufacturer to produce a million chain saws. The company introduced a new mini Mac 1–10 at 10½ pounds in 1965, and 1966 it introduced the world's first electric-starting chain saw. For the first time a small, handheld, gasoline engine could be started electrically by a self-contained starter, generator, and battery. The company claimed that this design would eventually put the starter pull rope on the shelf along with the automobile hand crank. Designated as the MAC3-IOE, it weighed less than fifteen pounds. In 1967 it produced the "lightest gear driven saws," and in the following year introduced the world's lightest chain saw, a Mac-6 model at 6½ pounds. This model was expected to revolutionize the chain saw industry. McCulloch added automatic oiling to some models in 1968, and also introduced vibration cushioning.

In 1971, its twenty-fifth anniversary year, McCulloch not only made its three-millionth chain saw, but became the first maker of snowmobile engines. In 1973 the company was purchased by Black & Decker. By the following year it had produced four million saws; nine years later, in 1981, with the introduction of four new electric models, its chain saws for consumer use sold for as little as fifty dollars.

In 1981 the company president, Bob McCulloch, purchased London Bridge and had it transported from England to span the Colorado River between Arizona and California at Havasu, the location of the main manufacturing plant.

Chain Saw Improvements

In 1952 Reed-Prentice introduced aluminum and magnesium parts to bring the weight of its new model down to about twenty-seven pounds. One of the earliest of the lightweight models, it was also notable for its automatic chain oiler, an innovation at the time.

In the face of many serious and often fatal accidents, chain saw manufacturers continuously stressed safety features. By 1968 there was at least one company

Fig. 23.4 Demonstration of a "new" lightweight McCulloch chain saw. Courtesy of the ISA Archives.

directly concerned with accident prevention. In that year the Continental Chain Saw Safety Guard Company introduced a new lightweight safety device for chain saws. A few years later in 1974 the Jonsered Company produced the first chain saw with electrically heated handles, the Jonsered 521. It was hailed as the beginning of the end of "white fingers," an occupational hazard for chain saw operators in cold climates.

In 1982 the Consumer Product Safety Commission (CPSC) reported that chain saws caused 122,000 injuries serious enough to require medical attention. In 1983 the CPSC announced a major design improvement—a new "technology chain" that promised to reduce the chain saw accident toll. The new device helped to prevent or reduce kickback, the hazard reported to cause 23,000 injuries per year. Weighing only an ounce or less, the Safety T-Tip was a one-piece unit consisting of a hardened steel top and a high tensile strength mounting screw simple to install and remove, measuring 2½ ! 2½ inches. Fitted over the nose section of the guide bar, it could be fastened by a mounting screw.

The Chain Saw Industry

The Asplundh Company may have been the first commercial arborist company in 1935 to use a power saw—a Reed-Prentice reciprocating bow saw. In 1939 the Asplundh Company first used a Disston saw. These early saws were crude, scarce, and heavy, had long blades (chain cycles) and required two men for operation. There is no other mention of a commercial arborist using a chain saw until after the war.

The Mall Tool Company in Chicago had purchased five Stihl saws in 1939, kept one for study, and sent four out for testing by others. It is said to have developed the first mass production of chain saws in the United States. By the early 1950s, it also made bars and chains.

By 1949 there were about thirty companies in the United States and Canada producing seventy-five different models of chain saws. There were also many foreign producers. The models available at the time included a variety of electric, pneumatic, and gas-powered saws as well as a wide selection of light models. Despite such variety, there were still only four kinds of chains—the Stihl, the Hassler, the Chisel, and the new Wolf. Of these only two appeared viable for future use. Although still in use, at this time the Stihl chain was considered almost obsolete, and the Hassler saw was superseded by a newer model, the chisel chain.

By 1952 the chain saw industry had become sufficiently important to publish a magazine called *Chain Saw Age*. Initiated in August 1952 by Jim Conroy, who was also the editor, it became the trade publication for the chain saw industry. Publishing its first issue in Portland, Oregon, its major advertisers were three major producers of chain saws—Homelite, Oregon, and McCulloch.

By 1954 there were 31 principal manufacturers of chain saws in the United States. Of these, eleven were the major suppliers: Titan, Jamieson, Lynx, Disston, Reed-Prentice, Poulan, Oregon, Atkins, Homelite, McCulloch, and Beaver.

THE WOOD CHIPPER

Following the introduction of the chain saw, the next significant development was the wood chipper. Asplundh pioneered chipper development beginning in 1949. Much of the information used here was drawn from an in-house history of the Asplundh chipper from 1949 to 1977 by Roy Rose, Asplundh Chipper Sales Coordinator at the company plant in Chalfont, Pennsylvania.

The wood chipper was developed to meet a growing need for disposing of brush in an orderly and efficient way. In its first twenty years from 1929 to 1949, the company faced an ever-growing problem of what to do with the enormous amount of brush debris from accelerated and intensive line clearing in urban areas. Every crew had its "brushie," the person with the least seniority whose job it was to gather, load, and compact the branches into the tightest load possible. With the advent of the new steel-covered trucks after World War II, this job probably became even more onerous than it had been with the open, stake-body trucks. Early efforts to get around this problem, involving a big wood burner or a series of mounted circular saw blades on the back of the open trucks, were unsuccessful.

Fig. 23.5 An early Fitchburg chipper demonstration. Courtesy of the ISA Archives.

By the late 1940s, the company turned to the Fitchburg Engineering Company in Massachusetts, which had a wood slicing machine with blades mounted on a rotating drum. At the request of the Asplundh Company this machine was modified by Fitchburg for chopping, so that it had a redesigned drum with three blades in pockets the full width of the drum and a spring-loaded pressure plate. This chipper became the first operating model of the Asplundh chipper and all subsequent wood chippers for most of the next thirty years.

Right from the start the Asplundh model was so successful that the company was soon making and selling its chippers to competitors. This success led in time to the rise of Asplundh as a major manufacturer of other kinds of tree care equipment.

The first unit connected to a Chrysler motor was mounted on the truck bed. Later units were placed on trailers for towing behind trucks. Other trials included a truck mount powered by the truck engine and tractor mounts on the rear of a farm tractor. One of the earliest crews to test the Asplundh chipper in the field was led by Harold Gentile. Known early on as "Hoppy," he soon became known nationwide in arboriculture as "Mr. Chipper" for his interest, enthusiasm, and skill in the use and operation of chippers, as well as in the chips they produced.

Successful development of the chipper gave the Asplundh Company a decided advantage over its competitors. In the early years of development it sold some machines to municipalities both large and small, as well as to Pennsylvania and Cornell Universities. Arborists at Cornell then began to explore the use of chips for mulch and other purposes. In 1950 the first chipper was exported to Germany. By 1953 the company began selling to its tree care competitors.

By 1956 it was becoming difficult to find enough manufacturing capacity to keep up with demands for chippers. Thus, in the following year the Asplundh Company purchased a building in Chalfont, Pennsylvania, and created its own manufacturing division, the Asplundh Chipper Company. By the end of 1957 2,000 of its chippers were at work in the United States.

Several significant changes were made to the various models in the first two decades of their manufacture. The first change in 1952 involved the addition of a flywheel and elimination of the springs from the pressure (or flapper) plate. In 1953 chipper operations in California experienced chute stoppage because of heavy foliage, including palm fronds. The problem was solved by attaching a blower to the flywheel. First added as an option, the flywheel became standard later. In the next year it was discovered that with the addition of the flywheel, the adjustable floor plate was unnecessary and potentially damaging. Thus, it was eliminated and the floor of the chipper housing was made solid. In 1955 the pressure bar and the cutter bar arrangement was simplified and the flywheel attachment modified for greater ease of operation.

In 1959 field workers complained of excessive time needed to change and set chipper blades. To counter this, the blade adjustment was made a part of the blade locking wedge so that adjustments could be made more easily. In 1961 another major change included a large machine housing, which led to a new model produced successfully from 1966 to 1974.

By the early 1970s, with public emphasis on ecology and environment, a call for less noise pollution led to development of a quieter model. Introduced in 1974, this became known as the Whisper Chipper. With no loss of efficiency, this model met most local requirements for noise levels in residential areas. By 1977 this chipper was powered by an even quieter-operating diesel engine.

New models from competitors, such as the Fitchburg Company, Mitts and Merrill in Michigan, and the Hall Machine and Iron Works, became available in 1957. The Fitchburg Company had retained the original model developed for Asplundh, but had failed to make significant modifications over a period of twenty-five years. The Mitts and Merrill Company claimed to have the chipper with the most experience behind it, noting its record of producing size reduction machinery for 100 years. Its model was not patterned on the Asplundh chipper. The Hall Brush Hog was seen by the Asplundh Company as an imitation of its own models. Throughout the 1950s all wood chippers were modeled on the drum type.

In 1960 Karl Kuemmerling of Ohio, an able and enterprising arborist, designed a side-feed brush chipper called the "Kuemmerling-Fitchburg." To promote his new model at the 1961 ISTC meetings in Minneapolis, he rented a circus

Fig. 23.6 The Asplundh Whisper Chipper. Courtesy of the ISA Archives.

barker's loud plaid jacket and straw hat. Keeping his unit under cover until he was ready to use the megaphone, he uncovered his model with a flourish, jumped onto its top and proceeded to ballyhoo its marvelous features, with a promise to paint it any color but Asplundh orange. Kuemmerling's chipper was only one of many to be introduced into the rapidly expanding chipper industry.

In the late 1960s Norval Morey of Morbark Industries in Winn, Michigan, developed a new type of wood chipper known as the disc knife chipper. The disc chipper was said to have significant advantages over the drum model. Claimed to be safer and quieter, it produced smaller and more uniform chips. Less trimming of side branches was required, and a reversible feeding mechanism made the machine safer. The major disadvantage was its slower chipping operation.

By 1970 Morbark had developed the first whole tree chipper for line clearance of rights-of-way (ROWs), and began selling a small model called the Eager Beaver brush chipper. By 1990 Morbark not only produced whole tree chippers, but brush chippers of various sizes and tub grinders for chipping stumps and other wood products.

By 1990 there was a growing demand for disc-type chippers. The older drum models maintained their niche in the chipper industry, even though drum chipper sales were declining. The popularity of the disc models is attributed by some arborists to new safety standards involving a minimum distance of thirty-six inches between the feeder table and pinch rollers. The disc chipper market kept expanding, and several companies offered both drum and disc models.

THE AERIAL LIFT

Coincident with the development of the brush chipper was the truck-mounted aerial lift. Like the chipper, the aerial lift was quickly improved by the Asplundh Tree Expert Company for line-clearing purposes. And like the chipper, it would soon become standard equipment in arboriculture.

Ordinary wooden ladders were used for high work in trees, which was plentiful in the early 1900s. By the mid-1920s the ladders were based on truck platforms, and later mounted as extensions of truck-mounted tree towers. According to the Asplundh history, ladder trucks were used in line-clearing operations throughout the 1940s and 1950s. However useful in their time, they were considered too hazardous for use around the higher-voltage wires. The Asplundh Company created a hand-cranked aerial platform. Under Lester Asplundh's direction, it was designed to be faster and safer than the ladders or towers, but the results were disappointing and impractical. The production of a truck-mounted aerial tower in 1950 was a significant mechanical development for aerial work.

The first of these, known as the skytower, was made in Milford, Connecticut, in 1950. Orin B. Maxwell, a fire equipment salesman from the West Coast, asked three engineers (Arthur Hunt, Wayne Pierce, and David Ritchie) in Connecticut to develop a bucket truck for use in apple harvesting. The first models produced essentially for tree work were sold for power-line work to the Niagara-Mohawk Power Company, to S. Kinder in Rhode Island, and to L. H. Meader.

The first aerial machines were crude compared to later models. They were not insulated, had steel booms and platforms, their control mechanism was jerky, they lacked continuous rotation, had no tool connections at hand, and their hydraulic systems were not well balanced or efficient. In addition, they were not equipped with safety features. Despite this, no other single device did as much to make the tree worker safe in the air. In the fifteen years following the introduction of aerial machines, climbing accidents declined by twenty-five percent.

Soon after acquiring "bucket trucks" in 1953, the Asplundh Company recognized the safety hazard in the lack of proper insulation of the booms constructed of steel or aluminum. When a boom came into contact with a high-voltage wire, the worker could be electrocuted, and there were fatalities. Lester and his Asplundh engineers sought for years to find a safer way to use the new aerial devices to preclude or minimize the hazard of electrocution. The solution came unexpectedly in 1958, when he saw in a small spool of wound fiberglass, a material stronger than steel, lighter than aluminum, and dialectrically sound, with a capacity for insulation against an electrical current.

Fig. 23.7 Demonstration of aerial lift devices at an International Shade Tree Conference. Courtesy of the ISA Archives.

Known as "spiralloy," it was first used commercially in the mid-1950s for rockets, missiles, and pipelines. The Asplundh Manufacturing Division used this filament-wound fiberglass in the boom winding operation, and the making of new model aerial bucket trucks. The first aerial bucket trucks with fiberglass boom trimmer lifts were made in 1958, and used in line-clearing operations in Pennsylvania, Louisiana, and California. By 1964 the Asplundh Company had more than 300 of its insulated aerial units in operation.

THE STUMP CUTTER

The elimination of tree stumps in North America has been a time-honored practice since colonial times when land clearing of trees was essential for planting crops. The grubbing out of stumps with fire, axe, spade, mattock, and horse pulling had not changed much by 1900. Early in the twentieth century blasting stumps out with dynamite or black powder was in vogue, and DuPont offered a special explosive for doing the job. In the 1920s one dynamiter in the Cleveland area offered his services for stump removal. Later in the 1920s, capstans and cables were used with hand-operated levers, provided one had an anchor base stronger than the stump itself. With increased use and development of the motor power of heavy trucks, winches, cables, and ropes came into use. Sometimes a heavy capstan was used with hand-operated levers to tighten ropes or cable attached to the stump.

TABLE 23.1
SIGNIFICANT TOOLS AND EQUIPMENT
USED IN ARBORICULTURE

ITEM	PERIOD FIRST USED IN NORTH AMERICA	NOTES
Axes and saws	Prehistoric	All manual: basic cutting
Automobile	1900	Easy and fast land travel
Sprayer	1920	Application of chemicals
Compressor	1925	Original source of power for tools
Chain saw	1940	Fast, massive cutting
Wood chipper	1950	Machine disposal
Aerial lift	1952	Efficiency and safety in tall trees
Stump grinder	1960	Machine removal
Spade tree mover	1960	Tree moving via machine
Machine pruners	1970	Fast cutting

Stump removal was augmented with block and tackle and pneumatic drills for both digging and cutting. Stump cutting below the soil was done with a new cutting machine, and stump chipping was possible to a depth of ten inches. Following World War II the problem of stump removal became more serious because Dutch elm disease and elm yellows created the need for thousands of large elm trees to be removed from city streets. Gasoline-powered jackhammers and wood-cutting chisels were often used. Later chain saws were combined with wood chisels. Despite these power methods throughout the 1940s and 1950s, the practice was still labor intensive, difficult to implement, and impractical.

The first successful stump cutter was built in the 1950s near Pella, Iowa, by two young farmers, Harry and Lonnie Ver Ploeg. They welded metal teeth to a barrellike cylinder that could be rotated by power. Bolted to a frame attached to a tractor, the rotor wheel could spin rapidly and move vertically. The Ver Ploeg machine was refined by Gary Vermeer, another imaginative farmer in Pella. He designed and built a new wagon hoist and produced it for sale. Another of his inventions, a portable power take-off for hammer mills and shelters, was also in demand so he began his own manufacturing company. Vermeer worked intensively with the Ver Ploegs on the stump cutter, experimenting and improving and adding safety features. The first model was introduced in 1957 and marketed directly by the Vermeer Manufacturing Company.

SUMMARY

The advent of the gas combustion engine led to the development of automotive power in the first decade of the 1900s and then to trucks, tractors, and trailers, all of which made the arborist's job easier. The rapid development of large, expensive equipment for use in arboricultural practice (i.e., aerial lifts, chippers, stump removers, and chain saws) is viewed largely as a response to the need to mechanize line-clearing operations because of increased labor costs.

Spraying

"Machine power revolutionized tree spraying" —Unknown

Spraying as an arboricultural practice is relatively recent compared to planting, pruning, and fertilization of trees. Although application of liquids and powders to plants is said to have come long after cultivation of crops was well established, it is not possible to say when plants were first sprayed. E. G. Lodeman's 1886 work, *The Spraying of Plants*, described how Parkinson, from England, used vinegar on tree canker in 1629. The concoction was strange but colorful, with dubious effects. Parkinson wrote, "Dresse it or wet it with vinegar or cows pisse, or cows dung or urine," from which Lodeman concluded that "the most offensive concoctions were considered the most effective."

In 1711 another liquid concoction was used against flies on ash trees. In this case, the water had been boiled in rue (*Ruta graveolens*), an herb with a foul odor and bitter taste, and applied using a small pump. But again, there was no record of success or failure. About fifty years later, in 1763, a more effective liquid was used in France against tree lice (probably aphids). The liquid was a mixture of water with slaked lime and tobacco juice. In this case the scale insects were killed.

In 1787 "flowers of sulphur" were used against "lice" on trees; in 1802 Forsythe, botanist to George III of England, used unslaked lime in water against tree aphids, which he applied by syringe. In 1850 Duchatel (probably in France) dusted grape leaves with elemental sulfur against powdery mildew. This was apparently the first use of dusting, the material being applied by a bellow spray apparatus. Early methods for application of chemicals to plants involved dipping and brushing, or dipping and shaking. Both the knapsack sprayer and barrel-pump sprayer were used before 1890. After bordeaux mixture was discovered, both the French and Germans moved to develop a machine to spread it. By 1886 a pressure spray machine and special cyclone nozzle were developed to spray this fungicide.

In much the same way, the growing menace of the gypsy moth in the north-eastern United States and the new lead arsenate compound made to control it would lead to advances in spraying machines and practices in North America. In 1886 M. Armand Cazenave de la Reole in France developed a revolving brush operated by three gears, which fed a mixture of lime and sulfur. A new machine also was developed by Nikolaus Pastor in Bernkastel, Germany. This latter spray machine was operated by a piston-pump device. The simplest version became widely accepted as a knapsack sprayer, probably the first of its type.

DEVELOPMENT OF TREE ORCHARD SPRAYERS

By 1880 the first U.S. spraying machines were devised to control the San Jose scale in California. In that same year Barnard developed the first "cyclone spray nozzle" to improve uniformity of chemical distribution. A significant development came in 1884 when the John Bean Company in San Jose designed the world's first continuous spray pump. The first machine, known as the "Bean Spray Machine," was quickly followed in 1887 by the development of the new and improved "Nixon Spray Nozzle." Bean spray machines would become standard American equipment for more than a hundred years.

According to the late Eric Haupt of the Bartlett Tree Expert Company, the Bean spray machines were originally developed for orchard work in California. By 1908 Bean had a power-driven pump for this work. Such a pump was the precursor of the hydraulic tree sprayer. In 1918, then located in Lansing, Michigan, the Bean Company was the first to feature control pump pressure on agricultural sprayers. By 1928 it was known as the John Bean Manufacturing Company. In 1929 the company became the Food Machinery Corporation, known familiarly as FMC. It was the first to introduce, in 1940, an air type sprayer, foreshadowing the ultimate development of the mist blower for shade tree spraying.

Development of a spray nozzle was an important step in the evolution of spraying equipment. Not surprisingly, the earliest models provided an interrupted flow of liquid. The first cyclone model developed by Barnard and modified by Vermorel of France avoided clogging. It was introduced about 1887 and was widely called the Vermorel nozzle. Modern nozzles now deliver a stream broken into many fine droplets on foliage surfaces.

Proper timing for best effect led to a need for machines that were more rapid, efficient, and lighter in weight. This, in turn, led to the revival of dusts about 1915 as alternatives to liquids, as the dust rigs could be much lighter. Airplane dusting, which would become even more popular, was not developed commercially until about 1930. Dusting technology eventually was used to drive liquid spray to surfaces of plants in a fine mist, depositing dust particles with less drift. This enhanced the total effectiveness of the toxic chemicals as well as additives such as spreaders and stickers. The last decade of the nineteenth century saw the first American backpack sprayer in 1890; the first use of liquid stream power developed for spray in 1894; the first gas engine for spraying in 1895; and the evolution of new nozzles and small hand pumps in 1896.

In 1884 B. T. Galloway, the first chief of the new USDA Plant Pathology Section, wrote what may have been the first book on spraying in the United States. In 1896 he noted the rapid advances achieved in combating insects and fungi. In that same year, E. G. Lodeman's book on the spraying of plants represented the state of the art at that time. Considered then the most complete and critical review of spraying as a practice, it is now seen as a classic.

EARLY SPRAYING IN ARBORICULTURE

Before the 1930s, it was commonly believed that any man with a rope, saw, and ladder who could climb trees to cut branches could become a practicing tree expert. By 1933, as the problem of tree insects turned from nuisance to oppressive, such a man needed a sprayer. Tree owners at this time were in such a panic over insects that it seemed to matter little whether the tree worker's machine was efficient, whether it had enough pressure, what he was spraying, or even if he knew what he was spraying for. Accordingly, the advent of spraying gave rise to a new crop of uninformed and unprincipled tree workers.

The early spray rigs used by arborists were cumbersome and powered by heavy machines with low-powered engines with one to two cycles. First mounted on wooden wheels, they progressed next to steel, then to tires, then to rubberized wheels, and finally were either truck mounted or towed on trailers with regular automobile wheels. The amount of power increased significantly during the first decade after introduction. Increasing from one cycle to four, from pressures of 100 to 600 pounds per square inch (psi), the output in gallons per minute had increased from 2 to 3 in the 1940s to 40 to 50 by 1953. When first used, power machines were apparently very noisy, but according to Blair of California, were considered good advertising, attracting the attention of potential clients.

Fig. 24.1 Spraying apparatus used in 1891. Courtesy of the Forest History Society.

The results of these changes were concentrated sprays of reduced volumes powered by high-velocity air blasts. The first mist blowers were small and portable, of the wheelbarrow type, with the ability to reach thirty-five feet in height. The later truck-mounted machines with engine capacities of twenty-five to thirty-five horsepower could reach higher, but only with horsepowers of forty to fifty was it possible to reach the tops of large trees.

The Bartlett Company began spraying in 1916. During the peak of the spraying season, it had forty workers active in the field. Fifteen years later the company claimed a larger fleet of motorized sprayers than any other company in commercial arboriculture.

Early spraying in arboriculture was laborious, to say the least. According to Lem Strout of the Bartlett Company, "In the early 1900s every tree that was sprayed, had to be climbed." Early spray jobs were done from barrels mounted on wagons drawn by horses. One early model, the "Gould Barrel Pump," required two men to operate. The "muscle man" had to pump by hand incessantly to get and keep pressure for the man with the spray nozzle, who sometimes had to climb trees up to fifty feet high. The barrel held fifty gallons and was commonly operated nine hours a day, six days a week.

Strout believed that the biggest improvement in tree spraying was the use of power to run a small pump. One sprayer produced in the early 1900s, the Arlington sprayer, was powered by a gasoline pump. It had a 100-gallon tank and gave 150 pounds of pressure. It was transported by train, or horse and wagon.

In those early years, tree companies such as Davey and Bartlett were operating on a shoestring; some of the early Bartlett Company spray rigs, or the trucks that carried them, were constructed from spare parts from dumps. In 1911 Lem Strout, jack of all trades, developed a gasoline spray pump that was still in use in

Fig. 24.2 Davey spray crew in action (1925). Photo by the Davey Tree Expert Company, courtesy of the ISA Archives.

1982. Later, he claimed that the first power sprayer mounted on a motor-driven vehicle was one that he had made in 1916. He tore the body off his old Ford car, bolted the sprayer on it, and used the Ford gas tank for a seat.

The Bartlett Company began spraying with the labor-intensive barrel pump, using a fifty-gallon pickle barrel with an attached iron pump handle. With the advent of the gasoline engine, spraying became power driven. No longer were strong arms needed to turn cranks or crawl around in tree tops dragging heavy hose. Spraying time went from several hours per tree to a matter of minutes per tree. The first hydraulic tree sprayers were small with low pressure, with volume of output at four gallons per minute (GPM). Gradually, pressure and volume increased, first to ten to twelve GPM, then to twenty to thirty-five and even to sixty. Meanwhile, as tank capacity increased, pressure per square inch (psi) rose to 1,000. Most significant for the arborist was the first spray machine that had the capacity to reach the tops of large, urban shade trees 100 feet tall.

In 1935 Strout of the Bartlett Company invented a hydraulic device for spraying called the Strout gun. Strout got a nozzle that produced both a strong stream and mistlike fog. It was licensed by the Bean Company for its sprayers. This led in time to the Bar-Way Manufacturing Company, a Bartlett subsidiary that made Strout guns and other hydraulic fittings.

Until 1920 the Davey Company had not been involved in many large volume spraying jobs because of the intensive labor involved and the limited chemicals available. Its first power rig was put together by Jerry Landis in 1921. Its first large sprayer, with a brand name of "Friend," had a 300-gallon tank and an output of 20 gallons per minute. Spraying against gypsy moths on a tour of northeastern cities in four states, Davey workers did $5,000 worth of business in five weeks. By 1960 spraying represented four percent of Davey's tree business.

The rapid development of power spraying in the 1920s stimulated a Davey search for larger and more powerful equipment. In 1926 the large-capacity machines were made of cast iron, were water cooled, and were heavy and cumbersome. Nevertheless, within that year it had sprayed 1.5 million gallons of liquid, a 2,000 percent increase over the total nine years earlier. That year, with 80 trucks, Davey consumed 47,000 gallons of gas.

AERIAL SPRAYING

An important step in the development of chemical application to plants in general and trees in particular occurred in 1921, when the chemical war against tree insects in the United States took to the air for the first time. With the cooperation of the U.S. Army, J. H. Houser, entomologist at the Ohio Agriculture Experiment Station at Wooster, directed dusting of arsenate of lead from an airplane against the catalpa sphinx in a grove of 4,800 catalpa trees near Troy, Ohio. This would be the forerunner of spraying large areas first from airplanes and later from helicopters. However significant this development, the dusts applied were not very satisfactory for use on shade trees.

Dr. F. S. Potts of the Connecticut Agriculture Experiment Station experimented with applications of arsenate of lead applied by "autogiro" (helicopter). Following this first demonstration in 1936, continued research on equipment and insecticide formulations led to successful development of aero-applied chemicals over large areas for insect and disease control. His work was the basis for the later development of the ground-level mist blower.

By the mid-1950s, many kinds of crop insects were being successfully controlled by airplane applications of insecticides. In 1951 the principle of mist-blower application was taken to the air with spraying by helicopter. Concentrated insecticide, piped into the engine exhaust and broken into extremely fine droplets, was forced downward over the trees by action of the rotor blades. This type of application was used successfully against the bark beetle vectors of the Dutch elm disease (DED) fungus and other shade tree insects.

EARLY SHADE TREE SPRAYERS

Before 1920 most spraying of shade and ornamental trees was done by hand. The early hand pumps had barrel capacities varying from five to fifty gallons, and had to be operated by two men—one man on the ground pumping for pressure, the other in the tree spraying from a hose. In the absence of water taps such as faucets or hydrants, the water required was suction pumped from any available creek or pond.

By 1922 there were four types of manually operated sprayers for home and landscape use. The knapsack sprayer consisted of a small tank that contained nonpressurized material. Low-level hydraulic pressure was developed with a manually operated pump. A slide pump sprayer operated on the same principle with pressure developed from a telescoping plunger, operated by two hands. The spray material was drawn from a separate container and discharged under pressure of the plunger stroke. The bucket or barrel sprayer was operated by a hydraulic piston pump held or mounted in a container of spray material. The spray material was drawn into and discharged by the sprayer. The wheelbarrow sprayer had a hydraulic pump, mounted on a wheelbarrow frame with handles, and one or two wheels. The spray material was siphoned from a separate container and discharged from the spraying apparatus.

According to one report the first mechanical sprayer for application of chemicals to trees was a model introduced in Germany in 1904. A machine-driven pump sprayer operated by steam was developed in the United States ten years earlier in 1894. Described as the first successful use of steam power for spraying, it was made by Stephen Hoyt of New Canaan, Connecticut. "Large trees were sprayed thoroughly and rapidly with most satisfactory results," according to the Connecticut Agriculture Experiment Station. Despite this, there is no evidence that this machine was ever developed as a practical mobile unit, a requisite for shade tree practice.

Commercial arborists in North America had their most significant stimulus for spraying to control the gypsy moth in the Northeast in the early 1900s. This development coincided with the institutionalization of arboriculture in the first decade of the current century, and would lead to the tree sprayer for use by arborists. The developments in this period included the iron drum spray tank in 1900; the first mechanical tree sprayer in 1904; the hand atomizer (a precursor of the mist-blowing sprayer) and the first hydraulic sprayer in 1907; and the first high tree sprayer in 1909, whose height range was increased in 1910. The high tree sprayer would become the first sprayer for automotive transport. Known as the hydraulic sprayer, it became the standard until challenged by the mist blower forty years later.

Fig. 24.3 A spraying demonstration in 1941. Courtesy of the ISA Archives.

Since controlling the gypsy moth in Massachusetts near the turn of the century was mandated by law, public funding for this purpose turned to machine spraying as soon as it became available. In the early 1900s there were no spray machines that could deliver chemicals in effective volume to the tops of high trees. Thus, it was a significant development for arboriculture when such a machine was finally developed in 1909 by Melvin Guptill and built by the Fitzhenry-Guptill Company in Malden, Massachusetts.

The first model was horsedrawn. The first power sprayer to be completely designed for shade tree work, it would become the model for future development of all hydraulic machines. Guptill went into partnership with Edward L. Fitzhenry, owner of a machine shop in Boston. By 1911 they had built their first truck sprayer, produced at their new plant in East Cambridge, Massachusetts, where all future design and production was carried out.

The Fitzhenry-Guptill sprayer was immediately sought after by the USDA and the state of Massachusetts. Over the next thirty years Guptill sprayers were in great demand for insect control—in fighting the Mediterranean fruit fly in Florida, the mosquitoes in New Jersey, and even fighting a sugar plantation fire in Cuba with a high-pressure sprayer from a truck. Guptill was a charter member of the first arborist organization in North America, the Massachusetts Tree Wardens and Foresters Association, and was active in the National Shade Tree Conference (now the ISA), until his death in 1942.

Guptill's machine was able to send a plume of spray into the tops of the tallest street trees in eastern cities. It not only revolutionized the work of insect control, but paved the way to the development of spraying as a major practice in

Fig. 24.4 An early mist-blower demonstration. Courtesy of the ISA Archives.

arboriculture in the following fifty years. Superseded by bigger and better machines, it was finally retired for field use only in 1950 after forty years of hard service. In 1965 the original machine was placed in the Smithsonian Institution. This sprayer is seen in retrospect as a milestone in arboriculture, as an invention that revolutionized the work in saving trees at a crucial time in the history of the scourge of gypsy and brown tail moths. It may also be seen as another tribute to those who rose to the challenge of gypsy moth damage. The first tribute had been the formulation of arsenate of lead, and the second, the hydraulic sprayer, which would dominate until the advent of the mist blower, and survive despite it.

By 1925 the means to apply chemicals against insects threatening trees were at hand with high-powered sprayers, dusters and even airplanes. First developed for field crops and orchards, they were now generally available for both forest and shade trees.

THE MIST BLOWER SPRAYER

The mist blower tree sprayer, which emerged after World War II, was one of the most significant machines in arboriculture in the 1950s. The combination of the chlorinated hydrocarbon insecticides such as DDT, and the new surge of DED because of the total absence of control efforts during the war, led to a huge demand for spraying landscape trees. With the chain saw, chipper, and the aerial lift, these new sprayers enabled the field of arboriculture to grow rapidly.

The mist blower sprayer was a large piece of equipment, mounted on the rear of a truck. It used a large fan to blow the spray material out in a cloud of mistlike droplets of microscopic size. In contrast to carrying chemicals to the trees by water as with the hydraulic sprayers, the chemicals were blown by air for deposition on tree surfaces. Relatively easy to operate, they were especially well adapted for use on city streets where trees were arranged in rows.

The development of the mist blower sprayer was made possible by the introduction in 1941 of aerosol insecticides propelled by liquid gases. The Experiment Station Office of the USDA, working with researchers at various State Agriculture Experiment Stations, was largely responsible for these developments. In cooperation with the Massachusetts Department of Conservation, it had been supporting research and development of tree spraying equipment since the 1930s.

After the war the USDA, working cooperatively with the Connecticut Agriculture Experiment Station, continued its development of both mist blower sprayers and chemicals to control insect pests of both shade and forest trees. As early as 1946 the USDA Bureau of Entomology and Plant Quarantine began testing the new mist blowing apparatus at Greenfield, Massachusetts. The development of liquid mist spraying machines by private companies followed, largely stimulated by the urge to test the new wonder insecticide, DDT. The miraculous results with DDT as an insecticide had a significant influence in furthering aerial spraying.

Mist-blown spraying had certain advantages over the older, hydraulic method. In addition to being easier to operate, and not having to wrestle with nozzles and hoses, mist blowing was associated with less chemical residue and runoff, and less buildup of insect pests following applications. In addition, it led to the development of custom spraying.

Spraying by mist blower was seen by many applicators as the most significant advance in the field of insecticide application since the advent of DDT. Such mixtures enabled good control of insects with greatly reduced volumes of water compared to conventional spray applications with water suspension of wettable powders. With one to two quarts of concentrated sprays of six to twelve percent DDT, the degree of insect control on large trees was as good as with forty to fifty gallons of the conventional, diluted spray. By 1953 spraying machines for airblast concentrates of chemicals were in common use by arborists.

By 1945 the Parker Brothers of Boston, Massachusetts, pioneers in mist blower technology, had developed the first high-pressure hose and couplings needed for commercial work. For shade tree work, the first suitable sprayer is said to have been a Buffalo turbine model, later known as the Lawrence Aero-Mist, made in 1946. At about the same time the Fitzhenry-Guptill Company, a pioneer in the development of hydraulic sprayers, added a mist blower sprayer to its line, appropriately named the "Mystifier."

The earliest ground-operated mist blowers were developed for application of small volumes of finely atomized concentrate sprays. They had several advantages over the hydraulic sprayers. The early machines varied in size and capacity. The smallest were portable in wheelbarrow fashion, and could reach up to thirty-five feet in height. Most early machines, however, were large enough to be truck mounted and had 25 to 35 horsepower capacity, 7,500 to 10,000 cubic foot capacity, and functional wind speeds of 125 to 140 miles per hour. These machines could reach tree heights up to 100 feet. Some machines were even larger and powerful enough to exceed heights of 100 feet.

The first applications of mist blown spray were insecticides, later followed by fungicides and ultimately compatible mixtures of both. The first insects to be controlled were leaf eaters, such as the gypsy moth and elm leaf beetle. The first large-scale use of the mist blower was in 1948 against the fast-spreading gypsy moth in Pennsylvania in a massive forestwide program. By 1951 mist blown spray had been applied successfully against scale insects on shade trees.

Probably the earliest of the national tree companies to use the new mist blower was the Davey Tree Company. According to company history, its mist blower was developed by George Daughterey of the Speed Sprayer Company of Orlando, Florida. After Red Jacobs studied this equipment, the Davey Company bought several units in 1948. This new method of spray application required additional knowledge and training and had some decided disadvantages, requiring a measure of sophistication not previously required.

By 1948 custom spraying had developed into a large-scale business, involving one or more operators in every moderate-sized community. Such operators were essentially in business only to spray, and thus began primarily as small businesses. The availability of such services had both positive and negative effects on the field of arboriculture. It enabled many small property owners to get quick and effective tree protection from insects and disease, and expanded spraying as a tree care practice to a new level. On the other hand, it attracted many poorly trained operators, and some outright phonies, who used the practice to defraud and hoodwink the public. Some of these unscrupulous operators sold unnecessary treatment at outrageous prices, and sold phony materials and treatments to control genuine problems. Given the increased need for greater sophistication, the poor quality of many sprayers' services gave spraying a negative public image, enhancing a call for regulation.

In 1952 the Bete Fog Nozzle Company of Greenfield, Massachusetts, introduced a unique fog spray nozzle devised especially for dormant oil base spraying for brush control. Designed to save on both materials and labor, it was seen as the

TABLE 24.1

DEVELOPMENT OF SPRAY MACHINES AND PRACTICES

YEAR	DEVELOPMENT OR PRACTICE	NOTES
1858	First garden engine	Europe
1885	First pressure machine	For bordeaux mixtures, Europe
	Bean spray machine	First in United States
1890	First backpack sprayer	United States
Until 1892	Manual application only	Brooms and syringes
1894	First mechanical tree sprayer	United States
1895	First gas engine for spraying	Europe
1896	New nozzles and hand pumps	United States
1900	Barrel pump operation	Hoses in trees
1907	Hand atomizer	Precursor to mist blowing
1909	Hydraulic sprayer	First power reach to tree tops
1921	Earliest spray via airplane	Insect control
	Earliest spray for brush control	Tanks
1930	First use of aerial devices	For tall trees

first practical solution to the problem of basal dormant spraying. Known as the HX5, this nozzle dispersed a flat, uniform fan pattern of the finest-size droplets, with no wasteful side horns or jets. Lightweight and inexpensive, it was built for easy operation by one person.

In 1955 a new type of dual nozzle was developed for the mist blower. With the earlier conventional model, the air velocity was not sufficient for deposition of tiny droplets at tops of large trees. The new dual nozzle system allowed for a coarser spray droplet as well as a fine droplet. This was suitable for deposition on leaves high in the tree crown. With a shutoff valve, the fine spray could still be used on lower foliage.

THE ROLE OF DED IN THE PRACTICE OF SPRAYING

After World War II research on chemical control of the elm bark beetle, carriers of DED, turned to DDT. By the 1950s DDT was shown to be highly effective in preventing new infections of DED by prevention of feeding by bark beetles, setting the stage for massive spray control programs in cities and towns throughout the eastern and midwestern states where the disease was prevalent. Dormant, foliar, or a combination of both sprays were applied either by the older hydraulic or the newer mist blower sprayers. While either machine could be effective in proper application, a never-ending controversy developed over claims that one machine was more effective than the other. The newer mist blowing machines became more popular with most young, new arborists, while the older hydraulic machines continued to be preferred by the older established arborists.

Another controversy arose in the 1950s concerning the effectiveness of spraying for control of DED compared to elimination of actual or potential sources of the bark beetle, carriers of the DED fungus (sanitation). From an economic standpoint, spraying was always more attractive. Spraying and sanitation were then the only direct methods for disease control. Spraying was far less expensive, had public visibility for positive action, and used the "wonder" insecticide of the postwar period—DDT—which seemed to conquer all insect problems. By contrast, sanitation required not only removal of diseased trees and potentially hazardous elm wood, but careful pruning of all elms on an areawide basis. This was expensive to the point of being economically prohibitive where wild elm populations were located near valued landscape elms. In addition, the public and some arborists viewed sanitation in a negative way, as in hauling away dead trees.

As a result, spraying grew to be hugely popular and a substantial rain of DDT fell on urban elm populations while the elmwood debris that bred beetle vectors and disease-causing spores was neglected for the sake of a false economy. Both entomologists and pathologists warned in vain that the effectiveness of spraying would be lessened without good sanitation. Each method, used alone, only reduced probability of infection by reducing both numbers of insect carriers and disease-causing spores. In time, the lack of sanitation would jeopardize the effectiveness of spraying, as beetle and fungus populations reached astronomical numbers, with a corresponding increase of infection pressure. The combination of its decreased effectiveness and the public outcry over environmental concerns contributed to the demise of spraying.

SPRAYING FOR BRUSH CONTROL

Until 1945 removal of brush in utility rights-of-way (ROWs) was entirely mechanical and mostly manual, involving axes, brush hooks, and mechanical girdling of larger stems. Brush control was radically transformed by the new silvicidal chemicals, broadly known as herbicides, and the means of their dissemination. First introduced directly into trees through ax cuts around the tree bole (ax frilling), they were later sprayed on foliage or on cut stumps, or a combination of both. Chemicals for woody plants on utility ROWs were first used in 1947. The first application by helicopter followed in 1950, although widespread aerial spray did not get under way until the mid-1960s. The first chemical to be widely used both on the ground and in the air was the herbicide 2,4-D, followed some years later by the very effective silvicide, 2,4,5-T, and then by mixtures of these and many newer chemicals.

By the 1950s chemical spraying for brush control had become a well-established practice in arboriculture, especially in rural areas on ROWs. One of the earliest preferred chemicals for a dormant basal application and on cut stumps was ammonium sulfamate (AMS) because of its lack of fumes. By the 1960s there were many more chemically diverse materials from which to choose, and with time their numbers increased even more. Their application in arboriculture led to a revolution in line clearing. Line clearing with chemicals, as opposed to mechanical means, was known as "brush control" in the late 1940s. More recently, it has been called "vegetation management" and "integrated vegetation management."

Each of the three national tree companies recognized the value of the new herbicides for brush control along utility ROWs. While the Asplundh Company had dominated utility line clearing since its inception, both the Bartlett and Davey Companies were sixty to seventy percent engaged and had a vital interest in anything affecting new developments. The Davey and Asplundh Tree Companies played leading roles in chemical brush control on the ground. The Bartlett Company was first to do so from the air. The Davey Company appears to have made an early, concerted leap forward, and Red Jacobs became an authority on chemical brush control. From his many reports and discussions, it became clear that in the first five years, the chemicals were often not as effective as expected. This was attributed to inexperience in using dosages and volumes that were too low. In the second five years, the efficacy and results were much improved, with better formulations, higher concentration and volume, and lower costs.

So successful was this new chemical brush control service offered by the Davey Company that its volume in this area increased steadily from $52,000 in 1946 to more than $700,000 in 1955. This was probably symbolic of the growth of chemical brush control for other arborist companies so engaged.

In cooperation with the American Chemical and Paint Company, the Asplundh Company began testing chemicals for brush control in 1946. It began by using small backpack tanks. Later, as operations expanded, it began using U.S. Army surplus vehicles, and progressed to devising new equipment of its own. Four-wheel-drive trucks were adapted for spraying. At first there were jeeps, then larger army M-6 trucks, caterpillar tractors equipped for spraying, and eventually spray trucks on railroad flatcars for ROW clearing along railroad lines.

The Asplundh Company began a series of schools on spraying in 1953 for its foremen. Later it conducted seminars for the edification of its utility clients in the

Fig. 24.5 Aerial spraying. Photo by the National Park Service, courtesy of the ISA Archives.

technology, strategy, and implications of large-scale spraying of ROWs. By the 1960s new tracked vehicles were used in the spraying fleet. The so-called "Muskeg Bombardier" with its continuous tracks was able to move spraying into unusually difficult terrain. By 1964 the old, heavy, cumbersome backpack tanks had been replaced by a newer, lighter, "Power-Pak" mist blower that made spraying faster, easier, and more effective.

The Bartlett Company first used helicopters for brush control in 1951. Its helicopter application operations grew rapidly so that within five years it acquired its own equipment for this purpose. In 1966, it created a subsidiary, the Bar-Fly Corporation, headquartered in Charlotte, North Carolina, from which they maintained and operated six machines for ROW inspection and spraying.

By 1975 numerous and varied herbicides were available for controlling unwanted plants to reduce the cost of vegetation management in ROW maintenance. In the same year, spraying as an arboricultural practice had become second in the field in dollar volume (eighteen percent), topped only by pruning (thirty-seven percent).

By 1977, largely by utilizing herbicides, vegetative management on utility ROWs had become a major service provided by tree companies. According to

Richard Abbott of Kent, Ohio, by then ground spraying with wheeled or tracked vehicles had become a minor portion of the operations, as a larger share of the spray application was performed by helicopter. Also by then, some utilities had begun to de-emphasize herbicides and use mechanical control with large rotary mowing equipment such as the Hydro-ax.

From Chemical to Mechanical

By the early 1960s the widespread use of chemicals on forest crops and shade trees had begun to raise disturbing questions about the impact of biocidal chemicals on the environment and their potential hazard to humans. In this decade more new tools and equipment for brush control without chemicals came into use. The mechanical methods avoided unsightly dead and dying foliage, as well as public resentment of herbicide use.

Arborists and foresters who understood the purpose, technology, and economics of brush control, disliked the offensive roadside scenery of dead and dying trees, and liked even less the burden of having to defend the practice on professional grounds. The problem of "brownout" may have been more influential in public support of the 1970 Environmental Protection Act than the perceived peril from DDT, which actually moved Congress to create the Environmental Protection Agency.

By the 1970s mechanical brush control was used seventy percent of the time compared to chemical brush control. As early as 1972 some members of Edison Electric Institute had discontinued herbicide programs. Others held on because of the high cost of alternatives. By 1975 the maintenance of ROWs in economically and environmentally acceptable ways was of much concern to utilities. Following a study to assess the situation, several conclusions were reached, bearing in mind that successful long-range vegetation maintenance was the goal. Initial ROW management had to begin with clearing of woody plants. Properly done, by whatever methods applied, clearing should be able to reduce future maintenance costs and be environmentally acceptable as well. Of the two spraying methods used, broadcast application by helicopter, fixed booms, or truck-mounted mist blowers was still dominant, but selective spraying was on the rise, using basal sprays.

By 1990 it was clear that the environmental movement, with its distaste for chemicals used on plants, was having an even greater impact on ROW maintenance. In earlier times, chemical use would be replaced by cutting brush in the face of opposition by environmentalists, only to be resumed again for its cost savings. By 1990 the utilities industry was still using both methods, but with some changes. With advances in technology, chemicals were more target specific and the volume of chemical use was declining. Low volume, selective spraying, and premixing were introduced to improve productivity as well as reduce environmental exposure.

By 1970 public concern with spraying chemicals into the environment gave the utilities good reason to be concerned themselves with the environmental quality of the ROWs under their management. Especially concerned that their most dependable herbicide, 2,4,5-T, might be curtailed, they urged that it not be used around homes, charging that a total ban would set back its vegetation management by twenty years. Despite public clamor for a ban of all dioxin-bearing chemicals, utilities noted that 2,4,5-T had such a small amount in its formulations that it posed virtually no threat as a carcinogen.

By 1975 spraying of shade and ornamental trees was a significant part of the business of commercial arborists, estimated by Richard Abbott, of Appraisal, Consulting, Research, and Training (ACRT), to be about eighteen percent. Trees in the urban environment appear to be especially vulnerable to insects and diseases. Often these biotic stresses followed previous stress by abiotic agents.

In the 1980s because of new regulations by the EPA and OSHA, chemical spraying became safer and more reliable. Safety training had become routine practice at all tree companies that complied with federal regulations. Despite these changes, the trend to deemphasize spraying continued. By 1985 spraying as a basic arborist practice was on its way out after a thirty-year period of near dominance.

By 1990 ROW maintenance had undergone several changes from the early years of almost total dependence on herbicides. The intensive use of herbicides had declined, although they were still used in combination with mechanical clearcutting. In fact sometimes company changes from use of chemicals to mechanical methods were reversed back to chemicals. Most companies used both methods in combination. In any event spraying became more selective, girdling was tried more often, and broadcast sprays to control seedlings were eased or even discontinued, and some spraying was confined to stumps.

SUMMARY

Spraying as an arboricultural practice had its origins in the initiation of tree spraying technology, including mechanical power and development of nozzles in England, France, and Germany during the 1800s. Later development and sophistication occurred in the United States, beginning with orchardists and culminating with precision machine manufacture and power.

After spraying reached its peak in the 1950s and 1960s, the practice began to decline. Spraying as a practice in arboriculture, while still significant, is no longer a dominant service by arborists.

CHAPTER TWENTY-FIVE

Injection

"To impart medicinal characteristics into fruits" —Granade, 1158

Injection in its original medical sense was used to indicate forcing a liquid directly into living tissue where there is no natural opening. Botanists have used the term in a broader sense meaning to introduce liquids into plants with or without force (infusion), or even to introduce nonliquid materials directly into plant tissues (implantation). Within this broader concept, the earliest information on tree injection dates back to 1158. According to a report by Granade of Moorish Spain in the 1400s, Ibn-Al-Awam of that region is said to have injected trees in 1158 to impart perfumes, flavors, and medical qualities to fruits and blue coloration to roses. His method involved removal and filling of the pith, or inserting musk, clove, and saffron between the bark and wood.

The oldest reference for liquid injection cited by many writers is from Leonardo da Vinci in 1602. Reported to have first begun injection of fruit trees with arsenic to deter thieves, he also is said to have injected other trees to make fruits sweet: "Fill the hole with honey and stop the hole with a haw-thorne branch, and the fruit will be sweet." Of special interest to arboriculture was his reference as to "how the worms are to be killed, if they be already in the tree." He advised: "Take pepper, laurel, and incense, and mingle all well together with good wine, and pierce a hole into the tree downward to the pith or heart of the tree, and pour this mixture into it . . . and the worms will die."

Following this, in the same century, Francis Bacon infused or implanted fertilizer into trees to increase growth. Cited in *The Rural Cyclopaedia* by J. M. Wilson, it involved the implantation of liquid mercury to destroy insects in trees and shrubs. This may have been the first evidence of the use of mercury as an insecticide

TABLE 25.1

SELECTED IMPLANTS USED IN TREE CARE

YEAR/PERIOD	MATERIALS	NOTES
1900	Sodium arsenite	Fruit trees
1931	Iron salts	Fruit trees
1940s	Iron salts	To cure chlorosis of cypress
1950s	Terramycin (antibiotic)	Used against bacterial fire blight
1960s	Iron salts	To cure chlorosis of pin oak
1978	Insecticides	Used against bark beetles
1980s	Medicaps	To treat zinc deficiency in pecan

in arboriculture, possibly preceding by a century the earliest use of mercury in medicine.

Mengol in France in 1709 showed that colored solutions moved upward into flowers and leaves attached to cut stems immersed in such solutions. In the following century several reports were published from plant injection experiments as the early plant pathologists sought to understand normal functions of liquids in plants. About 100 years later, Mayer in Germany showed the opposite movement of a solution dye, which moved from the surface of a cut stump into all but the finest rootlets.

Dr. Robert Hartig of Germany tried to arrest decay in trees in 1853 by infusing a liquid into a hole from a pre-established reservoir. In this way he improved on da Vinci's method by infusing large volumes of liquid into a hole. In 1886 von Sachs of Germany, using the Hartig method, infused iron salts of sulphate and chloride in a successful attempt to cure chlorosis (a noninfectious disease) of acacia trees, noting that only leaves above the injection point became green. This may have been the earliest case of successful injection designed to achieve a specific purpose in the care of trees.

Near the turn of the century the Russians began to report the use of injections in trees not only for therapy of infectious disease (gummosis), but for nutrition as well. Of special interest in their work was the use of pressure to facilitate the injections. This may have been the first real effort to cure infectious disease by injection, as well as the first attempt to use pressure to inject trees.

Just as many practices in arboriculture were borrowed from earlier Greek and Roman experience, the concept of injection was derived from medicine. Problems such as the trauma of tissue injury, infection, disease, and side effects of chemicals would also be seen in the early injection of trees in North America.

The first reported use of tree injection in the United States was by H. L. Bolley of North Dakota in 1906. After using water to break dormancy, he speculated on the possibilities of diagnosing nutritional needs by chemical injection. In writing of the practical difficulty of tree injection, Bolley noted that each tree appears to be a law unto itself, the wisdom of which is now appreciated by all who inject trees.

Little success was achieved with tree injection until the 1940s. The advent of the first systemic insecticides—the organophosphates—led to new trials of injection of chemical solutions into stems. A breakthrough with a new systemic fungicide in the late 1960s led directly to a new successful injection technology that established injection as a new practice in arboriculture.

THE EXPERIMENTAL PERIOD

The experimental period was a time of both discovery and minor advances, culminating with an established infusion technique that would later lead to limited success in therapy. The new technique was characterized by the use of new chemicals to achieve a variety of goals by one or more means of injection. It included injection first of inorganic chemicals such as sodium arsenite to destroy unwanted trees, and use of both inorganic and organic fungicides to control disease. There was moderate success with insects, but none with the more serious diseases.

The most controversial aspect of tree injection in this period was the theorized need to exclude air in tree holes made for liquid entrance. Boucherie in France had made no attempt to exclude air. Shevgrev in Russia stated that he obtained more and easier distribution of injected liquids after air was excluded. With claims of efficacy by both sides, this controversy persists to the present day.

Despite the many failures to control tree disease, iron injection, including implantation, had moderate success in preventing or curing iron chlorosis of trees. In 1928 the Davey Institute of Tree Surgery published a bulletin, *Injection of Shade Trees for Control of Insects and Disease.* This was the first publication in the United States that focused on tree injection. In 1939 the USDA Bureau of Entomology and Plant Quarantine published its first bulletin on tree injection. Publication E-467 contained ninety-seven references and abstracts. By 1950 there were more than 100 publications on tree injection.

INJECTION TECHNIQUES

Following the introduction of the chestnut blight fungus into North America sometime before 1906, and its subsequent spread and devastation of native American chestnut trees, there was a new interest in tree injection to control disease. In injection trials to control chestnut blight, C. Rumbold in 1915 found that the uptake of injected solutions was better when air was excluded in the injection process. A technique, commonly referred to as the funnel method, was developed to make an injection wound that excluded air. The funnel consisted of a water-retaining material wrapped around the stem, tightly bound to prevent leakage. The injection hole was then made by knife, chisel, or gouge into the water-conducting tissue (xylem) of the stem. Under tensile force, the sap stream absorbed the solution, and it ascended with the sap into smaller branches of the tree. Unfortunately, the nature of chestnut blight was too daunting to be controlled in this way. In 1932 C. W. Collins found that exclusion of air was not necessary for suitable uptake of chemical solutions. He was able to get satisfactory quantities into trees to effectively control insects such as bark beetles.

In 1930 Rush Marshall of the USDA demonstrated a simple tree injector at a conference of shade tree workers in Stamford, Connecticut. Adapted from an automobile grease gun, it required only a special fitting involving a brass tube threaded at one end to fit an Alemite bearing, and cut at the other end to form a wood screw. It was designed for injection with pressure of small quantities of heavy greaselike formulations into tree stems, and was used to force preservatives into pruning wounds, to inoculate trees with fungus cultures, and to attempt to control borers. Though unsuccessful, Marshall's "grease gun" was an early effort to use pressure in tree injection and may have been the earliest example of micro-injection.

A unique tree injection device was crafted by Cornell University to poison elms with silvicides in order to control Dutch elm disease (DED). Consisting of an ax, with a small chemical container, the "Cornell poison axe" made an incision and introduced the chemical in one stroke. Highly effective in killing elms, the method was ineffective in preventing the spread of disease.

The earliest successful use of injection as a shade tree practice would be in the area of nutrition to prevent or cure a noninfectious disease. The earliest materials injected were iron salts designed to cure chlorosis associated with iron deficiency. It was used again successfully with inorganic chemicals such as sodium arsenite to kill unwanted trees. It failed to control chestnut blight, however, and would be the first of many failures to control diseases caused by fungi. These failures may have been responsible for lack of sustained interest in injection for the next twenty years.

Following the unsuccessful trials to control chestnut blight by chemical injection early in the 1900s, Rankin of Cornell University may have been the first to attempt shade tree injection in 1917. Designed to prevent both disease and insect infestation, his efforts were unsuccessful. Around this same time Red Jacobs of the Davey Company tried to control both insects and disease by injection and published a bulletin on his work. There is no evidence, however, to indicate that he was any more successful than Rankin had been. Later, in 1926, injection was used successfully by others for the first time to control insect infestation of trees from borers and bark beetles.

The infusion period was dominated by attempts to control DED and oak wilt. It was also characterized by the advent of a new systemic fungicide developed for control of a broad spectrum of plant diseases.

Under a research fellowship grant from the Bartlett Tree Expert Company, Nestor Caroselli, a graduate student at Rhode Island State College (now University of Rhode Island), began a study in chemotherapy of bleeding canker of hardwood trees caused by a virulent fungus parasite, *Phytophthora cactorum*. Using chemical solutions in bottles attached by tubing to watertight drilled holes at the base of tree boles or in basal roots, the material was diffused into infected tissues. The chemical, known under a proprietary name of Carosel, was a di-amino-azo-benzene which was partially successful as a chemotherapeutant. This earliest demonstration of the possibility of chemotherapy in diseased trees provided the stimulus for testing many other chemicals by infusion, and in effect opened a new era for chemical testing, using a more refined technique for excluding outside air from the system.

INJECTION OF INSECTICIDES

Beginning in 1938 F. C. Craighead and R. A. St. George of the U.S. Forest Service showed that pine bark beetle infestations in trees under stress from drought could be prevented or minimized following injection of insecticides. This would lead to trials against the European elm bark beetles as vectors of DED. Injection of systemics against the elm bark beetles would come sharply into focus by the mid-1960s when Bidrin, produced by the Shell Oil Company, was injected by the Mauget method.

Walter J. Barrow and J. J. Mauget began experiments in Whittier, California, in the 1950s using solubilized iron in a cup of hot water attached by an aluminum tube into the phloem tissue of a tree. According to Barrow, "This had varied results, and Jim's (Mauget) people developed the two-part receptacle that when forced together created a small amount of internal pressure, thus forcing the chemical into the tree." Following refinements, this new device evolved into the Mauget system, which injected the chemical, not into the phloem as originally thought, but into the xylem tissue where upward water flow made distribution possible.

Following the advent of the fungicide benomyl in the late 1960s and the improved technology for tree injection, the Mauget Company developed its own systemic fungicide in 1972. Known under its trade name as Fungisol, by 1974 it had been registered for experimental use against DED, and by 1978 was being used against oak wilt in Texas. By 1964 capsules containing the insecticide Bidrin were first used for closed-system application to prevent feeding by elm bark beetles, the carrier of the DED fungus. By 1978 the Mauget Company had tested a variety of chemicals in liquid form delivered under light pressure of eight pounds per square inch into woody stem tissues. These included a complete fertilizer, the micronutrients, two systemic insecticides, and one fungicide. DuPont released its own form of the fungicide, Benlate, in the early 1970s. It was found to be both effective and systemic in preventing DED in healthy elms with application by soil amendment, trunk injection, or foliar spray. The new success with Benlate represented a major breakthrough in systemic fungicides, and was a stimulus for exploring new methods for improved tree injection.

Benlate itself, being insoluble in water, was not distributed sufficiently when injected. To overcome this problem, both the DuPont Company and the U.S. Forest Service made a concerted effort to solubilize it so that it could be distributed within the extensive vascular systems of elms and other trees. In addition, the forest services in both the United States and Canada, and researchers at the Illinois Natural History Survey, devised methods for injecting large volumes of solubilized benomyl compounds into elm trees.

After careful chemical manipulation and modification, the DuPont and Merck Chemical Companies produced several solubilized benomyl derivates suitable for a commercial market, and two in particular, Arbortect and Lignasan, were available for testing by 1977. The long-awaited success of a suitable material for successful chemotherapy of DED led to an explosion in injection technology, more critical evaluation of injection technology, and the testing of new chemicals. By 1970 the U.S. Forest Service had introduced the first pressure-injection system for introducing chemicals into elms in large quantities. By 1974 there were at least six other systems being tested.

Perhaps the most unique of these systems was one devised by Kondo of the Canadian Forest Service. Having found earlier that chemical distribution was better when injected in root flares than in stems, Kondo achieved the best distribution of all by injecting into excavated roots. By the 1980s it was generally accepted that his system was superior for distribution over any other. Excavating roots for injection, however, was very labor intensive and time consuming.

In the mid-1980s Phair and Ellmore of Massachusetts showed that precision of injection limited to the outer wood ring of elm resulted in the best distribution

TABLE 25.2
DEVELOPMENT OF SELECTED TREE INJECTION METHODS*

YEAR/PERIOD	METHOD	NOTES
1915	Funnel around tree	Incision below solution
1930s	Cornell injector	One-stroke wound and inject
1936	Marshall's grease gun	Early micro-injector
1940	Holes, tubes, and bottles	First successful chemotherapy
1941	Holes and reservoirs	Tubing connectors
1962	Mauget injector	Sealed system
1968	High pressure	Accessory pressure tank
1973	Excised root under pressure	Soil excavation required

Numerous, different models were devised; all are variants of one or more models noted.

yet observed for practical application. Their technique was known as the shallow pit method. Stipes of Virginia found that the shallow pit injection method was as effective for distribution as the flare root method of Kondo.

By 1973 injection with benomyl compounds produced good results for oak wilt and DED, first with Lignasan produced by the Dupont Company, and later by Arbortect produced by the Merck Company. Even later oak wilt was successfully held in check with injection of a new fungicide growth regulator, propiconazole. Tree injection was successful in controlling the yellows diseases of elm and palm with antibacterial chemicals such as the tetracyclines.

TREE GROWTH REGULATOR INJECTIONS

The early trials in the use of tree growth regulators (TGRs) to reduce growth, shorten pruning cycles, and reduce tree maintenance costs began with spraying such compounds as maleic hydrazide and alar in the late 1960s. By 1970 public opposition to spraying made the new injection technology attractive. By 1973, when the use of TGRs was established, the tree care industry turned to the possibility of replacing spraying with injection.

By 1976 researchers in England had been exploring the same possibilities and had developed new dynamic TGRs known as giberellic acid inhibitors. Developed for use on apple trees, these materials had the unique ability to reduce cell elongation without reducing cell division. The net result was healthy, shortened growth. By 1984 the English-born growth regulators with giberellic acid inhibitors were being injected into shade trees, especially on utility ROWs with improved injection systems. Tissue damage, however, emerged as a side effect of injection.

When injection to control DED was widely practiced, it soon became apparent that successful injection was not without serious problems. By that time, Alex Shigo, the foremost authority on wounds and decay in forest trees, had raised questions of potential damage from the numerous holes in trees required for satisfactory distribution of chemicals. While the older problem of phytotoxicity seemed not to be a factor in damaging foliage, it soon became a problem in woody tissues around and above injection holes where chemical doses were extremely high. Studies revealed that extensive areas of these tissues were killed, reducing storage capacity of the trunk and affecting future growth. In addition, when injection holes penetrated bacterial wet wood present in virtually all elms, the wet wood could be extended throughout the entire trunk.

IMPLANTS

Implanting materials in trees preceded genuine tree injection of liquids by either fusion or pressure, but it was not until the development of chelated iron salts in the 1950s that implantation became a serious practice in arboriculture. During the 1930s and 1940s iron salts were implanted successfully in holes drilled in stems to cure trees, such as fruit trees and cypress, of chlorosis caused by iron deficiency. After the advent of antibiotics in the 1950s, some, such as Terramycin, were found to be successful against bacterial fire blight. It was also in this period that the new iron sequestrene salts implanted in chlorotic pin oaks became both successful and popular. Research on iron chlorosis spawned more research and progress with implants than any other problem, so that a whole series of implants were devised in the 1970s and 1980s to control insects such as borers and bark beetles and many other deficiencies in addition to iron.

SUMMARY

Injection in North America progressed through three periods: experimental trials, from 1900 to 1940; infusion, from 1940 to 1970; and liquid injection, from 1970 to 1998. The first period was marked by early methods and materials, the exclusion or inclusion of air, success with nutrition implants, and the use of silvicides to destroy unwanted trees. The second was marked by new methods and materials, early successful chemotherapy and systemicity, the Mauget system, and the advent of benomyl fungicide. The last period was marked by a breakthrough for control of DED, and injection technology, the use of tree growth regulators, refinement and increased use of implantation, and chemical and physical damage from tree injection.

References

Abbott, R. E. "Commercial Arboricultural Practices in North America." *Journal of Arboriculture* 3 (1977): 141–45.

Alvarez, R. G. "Growth Regulators." *Journal of Arboriculture* 4 (1977): 94–100.

American Forestry Association. *The American Elm*. Washington, D.C.: American Forestry Association, 1937.

American Tree Association. *Forestry Almanac*. Philadelphia: J. B. Lippincott,1924.

Anderson, J. F. "The Gypsy Moth." *Frontiers of Plant Science.*" 32, no. 3 (1980): 1–8.

Anderson, R. F. *Forest and Shade Tree Entomology*. New York: Wiley, 1960.

Arbor Action. Amherst, N.H.: National Arborist Association, 1946.

Arbor Day Association. *Arbor Day Association Charter,* signed in New York, 1955.

Armstrong, N. "Importance and Place of Cavity Work in Arboriculture." *National Shade Tree Conference Proceedings*. 1935.

Arron, G. P. "Ontario Hydro as a Potential User of Tree Growth Regulators." *Journal of Arboriculture* 17 (1991): 103–6.

Asplundh Tree Expert Co. *A Spectrum of Asplundh Specialized Services*. Willow Grove, Penn.: Asplundh Tree Expert Co., 1978.

———. *The Asplundh Tree: 50th Anniversary Issue*. Willow Grove, Penn.: Asplundh Tree Expert Co., 1978.

———. *Asplundh Nationwide Storm Emergency Listing*. Willow Grove, Penn.: Asplundh Tree Expert Co., 1984.

———. *The Asplundh Tree: 60th Anniversary Issue*. Willow Grove, Penn.: Asplundh Tree Expert Co., 1988.

———. *The Asplundh Tree: 70th Anniversary Issue.* Willow Grove, Penn.: Asplundh Tree Expert Co., 1998.

Austen, R. *Treatise on Fruit Trees.* Reprint, Oxford, England: W. Hall for Amos Curteyene, 1553.

Bailey, L. H. *The Pruning Book.* New York and London: Macmillan, 1898.

Bain, J. *Dutch Elm Diseases: The New Zealand Experience.* Roturua, New Zealand: Ministry of Forestry, Forest Research Institute, 1990.

Baker, H. G. 1965. *Plants and Civilization: Fundamentals of Botany Series.* Belmont, Calif.: Wadsworth, 1965.

Baker, W. L. *Eastern Forest Insects.* Radnor, Penn.: USDA Forest Service, Northeast Forest Experiment Station, 1972.

Banker, H. H. "Arbor Day: The First 100 Years." *American Forests.* 1972. 8–11, 60–61.

———. *Arbor Day: Past and Present.* West Orange, N.J.: Committee for National Arbor Day, 1979.

Banker, H. J. "Arbor Day Renaissance." *Journal of Arboriculture* 8 (1982): 50–51.

Barrons, K. E. *Are Pesticides Necessary?* Chicago, Ill.: Regenery Gateway Books, 1981.

"Bartlett Organization: A Quarter Century of Scientific Progress." *Tree News* 10 (1931): 2–5.

Bartlett, F. A. *Bartlett: His Book on Trees.* New York: McKennae & Taylor, 1924.

———. *The European Elm Disease.* Bartlett Tree Research Lab Bulletin No. 1. Stamford, Conn.: F. A. Bartlett Tree Expert Company, 1928.

———. "Historical Background of Cavity Work." In *Proceedings of the National Shade Tree Conference.* (1935): 39–72.

———. *Radio Tree Talks.* Stamford, Conn.: F. A. Bartlett Tree Expert Company, 1932.

———. *Tree Talk.* Stamford, Conn.: F. A. Bartlett Tree Expert Company, 1913.

Bartlett, R. A., Sr. "Sprayers and Mist Blowers." Address to New Jersey Federation of Shade Tree Commissions, 1958.

———. Sr. "Sprayers and Mist Blowers." Address to New Jersey Federation of Shade Tree Commissions. *The Shade Tree.* New Brunswick, N.J.: Cook College, 1958.

The Bartlett Tree Organization: A Quarter Century of Scientific Progress. Stamford, Conn.: Bartlett Tree Co., 1931.

Barton, B. S. *Elements of Botany.* Philadelphia: Early American Imprints (Second Series No. 3763), 1803.

Beach, S. A., et al. "Spray Mixtures and Spray Machinery." In *New York Agriculture Experiment Station Bulletin 243,* 1903.

Beattie, R. K. "How the Dutch Elm Disease Reached America." *National Shade Tree Conference.* 109 (1933): 101–5.

Beatty, R. G. *The DDT Myth: Triumph of the Amateurs.* New York: John Day, 1973.

Beilman, A. P. "How to Feed a Shade Tree." *Missouri Botanical Garden Bulletin* 22 (1934): 113–26.

Bess, H. A. "Population Ecology of the Gypsy Moth, *Porthetria dispar* L. (Lepidoptera: Lymantriidae)." *Connecticut Agriculture Experiment Station Bulletin* (1961): 646.

Blair, D. F. "Keynote Address, ISA Western Chapter Meeting." *Western Chapter News* 10 (1984): 49–54.

Blair, M. F. *Practical Tree Surgery.* Boston: Christopher Publishing House, 1937.

———. "The Evolution of Arboriculture, Part I: A Résumé." *Arborist's News* 38 (1973): 109–12.

Bohmont, B. L. *The Standard Pesticide Users Guide.* Englewood Cliffs, N.J.: Prentice Hall, 1990.

Bolgiano, C. "Taking Aim at the Gypsy Moth." *American Forests* 95 (1989): 37–44.

Bolley, H. L. "Tree Feeding and Tree Medication." *North Dakota Agriculture Experiment Station Report* 14 (1904):55–58.

Bonnicksen, T. M. "The Development of Forest Policy in the United States." In *Introduction to Forest Science*, edited by R. A. Young. New York: Wiley, 1982. 7–36.

Brasier, C. M., and J. N. Gibbs. "Origin of the Dutch Elm Disease Epidemic in Britain." *Nature* 242 (1973): 607–9.

Breedlove, D. A., H. A. Holt, and W. R. Chaney. "Tree Growth Regulators: An Annotated Bibliography" *Purdue University Experiment Station Research Bulletin 989* (1989).

Brewer, E. G. "The Fight for the Elms." *American Forests* 47 (1941): 22–25.

Bridgeman, P. H. *Tree Surgery.* London: David and Charles, 1976.

Bridgeman, T. *The Young Gardener's Assistant.* New York: D. Mitchell Printers, 1840.

Brown, G. K. "Prototype Equipment for Commercial Pressure-Injection of Aqueous Growth Regulators into Trees." *Journal of Arboriculture* 4, no.1 (1978): 7–13.

Brown, R. C., and R. A. Sheals. "The Present Outlook on the Gypsy Moth Problem." *Journal of Forestry* 42 (1944): 393–407.

Buckley, A. R. *Trees and Shrubs of the Dominion Arboretum.* Agriculture Canada Publication 1697, Ottawa, Ont., 1980.

Burdekin, A. D., and H. M. Heybroek, eds. "Dutch Elm Disease." In *Proceedings of the IUFRO Conference.* Upper Darby, Penn.: USDA Forest Service, 1975.

Burgess, A. F. "The Dispersion of the Gypsy Moth." *United States Department of Agriculture Bureau of Entomology Bulletin 119* (1913).

Campana, R. J. "A History of Introduced Forest Tree Diseases in the United States." Master's thesis, Yale University, 1947.

———. "Dutch Elm Disease on the Prairie." *American Nurseryman* 1, no. 1 (1955): 13–14, 69–73.

———. "DED Controls: Will Systemics Work?" *Weeds, Trees and Turf* (May 1975):16–17, 71.

———. "Limitations of Chemical Injection to Control Dutch Elm Disease." *Journal of Arboriculture* 3 (1977): 127–29.

———. "Comparative Aspects of Dutch Elm Disease in Eastern North America and California." *California Plant Pathology* 41, no. 4 (1978): 1–4.

———. "Some Essential Aspects of Dutch Elm Disease Control." In *Symposium on the State of the Art of Dutch Elm Disease Control,* edited by R. Felix and F. Santamour. Washington, D.C.: National Arborist Association Symposium Proceedings, vol. 1, 1978. 42–53.

———. "Characteristics of Successful Systemic Chemicals." In *Proceedings of a Symposium on Systemic Chemical Treatments in Tree Culture,* edited by J. J. Kielbaso, H. Davidson, J. Hart, A. Jones, and M. K. Kennedy. East Lansing, Mich.: Michigan State University, 1979.

———. "The Interface Between Plant Pathology and Entomology in the Urban Environment." In *Perspectives in Urban Entomology,* edited by G. Frankie and C. Koehler, 459–80. New York: Praeger Publishers, 1983.

———, et al. "Isolation of *Ceratocystis ulmi* in California from Elms with Buried Infections from Previous Years." *Phytopathology* 70 (1980): 751.

———. "Dutch Elm Disease." In *Compendium of Elm Diseases*; edited by R. J. Stipes and R. J. Campana. St. Paul, Minn.: APS Press, 1981.

———. "Dutch Elm Disease in North America with Particular Reference to Canada: Success or Failure of Conventional Control Methods." *Canadian Journal of Plant Pathology* 3 (1981): 252–59.

———. "A History of Dutch Elm Disease in North America," In *History of Sustained-Yield Forestry: A Symposium,* edited by H. K. Steen. Portland, Ore: Forest History Society, for the International Union of Forestry Research Organizations, 1983.

Campbell, R. W., and H. T. Valentine. "Tree Condition and Mortality Following Defoliation by the Gypsy Moth." *USDA Forest Service Research Paper NE-236.* Upper Darby, Penn.: Northeastern Forest Experiment Station, 1972.

Carson, R. *Silent Spring.* Boston: Houghton Mifflin, 1962.

Carter, J. C. *The Most Promising Fungicide for Shade Trees.* Urbana, Ill.: Illinois Natural History Survey. n.d.

Carvell, K. L. *Environmental Effects of Herbicides Research Project (EEI Project RP 103).* New York: Edison Electrical Institute, 1973.

Catesby, M. *The Natural History of Carolina, Florida, and the Bahama Islands.* London: n.p., 1731.

Chadwick, L. C. "The Fertilization of Shade Trees in the Nursery." In *1934 Proceedings of the American Society for Horticultural Science.* Alexandria, Va.: ASHS, 1935.

———. "Fertilizer Trials with Shade Trees in the Nursery." In *1936 Proceedings of the American Society for Horticultural Science.* Alexandria, Va.: ASHS, 1937.

———. Fertilization of Woody Ornamental Plants. *Ohio Agriculture Experiment Station Bulletin* 25 (1940): 89–96.

————. "Shade Trees in Postwar Planning." *Arborist's News* 9 (1944): 17–19.

————. "Organic vs. Inorganic Fertilizers in Tree Feeding." *Arborist's News* 15 (1950): 68–72.

————. "3,000 Years of Arboriculture—Past, Present and Future." *Arborist's News* 35 (1970): 73–78.

————, et al. "NAA Can Prevent Flowering in Trees." *Arborist's News* 16 (1952): 82–86.

Clancy, T. "Back to the Farm: Tracing the Origins of Modern Equipment." *Tree Care Industry* (January 1990): 22.

Clepper, H. *Crusade for Conservation: The Centennial History of the American Forestry Association.* Washington, D.C.: American Forestry Association, 1975.

Clinton G. P., and F. A. McCormick. "Dutch Elm Disease." *Connecticut Agriculture Experiment Station Bulletin* 389 (1936): 701–52.

Clopper, H. S. "Observations of Lightning Injury and Protection for Trees." *Arborists News* 3 (1938).

Cody, J. B. *Vegetation Management on Power Line Rights of Way: A State of the Knowledge Report.* SUNY College of Environmental Science and Forestry. Applied Forestry Research Institute AFRI Research Report 28. 1975.

Collins, C. W., et al. "Bark Beetles and Other Possible Insect Vectors of the Dutch Elm Disease, *Ceratostomella ulmi* (Schwars) Buisman." *Journal of Economic Entomology* 29 (1936): 169–76.

Collins, H. M. "2,4,5-T Hearings." *Journal of Arboriculture* 1 (1975): 16–18.

Collins, J. F. "Tree Surgery." *United States Department of Agriculture Farmers Bulletin 1178* (1926).

Commercial Arborist, The. Amherst, N.H.: National Arborist Association, 1938.

Cooper, W. *In Search of the Golden Apple.* New York: Vantage Press, 1982.

Cornuti, I. *Canadiensium Plantarum Historia.* New York: John Reprint Co., 1635.

Coulter, L. L. "New Herbicides and Their Use." *Arborist's News* 16 (1950): 37–38.

Craighead, F. C. *Insect Enemies of Eastern Forests.* United States Department of Agriculture Miscellaneous Publication 657 (out of print). 1950.

Cran, H. J., Jr. "Charting Our Course for the 1970s." *Arborist's News* 36 (1970): 123–26.

Creed, L. D. "NAA as a Growth Retardant." *Arborist's News* 37 (1972): 25–29.

Cripe, R. E. "Lightning Protection for Trees." *American Nurseryman* 148, no. 9 (1978): 58–60.

Cronan, W. *Changes in the Land: Indians, Colonists and the Ecology of New England.* New York: Farrar, Straus and Giroux, 1984.

Crosby, A. W. *Ecological Imperialism: The Biological Expansion of Europe, 900–1900.* Cambridge, England: Cambridge University Press, 1986.

Dages, W. E., ed. *Tree Topics: 75th Anniversary Issue: Progress in Scientific Tree Care.* Stamford, Conn.: F. A. Bartlett Tree Expert Co., 1982.

Davey, J. *The Tree Doctor: A Book on Tree Culture.* Akron, Ohio: Commercial Printing Co., 1901.

Day, S. "Pruning: Selecting the Best Tool for the Job." *Colorado Green* (Winter 1988): 1–14, 40–41.

———. "The Influence of Sapstream Continuity and Pressure on Distribution of Systemic Chemicals in American Elm (*Ulmus americana* L.)." Master's Thesis, University of Maine, 1980.

Decker, G. C. 1948. "Recent Advances in Insecticides." *Arborist's News* (1948): 44–46.

Des Cars, A. *Tree Pruning: A Treatise on Pruning Forest and Ornamental Trees.* Translated by C. S. Sargent. London: Wilban Rider and Son, 1883.

"Development of a National Institution." *Tree News* Special Issue (Summer 1929).

Dietz, David. "The Politics of Pesticides." *Journal of Arboriculture* 9 (1948): 80–82.

Dimond, A. E. "Plant Chemotherapy." In *Plant Pathology: Problems and Progress. 1908–1958*, edited by I. C. S. Holton, et al. Madison, Wisc.: American Phytopathological Society, 1959. 221–28.

"Do It Right or Not at All." *The Davey Bulletin* 16 no. 10 (1928): 1–32.

Doane, C. C., and M. L. McManus, eds. "The Gypsy Moth: Research Toward Integrated Pest Management." *United States Department of Agriculture Forest Service Technical Bulletin 1584.* 1981.

Dodds, D. I. "Tree Care: Helping Nature with Science." *Weeds, Trees and Turf* (January 1974):14, 49.

Dodens, R. *A New Herbal or Historie of Plants.* London: E. Griffin 1619 (1578).

Dormir, S. C. "Chemical Control of Tree Height." *Journal of Arboriculture* 4 (1978): 145–53.

Dunegan, J. C., and S. P. Doolittle. "How Fungicides Have Been Developed," in *Yearbook of Agriculture.* Washington, D.C.: United States Department of Agriculture, 1953. 105–19.

E. I. DuPont de Nemours Powder Co. *Tree Planting with DuPont Dynamite.* Wilmington, Del.: DuPont, 1911.

Elgerama, D. M. "Factors Determining Resistance of Elms to *Ceratocystis ulmi.*" *Phytopathology* 57 (1967): 641–42.

Encyclopedia Britannica, s.v. "Surgery."

Evelyn, J. *Sylva: Or a Discourse on Forest Trees and the Propagation of Timber in His Majestie's Domain, Including an Historical Account of the Sacredness and Use of Standing Groves.* Reprint, London: Arthur Doubleday, 1908 (1662).

Ewan, J. *John Banister and His Natural History of Virginia, 1678–1692.* Urbana, Ill.: University of Illinois Press, 1970.

Facts About Dutch Elm Disease. Amherst, N.H.: National Arborist Association, 1949.

Fairchild, D. *Exploring for Plants.* London: Macmillan, 1931.

———. *The World Is My Garden: Travels of a Plant Explorer.* New York: Charles Scribner's Sons, 1939.

Felix, R. "The Arborist's Role in Urban Forestry." *Proceedings of the National Urban Forestry Conference, United States Forestry Service ESF Publication 80–003,* vol. 2. Washington, D.C.: United States Forestry Service.

———, and A. L. Shigo. "Rots and Rods." *Journal of Arboriculture* 3 (1977): 187–90.

———, and F. Santemour, eds. *The Current State of the Art of Dutch Elm Disease Control.* Amherst, N.H.: National Arborist Association, 1978.

Felt, E. P. *Our Shade Trees.* New York: Orange Judd Co., 1938.

———. "The Gypsy Moth Threat in the United States." *Eastern Plant Board Circular.* 1942.

———, and S. W. Bromley. "The Hurricane of September 21, 1938." In *Tree Topics.* Stamford, Conn.: Bartlett Tree Research Labs, 1938.

Fernow, B. E. *The Care of Trees in Lawn, Street and Park.* New York: Henry Holt, 1910.

———. *The Care of Shade Trees.* New York: Henry Holt, 1911.

Fertilize and Spray. Amherst, N.H.: National Arborist Association, 1948.

Filley, W. O. "The Nature of the First Four Shade Tree Conferences." *Arborist's News* 39 (1974): 87–126.

Fisher, S. W. "The Roots of Controversy: A Historical View of Pesticide Regulation." *American Nurseryman* (January 1987): 89–99.

———. "The Evolution of Insecticide Resistance." *American Nurseryman* (March 1990): 107–11.

Fitzherbert, J. *Boke of Husbandrie.* Theatrum Orbis Terrarum. Reprint, London: I. R. White, 1598 (1531).

"Fitzhenry-Guptill Sprayer Goes to Smithsonian." *Trees Magazine* (March-April 1968): 5.

Flemer, W. III. "Ornamentals: A Historical Outline of Plant Popularity." *American Nurseryman* (June 1990): 137–65.

Flexner, J. T. "George Washington in the American Revolution: 1775–1783." Boston: Little Brown, 1967.

———. *The Gypsy Moth: A Report of the Work of Destroying the Insect in the Commonwealth of Massachusetts.* Boston: Wright and Potter Printing, 1886.

———, and C. H. Fernald. *The Gypsy Moth. A Report to the Massachusetts State Board of Agriculture.* Boston: Wright and Potter Printing, 1896.

———. *On Healing of Tree Wounds. 50th Annual Report.* Boston: Massachusetts State Board of Agriculture, 1900.

Forsythe, W. *The Culture and Management of Fruit Trees.* New York: Ezra Sargent and Co., 1802. [Early American Reprint Series no. 2235].

———. *A Treatise on the Cultivation and Management of Trees.* London: n.p., 1803.

Fowler, M. E. "Tree Culture and Forestry." *Arborist's News* 23, no. 12 (1958): 89–94.

Frankie, G. W., and C. S. Koehler. *Urban Entomology: Interdisciplinary Perspectives.* New York: Praeger Publishers, 1983.

Fusione, A. E. "Arboretums and Botanical Gardens." In *Encyclopedia of American Forests and Conservation History,* edited by R. E. Davis. New York: Macmillan, 1983. 23–24.

Galloway, B. T. "Spraying for Fruit Diseases." *USDA Farmers Bulletin #38.* Washington, D.C.: United States Department of Agriculture, 1896.

Garrity, J. A. *The Great Depression.* New York: Harcourt Brace, 1986.

Gerstenberger, P. "Trees on the Move, South Florida Ordinances Spawn a Major Industry." *Tree Care Industry* (April 1992): 4–6.

Gibbs, J. N. "Intercontinental Epidemiology of Dutch Elm Disease." *Annual Review of Phytopathology* 16 (1978): 287–307.

"Glass Booms." The Asplundh Tree Expert Co., Spring 1985.

Gold, R. H. *Lightning Protection.* New York: Chemical Publishing, 1975.

Graf, V. "Thirty Years with the Chain Saw Industry: An Anniversary Retrospective." *Chain Saw Age.* (July 1982).

Gronovious, J. F. *Floria Virginica Exhibens Plants.* Apud Comelium Haar. Lugduni Batavorum, 1739.

A Guide for Fertilization. Amherst, N.H.: National Arborist Association, 1960.

"Gypsy Moth Damage." *Arborist's News* 37 (1971): 100–10.

Hackett, W. P. "Effective Use of Chemicals to Control Plant Growth in Landscapes." *Arborist's News* 72 (1972): 13–19.

Hamilton, W. D. 1984. "Sidewalk/Curb-Breaking Tree Roots: Management to Minimize Existing Pavement Problems by Tree Roots." *Arboriculture Journal* 8 (1984): 223–34.

Hanisch, M. A. et al. *Dutch Elm Disease Management Guide.* Washington, D.C.: United States Department of Agriculture, Forest Service and Extension Service, 1983.

Hardig, R. *Textbook of the Disease of Trees.* Munich, Germany: F. Straub, 1894.

Hariot, T. *A Brief and True Report of the New Found Land of Virginia.* Micro-opaque copy, 1588.

Harris, R. *Arboriculture: Care of Trees, Shrubs, and Vines in the Landscape.* Englewood Cliffs, N.J.: Prentice Hall, 1983.

Hedrick, U. P. *A History of Horticulture in America.* New York: Oxford University Press, 1950.

"Herbicides and Trees." *The Shade Tree* 59 (1986): 13–15.

Herrick, G. W. *Insect Enemies of Shade Trees.* Ithaca, N.Y.: Comstock Publishing, 1938.

Himelick, E. B. "Systemic Treatment of Nutrient Deficiencies in Trees." Symposium on Systemic Chemical Treatments in Tree Cultivation, Michigan State University, East Lansing, 1978. 59–63.

———. *Transplanting Manual for Trees and Shrubs.* 2nd ed. Revised. Urbana, Ill.: International Society of Arboriculture, 1981.

———. *Tree and Shrub Transplanting Manual.* Savoy, Ill.: International Society of Arboriculture, 1991.

Himelick, E. B., and D. Neely. "Recent Studies on Shade Tree Fertilization," in *Proceedings of the International Shade Tree Conference* (1966): 71–79.

———, D. Neely, and W. R. Crowley, Jr. *Experimental Field Studies on Shade Tree Fertilization. III.* Natural History Survey Biology Note 53, Urbana, Ill., 1965.

Hoagland, D. R. "Lectures on the Inorganic Nutrition of Plants." Waltham, Mass.: Chronica Botanica Co., 1948.

Hock, W. K. "Present Status of Research on Systemic Fungicides." *Arborist's News* 35 (1970): 57–60.

Holmes, F. W. Personal notes on the history of Dutch elm disease in the Netherlands, and personal communication. 1985.

———, and H. M. Heybroek. *Dutch Elm Disease—Early Papers: Selected Works of Seven Dutch Women Pathologists.* St. Paul, Minn.: APS Press, 1990.

Hopkins, C. G. *Soil Fertility and Permanent Agriculture.* United States Department of Agriculture Crop Reporting Board, 1910.

Hora, B. *The Oxford Encyclopedia of Trees.* New York: Oxford University Press, 1981.

Horsfall, J. G. "Principles of Fungicidal Action." Waltham, Mass.: Chronica Botanica Co., 1956.

Howard, J. "2,300 Years of Tree Moving." *Your Garden and Home* (July 1932).

Howard, R. A. "The Arnold Arboretum of Harvard University." *Arborist's News* 49 (1974): 78–82.

Hoyt, S. *Steam-Powered Pump Sprayer: 19th Annual Report, Connecticut Agric. Exp. Station.* New Haven: Tuttle, Morehouse, and Taylor, 1895.

Hubbard, F. T. *Nomenclatorial Notes on Plants Growing in the Botanical Garden of the Atkins Institution of the Arnold Arboretum at Soledad, Cienfuegos, Cuba.* Cambridge, Mass.: Harvard University Press, 1932.

Hyams, E. *A History of Gardens and Gardening.* New York: Praeger Publishers, 1971.

Irish, C. F. "The Process of Aeration and Fertilization of Tree Roots by Means of Compressed Air." In *Proceedings of the National Shade Tree Conference.* (1929): 35–37.

———. "Highlights in the Early History of Arboriculture." In *Proceedings of the National Shade Tree Conference.* (1932): 8–14.

Jackson, U. P. "Living Legacy of the CCC." *American Forests* (September-October 1988): 37–48.

Jacobs, H. L. *The Arboriculturist.* Kent, Ohio: Davey Tree Expert Co., 1946.

———. "Fertilization of Shade Trees. Part I: Fall vs. Spring Fertilization." Kent, Ohio: Davey Tree Expert Co., 1929. 28.

———. "A Modern View of 25 Years of Cavity Treatments." *National Shade Tree Conference Proceedings.* 1935.

James, E. O. *The Tree of Life: An Archaeological Study.* Leiden, Netherlands: E. J. Brill, 1966.

Johnson, W. T., and H. H. Lyon. *Insects that Feed on Trees and Shrubs.* Ithaca, N.Y.: Cornell University Press, 1988.

Jones, T. W., and G. F. Gregory. "An Apparatus for Pressure Injection of Solutions into Trees." *United States Department of Agriculture Forest Service Research Paper NE-233,* 1971.

Josselyn, J. *Account of Two Voyages to New England.* London: Giles Widdows, 1682. Reproduction of original in Harvard University, Cambridge, Mass.

———. *New England Rarities Discovered in Birds, Beasts, Fishes, Serpents and Plants of That Country.* N. p., 1672.

"Julius Worz: Chain Saw Industry Pioneer." *Chain Saw Age* (November 1985).

Kalm, Peter. *Peter Kalm's Travels in North America: The English Version.* 2 vols. New York: Dover Publishing, 1770.

Karnosky, D. F. 1979. "Dutch Elm Disease: A Review of the History, Environmental Implications, Control and Research Needs." *Environmental Conservation* 6, no. 4 (1979): 311–22.

Kastner, J. *A Species of Eternity.* New York: Alfred Knopf, 1977.

Kazmaier, H. E., D. E. Bell, R. G. Fuller, and J. H. Litchfield. *Summary of Results from Field Experiments Investigated During 1966–67 on Control of Tree Growth.* Columbus, Ohio: Batelle Memorial Institute, 1967.

Ketcham, D. E., and K. R. Shea. "USDA Combined Forest Pest Research and Development Program." *Journal of Forestry* 75 (1977): 404–7.

Kielbaso, J. J., and M. K. Kennedy. "Urban Forestry and Entomology: A Current Appraisal." In *Urban Entomology: Interdisciplinary Perspectives,* edited by G. W. Frankie and C. S. Koehler. New York: Praeger Publishers, 1983.

King, F. "American Gardens." In *The Story of the Garden.* Boston: Hale, Cushman and Flint, 1936.

King, G. C., C. Beatly, and M. McKenzie. *Polyurethane for Filling Tree Cavities.* Publication 58. Amherst, Mass.: University of Massachusetts, 1970.

Kirch, J. H. "Chemical Brush Control Enters a New Decade." *Arborist's News* 26 (1961): 33–39.

Klein, R. M., and D. T. Klein. *Fundamentals of Plant Science.* New York: Harper and Row, 1988.

Kondo, E. S. *A Method for Introducing Water-Soluble Chemicals into Mature Elms.* Informational Report O-X-171. Sault Ste. Marie, Ont.: Canadian Forest Service, 1972.

Kozel, P. C., K. W. Reisch, and G. E. Hull. "Chemical Control of Tree Growth." *Ohio Agricultural Research and Development Center Report* (September-October 1970): 104–5.

Kozlowski, T. T. "His Work in Trees." *Trees Magazine* 30 (1966): 16–17.

Kummerling, K. *Safe Practices for Arborists.* Amherst, N.H.: National Arborist Association, 1965.

Lacy, G. H. "Evaluating Chemicals for Tree Infusion or Injection to Control Diseases Caused by Mycoplasma-Like Organisms." In *Methods for Evaluating Pesticides for Control of Plant Pathogens,* edited by J. D. Hickey. St. Paul, Minn.: APS Press, 1986. 266–69.

Lane, F. C. *The Story of Trees.* Garden City, N.Y.: Doubleday, 1952.

Langenheim, J. H., and K. V. Thimann. *Plant Biology and Its Relation to Human Affairs.* New York: Wiley, 1982.

Lanier, G., and A. Epstein. "Control Tactics in Research and Practice." In *Dutch Elm Disease Perspectives after 60 Years,* edited by W. A. Sinclair and R. J. Campana. Ithaca: New York Agriculture Experiment Station, Cornell University, 1978.

———. "Vectors." In *Dutch Elm Disease Perspectives after 60 Years,* edited by W. A. Sinclair and R. J. Campana. Ithaca: New York Agriculture Experiment Station, Cornell University, 1978.

Latouche, R. *The Birth of Western Economy: Economic Aspects of the Dark Ages.* New York: Harper and Row, 1961.

Laut, J. G., and M. E. Schomaker. *Dutch Elm Disease: A Bibliography.* Colorado State Forest Service, Colorado State University, Fort Collins, 1974.

———, and T. M. Steiger. *Dutch Elm Disease: A Bibliography Addendum.* Fort Collins, Col.: Colorado State Forest Service, Colorado State University, 1980.

———, M. E. Schomaker, T. M. Steiger, and J. Metzler. *Dutch Elm Disease: A Bibliography (Revised).* Fort Collins, Col.: Colorado State Forest Service, Colorado State University, 1979.

Lawson, W. *A New Orchard and Garden.* Reprint, London: G. Sawbridge, 1676 (1597).

———. *A New Orchard and Garden.* Reprint, London: The Cresset Press, 1927 (1623).

Le Seur, A. D. C. *The Care and Repair of Ornamental Trees in Garden, Park, and Street.* London: Country Life Ltd., 1934.

Leighton, A. *American Gardens in the Eighteenth Century: "For Use or For Delight."* Boston: Houghton Mifflin, 1976.

Leonard, D. E. "Bioecology of the Gypsy Moth." In *The Gypsy Moth: Research Toward Integrated Pest Management,* edited by C. C. Doane and M. L. McManus. United States Department of Agriculture, 1981. 9–30.

Leonardo da Vinci: Codice Atlantico di Leonardo da Vinci-nella bibliotheca. Ambrosiens di Milano-reprodotto della Regia. Milan: Academia dei Lincei, 1884. (Folio 12R.a.)

"Lester Asplundh, 1901–1984." *The Asplundh Tree* (Summer, 1984).

Lewis, C. E. *Historic Outline of the Introduction of Woody Plants, Plant Collections and Nurseries into North America.* Farmingdale, N.Y.: SUNY Agricultural and Technical College, 1965.

———. "Our American Heritage—Trees." *Journal of Arboriculture* 2 (1976): 181–85.

Li, Hui-Lin. *The Origin and Cultivation of Shade and Ornamental Trees.* Philadelphia: University of Pennsylvania Press, 1963.

"Life Story of John Davey." *Davey Bulletin* 33, no. 6 (1946): 1–5.

"Life Story of Martin L. Davey." *Davey Bulletin* 33, no. 7 (1946): 1–21.

Little, E. L., Jr. "Fifty Trees from Foreign Lands." In *Yearbook of Agriculture*, 815–30. Washington, D.C.: United States Department of Agriculture, 1949.

Lodeman, E. G. *The Spraying of Plants.* New York: Macmillan, 1896.

Loudon, J. C. *An Encyclopedia of Gardening.* London: Longmans, Green and Co., 1865.

———. *A New Voyage to Carolina.* N.p., 1709.

———. *The Trees and Shrubs of Britain.* London: H.G. Bohn, 1854.

Mader, D. L. and R. N. Cook. *Soil Fertility for Urban Trees.* Washington, D.C.: University of Massachusetts and United States National Park Service, 1979.

Major, R. T. "The Gingko, the Most Ancient Living Tree." *Science* 157 (1967): 1270–73.

Making and Using Lime-Sulfur. Geneva, N.Y.: New York State Agriculture Experiment Station, n.d.

"Man of The Year: Hyland Johns." *Arbor Age* (February 1990): 46–54.

"Man of The Year." *Arbor Age* (January, 1987): 12–18.

Manchester, W. *The Glory and the Dream: A Narrative History of America.* Boston: Little Brown, 1974.

Marsh, G. P. *Man and Nature.* New York: C. Scribner, 1864.

Marshall, J. *Arbustum Americanum, or The American Grove.* New York: Hafner Publishing, 1785.

Marshall, R. P. "Scientific Aspects of Handling Tree Cavities," In *Proceedings of the National Shade Tree Conference*, 51–55. 1935.

Marvin, C. T. "Trees and Lightening Strikes." *Tree Talk* 3 (1938): 16.

"Massachusetts Forestry Association Condemns the Use of Concrete as a Filling Material." *Bulletin no. 38* (1924).

Massachusetts State Board of Agriculture. *Exterminating the Gypsy Moth: Annual Reports of the Massachusetts State Board of Agriculture.* Boston: Wright and Potter Printing, 1891–99.

Mathieu, T. F. "Methods and Practices of Moving Small Trees." *Arborist's News* 16 (1951): 21–25.

Matthews, W. E. "The History of Arboriculture in the United Kingdom." In *IUFRO Proceedings on Urban Forestry*, edited by J. Andersen, 150–57. 1976.

Mauget. "Forced Feed for Trees." *Western Fruit Grower* (January 1958).

May, C. "Methods of Tree Injection." *Trees* 4 (1941): 10–12, 14, 16.

McNew, G. L. "Landmarks During a Century of Progress in Use of Chemicals to Control Plant Diseases." In *Plant Pathology: Problems and Progress 1908–1958*, edited by C. S. Holton et al. Madison, Wisc.: American Phytopathological Society, 1959. 42–54.

"Medicines for Plant Health: Fungicides." *Phytopathology News* (November 1990): 181.

Meister, R. T. *Farm Chemicals Handbook.* Willoughby, Ohio: MeisterPro, 1986.

Merrill, E. D. "Eastern Asia as a Source of Ornamental Plants." In *Proceedings of the National Shade Tree Conference*, 41–47. 1933.

Metcalf, W. *Introduced Trees of Central California.* Berkeley, Calif.: University of California Press, 1969.

Meyer, F. G. "Plant Cultivation in Colonial Gardens in the South." *The Harvester* 2 (1976): 3–24.

Meyer, F. G. *Plant Cultivation of Introduced Trees in Southern States.* Decatur, Ga.: Georgia Horticultural Society, n.d.

Meyer, P. W. "John Bartram: Botanist and Horticulturist." *Journal of Arboriculture* 4 (1978): 165–68.

Meyer-Wegelin, H. *Astung [Pruning].* Trans. USDA Forest Service. Hanover, Germany: M & H Schaper, 1936.

Michaeux, A. *Flora Boreali-Americana.* Parisiis et Argentorati: Apud Frates Lebrault, 1803.

Michaux, F. A. *The North American Silva.* Paris: C. d'Hautel, 1819.

Miller, K. C., and R. E. Abbott. "Results of TGR Survey." *Journal of Arboriculture* 17 (1991): 44–48.

Mitchell, J. W., and R. R. Rice. "Plant-Growth Regulators." *United States Department of Agriculture Miscellaneous Publication 495* (1942).

Monteath, R. *Monteath's Foresters Guide.* Edinburgh: W. Blackwood, 1829.

Morrison, M. "Tree City USA." *Journal of Arboriculture* 2 (1976): 123–232.

Morton, S. *Arbor Day Resolution.* Lincoln, Nebr.: State of Nebraska Board of Agriculture, 1872.

National Academy of Science. *Weed Control: Principles of Plant and Animal Pest Control.* Vol. 2. Washington, D.C.: National Academy of Science, 1968.

National Arborist Association. *National Arborist Association: Its History, Objectives, Activities, Accomplishments.* Amherst, N.H.: National Arborist Association, 1960.

———. *Pruning Standards for Shade Trees, Revised.* Amherst, N.H.: National Arborist Association, 1988.

National Fire Protection Association. *Lightning Protection Code.* Boston: National Fire Protection Association, 1980.

National Shade Tree Conference. 1929–1960. Annual Proceedings

Neely, D., ed. *A Standard Municipal Tree Ordinance.* Urbana, Ill.: International Society of Arboriculture, 1978.

———. "Healing of Wounds on Trees." *Journal of the American Society for Horticultural Science* 95, no. 5 (1970): 536–40.

———. "Tree Wounds and Wound Closure." *Journal of Arboriculture* 5, vol. 6 (1979): 135–40.

———, and E. B. Himelick. "Effectiveness of Vapam in Preventing Root Graft Transmission of the Dutch Elm Disease Fungus." *Plant Disease Reporter* 29 (1965): 106–8.

———, E. B. Himelick, and W. R. Crowley, Jr. "Fertilization of Established Trees: A Report of Field Studies." *Illinois Natural History Survey Bulletin* 30, no. 4 (1970): 235–66.

Netton, S., ed. *Gardens and Arboreta of Philadelphia and the Delaware Valley.* Philadelphia: University of Pennsylvania Morris Arboretum, 1981.

New Formulation of Lime-Sulfur Prepared for Self-Boiling, A. Geneva, N.Y.: New York Agriculture Experiment Station.

Nicol, W. *The Practical Planter.* London: Printed for J. Scatcherd and H. D. Symonds by C. Wittingham, Printer, 1803.

Norris, D. M. "Systemic Insecticides in Trees." *Annual Review of Entomology* 12 (1967): 127–48.

Nuttall, T. *Genera of North American Plants and a Catalogue of the Species.* Philadelphia: D. Heartt, 1818.

———. *North American Sylva: Trees Not Described by F. A. Michaux.* Philadelphia: Smith & Wistar; New York: G. P. Putnam, 1849.

Pack, E. L. *The School Book of Forestry.* Washington, D.C.: The American Tree Association, 1922.

Parkinson, J. *"Paradisis": The Ordering of the Orchard.* N.p., 1629.

Parliman, B. J. "The Plant Introduction and Quarantine System of the United States." *Plant Breeding Reviews* 3 (1985): 361–434.

Parmenter, S. W. "Liquid Feeding of Trees by the Jet Method." *Arborist's News* 16, no. 7 (1932): 65–68.

Parris, G. K. *A Chronology of Plant Pathology.* Starkville, Miss.: Johnson and Sons, 1968.

"Pedigreed Shade Trees." *The Shade Tree* 35 (1951): 38–39.

Peets, E. *Practical Tree Repair.* New York: McBride, 1926.

Perry, T. O., F. S. Santamour, Jr., R. J. Stipes, T. Shear, and A. L. Shigo. "Exploring Alternatives to Tree Injection." *Journal of Arboriculture* 17 (1991): 217–26.

Pershing, H. A. *Johnny Appleseed and His Times.* Strasbourg, Va.: Shenandoah Publishing House, 1838.

Pfleger, R. E. *Green Leaves: A History of the Davey Tree Expert Company.* Chester, Conn.: The Pequot Press, 1977.

"Phenoxy Herbicides." *Weed Science* 23 (1975): 252–63.

Pimentel, D., and C. A. Edwards. "Pesticides and Ecology." *Bioscience* 32 (1982): 595–600.

Pinchot, G. *Breaking New Ground.* New York: Harcourt Brace, 1947.

Pirone, P. P. *Maintenance of Shade and Ornamental Trees.* New York: Oxford University Press, 1941.

———. *Pests and Diseases of Ornamental Plants.* New York: Ronald Press, 1978.

————. *Tree Maintenance,* 5th edition. New York: Oxford University Press, 1978.

Piser, H. "Arbor Day Needs Support." *Nature* 48 (1955): 522–25.

————. "The Place and Purpose of an Arbor Day Association." In *Proceedings of the National Shade Tree Conference,* 81–91. 1954.

Pomerleau, R. "History of the Dutch Elm Disease in the Province of Quebec." *Forestry Chronicle* 37, no. 4 (1961): 356–67.

Pontey, W. *The Forest Pruner: A Treatise on the Training or Management of British Timber Trees, Whether Intended for Use, Ornament or Shelter.* 3rd ed. London: Hardy, White, Mawman, 1810.

Potts, S. F. "Control of Forest and Shade Tree Insects with Concentrated Sprays Applied by Mist Blowers." Quarterly Tree Pest Leaflets 31 and 54. Washington, D.C.: United States Department of Agriculture Bureau of Entomology, 1950.

Proceedings of the Eastern Shade Tree Conference. Bronx, N.Y.: New York Botanical Gardens, 1938.

Pruning Standards for Shade Trees. Amherst, N.H.: National Arborist Association, 1958.

Pursch, F. *Flora America Septentrionales.* London: White, Cochrane, 1814.

Radke, R. O. "Herbicide." In *Encyclopedia of Science and Technology.* 6th ed. New York: McGraw Hill, 1976.

Rae, W. "Tree Fertilization." *Tree Care Industry* 2 (1991): 8.

————. "Tree Transplanting." *Journal of Arboriculture* 2 (1976): 133–35.

Reed, H. S. *A Short History of the Plant Sciences.* Waltham, Mass.: Chronica Botanica Co., 1942.

Rehder, A. *The Bradley Biography.* Cambridge, Mass.: Riverside Press, 1900.

————. *Manual of Cultivated Trees and Shrubs.* New York: Macmillan, 1940.

————. "On the History of the Introduction of Woody Plants into North America." *National Horticulture* 15 (1935): 245–57.

————. *On the History of Introduction of Woody Plants into North America.* Boston: American Horticultural Society, 1936.

Rhode, E. S. *The Story of the Garden.* Boston: Hale, Cushman and Flint, 1936.

Ringenberg, S. "Cabling and Bracing." *Arbor Age* (June 1990): 12–24.

Ritz, C. President, Karl Kuemmerling, Inc., Massilon, Ohio. Personal communication, 1987.

Rodgers, A. D. *Berhard Edward Fernow.* Princeton, N.J.: Princeton University Press, 1951.

Roosevelt, T. *White House Address on Arbor Day.* Washington, D.C.: U.S. Government Printing Office, 1907.

"Root Barriers and Root Pruning." *Arbor Age* (June 1990): 38–45.

Rose, R. H. "Asplundh 50th Anniversary Issue." *The Asplundh Tree* (Fall 1978).

Rumbold, C. "Methods of Injecting Trees." *Phytopathology* 5 (1915): 225–28.

————. "The Injection of Chemicals into Chestnut Trees." *American Journal of Botany* 7 (1920): 1–20.

Ryan, H. D. "Professional Pruning." *TCI Magazine,* 2, no. 11 (1991): 17–20.

Sachs, R. M. et al. "Chemical Control of Plant Growth in Landscapes." California Agriculture Experiment Station Bulletin 844.

Santamour. F. S., Jr., and R. Felix, eds. *The Current State of the Art of Dutch Elm Disease Control.* National Arborist Association Symposium. No. 1. Washington, D.C.: United States National Arboretum, 1977.

Sargent, C. S. "The First Fifty Years of the Arnold Arboretum." *Journal of the Arnold Arboretum* 3 (1922): 127–71.

———. *Report on the Forests of North America.* Washington, D.C.: U.S. Government Printing Office, 1884.

———. *The Silva of North America.* Boston, New York: Houghton, Mifflin, 1891.

Scanlon, E. "Fitzhenry-Guptill Sprayer Goes to Smithsonian." *Trees* (March–April 1968).

Scheffer, R. J. 1991. "Dutch Elm Disease Control: Microorganisms or Sterol Biosynthesis Inhibitors to Control a Major Vascular Wilt Disease." In *Applications of Biotechnology to Tree Culture, Protection and Utilization,* edited by B. E. Harsig et al. United States Department of Agriculture Northeast Forest Experiment Station, 1991.

Schlesinger, A. M., Jr. *The Age of Roosevelt: The Coming of the New Deal.* Boston: Houghton Mifflin, 1958.

Schofield, E. K. "Pesticides from Plants." *American Horticulturist* (December 1986): 10–13.

Schreiber, L. R. "A Method for the Injection of Chemicals into Trees." *Plant Disease Reports* 53 (1969): 764–65.

Schuster, J. A. *Translocation of Fungicides in American Elms.* Master's Thesis, University of Illinois, 1970.

Scientific Tree Topics. Stamford, Conn.: F. A. Bartlett Tree Expert Company, 1939.

Seitz, S. "A National Disaster." *Arbor Age* 1 (1981): 10–11, 28–29.

Shade Tree Work for Veterans. Amherst, N.H.: National Arborist Association, 1945.

Shigo, A. L. *A New Tree Biology Dictionary.* Durham, N.H.: Shigo and Trees, Associates, 1986.

———. *A New Tree Biology.* Durham, N.H.: Shigo and Trees, Associates, 1986.

———. *Modern Arboriculture: Touch Trees.* Durham, N.H.: Shigo and Trees, Associates, 1991.

———, and N. G. Marx. "Compartmentalization of Decay in Trees." *USDA Forest Service Agriculture Information Bulletin 405* (1977).

———, and R. Felix. "Cabling and Bracing." *Journal of Arboriculture* 6 (1980): 5–9.

———, and W. C. Shortle. "New Ideas in Tree Care." *Journal of Arboriculture* 3 (1977): 1–6.

Shurtleff, M. C., and G. W. Simone. "Fungicide Inventory and Disease Control Spray Programs for Woody Ornamentals." *Journal of Arboriculture* 3 (1977): 41–53.

Sinclair, W. A. "Range, Suscepts and Losses." In *Dutch Elm Disease: Perspectives after 60 Years,* edited by W. A. Sinclair and R. J. Campana, 1–52. New York Agriculture Experiment Station, Cornell University, Ithaca, 1978.

Smalley, E. B. "Systemic Chemical Treatments of Trees for Protection and Therapy." In *Dutch Elm Disease: Perspectives after 60 Years*, edited by W. A. Sinclair and R. J. Campana. New York Agriculture Experiment Station, Cornell University, Ithaca, 1978. 34–39.

Smith, R. F., T. E. Mittler, and C. N. Smith, eds. *History of Entomology.* Palo Alto, Calif.: Annual Reviews, Inc., 1973.

Smith, S. "Riding the Technology Express." *American Nurseryman* (June 1990): 168–97.

Society of Municipal Arborists. 1935–1975. *Trees Magazine.*

Solotaroff, W. *Shade Trees in Towns and Cities.* New York: Wiley, 1911.

Soper, J. H. "Arboretum." In *The Canadian Encyclopedia.* 2d rev. ed. Edmonton, Alberta: Hurtig Publishers, 1988. 90–91.

Spongberg, S. A. "Establishing Traditions at the Arnold Arboretum." *Arnoldia* 49, no. 1 (1989): 11–20.

Spraker, L., and J. Walker. *Tulip Trees and Quaker Gentlemen: 19th Century Horticulture at Longwood Gardens.* Kennett Square, Penn.: Longwood Gardens, Inc., 1975.

Stewart, H. *The Planter's Guide,* 2nd ed. Edinburgh: J. Murray, 1828.

Steuart, H. *The Planters Guide.* 2nd edition. Edinburgh: J. Murray, 1828.

Stipes, R. J., and R. J. Campana. *Compendium of Elm Diseases.* St. Paul, Minn.: American Phytopathological Society, 1981.

———. "Introducing and Evaluating Liquid Fungicides in Elm Trees for the Control of Dutch Elm Disease." In *Methods for Evaluating Pesticides for Control of Plant Pathogens,* edited by K. D. Hickey. St. Paul, Minn.: APS Press, 1986.

Stone, G. E. *Tree Surgery.* Amherst: Massachusetts Agriculture Experiment Station, 1915.

Strout, L. "Fifty Years Observation." *Tree Topics* 31 (1962): 6–7.

Sutton, S. B. *Charles Sprague Sargent and the Arnold Arboretum.* Cambridge, Mass.: Harvard University Press, 1970.

———. *The Arnold Arboretum: The First Century.* Peterborough, N.H.: Noone House, 1971.

Tannehill, I. R. *The Hurricane.* United States Department of Agriculture Miscellaneous Publication 197. Washington, D.C.: United States Department of Agriculture, 1939.

Theophrastus. *De Causis Plantorum,* 3 vols. 300 B.C. Reprint, Cambridge, Mass.: Harvard University Press, 1976.

Taylor, R. L. *Plants of Colonial Days.* Williamsburg, Va.: Colonial Williamsburg, Inc., 1952.

———. *A New Policy for Botanical Gardens in Canada.* A Symposium on the National Botanic Garden System for Canada sponsored by the Royal Botanical Gardens. Technical Bulletin #6, 10–21. Hamilton, Ont.: Royal Botanic Gardens, 1972.

———. "Role of Botanical Gardens in Urban Forestry." In *IUFRO Symposium on Trees and Forests for Human Settlements.* 1976. 399–404.

———. "The Canadian Flora, 1534 to 1900." In *Man's Impact on the Canadian Flora.* Canadian Botanical Association Bulletin 9, no. 1. 1976 1–30.

———. "Botanical Garden." In *The Canadian Encyclopedia,* 254. 2d rev. ed. Edmonton, Alberta: Hurtig Publishers, 1988.

Thacker, C. *The History of Gardens.* Berkeley, Calif.: University of California Press, 1979.

Theophrastus. *De Causis Plantorum,* 3 vols. 300 B.C. Reprint, Cambridge, Mass.: Harvard University Press, 1976.

———. *Enquiry into Plants.* Adud Laurentium Amstelodami. 1644.

"Thirty Years with *Chain Saw Age*: An Anniversary Retrospective." Portland, Ore.: Chain Saw Age, 1982.

Thompson, A. R. *Lightening Protection for Trees.* Washington, D.C.: U.S. Park Service, 1938.

———. "Tree Bracing." *United States National Park Service Tree Preservation Bulletin 3,* Washington, D.C., 1959.

———. *Tree Preservation Bulletin No. 8.* Washington, D.C.: United States Department of the Interior.

Thruelsen, R. "Treeman: Men at Work." In *Saturday Evening Post.* Reprint, 25 September 1948 issue.

Tilford, P. E. "Tree Wound Dressings." *Arborist's News* 6 (1940): 41–49.

———. "A Half Century with Trees and Their Friends." *Journal of Arboriculture* 1 (1975): 131–36.

"Tree Growth Regulator Research." *Arbor Age* (February 1990): 33.

"Tree Growth Regulators Move into the Mainstream." *Arbor Age* (August 1989): 49–53.

Tree Evaluation Book. Amherst, N.H.: National Arborist Association, 1957.

Tree News. Stamford, Conn.: F. A. Bartlett Tree Expert Company, 1924.

"Tree Surgery to Date." *Tree Talk,* 5, no. 7 (1923).

Tree Tips. Stamford, Conn.: F. A. Bartlett Tree Expert Company, 1984.

Tree Topics. Stamford, Conn.: F. A. Bartlett Tree Expert Company, 1932.

"Tree Trimming Equipment." *Arbor Age* (September 1990): 12–16.

"Trees May Become Infected." *Tree Talk* 9 (1927): 25–26.

Troy, G. "Gypsy Moth Invasion Runs Arborist Ragged." *Weeds, Trees and Turf* (September 1981): 28, 32, 34, 108–10.

Troyer, L. C. "Seventy-Fifth Anniversary of the Davey Tree Expert Company: A History." *Davey Bulletin* 73 (1984): 1–34.

United States Department of Agriculture. *Plant Exploration and Introduction.* Multivolume Record of Introductions since 1898. Washington, D.C., 1898.

———. *Arbor Day, Its Purpose and Observation.* Washington, D.C.: United States Department of Agriculture, 1940.

———. *Dutch Elm Disease. A Report to the President and Congress of the United States.* Washington, D.C.: United States Department of Agriculture. 1977. United States Department of Agriculture, Bureau of Entomology. *The Elm in the United States.* Unpublished internal report. Washington, D.C., 1938.

United States Department of Agriculture News Service. *Searching the World for Garden Beauty.* Washington, D.C., 1969.

"U.S. Agriculture Hall of Fame Introductory." Kansas City, Mo.: 1988.

U.S. Area Zone Map for Plant Hardiness. USDA-ARS Miscellaneous Publication No. 1475. Washington, D.C.: U.S. Government Printing Office, 1990.

van de Werken, H. "Fertilization and Other Factors Enhancing the Growth Rate of Young Shade Trees." *Journal of Arboriculture* 7 (1981): 33–37.

Vaux, C. *Villas and Cottages.* New York: Harper & Bros., 1857.

Verall, A. F., and T. W. Graham. "The Transmission of *Ceratostomella ulmi* Through Root Grafts." *Phytopathology* 25 (1935): 1039–40.

"Vermeer Celebrates 40th Year." *Arbor Age* (September 1988): 7.

Wachtel, C. L. "Tree Surgery in Modern Arboriculture." In *Proceedings of the International Shade Tree Conference* (1965): 26–30.

Wagar, J. A. "Reducing Surface Rooting of Trees with Control Planters and Wells." *Journal of Arboriculture* 11 (1985): 165–71.

Wait, L. C. *Fairchild Tropical Garden: The First Ten Years.* New York: Ronald Press, n. d.

Walker, J. C. *Plant Pathology.* New York: McGraw Hill, 1969.

Wallner, W. E., and K. A. McManus. *Lymantriidae: A Comparison of Features of New and Old Tussock Moths.* United States Department of Agriculture Northeast Forest Experiment Station, 1989.

Ware, G. W. *Pesticides: Theory and Application.* San Francisco, Calif.: W. H. Freeman, 1978.

Warder, J. A. *American Pomology.* New York: Orange Judd and Co., 1867.

Warner, O. F. "Bracing Material and Methods." *Arborist's News* 5 (1940): 9–14.

Warnick, H. "The RPAR and 2,4,5-T." *Journal of Arboriculture* 5 (1979): 21–24.

Watson, D. G. *Shade and Ornamental Trees in the Nineteenth Century Northeastern United States.* Ph.D. thesis, University of Illinois, 1978.

Way, R. *Ontario's Niagara Parks: A History.* 2d ed. Fort Erie, Ont.: Review Publishing Co., 1960.

Weaver, R. J. *Plant Growth Substances in Agriculture.* San Francisco, Calif.: W. H. Freeman, 1972.

Webster, A. D. *Tree Wounds and Diseases.* London: Williams and Norgate, 1916.

Weidhass, J. A., Jr. "Current Status of Shade Tree Insect Research in the United States." *Arborist's News* 48, no. 3 (1972): 65–80.

Welch, D. S. "Treatment of Tree Cavities." *Trees Magazine* (Jan. 1939).

Westcott, C. *The Gardeners Bug Book.* New York: Doubleday, 1964.

Western Shade Tree Conference. 1934. *Proceedings of the First Western Shade Tree Conference, Golden Anniversary Issue.* Anaheim, Calif., May 1983.

Wilson, E. H. *Aristocrats of the Trees.* Boston: The Stratford Co., 1930.

Wilson, J. M., ed. *The Rural Cyclopedia of Agriculture: and of the arts, sciences, instruments, and practice necessary to the farmer.* Edinburgh: A. Fullerton and Co., 1847–49. (microform).

Wolfe, W. D. *A Scientific and Economic Review of Systemic Implants in Tree Culture.* Symposium on Systemic Chemical Treatments in Tree Cultivation, Michigan State University, East Lansing, Mich.: 1978.

Wright, R. *The Story of Gardening.* Garden City, N.Y.: Garden City Publishing Co., 1938.

Wyman, D. "Growth Experiments with Pin Oaks Which Are Growing Under Lawn Conditions." *New York Agriculture Experiment Station Bulletin 646.* (1936).

———. *The Arboretum and Botanical Gardens of North America.* Waltham, Mass.: Chronica Botanica Co., 1947.

———. *Trees for American Gardens.* London: Collier-Macmillan Ltd., 1965.

———. "The History of Ornamental Horticulture in America." *Arnoldia* 33, no. 1 (1973): 97–112.

———. *Wyman's Gardening Encyclopedia.* New York: Macmillan, 1986.

Young, G. F. *The Medici.* New York: The Modern Library, 1910.

Young, H. C., and P. E. Tilford. "Tree Wound Dressings." *Arborist's News* 2 (1937):1–4.

Index

345–46
Central Park, development of, 24,25
Ceratostomella ulmi, 210
Cercidiphyllum japonicum. See katsura tree
Chadwick, Lewis C.: *v,* and the Eastern Shade
Tree Conference, 207; as editor of *Arborist's
News,* 171; and fertilization of shade trees,
318, 320, 321, 322; and hospital
landscaping, 141; ISA Award of Merit, 179;
and NSTC Memorial Research Fund, 175; as
officer of the NSTC, 2, 152–53, 154, 155,
156–57; and quality of workmanship
among arborists, 289; and revised NSTC
constitution, 150; survey of hurricane-
damaged trees, 207; and wartime controls
on fertilizer, 137, 139
chaining and bracing. *See* cabling and bracing
Chain Saw Age, 370
chain saws: "A" model, 367; "K" model, 367;
deck, 366; development of, 141, *142,* 365–
70; electric starting, 368; injuries caused
by, 369; McCulloch models, 368; principal
U.S. manufacturers of, 370; safety devices
on, 369; Stihl, 366; use of in pruning, 296,
297
Chapman, John, 20–21
chemotherapy: as Dutch elm disease control
method, 224, 225–27, 270; use of to treat
plant disease, 269–71
cherry trees, 32, 42
chestnut, 4
chestnut blight fungus, 42, 44, 93, 399–400
chinaberry, 34, 36, 40
Chinese scholar tree, 40
chipper. *See* wood chipper
chisel pruner, 294
chloranil, 267
chlordane, 256
chlorflorenol (CF), 281, 284
chlorinated hydrocarbons, 257
chloro-p-benzoquinone. *See* chloranil
chlorosis, 322, 398, 399, 400, 404
cinchona, 37
citrus fruit trees, introduction of to U.S., 32
Civilian Conservation Corps, the (CCC), 197–99,
200, 205, 206
clam shell bucket digger, 303
Clark, William S., 18, 41
Clayton, John, 15–16, 64
Clearway, 191

climbing ropes, use of, 119
Clinton, G. P., 156
Clopper, H. Stevenson, 357, 358
CO 11, 282
coal tar, as wound dressing, 326, 327, 328, 329,
339, 340, 346
cocoa plant, introduction of to U.S., 34
Codding, George M., 119, 124, 316
coffee, introduction of to U.S., 34
"collar cut," the, 293
Collins, C. W., 400
Collins, J. F., 328, 346
Collinson, Peter, 15, 16, 35, 63
Colutea arborescens, 35
Commercial Arborist, The, 238
Commercial Arborist Committee, the, 166
Committee for a National Arbor Day (CNAD),
53–55, 57
Committee on Street Lighting and Tree Planting,
163
Connecticut Tree Protection Association, the, 141
Conroy, Jim, 370
conservation, early American efforts at, 26–28
container trees, 309–10
copper carbonate, as fungicide, 264, 266
copper sulfate, in control of Dutch elm diseases,
223; as fungicide, 263–64, 265; as
herbicide, 273, 275; in tree wound
treatment, 328, 333
cork tree, 41
"Cornell poison axe," the, 400, 403
Cornuti, Marie Victorin, 13
Cory, E. N., 150
Cotinus coggygria, 35
cottonwood, 21
Council of Tree and Landscape Appraisers, the,
240
Cowan, R. Douglas, 114
Craighead, F. C., 401
Cran, Herbert J., 164, 178
Creech, John, 70
creosote: as fungicide, 265; as wound dressing,
327, 328, 329, 339
crown gall, 269
Cupressus sempervirens. See cypress, Italian
Custis, John, 35
cyclohexamide, 269
cyclone spray nozzle, development of, 380
cypress: Italian, 33, 36; pyramidal, 18
cytokinins, 280–81

Felix, Robert, *234,* 234–35, 241
Felt, Ephraim Porter, *121, 148;* and creation of the
    National Shade Tree Conference, 147; as
    director of Tree Research Laboratories, 125;
    and the Eastern Shade Tree Conference,
    206; as editor of *Tree Talk,* 120; and gypsy
    moth control 84; as National Shade Tree
    Conference editor, 149, 170–71
Fenner, Carl, 153, 318
ferbam, 266, 268
fermate, 267
Fernald, Charles H., 83
Fernow, Bernard Eduard, *27,* 27–28
ferric citrate, 315
ferric dimethyldithiocarbamate. *See* ferbam
ferric sulfate, 274
ferrous ammonium citrate, 315
Fert-O-Ject, the, 319
fertilization: application methods, 312–15;
    chelation in, 322; development of
    knowledge and techniques of, 313; earliest
    instances of, 287, 311, 354; foliage, 320–
    21; injection and implantation of, 315;
    liquid, 318–20; materials used as, 314;
    slow-release, 322–23; wartime regulation of
    distribution of, 135, 136
fiacre, 326
figs, 34
Filley, W. O., 146, 147, 156, 206
fir, red, 38
fire blight, 269
Fitzhenry, Edward L., 386
fixed copper, 137
flannel bush, 38
Flexfil, 119, 346
floraprimadol, 285
Florida Forestry Corporation, 186
Florida Shade Tree Conference, the (FSTC), 151
fluoride, as insecticide, 256
flush cutting, 292, 293
foliar analysis, 320, 321
Food Machinery Corporation, the (FMC), 380
Forbush, E. H., 340
forest reserve law, the, 27
Forsythe, William, 10, 11, 98, 325, 338, 379
Fournier, Yvon, 166, 176, 179
Franklin, Benjamin, 21, 357
Franklinia, 17, 35
Franzen, J. J., 209
Fraxinus greggii, 38

Frederick Law Olmsted Award, 58
Frederick Louis, Prince, 63
Freeman L. Parr Award, 243
Fremont, John C., 38
Fremontia californica. See flannel bush
French, Caroline Joy, 48
Frost and Bartlett, 116
Frost, Harold L., 116, 343, 346
fruit trees, importance of to colonists, 19
fungicides: antibiotics, 269; decline in use of, 271;
    development of, 263; inorganic, 263;
    organic, 266–68; systemic, 270–71, 402;
    use of additives with, 268; wartime effect
    on usage of, 137
fungisol, 402
Funk, Roger C., 113

GI Bill, the, 141–42
Gaffney, John A., 190
Galloway, B. T., 381
gardenia, 36
gardens: Babylonian, 3; China, 4; earliest known,
    7; Egyptian, 2; Greek, 4; Persian, 3–4; post-
    Renaissance Europe, 8; Roman, 6, 7
Gardona, 91
Gentile, Harold "Hoppy," 371
germicides, in tree wound treatment, 331, 333
gibberellins, 280, 403
ginkgo tree, 36
Gleditsia sinensis, 37
Gold Leaf Awards, 57
"golden juice," 271
goldenraintree, 35, 40
Gonzenback, J., 230
Good Steward Award, 58
Gosnell, Tom, 167
Gotelli, William T., 71
"Gould Barrel Pump," the, 382
grafting, earliest instances of, 287
Gray's Manual, 19
Gray, Asa, 18, 19, 40, 67
grease, as wound dressing, 326
Great Northeastern Hurricane, the (1938):
    cleanup of, 199, 203, 204–6; damage
    caused by, 203–4, 205; lessons from, 207;
    path of, 202–3, 205; positive impact of,
    208; trees more and less resistant to, 204
Grecian laurel, 33
Gregg, Josiah, 38

John Bean Company, the, 380
"John Davey Elm," the, 106
Johns, Hyland R., *179, 190;* as Asplundh Tree
    Expert Company board member, 190; and
    Asplundh Supervisory Training Program,
    186, 189; and formation of the Interna-
    tional Society of Arboriculture, 158; and
    ISA Research Trust, 176, 194
Johnson, Ken, 249
Johnson, Lady Bird, 179
Jordan, West, 185
Joshua tree, 38
Josselyn, J., 32
Journal of Arboriculture, The, 158, 171–72, 173
Joy, John W. (Jack), 114
juglone, 281
juniper, 21

K̲alm, Peter, 16
katsuratree, 40, 41
Kendrick, William, 36
Kentucky coffee tree, 14
kerosene, use of as insecticide, 252, 254
Kew Gardens, 63
Kilner, Fred R., 179
kinetin, 280
King, G. C., 349
Kirk, Kenneth B., *245*
Kirk, Vi, *245*
Koelreuteria paniculata. See goldenraintree
Kornenek, Albert H., 307
Koslowski, Theodore T., 175
Kramer, Paul, 175
Kruidenier, William P., 156, 160
kudzu vine, 44
Kuemmerling, Karl, 242, 362, 372

L̲'Enfant, Pierre Charles, 17
Lagerstroemia indica. See myrtle, crape
Lakehead University Arboretum, 74, 76
Landis, Jerry, 383
Langford, George S., 158
larch, Japanese, 41
laurestinus, 33, 36
Laurus nobilis. See Grecian laurel
Lavallee, Alphonse, 64
Lawrence Aero-Mist, the, 388
Lawrence, Clinton C., 117, 122, 132

Lawson, George, 74
Lawson, John, 9, 15
Lawson, William, 290, 293, 301, 337
lead arsenate, use of as insecticide, 254, 255,
    256, 260; use of against gypsy moths, 88,
    93
lead paint, as wound dressing, 326, 327
leaf curl, 265
leaf spot, 265, 267, 268, 269
Leonard, C., 322
Lewis and Clark Expedition, the, 18
Lewis, Clarence E., 56
Lewis, Meriweather, 18
"Liberty Elm," the, 14
lightning protection, trees, 120, 354, 357–59
Lignasan, 226, 227, 271, 402, 403
lilac, 33, 35, 41
Lilly, Sharon, 166, 168
lime sulfur: as fungicide, 264, 265, 266, 267; as
    insecticide, 136, 254; insect resistance to,
    255
lime trees, 14
lime: use of in cavity filling, 337; use of as
    fertilizer, 312, 314
lindane, 256
linden, 33, 34, 40
line clearing, 134–35, 297
Linnaeus, 16
Linnean Botanical Garden and Nursery, the, 17
Liquidambar orientalis. See sweetgum, Oriental
locust, 14, 15
Lodeman, E. G., 381
London purple, 254-55
Longwood Gardens, 66
Loudon, J. C., 11, 12, 339
Lowden, R. D., 167
Lymantria dispar. See gypsy moth
Lyte, James, 8

M̲'Glashan's transplanting machine, *304*
M'Mahon, Bernard, 23
M. cordata. See magnolia
MAG-AMP, 322, 323
magnesite, 329
magnesium ammonium sulfate. *See* MAG-AMP
magnesium sulfate, 259
Magnolia liliflora, 37
Magnolia Plantation, the, 15
Magnolia stellata, 41

woody plants, introduction of to U.S.: Asian, 33,
40–43; colonial period, 32–36; Dutch, 33;
English, 33, 34, 35; Mediterranian, 33;
Spanish, 32; by U.S. government, 42–43
Works Progress Administration, the (WPA), 109–
10, 197, 199–201, 205–6
wound closure, tree, 330
wound dressings, tree: 326–30
wound treatment, tree: dressings used in, 326–
30; earliest instances of, 5, 9, 10, 11; lack of
necessity for, 333; publications on, 332;
sterilization in, 328, 340; use of insecticides
and germicides in, 331, 333
Wright, Charles, 38
Wyman, Donald, 31, 179, 317
Wysong, Noel B., 155, *158*, 171, 233

Yelenosky, George, 175
yellows. *See* elm yellows disease
yew, English common, 34
York, H. H., 149

Zeidler, Othman, 257
Zelkova carpinifolia. See zelkova
Zelkova, 40
Zentmeyer, George, 140, 226
zinc chloride, as fungicide, 264, 265
zinc dimethyldithiocarbamate. See ziram
zinc oxide, in tree wound treatment, 328
zineb, 267, 271
ziram, 267